SUCCESS HABITS
OF
SUPER ACHIEVERS

To

From

I wish for you a life of wealth, health, and happiness;
a life in which you give to yourself the gift of patience,
the virtue of reason, the value of knowledge, and the
influence of faith in your own ability to dream about and
to achieve worthy rewards.

– Jim Rohn

Published by
Kyle Wilson International
KyleWilson.com

Distributed by
Kyle Wilson International
P.O. Box 93927
Southlake, TX 76092 817-379-2300

ISBN-13: 978-1-7357428-0-9

Printed in the United States of America.

SUCCESS HABITS
— OF —
SUPER ACHIEVERS

Join the Success Habits Book Facebook Community!

Share with us your testimonials and comments and get daily insights from authors in the book.

Access the *Success Habits of Super Achievers* Podcast

Receive Special Bonuses When Buying
The *Success Habits of Super Achievers* Book

To access bonus gifts, plus links to the *Success Habits* Book Facebook Group and the *Success Habits of Super Achievers* Podcast, send an email to

gifts@successhabitsbook.com

DISCLAIMER

The information in this book is not meant to replace the advice of a certified professional. Please consult a licensed advisor in matters relating to your personal and professional well-being including your mental, emotional and physical health, finances, business, legal matters, family planning, education, and spiritual practices. The views and opinions expressed throughout this book are those of the authors and do not necessarily reflect the views or opinions of all the authors or position of any other agency, organization, employer, publisher, or company.

Since we are critically-thinking human beings, the views of each of the authors are always subject to change or revision at any time. Please do not hold them or the publisher to them in perpetuity. Any references to past performance may not be indicative of future results. No warranties or guarantees are expressed or implied by the publisher's choice to include any of the content in this volume.

If you choose to attempt any of the methods mentioned in this book, the authors and publisher advise you to take full responsibility for your safety and know your limits. The authors and publisher are not liable for any damages or negative consequences from any treatment, action, application, or preparation to any person reading or following the information in this book.

This book is a personal collaboration between a number of authors and their experiences, beliefs, opinions, and advice. The authors and publisher make no representations as to accuracy, completeness, correctness, suitability, or validity of any information in the book, and neither the publisher nor the individual authors shall be liable for any physical, psychological, emotional, financial, or commercial damages, including, but not limited to, special, incidental, consequential, or other damages to the readers of this book.

Excerpts from
Success Habits of Super Achievers

The deck is stacked against you. There's no question about it. And to get out of where you are, you gotta be hungry! Jackie Robinson said, don't level the playing field. Just let me on the field, and I'll level it myself. People that are hungry level the field, all they want is access in the game. When you are hungry, your gifts will make room for you. Bring what you have, do the best that you can, and God will do what you can't do.

– **Les Brown**, Iconic Motivational Speaker and Author

As an artist development coach, you are also a life coach. I take that seriously. I pour myself into my clients, as the training is not only about a music business career but about their personal ability to get up after being knocked down. The industry is full of armchair critics who enjoy the art of serving up their opinion publicly.

– **Linda Septien**, Kingpin of Pop Talent

That was the only time during my amateur, professional, and minor league baseball career where I had self-doubt. I almost walked away. I didn't have the vision that I would get called back to the big leagues, play for 15 years, or play on three World Championship teams and get paid tens of millions of dollars. I didn't know I was going to play for a Hall of Fame manager or that a lot of my teammates were going to go to the Hall of Fame.

I couldn't see any of that because I was ready to quit. Where I was is where most people quit, and not just in sports, but in life, from a marriage, job, or situation. It's where they decide they're just not good enough. It's a wall you run into that you either get over or around, or the wall becomes your ceiling forever.

– **Todd Stottlemyre**, 15-Year MLB Player and Entrepreneur

For me, much more important than being the guy on stage is helping other dreamers get there. That realization launched me into my incredibly successful role behind the scenes as a songwriter and Grammy-winning producer, which in turn, has given me the platform to mentor up-and-coming musicians on their journeys. The irony is that serving led me to success.

– **Seth Mosley**, 3x Grammy-Winner, Producer, and Songwriter

When I got back from serving in Afghanistan, I decided I wanted to compete in the US Memory Championships. I hired a coach, United States Navy SEAL TC Cummings. He taught me a lot about mindset and discipline. He had me memorizing cards underwater. He had me memorizing cards in noisy bars. He had me changing my diet, getting up early, and training like a Navy SEAL would train for war so that I would be a well-trained brain athlete for the memory tournament.

– **Ron White**, 2x US Memory Champion

The happiest people in the world are those who feel absolutely terrific about themselves, and this is the natural outgrowth of accepting total responsibility for every part of their life. They make a habit of manufacturing their own positive expectations in advance of each event.

Never complain, never explain. Resist the temptation to defend yourself or make excuses. Develop an attitude of gratitude, and give thanks for everything that happens to you, knowing that every step forward is a step toward achieving something bigger and better than your current situation.

– **Brian Tracy**, Iconic Speaker and Trainer

To do a few things excellently, you've got to say no to a lot of things. I've found that one hard no then makes a thousand little no's easy. I look for opportunities where I can make one decision that then makes a thousand decisions behind it.

– **Darren Hardy**, Speaker, Author, Former Publisher of *SUCCESS* Magazine

School sports helped pull me out of that home environment. I was not a great athlete, but chose to show up, suit up, and get in the game. That was my attitude—get in there and do the very best I could.

– **Tim Cole**, 31-Year Marine Colonel

I recognized I had an addiction when I realized I couldn't remember things. On my ex-girlfriend Liz's birthday in April 1987, we were in Paris having a glass of champagne, and I said, "I'm not drinking after this." We went to India the next day, and I quit cold turkey.

The benefits were outrageous. I got two extra hours a day that I wasn't spending recovering or just feeling not great. That's when I started working out because I actually had time to burn.

– **Phil Collen**, Lead Guitarist of Def Leppard

Success doesn't reveal as much about who you are as failure does. I've learned on my journey that wherever you look, there are corresponding opposites, and those opposites are ultimately inseparable. We need them both—the success and the tragedy. We cannot fully know one without the other. In my lowest low, I discovered my authentic soul.

– **Mike Muhney**, Co-Founder of *ACT!* Software

I had to step out of myself and ask, "Do people really want you to be like Zig Ziglar on stage?" The answer was no. They want me to have the same principles and values but to be the best version of myself. When I am not myself, it comes across as fake, a mask. That put the pressure in the right place, in developing myself and understanding what people needed. I realized it wasn't about me or the opportunity I had to speak. It was about every person in the room.

– **Tom Ziglar**, Speaker, Author, and CEO of Ziglar

I had run nine marathons and was getting into ultra-marathons, which are longer than 26.2 miles. I had just completed an Ironman triathlon and my first 100-miler on a track course, and I was looking forward to a second 100-mile ultra-marathon in the mountains. I started experimenting with breathing without changing my running or strengthening routines. I started getting faster and running became easier. I could run a marathon, do my specific breathing technique during and afterward to calm down, then get up and walk normally, and the next day go for a run again. With no other changes in my training, I dropped 14 minutes off my marathon time within seven months—a huge triumph. Most importantly, I knew I had to start using this to help other people develop a new breathing habit.

– **Dr. Amy Novotny**, Breathing and Chronic Pain Specialist

You have to believe in and fight for your dreams and goals. Who are you going to be? What are you going to be? What are you chasing? I figured out at 17 years old that I didn't have to please everybody including the friends around me. I had this dream of being a sportscaster. That's all I needed to work on—my dream.

– **Newy Scruggs**, 8x Emmy-Winning Sportscaster

The question is, what's holding you back? Whatever it is, limiting beliefs, low self-worth, fears, we know how to fix that. The key is: Are you willing to do the work necessary to eliminate the obstacles, so you achieve the dream? If you're not willing to do the work, stop complaining and stop having these big goals and dreams.

– **John Assaraf**, #1 *NY Times* Bestselling Author

Jack and I set BIG goals! And the results eclipsed even our lofty goals! As of today, we have sold over 500 million Chicken Soup books worldwide. If you think, "I can't do it. I'm not strong enough. I'm not enough," you won't be. But, if you start saying, "I really have a wonderful mind and powerful resources," you are setting yourself up for unlimited achievement, success, and opportunities galore.

Everyone's got a genius talent, skills and abilities, but it's different for each of us and requires enormous self-discipline to action. Everyone has a destiny. It's your job to discover what that is and then go fulfill it.

– **Mark Victor Hansen**, Co-Creator of *Chicken Soup for the Soul*

Over the next five years, I went to 15 countries to visit orphanages and asked the children the same three questions: Is God fair? If you had one wish, what would it be? Who in the world would you want to meet and why? *That ended up becoming a book,* Whispers from Children's Hearts. *That book launched my speaking career. I spoke in schools and gatherings across the globe, sharing the words of the unheard children.*

– **Lisa Haisha**, Producer, Speaker, and Coach

Over the past 30 years, I have had to innovate and reinvent many times over. The tactics change as technology changes, but the marketing principles do not. I think too many people confuse technology with marketing. I can hire the tech piece. It is the marketing that I need to make sure I never relegate. Once you understand that the principles of marketing don't change, it is just the tactics that change, you can then adjust accordingly.

– **Kyle Wilson**, Marketer, Strategist, and Founder of Jim Rohn International

To me, a legacy is about listening. A legacy is about sharing. A legacy is about depth...staying a little longer in conversations with people. It's about impacting and inspiring. A legacy is about others first. It's not about having success, but about what I do with that success. Most legacies are built on sharing and caring, not how high you went up the ladder.

– **Kevin Eastman**, 12-Year NBA Coach, Speaker, and Author

My dad told me that he felt my purpose in life was not to learn a trade. My purpose in life was to be a leader, to help and elevate people and to do it without expecting anything in return. He felt I could not be a great leader unless I understood and related to people doing the hard work who often felt underappreciated and passed by in life. That is why he assigned me all those dirty jobs, so I could walk in their shoes.

– **Robert Crocket**, Entrepreneur, Speaker, and Author

In reality, success is not all that difficult. But it does take effort. And it's nearly impossible to do it alone. Which is why one of my greatest personal success secrets is forming, developing, and nurturing fantastic, productive, authentic, win-win relationships.

– **Robert Helms**, #1 Real Estate Podcast, Real Estate Developer

I've learned to be a role model, not a critic. If they shouldn't be doing it, neither should you. Be someone worth emulating to your children. Set the example in your life. By preaching, I never got anywhere. I'm a highly sought-after professional speaker, I give a good lecture, but still, they watched me more than they listened to me talk.

It's much better to walk your talk. If you point out people's shortcomings, they manifest those. It's very hard to come away from what you're being preached not to do. Instead, lead them toward the desired result.

– **Denis Waitley**, Iconic Speaker and Author

Dedication

To all the mentors and influences that have shaped the lives of each of our authors. To our families and loved ones who fan our flames and inspire us. To all those that read this book and are inspired to believe in their ability to achieve great things, take action, and persist.

Acknowledgments

To Takara Sights, our editor and project manager extraordinaire, for your endless hours of work and passion in this book! Despite the complexities involved with a project like this, you kept the process a pleasure and always provide first-class results. A thousand praises! You are a ROCKSTAR!

Thank you to Kathi Laughman, Adrian Shepherd, Gary Pinkerton, Felecia Froe, John Reynolds, Heidi Wilson, Jim Gardner, and Vanessa Canevaro for being our second eyes and proofreading the manuscript as needed. We so appreciate it!

To our amazing authors and world-class thought leaders who shared their wisdom and stories with us — THANK YOU!

INTRODUCTION
by Kyle Wilson

It was June of 2018, and I was hosting Memory and Marketing, an annual two-day event I do with longtime friend and 2x US Memory Champion, Ron White.

I had just interviewed friend, mentor, and 31-year Marine Colonel Tim Cole, and after some audience Q&A, we took a 15 minute break. Then one of our attendees and a good friend, Michael Blank, came up and said, "Kyle, that was amazing! When are you going to start your podcast? When you interview members and attendees at your Inner Circle Masterminds and now today at this event, I always learn something new. Plus you know everyone in the speaker world. I think a podcast is way past due for you!"

I was flattered and thanked Michael. A podcast was something I had long been considering, but I wasn't quite ready. I knew the work involved and that once I pressed "go," it was going to be a permanent commitment.

After much thought, I decided on the topic and format of the podcast. I wanted to be able to bring into the living rooms, workout rooms, and cars of listeners an intimate conversation, filled with wisdom and insights from the many iconic thought leaders I've been honored to work with. Thus the *Success Habits of Super Achievers* podcast was born.

To kick it off, I sat down with longtime friends and collaborators including **Darren Hardy**, **Les Brown**, **Brian Tracy**, **Phil Collen**, **Lisa Haisha**, **Denis Waitley**, **Mark Victor Hansen**, **Robert Helms**, **John Assaraf**, **Ron White**, and **Todd Stottlemyre**.

I made an early decision to do long-form podcasts rather than the standard 15 to 20 minute podcast. If I have the opportunity to sit with Darren Hardy, Denis Waitley, or Phil Collen of Def Leppard in their home and interview them, I want to get as much of their wisdom and brilliance as possible for my own benefit and that of my listeners.

And from the podcast was born this book, *Success Habits of Super Achievers*.

I've interviewed over 80 thought leaders, entrepreneurs, professionals, coaches, and experts and distilled from our conversations, both private and published on the podcast, some of their biggest lessons, strategies, advice from mentors, success habits, and more.

Creating this book was a BIG idea and undertaking, and it was a BIG responsibility to steward and share the stories and lessons from each interview. Editor Takara Sights and I ambitiously took it on, with the expectation of what the potential result could be.

You will find common themes among the stories that include resilience, overcoming massive challenges and difficulties, exercising faith in uncertain times, leveraging mentors and coaches, and serendipitous forks in the road that helped these leaders find a new opportunity that has brought them to where they are today.

They all have a philosophy of bringing and creating value in their relationships as well as to the marketplace—a principle my mentor, Jim Rohn, taught me early on.

I'm excited and honored to introduce you to the people in this book. Each of them has made a difference in my life. Many are good friends and people I get to work with, hang out with, and learn from.

Feel free to start at the beginning and read this book cover to cover or go to the table of contents and choose a name or title that jumps out to you.

Either way, I encourage you to read all the stories in the book. Feel free to share key lessons and quotes on social media (using the hashtag #successhabitsbook) and with your audience and spheres of influence. Also let the authors and me know when a story, lesson, or idea impacts you. You will find their contact info at the end of each story.

Enjoy!

Kyle Wilson
Publisher, Speaker, Author, Founder of KyleWilson.com and Jim Rohn International

TABLE OF CONTENTS

As God's carefully sculpted masterpieces, all of us have got to chip out our imperfections and self-sabotaging behaviors. Stories subtly help each of us to do that. Reading other people's stories either builds you up or helps you to realize your weaknesses and mistakes and gives you the chance to overcome them.

– **Mark Victor Hansen**, Co-Creator of
Chicken Soup for the Soul

KYLE WILSON
Sharing Jim Rohn's and Others' Messages with the World

Kyle Wilson is a marketer, strategist, publisher, and speaker. He is the founder of KyleWilson. com, Jim Rohn International, and LessonsFromNetwork.com. He's worked with the top names in the personal development industry including his 18-year business partner, friend, and mentor Jim Rohn, as well as Brian Tracy, Les Brown, Darren Hardy, Denis Waitley, and more.

Early Years
I grew up in a small town, Vernon, Texas. I was fortunate to be raised in a loving and supportive family. As a kid, I was always industrious and would go around the neighborhood selling different things. I got my first job at age 14. I've been working ever since.

Unfortunately, as a teenager, I got into drugs for a few years. But at age 19, I had a significant emotional experience which radically changed my life.

I started my first official business at age 19. It was a detail shop washing and cleaning cars. Then I added oil changes and eventually took over running a service station. That led to opening Wilson's Texaco, a station located on a high-traffic freeway. I had 10 employees and was open 24/7.

Things were going well. But by 26, I really wanted something different. I felt compelled to move away from the town I was born and raised in. I didn't have much of a plan, I just felt strongly the desire to move to a bigger metropolitan area. I ended up in Dallas/Ft Worth.

Getting Into the Seminar Business and Filling Large Rooms
After moving to Dallas, I attempted a couple of different entrepreneurial ventures. Then 18 months after moving, I was serendipitously invited to attend a seminar. I met the promoter, Jerry Haines, and at the end of the seminar, Jerry said he was looking for sales reps to help him market his events.

The job entailed making 50-100 prospecting phone calls a day to book myself to speak at a company's weekly or monthly sales meeting. The presentation was designed to bring value to both salespeople and managers, and at the end of the talk I invited those in the audience to buy a ticket to an upcoming seminar.

The thought of getting up and speaking in front of a group was terrifying to me, but I really felt I was supposed to give it a shot. I did everything Jerry told me to do. I made the phone calls. I followed up. I learned the presentation. I learned the close. And I went to work.

After just one year, I became Jerry's top guy, but I was hardly making any money. The model was broken. So, I decided to go out on my own. I convinced my wife Heidi to leave her job, and we began to travel the country putting on events. We got really good at it, eventually getting 2000 plus people in each city. We would hire Jim Rohn, Brian Tracy, and Og Mandino to speak at our events.

Launching and Growing Jim Rohn International
In 1993, Jim Rohn and his business partner split up. I told Jim I really believed he was the best speaker in the world, and that I was a pretty good promoter, and asked him for exclusive rights to promote and market him and his products. In two of Jim's previous partnerships, he had lost over a million dollars combined, so when considering another partner, he was reluctant. So I proposed the idea of it being my company. I would cover all the expenses and overhead,

pay Jim's speaking fee off the top like a speakers bureau, plus give him a royalty on all the products we would create and sell. That way it was all profit for Jim with zero overhead and no risk of losing money.

Jim said yes. We did a handshake agreement which lasted for over 10 years until we finally put our agreement in writing in 2003.

In the beginning, Jim did not have a customer list and had only a handful of products to offer. I knew I needed to go to work on both.

Game Changer, The Wheel

That first year, I took Jim from 20 speaking dates with a fee of $4,000 per date to 110 speaking engagements at $10,000 each that eventually we raised to $25,000.

The game-changer for me was a concept called The Wheel.

I remember sitting down and drawing on a piece of paper a big circle with a small, center hub with multiple spokes—a wheel. Each spoke was an existing product or service Jim had, including a book, an audio series, one and two-day live seminars, plus his corporate and public speaking. The goal of the wheel is, once someone gets on the wheel, you then take them around it to experience other products and services you offer that may be a good fit for them. The key is to have GREAT products and services!

Since we had only a handful of products, the next logical action would have been to create more products... but what I really was asking myself was where were are all these people that I needed to get on the wheel going to come from?

The primary criteria I teach for adding a new spoke on the wheel are:

- It needs to be synergistic to your core business

- It focuses on your main customer avatar

- It is built around your secret sauce, what makes you special

- It is strategic and something that will knock down the rest of the dominoes

- It helps get new prospects and customers on the wheel

Being a wordsmith was part of Jim's secret sauce. He had the ability to take the complex and make it simple in a few words. So for the first new spoke, I went through all of Jim's speeches and came up with almost 1000 Jim Rohn quotes. From there, I got it down to 365 quotes and divided them into 60 categories. That became a hardbound book, *The Jim Rohn Treasury of Quotes*. But I really wanted a smaller gift booklet our customers and advocates could buy in multiples and give away. So I created a smaller version with 110 quotes, *The Jim Rohn Treasury of Quotes Excerpt Booklet*. The excerpt booklet had a page in the front with a special To and From and a place to write a personal note. It also had our product catalog in it with how to buy more booklets at a highly discounted rate. It was a viral tool we ended up moving millions of. It checked every box.

Your Success Store and Online Marketing

After I would book Jim to speak at companies, and once someone bought all his products, then what? I found that once people discovered Jim Rohn and his message, they wanted more.

So I started another company called Your Success Store. In addition to Jim Rohn, I started booking other speakers—including Brian Tracy, Les Brown, Mark Victor Hansen, Denis Waitley, Bob Burg, and others—and selling their products to my customers. I also created quote booklets, similar to what I did for Jim, for Zig Ziglar, Brian Tracy, Mark Victor Hansen, and Denis Waitley.

I found each speaker and product would attract new people onto the overall marketing wheel.

Then in 1999, I dove headfirst into the internet and was one of the first people to build a 1,000,000 plus email list. By 2002, I had multiple publications and over 300 different products (including digital) by Jim Rohn and other authors and speakers I was working with.

Marketing Is Marketing Is Marketing

I often talk about seven key principles to marketing. Over the past 30 years, I have had to innovate and reinvent many times over. The tactics change as technology changes, but the marketing principles do not.

I think too many people confuse technology with marketing. I can hire the tech piece. It is the marketing that I need to make sure I never relegate. Once you understand that the principles of marketing don't change, it is just the tactics that change, you can then adjust accordingly.

If you focus on having great products, services, and customer service and being consistent and relational (not churning through people), then the rest is simply finding the most efficient and strategic way to connect the dots between your products and services and a prospect or client.

Selling It All in 2007

In 2006, one of the few companies that I felt could steward Jim's message and also take the other speakers and authors I managed to the next level wanted to buy me. They were also in the process of buying *SUCCESS* magazine.

I had over 20 employees plus I was representing several speakers.Things were going well, but I was tired and burnt out and my kids were growing up fast. I felt maybe the timing was right to hand it all off. I was able to negotiate a great deal for my team to stay on plus pay them profit sharing on the sale of the company. It felt like it was a win/win for my team, the speakers, and the company wanting to buy me. So, in late 2007, I sold the companies. I stayed on to help them transition up until the unexpected passing of Jim in December 2009.

Lessons From Jim Rohn and Other Mentors

Meeting Jim in 1989 and then launching Jim Rohn International in 1993 was one of the great honors of my life. Jim and his teachings and mentorship changed my life!

Jim said for things to change, I had to change. Not the government, or the economy, or circumstances. He taught me that the biggest influences in my life, I have control of. My attitude, my work ethic, the books I choose to read, and the seminars I attend instead of mindless TV. It was all in my control and those things were the greatest determining factor to my future success.

Jim showed me that success was predictable, just like planting tomatoes in a garden. If I plant the right seed at the right time, water it, and keep the weeds out, the odds were massively in my favor to reap a harvest. I didn't have to go for the quick fix or the too good to be true. I could have predictable success as a result of the predictable steps I took. And if I continued to do the steps, my success would start to compound over time.

Jim told me that if I wanted to be successful I must find ways to bring value to the marketplace. He said money is an exchange for bringing value. And he added, if you want to be wealthy, learn to bring value to valuable people. Always lead with bringing value.

I was blessed to also work with many other mentors including Brian Tracy, Les Brown, Mark Victor Hansen, Paul J Meyer, Zig Ziglar, and more. I share those lessons in a free book called *52 Lessons I Learned From Jim Rohn and Other Legends I Promoted.*

Coming Back Out of Retirement

In 2013, I started getting the itch. I tested the waters a bit and knew it was time to get back into the industry that had changed my life.

Being the promoter and marketer for others was my comfort zone. I didn't want to be the talent. But I found it necessary to come out from behind the curtain and start to share my knowledge and experience with others.

Today I focus on four core things.

The first is my Kyle Wilson Inner Circle Mastermind, which is something I love. I started the group for me. Jim said who you spend time with matters. We have the best members from all over the country, some from around the world. It's an incredible community.

Second is publishing books like this one, *Success Habits of Super Achievers*, where we get to connect amazing thought leaders with the marketplace.

Third is the Lessons From Network, a platform to help connect entrepreneurs and business owners with the marketplace. It's an idea that started when I bought the domain LessonsFromSports.com in 2007 after interviewing a successful football coach.

And fourth is coaching, consulting, and speaking.

I still get to be the promoter and shine the light on others and their talent through my Inner Circle, books, LFN, and podcast. But I'm now also the face (reluctantly at first) of the platforms.

Starting the *Success Habits* Podcast

In November of 2019, I started the *Success Habits of Super Achievers* podcast. People ask why success habits? Why not a marketing focused podcast?

First, I really wanted a platform that would allow me to host many of the iconic thought leaders I've been honored to work with. Going into the homes of Darren Hardy, Brian Tracy, Denis Waitley, Phil Collen of Def Leppard, etc. and talking about what makes them tick with a goal of extracting their wisdom, lessons, and insights is something I love and benefit from, as do my listeners.

Second, I'm turned off by so much of the current marketing advice out there. So many are selling the dream, often in areas they have never had success themselves and ignoring marketing principles. So, I decided to stay out of that noisy conversation. Based on the feedback from listeners, I'm glad I made that choice.

I've learned that we all have a message of value to share. And I'm blessed I get to share others' valuable messages with the world!

Go to KyleWilson.com to learn more about the Kyle Wilson Inner Circle Mastermind, Kyle's consulting and speaking for your organization, receiving the FREE 52 Lessons book, and to get links to episodes of the Success Habits podcast. Follow Kyle on IG @kylewilsonjimrohn

CARLOS DELHERRA
Straight Out of Compton: Embracing Poverty to Find Prosperity

Carlos Delherra is an entrepreneur, real estate investor, developer, syndicator, and philanthropist in Southern California. His nearly $100 million in total asset value property management and investment firm focuses on student housing. Carlos is married and a proud father of two children.

My Early Years in Compton

I am the son of immigrant parents who landed in California in the 1970s. I was born and raised in Compton, at the time, one of the most violent, dangerous places to live in the United States. My father came to this country in the 1960s under the US Bracero program, which imported cheap, seasonal farm labor from Mexico. He later worked as a janitor and never made more than minimum wage. My parents were hard-working people with third-grade educations who made the bold move to uproot and create better opportunities for their family.

We struggled like most immigrants, facing the uphill climb of adapting to a foreign land. We lived in a one-bedroom dilapidated shack with inconsistent gas and electricity, concrete floors, and no insulation behind a single family home occupied by a family involved in gangs. I will never forget relying on government subsidies like food stamps and being dragged by my mother as a five-year-old child to the welfare office, feeling like a beggar. I will never forget going to a local church as they handed out government cheese and powdered milk.

My mother always hustled to make a few extra dollars on the side. She sold used clothes at a local flea market, sold sweet Mexican corn as a street vendor, and at times hauled around a shopping cart picking up cans on the street. She usually dragged me along, and I would begrudgingly go, knowing my neighborhood friends would later laugh at me. The pain and shame of poverty impacted me tremendously.

My parents worked very hard and also did not want to rely on help. They did their best with the limited opportunities and resources they had. While we were financially poor, we always had a roof over our head and never went to bed hungry. My parents taught us the fundamental values and ethics that shape the person I am. Work hard, say thank you, respect your elders, and be good human beings.

Feeling Powerless

On top of growing up in one of the most dangerous cities in Los Angeles, I had to deal with dreadful public schools, an inept and corrupt local government, and a police force which was feared and distrusted. At times, I felt an overwhelming sense of powerlessness. I had to be laser-focused and determined to overcome the ever-present obstacles. A misstep and a little bad luck, and my life could have taken a deadly turn.

My earliest memory is of my neighbors getting shot by a rival gang in the middle of the night. I must have been two or three, but I vividly remember them running into our house crying hysterically, telling us their mother had been shot.

When I was 12, a random person, visibly high on drugs, put a gun to my head and threatened to kill me. I talked my way out, persuading him that killing me wasn't worth it. I barely escaped death that day yet did not lose any sleep over it. This was normalcy, and deathly violence was numbing. Later in life, I would always measure any difficult situations by this unique experience.

Embracing the Hardships

For most of my life, I believed I had the worst luck growing up in Compton. But now I have fully embraced it. I consider myself incredibly lucky, to live in the greatest country in the world. I am proud to have overcome poverty and honor the courage of my parents who gave their kids a better life.

Enduring this harsh environment built survival skills that gave me an edge. Most of life's challenges seem trivial in comparison. If you accept challenges and adopt a different philosophy, you can not only survive, but also thrive. Compton was my training ground to over-prepare me and forge a resilient armor, which proved essential for the real world challenges that lay ahead.

But first, I had to get out. If I could focus on education, I had a chance.

Finding Freedom Through Education

When I was seven-years-old, there was a city boundary change that forced everyone on my block to attend Compton public schools. That was a major turning point in my life. As a third-grader, I could not believe the chaos, danger, and grossly unqualified teachers. I attended for one week, then told my mother I was never going back. I told her I could learn more teaching myself. I was seven years old. A kid that age should not have to take such a deliberate and forceful role in his education, but I had no choice. I look at my seven-year-old daughter today and cannot fathom her having to take decisive action like this. I knew that if I stayed in that school, my life would have turned out differently.

At this point, I realized my parents had taken me as far as they could, and it was up to me to forge ahead.

As a senior in high school, my English teacher Mrs. Budak instilled confidence in her pupils and gave us a belief we did not know existed. I vividly recall when she made it a requirement to fill out college applications to several universities. If she had not, I do not think I would have attended UC Berkeley.

The education I had received left me ill-prepared for a top-notch university. It was a huge risk to leave home and attend. But when you come from nothing, there is nothing to lose.

Be Uncomfortable and Unconventional

Attending Berkeley proved to be the challenge I expected. On my first exam, I received a C+. I had never received a grade that low, and I was in shock. My choices were clear: fail and go back to Compton or graduate from one of the top universities in the world and open up unfamiliar opportunities. I grew up without a safety net in an environment where a misstep can drastically alter or end your life. Most of my classmates attended excellent high schools and had an insurmountable head start. But the race was long, and my parents instilled in me a strong work ethic. I remembered the sage advice Mrs. Budak gave us: "You will always encounter people who are two or three times smarter than you. So you just work two or three times harder than them." I could not control being born without special privileges, but outworking my fellow classmates seemed tangible and achievable.

I graduated from UC Berkeley with a 3.5 GPA, was accepted into their prestigious and ultra-competitive Haas School of Business undergraduate program, and was even able to squeeze in a year studying abroad. I did this while working 20 hours a week with a full class schedule.

I got the travel bug studying abroad in Madrid, Spain, and decided to seek a job that included plenty of travel and a great training program. I found a top management consulting company named Accenture (formerly Anderson Consulting). While I was qualified, it was a job that was out of my comfort zone. I was not the pedigreed candidate they typically hired.

Rising to the executive management level, my career at Accenture lasted over seven years and gave me the opportunity to consult and work for several Silicon Valley start-up Fortune 500 companies like Microsoft, Verizon, and Yahoo!. I worked all over the United States and Europe, living in major cities like San Francisco, Seattle, and Amsterdam. While Accenture provided me invaluable training and skills and a global network of people, I realized that climbing the corporate ladder was not for me. Consulting was challenging, testing me daily and forcing me to become solution-oriented and adaptable. It helped lay the groundwork for the next chapter in my life: becoming an entrepreneur.

Failing Forward

After reading Robert Kiyosaki's *Rich Dad Poor Dad* in 2001, I decided to start investing in real estate while keeping my corporate job full-time. I joined The Real Estate Guys Mentoring Club and began laying an educational foundation in real estate investing. I attended their goals retreat and learned the powerful skill of goal setting. I figured out what I wanted out of life, why I wanted it, and how to do it. It was simple: I wanted to start my own business and produce enough passive income through real estate to achieve financial freedom by age 35.

I struggled to find a business venture so I focused on my real estate portfolio. I started buying properties and assembled a multi-million dollar portfolio in California, Nevada, and Texas. Then, 2007 happened, and the world was turned upside down with the mortgage meltdown and the beginning of the Great Recession. I not only lost it all, but also woke up one day and found out my net worth was *negative* half-a-million dollars!

The problem was my strategy. I relied on equity appreciation rather than positive cash flowing properties. When the dust settled, my credit score collapsed, my reputation took a hit, and my confidence was shaken.

Conventional wisdom (and many friends and family) told me I should quit the real estate game. At the time, most people quit. Instead, I came across Warren Buffett's words: "Be fearful when others are greedy and greedy only when others are fearful." Real estate prices had plummeted, and it was time to double-down! Quitting was never an option. I needed to learn from my mistakes and make the necessary adjustments.

If I had a positive cash flow strategy from the outset, my real estate crash and burn would not have happened. I simply had to find positive cash flowing properties and identify the right niche to get rich!

Finding My Passion

That's when an opportunity of a lifetime in student housing appeared. My current business partner George Alva saw an opportunity to purchase a large house for a student group seeking a home near the University of Southern California (USC). It was the perfect storm in a strong cash flowing niche: historically low real estate prices, minimum competition, at a tradition-rich university with increasing demand in an improving neighborhood. This set me off on a course that would far exceed my expectations.

George and I have been in business for over 10 years now. We started out wanting to replace our corporate incomes and managed to build a meaningful business together. Our top-notch property management company has 10+ employees and oversees approximately 100 units and 600 tenants. Our real estate investment firm and development company has a portfolio approaching $100 million in asset value. We are currently entitling a mixed-use, seven-story, 75,000 square foot development near downtown Los Angeles. Along the way, we raised millions of dollars from friends and family and recently brought in a long-term capital partner for our next phase of growth.

None of this happened by chance. Every year we dedicate three days to map out our future and set far-reaching goals. We also made a concerted effort to live well below our means and could not have achieved our goals without the faithful support of our spouses.

They say luck is when preparation meets opportunity. Everything that has happened, especially the failures, helped me prepare for this amazing opportunity. But I had to see it, seize it, and put in the hard work.

My experience demonstrates that the American Dream is alive and well. If you are willing to put in the work, this country will provide the opportunity for prosperity and success.

Carlos Delherra is the co-founder of Mosaic Student Communities and Mosaic Investment Partners. Contact Carlos about investing, speaking engagements, and philanthropy by email at carlos@livewithmosaic.com and on Facebook as Carlos Delherra Delgado.

LINDA SEPTIEN
Kingpin of Musical Talent

Linda Septien, CEO and founder of Septien Entertainment, is a music artist development professional with 25+ years of experience. Some of her most recent famous artists include Demi Lovato, Selena Gomez, Kacey Musgraves, Beyoncé, Rudi Aliza, Jessica Simpson, members of Why Don't We, Leon Bridges, and scores of other profitable musicians. Linda has been coined by popular media as the "Kingpin of Pop Talent."

Growing Up With Music

I was raised in South Louisiana, two hours from New Orleans, where music is the city's flavor, nightlife, and culture. The food, Cajun music (Zydeco), and the locals are premium fun-loving peeps who truly enjoy life and are all one big gumbo of colors.

My musical family was my example of everyday life. The upright piano plunked at all times, my mother practiced for her upcoming gigs, and my dad played country tunes on his old Fender. My sister, nephews, and sons are in the music industry as well. My 94-year-old mother still gigs today in her tart ragtime style. When my family said "Get a real job!", we all understood that to be in the music industry.

The Turning Point

As a trained classical singer, my career was in touring. One summer while singing in Italy, I made a lifetime decision to quit classical touring life and join the commercial world of music. Pop artists seemed to be having much more fun than those of us on stage who stood still and sang out foreign words.

I combed through hundreds of pieces of original music for my new project. After months of choosing, learning, and memorization, I was ready for my recording debut in the pop world! Off to Nashville I went! I just knew I would be offered a record deal by 5:00 p.m. the same day.

I began singing my first song in a beautifully equipped Nashville studio and waited for reactions….and waited…and waited. On the other side of the studio window sat two producers with their mouths wide open. I just knew that deal would arrive soon.

…But for 30 minutes on the other side of that window, I stared at them as I could see them discuss among themselves. My inner thoughts were killer, right? "Okay, I am paid to go on tours, so SOMEONE must think I'm good. Or, are they mesmerized by the beauty of the sound and have been left speechless? Are they discussing the many labels they could offer me to?"

I finally had the nerve to ask. "Wa.a.a.a.assss that alright?"

One producer turned from the other and said, "Are you going to sing like THAT?"

I thought, *Uh, that's the only way I know how to sing.*

He continued, "That totally sucked…Just sucked."

I have never been one not to accept reasoning as I always believe that each of us say things either in truth or from pain. Much can be learned from both outcomes. While I shot eye darts at the glass between us, I came to three conclusions 1) I knew I could sing. How would anyone pay me on tour if I couldn't? 2) Maybe I had hired a jerk, but didn't he know I could fire him as well? 3) Ok, he did discuss it for 30 minutes so, maybe he was really trying to figure out the best way to tell me?

I took #3.

"Tell me how I suck."

"You have no feeling. Your words have no meaning. You have no presence in your body, nor pre-thoughts as to HOW you would like to express the words through your song. You aren't telling a story through accents, nor emphasizing YOUR meaning behind the lyrics. What are you thinking while you sing? Just as we tell a story with added exclamatory sounds, you need to do the same in songs! This isn't karaoke night at Bob's Bar! No scatting, no rhythmic structure, no colorization, no texturization, no nothing of anything. When you tell a story, are you that boring?"

Whoa….the worst part? I had no idea what he was talking about. "We don't do all that 'stuff' in classical singing."

At the time, I was also eight and a half months pregnant and pondered if the only "pop" in my life would be my husband. But before I could tuck my tail and leave, my producer gave me some amazing, life-changing words that back then didn't seem so life-changing. "Here's what you should do. Become a diesel sniffer a.k.a. 'groupie.' Follow 18-wheeler tours of popular bands around the world and take notes on what moves their fans and how they express their emotions through a song. Watch their moves, their lips, their timing, their stage banter, and write a manual about every discovery you make."

I wrote 27 manuals in two years.

And for those two years, my new job groupie status was pretty darn fun. Mick Jagger, Bruce Springsteen, Sting, Freddie Mercury, Michael Jackson, Billie Joel, Elton John, Green Day, Nirvana, and a host of other amazing performers taught me what entertainment was about. I studied A-listers from the '50s and '60s… Elvis, Dean Martin, Bing Crosby, and Sammy Davis, Jr., to discover their 2% factor. I got to see Frank Sinatra in Vegas! I made a special trip as I had heard so much about him from my mother. I learned the most from him… I was bored stiff. He talked and talked about himself. His old stories were boring! I realized music was generational. That was an "aha" moment.

One year later, I began the launch of Jessica Simpson. Jessica is now worth over $1 billion. Jessica got "fresh off the press" ideas to the formula of success… not just as a singer, but also as an A-lister that fans want to follow. My company grew to what it is today with testing facilities, songwriting rooms, practice stages, full production studios, and lots of stage candy and equipment… all to assist the modern performer to entertain today's fans. The keyword is TODAY! Today's sound, today's look, today's generation, and today's stage banter. Septien Entertainment Group (SEG) has now trained over 17,000 artists!

The Formula to Uniqueness

The most integral step to branding is discovering the X factor! What does this artist have to offer that's different from anyone else? Nationality? Sound? Look?

Once we have an educated guess of the initial X factor, we train the artist to match up with an "8 Point Artist Cocktail."

Branded Voice + Branded Style + Stage Entertainment + Socials + Brand +

Hit Songs (Remix or Original) + Gig Experience + Community

The cocktail consists of training an artist to mutate their voice into a style that can sell to enough fans that would sustain a living. Whether the singer is pop, country, soul, Christian, rock, an independent singer like Billie Eilish or multi-platform artist like Taylor Swift, our team aligns each element into the product that will attract a specific demographic. After enough fans are accumulated, music styles can be changed, but at first, the brand must be focused and consistent in one lane. From stage wear, branded social media, song content, song style to videos, gigs, and interviews, everything must line up for a powerful punch. Today's artists have to cut through way too much noise in fan-land.

Launching an artist today is 180° from before. Micro or macro-influencers help us push an artist out digitally. Whether the influencer is a cook or makeup guru on TikTok or IG Reels, top influencers on these platforms work to the benefit of our emerging artists.

The Healing Power of Music

This industry attracts many heart-seeking individuals because of the therapeutic nature of music, especially those that have something to write about! When writing personal stories and turning them into songs, a little bit of pain bleeds out. Sometimes this can result in a bit of inward behavior as the focus becomes about personal lives, stats, and fan base growth.

SEG Leadership Program is an additional track offered that trains in healthy thought processes and metaphysical understanding of life, but also includes financial programs such as stock market training, budgeting, and algorithm training. Similar to a home-based program, our leadership training program encompasses both regular school and areas where school completely misses the mark.

Everyone wants to be a star in some way, but singers must be a star to make money. The definition of a star is mass approval. Singing is not your true identity. It's just a job. When your job is your identity, you're in trouble. If it dies, you're dead. It's not what comes TO you in life, but what comes THROUGH you. That is what is important. It's what are you going to give, not what's going to be given to you.

Understanding the Music Business

SEG trains over 200 artists at any given time. My time is limited to 10 clients, but I continue to train because of the importance of staying on the "street." My artists have a pulse on music trends.

It is a difficult transition to convert from the talent to the coach to running a business with continual training needed. It is important to begin business each day as if this is your opening day. Going from a complete creative to running a business is a life change. Each difficult decision forces me out of my comfort zone and into a new and bigger space. I go back to school often, study daily online, read two hours every morning and love the pull. The biggest lesson I've learned in 30 years is the importance of knowing what doesn't work; that's the definition of a seasoned business. The combination of an experienced team and trendmakers from Gen Z is and always will be a perfect formula.

SEG Entertainment Divisions

SEG is divided into a pro division and a newbie division. Septien School of Music offers services for newbies to discover the opportunities in the world of music.

Pro divisions provide artist development to singers who seek financial gain in the industry. "Tweenation" is our pro division for tweens to help them gain entry into Disney, Nickelodeon, etc. "Emerging Master" is our division for teens who want to start a complete program in the "Artist's Cocktail." Our adult division is divided into three categories depending on the viability of the artist. Some artists have been successful before and want to recreate their brand.

"The Song Hatchery" is our pro-school of songwriting and now encompasses a 1000 song catalog, written by clients of all ages. Grammy award-winning writers train new and seasoned songwriters to write, produce, loop, trend, and edit for sync and licensing.

"Pulp Social" is the newest division of social media branding. Our team researches monthly the top 20 digital marketing companies for musicians. They change often. Next, we extract the winning ways to create a branded artist. We then join forces with influencers working for each company. **Musical artists today are trending influencers who sing rather than singers who influence.**

The Tools for Training a Voice

I can teach anyone to sing who has healthy folds, because the vocal cavity is no more than an instrument to be honed and built according to the law of physics. As medically trained vocologists, touring singers must build a healthy vocal instrument. Touring is tough on the body. But even more difficult than maintaining a healthy set of cords is singing while entertaining because of the intense energy it requires and the number of calories you need to perform. My studio looks more like an athletic center. From treadmills to weights, the artist must work out while he or she sings. In one session, a singer can burn 400 calories. Since a singer's body is active at all times on stage, an additional 400 calories will be lost through pure sweat and nerves. You MUST be in shape!

The pivotal career move is the entertainment factor! Are they able to move with an instrument? What's going to come out of their mouth? Is their stage banter cautious and uninviting? Do they know how to connect? Timing working? Have smooth transitions? In my work with *American Idol*, *The Voice*, and *America's Got Talent*, it is easy to identify the entertainers within the first moments of a song. It is predictable who the audience will gravitate to long before the season launch.

How I Replenish My Joy

As an artist development coach, you are also a life coach. I take that seriously. I pour myself into my clients, as the training is not only about a music business career but about their personal ability to get up after being knocked down. The industry is full of armchair critics who enjoy the art of serving up their opinion publicly.

I caution my team to give back to themselves as I must do. While serving others, are they serving themselves? I read, reread, and unlearn things in my head to ready my heart for the day. A 30-year student of personal development, I enjoy thought leaders like Jim Rohn, Zig Ziglar, Eckhart Tolle, and many others. I learn from those who have been through life and can now help ME know what not to repeat! When I feel a bit down, I just take a walk outside, especially if it is raining. I lay down in the grass as the water drips down. It is remarkable how the tears from clouds will bring a smile, renew your life, and cleanse your soul.

Linda Septien is the CEO and founder of Septien Entertainment Group. For more information, go to www.septiengroup.com or social platforms.

DR. TOM BURNS
Doctor, Investor, and Lifestyle Advocate

Tom Burns is an orthopedic surgeon and a physician for the US Olympic ski team. He is a real estate investor, author, and speaker. He promotes financial education and service through the Rich Doctor Company, and he is co-founder of Presario Ventures, a Texas-based private equity firm.

Design Your Future

I didn't always want to be a doctor. When I was young, all I did was play sports. It took me a while to realize that, although I was reasonably talented, I probably wasn't going to become a professional. So, I decided to pursue orthopedics and sports medicine to remain part of the athletic world.

Near the end of my medical training, I started to look at my chosen career and what life would be like for the next 40 years. Surprisingly, I noticed that the doctors I was supposed to emulate were constantly complaining about lack of time and control. They were making money, but they weren't happy.

I realized this was not the future I wanted. I enjoyed medicine but didn't want to be trapped in a life that didn't give me joy and satisfaction. I wanted to be excited about the future, so I decided to create some income that wasn't dependent on the world of medicine.

I wanted to control my own destiny, so I started looking for opportunities. One of the first things I did was to attend a free seminar hosted by a financial planner. While I didn't become a client, I understood the numbers, and it put my brain into overdrive. The more I learned, the more I knew I was on the right path. I wanted money to work for me, rather than the other way around.

Of all the financial opportunities I researched, real estate made the most sense to me. It moved slow, could be done part-time or full-time, and could be accomplished solo or with partners. Most importantly, real estate provided passive income, which I believed was the key to freedom and control of my future life.

After finishing my regular physician training, I went to Vail, Colorado for additional sports experience. I was working hard but was dead broke in the midst of extraordinary wealth. Although I hadn't taken a step into real estate, I was learning from mentors all around me. I was exposed to financial icons like Arthur Rock, the father of venture capital. I spent time with sports stars, film stars, billionaires, and even a former US president. I was soaking up their wisdom, whether they knew it or not. I was building a foundation.

Action Leads to Opportunity

Once I got a real job, we lived frugally, and I paid off my debts. This gave me freedom to enter the entrepreneurial world with somewhat of a cushion. I knew I would make mistakes and didn't want my family to pay for them.

I went straight into action mode and boy did I make mistakes! I tried more things than Kim Kardashian has followers. Some were winners and some were losers. But during the process, I was learning, and of course, I learned more from my failures than from the victories.

I needed more education, so I hooked up with a real estate partner who taught me what he knew, and I continued to read and attend seminars. I wasn't wealthy and I was not financially free, but my mindset and my attitude were becoming rich.

One day I bought an obscure book by an unknown author while getting my car washed. I was reading everything I could get my hands on, and the title caught my eye. Somebody who titled their book *Rich Dad Poor Dad*, and proclaimed that the rich teach their kids differently than the poor, had to have something of value for me.

That turned out to be an understatement. That "somebody" turned out to be Robert Kiyosaki, and that "obscure" book is now the bestselling personal finance book of all time, with over 40 million copies sold. I was apparently the first person in the world to buy a copy. I've often wondered if that was luck, or the universe rewarding an open and curious mind.

Through various circumstances, Robert and I became friends and have stayed in touch for over twenty years. I have continued my education through his books, seminars, and personal conversations. I am eternally grateful to be part of his world.

Why Doctors Don't Get Rich

One day, while at Robert's Advisor Mastermind in Phoenix, he turned to me and said, "You know, you've got a story, Tom. You need to tell it. You should write a book."

I hadn't written a book before, but in my typical "shoot, ready, aim" fashion, I said "Sure!" He even came up with the title, *Why Doctors Don't Get Rich*, so how could I turn him down?

Writing a book is like setting a huge, almost unobtainable, goal. It's not reaching the goal that's important, but who you become in the process. Writing *Why Doctors Don't Get Rich* has been a life-changing process. I have learned more about myself and my medical colleagues than I would have otherwise.

This journey has sparked a passion that I cannot deny. Physicians worldwide are disenchanted with medicine, and unhappy doctors lead to unhappy patients. This creates a healthcare system that can become sterile and sometimes heartless. I want to change that.

Statistically, half of American physicians have wanted to quit medicine at one time or another. That fact saddens me. I have been in a position to retire for over a decade, but medicine is fun for me. It's hard for me to imagine not connecting with my patients regularly and playing a part in making their lives better.

The truth is, practicing medicine is completely different when you choose it out of passion, rather than the need for a paycheck. Now that I've experienced this freedom, I want all doctors to have freedom, choice, and control over their life and their work.

I frequently speak to physician groups about medicine, money, and real estate. Typically, I give them a glimpse of the freedom provided by passive income. Afterwards, I invariably hear, "Thanks. I never knew this was possible." "I can see light at the end of the tunnel." "I felt so trapped until I heard you speak!"

Education and action provide the opportunity to make choices. *Why Doctors Don't Get Rich* is designed to open the mind and give direction. It's written to give "trapped" people hope. It won't teach you how to flip a house or buy an apartment complex, but it will build the foundation of your mindset. Wealth starts in the mind.

Having the Choice

Financial independence gives you the freedom to choose how you spend your time. It grants you control over your life and the option to do what gives you meaning and joy, regardless of whether it pays well. That might be working 60 hours a week at a job you love or playing golf every day. The good news is that financial independence gives you the choice.

Does that goal seem too big right now? Well, there's hope. You can attack freedom in small pieces. You don't have to be fully financially independent to be happy. A small amount of passive income will relieve some pressure. If you don't have to worry as much about your house or car payment, life becomes a little softer, and you might smile more.

All I want to do is help people smile more and like what they're doing. Once some pressure is relieved, or someone reaches financial independence, it is my hope that they will follow their passion and improve the world. Some will retire, and I applaud them. Others will feel there is unfinished work and will create magic.

Keep Growing

My humble advice for anyone is to keep learning and growing. When we stop growing, our mind stagnates, and we lose the ability to foster the greatness that is within us. Read books and listen to podcasts. Make it a point to seek out those who are creating positive change. Find people moving in the same direction as you. Their vibes will help you move faster.

Don't be afraid to make mistakes. You'll make plenty, but they will be your best teachers. I could write a whole book on mistakes because that's gotten me to where I am today. Never waste a good mistake. As Albert Einstein said, "Anyone who has never made a mistake has never tried anything new."

Write down the things that you care about the most. When you whittle that down to your top three, you will have an idea of your purpose in life. Chase that purpose with passion, love, honesty, and humility. That's a formula for a life worth living.

Create your freedom.

With love and gratitude,

Tom

To take advantage of free wealth-building resources and access Tom Burns' new book, Why Doctors Don't Get Rich, *visit www.richdoctor.com. You can also connect with Tom, book a speaking engagement, or explore educational opportunities by emailing tom@richdoctor.com*

GREG ZLEVOR
The Reflective Journey: The Joys of Slow-Growth Success

Greg Zlevor, president of Westwood International, has worked with Johnson & Johnson, The Singapore Police Force, Volvo, General Electric, and many other high-profile companies, authored four #1 bestselling books, and shared the stage with greats including Jim Rohn, George Land, and M. Scott Peck.

In Pursuit of the Mind and Spirit

In college, I realized that my life was going to unfold differently than I'd always thought. I was a biology major at Lawrence University and hoped to go to medical school. But halfway through, I realized I'd rather work with the mind and spirit than the body. I found that in my free time, I was reading books by authors like Mohandas Gandhi, M. Scott Peck, and Dietrich Bonhoeffer. Many books were science-related, but more were about psychology, spirituality, and development. I came to understand that I was more interested in personal growth than physical growth. I stuck with my biology degree but decided not to go to medical school.

The problem—at least temporarily—was, even though I knew I was following my passion, I wasn't sure how to translate that into a career. Luckily, a local school needed some help. For four years after college, I was a science teacher and football coach at Xavier High School in my home state of Wisconsin. I'd come from a family of hardcore Packers fans, and football was a big part of my life. But in the back of my mind, the desire to go to graduate school wouldn't go away. I just didn't know what to study.

Someone said to me, "Why don't you go for what's important to you?" I came to realize nothing was more important to me than my spiritual journey. It had been a gradual awakening, but there were some peak experiences like my decision not to go to medical school and the summer I'd spent living at Madonna House, a Catholic community in Ontario. That question— Why shouldn't I go for what is important to me?—unlocked new thinking and clarity. I made up my mind and decided to get my master's degree in spirituality.

The Slow Path

I started applying to graduate schools. I was most excited about the University of San Francisco…and the program would kick off with a 40-day silent retreat. Intense.

The priest who had taken on the role of spiritual director in my life asked me, "Greg, have you been on a 10-day silent retreat?" I hadn't. In fact, I had never been on any kind of silent retreat. He asked, "Don't you think you should go on a three or five-day retreat before you go on a 40-day?" Thanks to his insight, I realized that I was potentially taking a leap too far, too soon.

I took a left turn and decided to go to Boston College. The program at BC included classwork, reflection, and a master's thesis but did not have an intense silent retreat component.

It's amazing how someone who loves and respects us, who really listens, and who asks questions that make us think has the power to affect us. That mentor changed my life forever because of a 10-minute conversation and a couple of simple questions. It's also a reminder that in spite of the fast-paced world we live in, sometimes it's best to take things at a slower pace. Starting graduate school with a 40-day silent retreat could have gotten me on the right foot faster, but it could have burned me out just as quickly.

One Step at a Time

For nine years, I stayed at Boston College, first as a graduate student, then as a chaplain designing and running leadership programs, mission trips, and retreats. Within a few years, I was hosting community-building workshops and studying group dynamics. Based on my work, companies began asking me to work with them. When a few of them offered me retainers, I realized each one would pay more than I made in a whole year as a chaplain. I decided that I had better give training others a try. I left the university and embarked upon what has been my career ever since.

I didn't plan any of it in advance, nor did I think that one step was going to lead to the other. But the combination—my degree in biology, training in spirituality, and work in mindfulness, meditation, and emotional intelligence, merged with my understanding of the importance of serving and building communities led me to where I am today. It was crucial that I took this all one step at a time and that I slowed down when the instinct was to act fast, like with that 40-day meditation retreat. The world changes. We change. Often, building the lives we want to live isn't about meticulous, years-in-advance planning, but in slowing down, reflecting, and adapting.

Taking the Journey

Spiritually, we're all individuals from different traditions and life paths. But most of us struggle with the same questions. We want to serve, be happy and content, and use the most of our gifts. Getting there is a journey of questioning, community, feedback, ups and downs, and discovery.

I've worked with quite a few mentors and spiritual directors in my life, but their role is to open up your own conscience, not to tell you what to do. The spiritual journey is one you have to walk yourself. And, increasingly, that journey is relevant to other areas of your life. I find it fascinating how much businesses, even masterminds and personal development circles, are being called upon, not necessarily consciously, to do work that used to be handled by churches and spiritual centers. In his seminal 2000 book *Bowling Alone*, Robert D. Putnam explores the decline of institutions that fulfilled Americans' need for social connection and spiritual fulfillment. Two decades later, his message is even more resonant. Those needs don't go away. So now, how do we, as entrepreneurs, business leaders, and executives fill that role in a way that has integrity and depth?

It's not an easy task. When I go into the corporate world, I might not even mention the word spirituality. But, it is important that I listen, serve, and stay calm in a crisis. And it's important for the people I work with to know there's something bigger than themselves. When they do and when they share their personal agenda in a calm way, they can bring others together. That's the ultimate form of teamwork and connection. That's human spirituality. We have learned this through the centuries, and today we can adopt these truths within the framework of technology to fit our 21st-century world.

Daily Rituals

Creating rituals has significantly aided my journey. My rituals include:

Meditation. I begin every morning early with meditation. It helps me stay focused and calm even when things get difficult. I started with 15 minutes and now I am pretty consistent with 45 minutes every morning.

Your tribe. Find people who can support you and keep you on track. These are the people you trust enough to ask for opinions on your ideas, methods, and challenges. They're the ones who will challenge you by asking you what you really want and what decisions you ought to make. I can tell you, going to my three or five confidants helps balance me and keep me on course. Without them, I would potentially be doing fine, but I would quite likely be 10-15%

off the trajectory of my desired course. At first, 10-15% isn't much, but over time, as you get further from your launching point, that difference amplifies and becomes a big problem.

Journaling. Keeping a productivity journal in which I map out my intent for each day and my schedule helps me get clear and stay focused. Since I have implemented this practice, I have seen huge improvements in my mindset and what I can get done. It allows me to set and accomplish realistic tasks every day.

How to Create Miracles

One of my favorite phrases from entrepreneur and motivational speaker Jim Rohn is, "You do not have to do extraordinary things to get extraordinary results. You only have to do ordinary things extraordinarily well to get extraordinary results." Miracles aren't random or reserved for rare geniuses; they happen because you've been diligent. Miracles happen because you decide to read all the books you need to, do all the action steps you need to, talk to all the people you need to, and walk the path until you get your answer. Teams are looking for these miracles, and helping them achieve them is priceless. Diligence is so mundane in theory, and yet so few people follow their journeys with this mindset.

We live in a world that simultaneously worships the idea of "move fast and break stuff," a phrase made popular in Facebook's early days, and the expectation that you have your 5- and 20-year plan sharply in your headlights. Neither is realistic. Committed, slow discipline gives you the expertise to create miracles in your work. It's wildly underappreciated. But it works.

I've gained immense advantages in business from obtaining a graduate degree in spirituality and serving as a chaplain. You have to get good at contemplation. Everyone's looking for a better bottom line, more productivity, better efficiency, and ways to find and retain talent. Most companies either want more of the market share or to create an innovative team that can find that next leading edge. The tricky part is that when problems show up, many companies and executives are quick to look for solutions to these challenges outside their companies. They don't stop to breathe and contemplate. When I work with companies, I'm there to show them that their real challenges are likely on the inside.

People who have spent years meditating can tell you that there is beauty in slowness, in turning inward. As it turns out, it may also be key to solving some of the most pressing issues that face your business, no matter how intense they seem.

If you are too busy to think and reflect, you are too busy. Slow down and give your journey the reflection it needs.

Contact Greg Zlevor about his books, coaching, leadership development, and speaking at gzlevor@westwoodintl.com or look for Greg Zlevor on LinkedIn.

LYNN YANGCHANA
I Too Can Conquer the World

Lynn Yangchana specializes in commercial real estate primarily in office buildings in the Inland Empire areas of Southern California. Lynn has been directly involved in over $500 million in transactions at MGR Real Estate since 2005. She's an investor with an amazing story and the mother of twins.

The Black Sheep

I was born in Thailand and grew up in a Chinese family that had traditional Asian values: superior status for males, entrepreneurial spirit, and a strong belief in the value of real estate.

Growing up, I observed my father's motto: "work hard, take risks, and enjoy life." From her hard childhood, my mother had a traditional belief of "work hard, play later, and wealth accumulation is the goal in life."

I may be something of the black sheep of the family. My motto is "work hard and remember what's important in life." And I believe that as a female, I can do as good a job as anyone. As long as I commit to fully engaging my mind and my efforts, I can definitely succeed in the world.

A New Life at Age Six

When I was six years old, my mother took me to an assessment for placement at a private school, hoping that I would get in as my two older sisters had. I remember the teacher handing me a sheet of paper with a picture of an apple, a doll, and a few other items for me to mark up the relationship between the pictures and the words. I understood the instructions but did not do anything the whole time.

I ended up not being accepted, and my mother convinced my father to send me to Taiwan to live with my maternal grandparents to learn Chinese. I only spoke Thai at the time and was thrown into the unknown of a different culture and language. Within a year, I was able to speak simple Mandarin Chinese, get on the school bus myself, and make friends at school. Living away from home at the age of six and having to suddenly learn a second language in a different country taught me independence quickly. It was a major challenge at the time, but I am grateful that my parents set me on that path. That experience gave me a thirst for new experiences, taught me resilience, and instilled a lifelong love of traveling.

I also came away with a deep-seated ability to listen, internalize, and understand others. I tend to notice body language and emotion more than others. I learned early to fend for myself by observing the world and people around me. I had to do this just to make my way at only six.

In my twenties, my interest in communication and new experiences continued to grow, and I moved to the United States to complete my master's degree in communications from California State University, Fullerton. I began my career learning and exploring the art of marketing by working for an advertising agency.

A Family Culture of Real Estate

I grew up with real estate. On my family's property in Bangkok, we were surrounded by rental houses. When I was young and playing with our tenants' kids, my mom would ask me to pick up the rent checks from their parents. Everything my parents talked about was either real estate, investments, or business.

My father was looking forward to building a property in Bangkok. I remember seeing a rendering of a tall building on his desk and thinking, "Wow! That's such a big goal. That would be so wonderful to build this building ourselves." Unfortunately, he became ill and passed away before realizing his dream.

The picture of the tall, white, beautiful building was always in my mind, and that image gave me the desire to get my real estate license and explore the real estate investment arena.

Commercial Real Estate

Day one, I was attracted to commercial real estate. I love being surrounded by large buildings. I asked myself, "If I want to be the owner of such a building, what do I need to do?" It is not just about having the money and making the purchase. How would I buy it right and keep it going? That thought led me to finding and working with the company I am with now.

I started one step at a time and over the years began to understand the importance of cash flow. Cash flow is 100% about finding and selecting tenants carefully, mitigating turnover, and supporting them with active property management. I have had the pleasure of working with clients from small business owners to national corporate clients and learning the best practices of sound management and underwriting of investment properties. Every deal and relationship is the basis of a new learning curve and the foundation for the next level.

In leasing, I work from multiple perspectives. From the building owners' perspective, I need to understand the tenant business, their rental and financial history. When I started in the business, tenants were just names and numbers because I did not know what to look for. Today, I can tell early on with a pretty high success rate how their story is going to unfold. Based on a tenant's background and how they show up and negotiate, I can judge whether this would be a good move for both parties.

What I enjoy most about leasing is the opportunity to meet with business owners and entrepreneurs. These are all very creative people with great conviction for the future. It feels great when I walk the empty space with them and get into the details of envisioning how they will build their business in the space. Once a business has moved in, the relationship continues. They will call me months and years later as they continue to expand because, from the start of our relationship, I shared their vision.

I tell my mentees today that effective leasing is the blood and soul that makes this asset class profitable.

A High-Level Chess Game

My greatest strength in the deals I do is managing relationships and crafting win-win agreements. Acquiring a second language the way I did gave me lots of practice in noticing patterns. My secret to successful contracts is understanding their patterns and uncovering hidden landmines as well as unintended consequences.

For me, these negotiations are like a challenging chess game. It is my responsibility to manage a dynamic of the right tenants, maintaining efficient space plans, and projecting the current and future cash flow while also preparing for any turnover. I juggle a great many elements in addition to attending to underwriting and acquisition opportunities. I just love the game.

#1 Advice from My Mentor: Setting the Table

Having a mentor is essential. I never could have come this far this fast without great mentors. I wish I had met my current mentor much sooner because he has greatly expedited my learning curve.

His first lesson was "how to set the table." I wanted to learn real estate, sales, and leasing. Why did he want me to set the table? It took me quite some time to fully understand the essence of setting the table. And it is applicable to every team, business, family, and relationship.

Setting the table is all about the power of proper preparation. If you are going to have a meeting, how do you prepare the night and days before? If you are going out for a leasing appointment, what do you need to prepare for? You need to understand your inventory, the market, the tenant's requirements, and most importantly, always consider who they are and where they want to be.

This is preparation. You want to be thoughtful about the process to ensure the good outcome that you envisioned and prepared for.

Not only do I need to have the right materials, I also need to look presentable, be professional, and be on time. These are all the preparations. I am teaching my kids to "set the table" before they go to school, especially if they have a test. It is how you set yourself up to be successful.

I love this quote from Napoleon Hill: "Whatever the mind can conceive and believe, the mind can achieve." That is setting the table—creating a picture of how that meeting's going to go and how it's going to finish.

Love Conquers All

At my core, my deepest value is love of my family and love of pursuing what I enjoy in my career. Despite a very competitive real estate environment, I tend to have tunnel vision for my love of the game and for what I would like to achieve. Love gives me the greatest energy to overcome obstacles and be resilient.

My husband and I encourage our kids to find their true love by continuing to keep dreaming with an open mind. We teach our kids that you will succeed at anything you love to pursue if you persevere. It is easy to say, but not easy to accomplish. Ultimately, I believe that if you have a passion for your work and love what you do, you will achieve your goals. Because love really does conquer all.

Reach Lynn Yangchana about office investments in Southern California from East San Gabriel Valley to West Inland Empire markets at 1-714-273-0208, lynn.yangchana@gmail.com

DARREN HARDY

Former Publisher of *SUCCESS* Magazine Shares
How to Grow Your Business Bigger, Easier

Darren Hardy is NY Times *bestselling author of* The Entrepreneur Roller Coaster, Living Your Best Year Ever, *and* The Compound Effect. *He's a recognized speaker awarded the Master of Influence designation by the National Speakers Association, a high-level advisor to his clients—including billionaires, and the former publisher of* SUCCESS *magazine. As an entrepreneur, Darren built a major 8-figure a year company. He is the creator and host of* DarrenDaily *reaching over 350,000 subscribers.*

Early Years

My parents divorced when I was 18 months old. My mother walked out the door and never looked back. My dad was 24 years old when I was born, and he had just moved from the Bay Area where all his family was to New Mexico to take a job as a university football coach.

He was super alpha male. He coached football by demoralizing people, challenging them to get better to earn his respect. That's where I learned about determination and hard work.

My father's love language was achievement. The only way you got love or attention from my dad was to achieve. If you didn't, it was a dark, cold place to live. He was the only person I had to depend on for survival. All I wanted to do in life was make this man proud. This became the engine for my pursuit of greater and greater success.

I have so much gratitude for my father. He taught me determination and my work ethic. He took on the burden of raising me when even my mother wouldn't do it, and he did all that he had to do to make that possible.

But he could only bring me to a certain point.

It wasn't until I went to my first personal development seminar that I saw the possibility of a whole other world, a world of abundance and achievement beyond one's upbringing.

Meeting Jim Rohn

I first heard Jim Rohn speak in November,1994 at the Harvey Hotel in Dallas. I was 23 years old. I don't remember a lot because life can be a blur when you're always thinking about the future, but I remember that day. I was there to meet the promoter of the event and Jim's agent and business partner, Kyle Wilson. The event was still going on, so I went in to sit in the back of the room. I'd never heard of Jim Rohn before.

Jim asked the audience, "How many of you here want to have more? Raise your hand." I instinctively raised my hand. I'm a student. I pulled out my little notepad from my coat jacket thinking, *What is it he is going to tell me to do? What else can I do?* At that point, I was working seven days a week, maximum hour days, running myself ragged. Outworking everybody else was my go-to success strategy. But I was listening, and if there was one more thing, I would do it.

Jim said, "If you want to have more, you have to become more."

Now that was a twist of logic that changed my trajectory from that moment forward.

He said, "What you pursue eludes you. It's who you become. Then, you attract the success you seek based on the person you become."

Instead of *what* I need to do next it was **who** I need to become next to get what I want. That really amplified my personal *development* journey and started my lifelong love of Jim. He was the grandfather I never had. I loved that it wasn't about antics. It wasn't theater. It was a mindset. It was philosophy.

When I was sitting in the back of the room at that event, I was at my ceiling for all that my dad, my first mentor, had taught me. I couldn't go any further. I couldn't work any harder. Jim brought me the rest of the way.

Then there was a point, I talk about it in *The Entrepreneur Roller Coaster*, when I graduated from wanting to please my dad to wanting to pursue my passions for my own interest. For a long while my achievement was literally rooted in making my dad proud. That desire propelled a lot of my early success, but when I developed my self-interest, I grew to new heights.

Embracing Our Weakness

I think part of my drive comes from my mother walking out and having to vie for love and attention from my father. As a result, I want to do whatever it takes to assure that what I put out is worthy, to the point that what I create is over-produced. I won't put anything out if it's not excellent. And I think it's in response to this driving issue.

I believe a lot of times people's highest skills are rooted in their dysfunction.

I've learned to not fight it and to appreciate it. I'm so grateful that I've had this drive to seek significance because I'm going to impact 1.5 billion people this year through our work.

Why I Say No

To do a few things excellently, you've got to say no to a lot of things. I've found that one hard no then makes a thousand little no's easy. If I don't do any podcast interviews, then saying no to every podcast interview request is easy. If I don't write the foreword to anybody's book, then all the requests to write forewords that come in are easy to say no to.

I look for opportunities where I can make one decision that then makes a thousand decisions behind it.

There are always exceptions to the rule, but you need rules if you want to maintain your focus and flow.

Business Mantra

One of the mantras in our business is we want to grow bigger, easier. We want to grow bigger, yes. But we also want to make everything that we're doing to grow bigger, easier.

There are three tenets.

Number one is people. Do you have the right people in the right positions doing the right things the right way? You accomplish this first through recruiting, then through assessing vital functions of your organizational chart, whether the right positions are doing the right things, then finally through aligning your vital metrics with their vital functions which roll up to the goals of the organization. And doing it the right way. I walk through this in my INSANE PRODUCTIVITY program.

Second are systems. All the dumb things we're doing over and over that are costing time, energy, and effort can be optimized through systems. Then, how do you leverage systems in order to create scale? A lot of the technologies that are powering our capabilities as a company didn't even exist three to five years ago, including all the video conferencing that I run a virtual team with. My team is 100% virtual.

I work here in my home, and I run a major business with employees all over the country. The tools and technology we have today offer the opportunity to go find incredible talent no matter where they live and keep them emotionally engaged.

The third one is the hardest. And that is choices. The decisions that you make along the way, all those things that you say YES to are also a NO for something else.

You've got to figure out the highest possible outcome for the allocation of your resources. Here's an analogy.

A mouse can walk in front of a lion, and the lion will disregard it even though it could kill the mouse and it would be nutrition. But, if a lion, who is the greatest killing machine nature has invented, went around chasing and killing mice all day, it would eventually die of malnutrition. A lion can only sustain its life and its pride's life on antelope—big game. And it takes a tremendous amount more energy and effort to capture and kill an antelope than it does a mouse. But when captured, an antelope will feed its pride for a week.

It's the same thing in our lives. There are a lot of mice opportunities around us all the time. And even if a mouse opportunity provides a little bit of nutrition, a little bit of revenue, a little bit of reward, you will die of malnutrition over time. These are the trivial tasks and opportunities people pursue. Be the lion and only go after antelope, big game, big outcomes, big opportunities, things of high value. As Jim Rohn would say, "Don't major in the minors."

The Story Behind *DarrenDaily*

I was doing my best to give back. I was on boards of a lot of nonprofit organizations to try to contribute, not just money, but also time and expertise. I found myself sitting in meetings where they were going through the financials and I had nothing to contribute, but I was burning my time, my most important asset. I'm fastidious about how I spend my time. I thought this wasn't serving them or me. So how could I take the same time and the same money, but have a greater impact? And I thought, *Well, what do people want from me that they can't necessarily afford? They want mentorship.* So on the 20th anniversary of when I first met Jim Rohn, to honor and pay forward what Jim paid to me, I announced a give back program, a year of free mentoring every single morning.

I would pay for the whole production and send it out for free. I wanted to make a contribution into people's lives for anyone interested. And that's all *DarrenDaily* was, a charitable endeavor motivated to reallocate time and resources. But the effect it had on people was unimaginable. I mean, moms were playing it for their young boys who were fatherless to replace the male influence in their life. Parents listened to it in the car while taking their kids to school. It brought marriages together because of something they heard that they hadn't considered. They could see in a new way how they might be affecting their spouse. All these amazing stories started coming back, and I was like, *Alright, I'll just keep doing it.*

The thing that really struck me was how powerful it is to be an anchor in somebody's routine on a daily basis. *DarrenDaily* becomes a part of their routine. I am embedded into the routine of people's lives, and that's a whole different relationship than an occasional podcast or a weekly or a monthly magazine subscription. People get up in the morning, make their coffee, sit down, and watch *DarrenDaily* without conscious thought as part of the rhythms of life. It builds an emotional relationship and a connection. That's why, five years later, I'm still doing it. Not only is *DarrenDaily* still an opportunity to deposit into people's lives, but also having 350,000 people who are relationally connected to you through their routine has massive influential power.

I'm in Pursuit of...

I'm in the pursuit of getting better every day. Why? Because getting better every day makes me happy. I just want to be better today than I was yesterday. That's what's going to then check all the other boxes.

Darren Hardy is the CEO of Darren Hardy, LLC. Follow Darren Hardy and Receive His Free DarrenDaily *at DarrenDaily.com*

To Learn More About Darren's Massively Successful INSANE PRODUCTIVITY Course go to insaneproductivity.com

GARY PINKERTON

Enabling the American Dream – Pursuing Your Unique Genius

Gary Pinkerton uses 30 years of ethical leadership gained at the US Naval Academy and honed as a nuclear attack submarine Commander to improve the lives of his clients through his work as a wealth strategist with Paradigm Life and as an entrepreneur, motivational speaker, and real estate investor.

Chip on My Shoulder

I grew up in southern Illinois dairy farming. My father would be milking the cows at three o'clock in the morning and then again in the afternoon, rain, snow, or shine. I remember 10 plus years where he didn't take a vacation more than a few hours.

In high school, I was going to school in an embarrassing old car wearing hand-me-down clothes. Our worn out farm equipment often failed, and we'd have to manually collect and stack all the hay, 10,000 bales a year, into the barn. My friends would go to sports practice then come over and get paid to help us. There'd be no paycheck for me and no ability to go to sports.

This was the mid-1980s, and we hadn't yet broken high interest rates—18% variable interest rate loans on our farm. We would get a new loan, and then a couple years later the introductory "teaser" rate would go away and the payments would be crushing once again. Soon the bank foreclosed, and we were broke, living in a trailer on my uncle's land.

All I was thinking about my first 20 years as an adult was monetary wealth, and that my kids weren't going to live this future. Now though, I feel like my children are probably disadvantaged. My background created this chip on my shoulder. I had motivation to change my situation and worked as hard as I could to get straight A's and get accepted to the Naval Academy, then submarines, and finally, my own boat.

Nuclear Submarine Commander

I commanded the USS Tucson, a Los Angeles class, one of the last ones built in the late 90s. That seems old, but it was a third of the way through its life when I had it in 2009-2011. Submarining is certainly a unique lifestyle. I think the longest that I've been underwater without opening the hatch is probably 70 days. But there are people who have gone quite a bit longer. Once you know there's a good chance you may be out for a while, you bring about 90 days worth of food with you. After that, you get creative, as in figuring out new ways to eat the three bean salad out of a metal can. We made our own water and air onboard. We had 30 years of fuel and energy, lots of parts, and the ability to make more parts. So with the exception of food or a very unique part, we could operate indefinitely.

In command of a submarine, you have a team of 150 people. It's an amazing group. They're the best of the best in the military. They're not all extremely excited to be there every day, but they're motivated, and equally important to their patriotism, they're extremely smart. When I took over, the ship had just been through an almost two-year overhaul. Everything was made brand new with the latest systems. But the crew had to learn how to go to sea all over again. They eventually succeeded and we took her on her first deployment in Asia. It was just incredible—a very difficult challenge at the beginning with a tremendous result at the end. It's something I'll never forget. I'm truly humbled and honored. Yet as I finished that tour that brought many accolades, my personal life was crumbling.

Needing a Change

Initially, I thought I just needed to be in a different role in the military. For years I was consumed by how amazing it would be to command a submarine and then to be promoted to Admiral. But I was married and a dad. And to be honest, I was gone so much that I didn't really know my kids and they didn't know me. Reflecting on all I learned from my dad in those long hours on the farm, the legacy of experiences and lessons he'd left me, I realized how fortunate I'd been, not for the work or hardship, but that it had given me so much time with my father and mentor. I needed to be around my kids much more and could not achieve that climbing the ranks within the military.

I spent most of my last years as a Navy Captain in the DC area working in big government leading a division for the Chairman of the Joint Chiefs in the Pentagon, another incredibly rewarding opportunity to work with the best of the best, and this time across all the Services. This experience taught me something very important about myself: Senior military roles and big government life were not for me. I realized that my love for America was not about patriotism, but rather our constitution's enduring focus on protecting the rights of individuals, their life, liberty, and property. I wanted to help sustain this 250-year-old experiment that our founding fathers started.

I shifted my focus to helping business owners and entrepreneurs prosper by improving their finances and sharing their unique genius with the world, the practices I saw and loved when I was a kid on the farm. Back then, there was no Amazon, things we needed were made locally. Someone just started making it, and often, a thriving business was born. My dad and I made apple crates for orchards for a few years because they needed them and we had trees, a sawmill, and were paid well to solve that challenge. I love that about America.

But DC taught me when you have a big government whose goal is to get bigger, it takes more taxes, which is crushing for the small business owner and the exact opposite of what our founding fathers intended. There's an important reason the Bill of Rights says that all rights not specifically given to the government are to be withheld for the people. It is essential to limiting government overreach and taxes. Every organization and company, once created, takes on its own life, and like organisms, its primal function becomes "sustaining life." Historically, this leads governments to greater bureaucracy, larger budgets, and tyranny or socialism. Even in America, government ends up working against its charter to protect people's rights and get out of the way so that they may flourish. My Pentagon time included a government shutdown. Everyone showed up but no work was done; all effort was on not being the organization that got eliminated or reduced.

The American Entrepreneur

If somebody were to hear me talk about this, they would ask, "Are you saying government is bad?" Absolutely not. I think our government is amazing. It gives people the confidence that if they do the work and put the money in to create something, whether it's a product or a service, they get to benefit from it. 250 years ago, America was first to try this experiment and the results are obvious. Countries that followed have similarly prospered.

Those who know Napoleon Hill know the phrase _think_ and grow rich. If any part of that is true, and I believe it to be, the potential of the human mind is massive. Yet there are millions of people that come to the end of life not having shared their unique genius with the world because their environment doesn't support it, their time is consumed making ends meet, and they've been beaten into belief that it's not possible. Helping people set up a personal economy so that they can focus on their passion and achieve greatness is what inspires me.

It comes down to people having the ability to, first, focus on what they're uniquely good at or interested in and, second, prosper from that. What does my business of high cash value life insurance have to do with that?

Funding a Personal Economy, a Foundation to Wealth

I help people build a personal economy where they've got control over how they use their resources and what they choose to do in life. A personal economy lays a foundation that enables you to invest in yourself and your business, far more important than investing in your 401K. And to be successful long-term, you need reserves in a place that are protected and private, and you need to offset risks that typically cause many families and small businesses to fail, like inflation and high taxes.

I use insurance-based financial planning and services to solve that foundational level. At the core, my team educates on the use of an insurance policy as a vehicle where you store emergency money, reserves for your businesses or properties, and cash for upcoming major expenses and investments, where it's protected and can grow three or four times as fast as it would in a savings account and without the impact of taxes.

This financial foundation, the life insurance benefit, privacy, protection, and tax-free wealth available through this strategy is amazing. And it is the best vehicle for enabling financial dreams and growing permanent wealth. Let's keep America great!

Contact wealth strategist, entrepreneur, motivational speaker, and real estate investor Gary Pinkerton to learn more about insurance-based financial products, real estate, private banking, alternative investments and guaranteeing a better future at garypinkerton.com or directly at gary@garypinkerton.com.

ROBERT CROCKETT
Serve Others Without Expecting Anything in Return

Robert Crockett has founded, managed, and reorganized numerous businesses and is the proud father of two amazing children. Today, he owns and operates Advanced Personal Care Solutions, a home health company he founded in 2004 employing over 240 employees and is an author and speaker.

Most Valuable Lesson

I started working in my father's construction company when I was 10 years old. Since he was also a university professor, he often left me at the construction site with a list of tasks to accomplish. Over the years, he hired several of my friends to work with various subcontractors. If there was a tough, dirty job to be performed, I was the one to do it. Over the next ten years, I watched my friends work with electricians, plumbers, roofers, and sheet rockers while I cleaned, dug trenches, moved materials, and did everything else that nobody wanted to do.

When I was in my mid-twenties, I was working as an assistant controller at an agricultural company and decided to resign and move from Denver to Los Angeles. I was talking to my father about my decision and mentioned my disappointment in spending so many years in the construction company doing things that added no knowledge or value to me while my friends learned tasks that I never got a chance to learn. His response shocked me.

He told me that he felt my purpose in life was not to learn a trade. My purpose in life was to be a leader, to help and elevate people and to do it without expecting anything in return. He felt I could not be a great leader unless I understood and related to people doing the hard work who often felt underappreciated and passed by in life. That is why he assigned me all those dirty jobs, so I could walk in their shoes.

It was the most valuable lesson I've ever been taught. As I look back on the events in my life, I've come to realize that a lot of my success has come from helping people without expecting anything in return from them.

Forced to Sell

Later in my career, I was COO of a telemedicine startup. The company had received FDA approval for a telemedicine device and hired a sales force for the Eastern United States while I set up the internal operations of the company.

The technology used at the time was revolutionary, and since there wasn't a standard way to get reimbursed, the sales force wasn't having a lot of success in getting health care companies to commit the money and effort required to implement the system.

After two years of little to no sales, I was called into the office of the CEO and told I was now the vice president of sales of the western United States. I was to relocate from the Midwest to the Western United States, hire and train a sales force, and start selling the product. I was devastated. I HATE SELLING! My professional experience up to that point was in operations and finance. I didn't like giving presentations, knew nothing about selling, and had absolutely no idea how to hire and train a sales force. The CEO told me I didn't have a choice. We were burning through our cash reserves and this was an "all hands-on deck" event. Everybody had to sell.

I moved to Phoenix the next month, hired my first sales rep, flew the sales rep to Phoenix, and we went on our first sales call. If there was a list of what not to do during a sales presentation,

I checked all the boxes. I didn't really talk much about the product. I never asked for the sale. Instead, I just talked about the owner's business, and we talked about both of us growing up in the Midwest. During a tour of the facility, he mentioned that he liked the product and could see the value, but he needed to buy a new facility and didn't have the money.

I noticed during the tour that most of the space was in the warehouse, and it was a mess and not organized efficiently. This was my area of expertise. I was pretty sure I was going to fail as a sales person, so I asked if I could come back and organize his warehouse after I dropped my sales rep at the airport.

He agreed, and I started working on his warehouse a couple of hours later. We worked through the night, throwing away broken equipment, palletizing slow-moving product and placing them on storage racks, and moving fast-moving product down to the floor for easy access. When we were finished, the warehouse was half empty.

The owner looked at the progress we had made in just a couple of days and asked me to wait while he went and got something. He came back with a signed contract for the product. He told me that what I had saved him in the cost of a new facility far exceeded the cost of the product, and if this was an example of what working with me was like, he definitely wanted to work with me and the product.

At the time, the contract he signed was not only the largest contract signed in the history of the company, it was also the largest contract ever signed in the industry.

And this was all because I served someone without any expectation of getting something in return.

It cemented the lesson from my father, and it wouldn't be the last time it would serve me.

Head of the Better Business Bureau

In 2010, I was on the board of directors of the Better Business Bureau (BBB). There had been a news report about the BBB selling ratings, and the Las Vegas BBB was in disarray. Not only was there an issue with ratings, but also the systems didn't work, the membership records were a mess, a lot of the ratings were wrong, and the CEO was sick.

I told my father how distressed I was. I felt responsible, and worse, I didn't think anyone was interested in solving the problem. He told me I could either resign and wash my hands of the mess, or I could fix it even though there wouldn't be any benefit to me.

When the CEO was too sick to work anymore, I volunteered to be the CEO, working for free until the issues were resolved. People couldn't understand why I would volunteer for something like that, but for me it was my only option. Over the next couple of years, with a ton of effort from the staff at the BBB, we managed to resolve the issues and turn everything around.

During that time, I met an older woman who wanted to join the BBB who started a home care agency with her daughter. She was trying to get a contract with the state of Nevada and didn't know what was required. Since I had a lot of experience in that industry, I gave her my policies and procedures and walked her through the contracting process. I stayed in touch with her over the years, answering questions and providing support whenever I could.

At the end of August 2016, she called and asked if we could meet. During the meeting, she explained that she had one daughter who had cancer, her other daughter had left her agency, and her husband had dementia. She tried to sell her agency, and finding no interest, asked me if I would take over her agency as soon as possible so she could take care of her daughter and husband. The only thing she asked of me was that I take care of her clients and employees, who she considered part of her extended family. A month later, we had put all of her employees through our training and transferred her clients into our agency.

Taking on her 60 employees plus her clients, and acclimating them to our culture was difficult, and there were times we were sure it wasn't worth the effort. Despite that, we never wavered in our decision because she needed help to take care of her family. Four years later, we have a larger pool of dependable, valuable employees, and everyone has benefited.

Core Philosophy, Legacy

The lesson my father instilled in me was invaluable. Over the years, I have seen it proven true time and time again that seeing the world from other people's perspective and serving without expecting anything in return inadvertently leads to incredible rewards. I could easily list a dozen examples of this happening in my lifetime. Serving without expectation has become one of my core philosophies, and I have tried to instill this in my children as my father taught me.

Reach out to business coach, speaker, and author Robert Crockett

Email Robert@rpcrockett.com

Website rpcrockett.com

Twitter @RobertPCrockett

RYAN PETTITT
Transforming Challenges Into Endless Possibilities

Ryan Pettitt is an entrepreneur and real estate investor with 12 years of experience and is well-versed in leading multimillion-dollar initiatives as a certified Project Manager Professional. Ryan has a diverse investment portfolio of agriculture, hospitality, residential, and land in the US and internationally.

Early Years

I grew up in South Carolina and have always been ambitious. At a young age I strove for excellence being an honor student, earning the Eagle Scout award, graduating with a 4.0, playing the cello, and swimming on the varsity team.

I stayed close to home and attended the University of South Carolina. While attaining my degree in entrepreneurship management and marketing, I was active with student housing, held leadership positions in honor and business fraternities, created an organization to raise awareness of sexual assault and violence prevention, and completed a minor in psychology.

Persistence, Hard Work, and Dedication

In 2009, I started my career directly out of college in a leadership development program with a major corporation. Earning the position was a roller coaster due to the economic climate. I interviewed with several companies, received offers which were later rescinded, and witnessed what appeared to be thriving businesses close their doors. After receiving an official offer, I found out I was an alternate to another candidate. I knew I had something to prove.

I started soaking up the industry knowledge and willingly worked 11 to 14-hour days, often beginning before 5 a.m. I took over a district struggling with sales and execution. It was an awkward transition, but over the course of the next year, I was able to build a new team, drive results, and improve operations. When I was promoted to my next role, I was able to get the region back on track for training initiatives which were lacking for over a year and exceed all of the objectives within a nine-month period. I started to feel like I was proving my worth and had aspirations of continuing as a high-performing employee.

Success Is Not a Straight Line

Shortly thereafter, the company restructured. I was the lowest on the tenure list, which resulted in being laid off. I was shocked. I racked my brain trying to understand how I could be so easily disposed. What affected me the most was a lack of expressed care or concern from co-workers I considered friends and mentors. It was as if I were a leper and no one knew how to interact with me. My ego was bruised, and the wind was taken out of my sails.

After applying to other jobs and many conversations with my husband, I shifted my focus to the coffee and tea shop we purchased the prior year. I started to work there full-time covering shifts and acting as the operations manager. I fell into the trap of getting caught up in the minutia, working in the business instead of on the business. My life revolved around the day-to-day operations of the shop.

We opened a second location near the university which brought in a different demographic and more consistent traffic. However, we were continuing to contribute personal funds to the business without paying ourselves. It quickly became evident that the business was not sustainable. As we approached the three-year anniversary, staring down the possibility of bankruptcy, it was time to make a change.

Failure Is a Learning Experience

We attempted to sell the business, but in the long run we were forced to liquidate all of the assets. After coming to the realization I needed to return to the workforce, I began discussions with my previous employer about a sales manager role across the country.

It was time to start a new life.

I experienced two major setbacks in a short timeframe, and I was embarrassed. I found it difficult to come to terms with the situation feeling as though we had let ourselves, family, and friends down. It was a challenging transition, and we lost contact with several people from the community who supported our business over the years. We considered it a failure.

Focus on the Possibilities

Being laid off and closing a business was extremely taxing on me, but it has turned into a blessing for my growth and personal development. I am surrounded by an amazing network which provides tons of encouragement and challenges me to excel. I have found my passion in real estate.

I've learned what I previously considered failures have actually been the best form of education. The trajectory of my life has forever changed as a result. It's all about perspective. The struggle I experienced continues to be my motivation to build a path of financial freedom through cash flow. I vowed to no longer allow a corporation to hold me hostage to potential downfall. My first business venture was the stepping-stone to building a bigger and brighter future for myself and those around me. I'm grateful I didn't give up, shifted my focus to real estate, and improved my network. All of these things have been transformational and have opened up limitless possibilities.

My advice is, don't focus on what happened in the past or your current situation in the present. Focus on what could be next and don't lose sight of the possibilities that are ahead.

Don't Say No Immediately

Take time to reflect and understand.

Before Kurtis and I met, he bought and renovated a couple of single-family homes to lease as rental properties. He had the real estate itch and wanted to grow his portfolio. My only experience was in college when I bought a property with my parents, rented out the rooms, and lived almost rent free (with the exception of a few utilities). I didn't understand real estate and definitely didn't consider it as a vehicle for making money. He started exposing me to podcasts and books. I soaked up the material, but I was nervous about taking a leap into the investing world. Finally, I came to the realization it was time for me to face my fears and anxiety in order to create a better version of myself.

After relocating to Oregon, we started working with turnkey property providers. In our first year, we were able to purchase five rental properties with the support of our W-2 income. That year we also opened a real estate business for sales and acquisitions. Since then, we've done hundreds of transactions with our small team (myself, Kurtis, and our manager) while maintaining corporate positions.

Balancing a marriage and a business partnership is unarguably a challenge. Fortunately, we have complementary skill sets. I do a lot of the tactical, operational interfacing with vendors, legal and accounting team, as well as investor relations. On the flip side, Kurtis focuses on the future and our growth potential. He's more of the visionary. We support one another and have learned communication is vital to achieve success.

Your Network Defines Who You Are Becoming

Your experience and relationships define your wealth.

A few years ago, we started discussing a syndication business. After thinking about it, I agreed to keep an open mind. When I attended my first syndication event with The Real Estate Guys, I was immediately hooked because of the people I met. Since that time, we've exponentially expanded our network, built amazing friendships, and are continuously exposed to new concepts and experiences. Through GoBundance, Kyle Wilson's Inner Circle, Syndication Mentoring Club, and various investing groups, I've learned family doesn't have to be blood related. Instead, family can be created and chosen. I make a conscious effort to immerse myself with authentic, open-minded, socially conscious, resilient, supportive, and diverse people with an abundance mindset. Surround yourself with people who encourage greater potential and are ahead of where you strive to be.

Creating Win-Win Solutions for Others Through Syndication

Today, real estate syndication is our core business. We work with investors to present real estate projects in which they can contribute capital for passive cash flow. Investors can leverage our experience, network, team, knowledge, and strategic relationships to participate in opportunities which may have been too large for one person.

We strategically analyze opportunities and present creative offers to achieve win-win scenarios. That is our ultimate goal. We want everyone involved, (seller, buyer, and investor), to walk away with more than they started. We've built our business model around the concept of mutually beneficial solutions.

Giving Back

I have a passion for supporting children in need. One of my long-term goals is to provide safe and stable housing for foster care children with positive role models. I am also a benefactor to St. Jude's Children's Hospital and Le Bonheur Foundation, as these organizations have supported children and families in our lives.

We are passionate about making an impact personally and through our business. Our residential investments provide safe, affordable, clean housing, and we strive for sustainability. We're also having conversations with non-profit organizations to incorporate philanthropic efforts into our projects. This is why *impact* is our word for the current decade.

Don't have any regrets. Instead, focus on what you can start, stop, and continue doing to live your best life.

Connect with Ryan Pettitt at Prosperity Aid Capital Group for a personalized investment strategy consultation call by visiting www.prosperityaid.com or emailing him at ryan@prosperityaid.com. His goal is to throw down the rope and support those who are interested in changing their financial position through cash flowing assets.

DR. AMY NOVOTNY
The Breathing Habit to Eliminate Chronic Pain and Anxiety

Dr. Amy Novotny is an ultra-marathon runner, photographer who has traveled to six continents, and the founder of the PABR® Institute, where she helps people reduce and eliminate pain, stress, anxiety, sleep deprivation, orthopedic surgery, and the need for medication. She teaches how to calm the nervous system to relax the muscles and body through breathing and body repositioning techniques.

Under Control Until I Escaped

Stress started early in my life. It has been there as long as I can remember.

I grew up with a mother who was mentally ill, but I didn't know it at the time. I adored her and thought I had a normal childhood like everyone else, even though I never knew which personality would show up each day—Dr. Jekyll or Mr. Hyde. After I finished elementary school, she decided she couldn't handle living in the same state as my father. Within a matter of days, she sold almost everything and flew us from Arizona to Hawaii. After two weeks there, she realized our dad figured out where we were, so we headed to Iowa, where she had grown up.

She decided she didn't like the memories of Iowa, so she drove us to Henderson, NV. It didn't live up to her vision, so we headed back to Mesa, AZ, where we lived in a hotel for several months. She spent all of her savings, and I missed school for six months. Somehow I didn't fall behind and jumped right into advanced classes when I returned.

When I let her have complete control over me, things were fine. I didn't go out with friends and came straight home after school. Some days she was happy-go-lucky. Other days, she yelled that I was an ungrateful, selfish daughter and threatened to send me away. It took a long time to realize that it wasn't me or my actions. I couldn't make her happy, no matter how good or perfect I was. I never drank or have been drunk. I didn't smoke, do drugs, or have boyfriends. I didn't do anything but get straight A's. If I got less than a hundred percent, I was devastated. I wasn't allowed to make mistakes, but I couldn't sit or stand or talk without getting in trouble. I was scared to speak most of the time and often went most of the day without talking. Nothing made her happy.

I spent four years in high school and then the first two years as an undergraduate at Arizona State University tutoring my mom six to eight hours every night to help her get her undergraduate and master's degrees. I used studying abroad in college as my escape. I knew that my leaving would change everything. I needed relief.

I found a new life in France. I lived with a French family and learned the language and culture. I learned what it was like to have a French mother who trusted me and allowed me to grow and explore. My own mother tried to continue controlling me and threatened suicide while I was away. I didn't give in. Afterward, I backpacked Europe for three months. I knew when I came back she was going to kick me out, and I didn't look back. I moved out and began to work on me.

Reconciliation

I didn't speak to my mother for nine years. The stress of her in my life had become unbearable, and I couldn't face the unavoidable verbal beatings, so I had to cut her off to survive. On April Fool's Day 2014, I found out she was dying from cancer—within a week or two. I dropped everything and ran to the hospital. When I saw her, I burst into tears and apologized. She did the same. She said my coming back into her life gave her the energy and will to live. Her two-week prognosis turned into seven months, part of which she lived with me under hospice care.

There were times during those seven months that she reverted back to her old behaviors. She ordered me around, even knocking things on the ground so I had to pick them up. Once a week, I fought back verbally because the stress had become too much. I was beginning to develop a new breathing habit to calm me, but I wasn't quite skilled enough to implement it effectively in this high-stress situation. I accepted this wasn't the time to change her behavior; rather, it was time to provide care and comfort.

Her last promise to me was that she would celebrate my birthday with me. Even though she was nonverbal in the last minutes, we were able to reconcile. She had been comatose for a couple of days; but she came to, smiled, and squeezed my hand. I told her I knew she did the best she could and I loved her.

She made it two minutes into my birthday. Her mother was born that day. I was born that day, and she passed away that day. I had never seen her look so beautiful until the moment the stress of living left her body and all the wrinkles in her face faded away.

Breaking Away from Physical Therapy

The constant push from my mother to be perfect as a child seeped into my academic life. I was one of the top three scholars at ASU. In grad school, again, I was valedictorian and the only person to get straight A's throughout my doctoral program. I wanted to see if I could get lifetime straight A's because I wanted to learn everything I could.

When I finished my studies, I went the traditional route and worked as a physical therapist in a clinic. I saw some patients with chronic pain, especially back and neck pain, and I treated the standard ways: look at the joints above and below the injury, tighten the core, strengthen, stretch, and perform joint and soft tissue mobilizations. But it wasn't enough. I knew there had to be more to it. I was not analyzing the whole person, only addressing parts of the body. That's when I started to look at breathing. I became a director of a clinic for another company and started taking courses through the Postural Restoration Institute®. I started looking at how breathing and asymmetries in the body play a role in mobility. Then I started working on my own breathing habit.

Running 100 Mile Marathons

At the time, I was running marathons looking to qualify for Boston. I had run nine marathons and was getting into ultra-marathons, which are longer than 26.2 miles. I had just completed an Ironman triathlon and my first 100-miler on a track course, and I was looking forward to a second 100-mile ultra-marathon in the mountains. I started experimenting with breathing without changing my running or strengthening routines. I started getting faster and running became easier. I could run a marathon, do my specific breathing technique during and afterward to calm down, then get up and walk normally, and the next day go for a run again. With no other changes in my training, I dropped 14 minutes off my marathon time within seven months—a huge triumph. Most importantly, I knew I had to start using this to help other people develop a new breathing habit.

This realization and accomplishment coincided with my mother passing away a month and a half later. That's when I started looking at the impact of breathing on the nervous system and stress.

I wanted to see how much I could stress my body and still recover. I already had severe mental stress from losing my mom, but what about body stress? I started doing back-to-back races to see if my process would hold up. In 2017, I faced my greatest challenge: a fast road marathon, six days later a 102-mile mountain ultra-marathon, four weeks after that a 62-mile mountain ultra-marathon, seven days later a road marathon, and seven days after that a 50-mile mountain ultra-marathon. I came away without injury and just a little tired. I was onto something special.

Helping Robert Kiyosaki

I founded the PABR® Institute, **P**ain, **A**wareness, **B**reathing **R**elief, in 2018 to address our different pains, whether that pain is physical, stress, or anxiety. The PABR® philosophy uses awareness training of body position and muscle use along with a specific breathing technique to move us from our pain to relief. The focus is to help us sense the "fight or flight" nervous system calming down and regain control over our body. Ultimately, we develop a new breathing and body position habit.

I began shifting my life plans after reading the book *Rich Dad Poor Dad* in 2018. I then met the author, Robert Kiyosaki, on a cruise during a public book signing, where he told me that he was having pain in his hand. He shared that he had experienced a fall a year prior and had been checked out and told nothing was wrong. He still suffered from hand pain, so I offered to help.

Robert is a famous and high-achieving person. People come at him all the time, and he has a well-developed drive to perform. The military also taught him "chest out, shoulders back," which puts a nervous system on edge and a person in fight or flight mode. During his time as a pilot, he also had several crashes. Very clearly, his body was in protection mode and had been for a very long time. In a public lounge, I asked him to sit in a chair and walked him through some breathing and position training. Within a few minutes, he was practically asleep. When I woke him, he told me his pain was going away, even the pain in his neck and shoulders.

We needed to change how his nervous system works, so I asked him to continue practicing with me. It would take more than one session, especially since the nervous system resorts to old habits while sleeping. The next day, I met him in the cruise ship gym. I calmed him down enough to put him in a deep sleep and relax his whole body on a mat. He said he felt fabulous and the pain had gone away. The next day, I heard people on the cruise saying Robert Kiyosaki was looking for his body healer. He found me at lunch and exclaimed in front of the table that this was the first time in a year he had been able to sleep pain-free and without waking. Here's someone who gives and gives to others, and I gave him relief.

The Body and Its Stressors

As I've learned throughout my childhood and professional life, every stressor in life kicks us into fight or flight mode with physical repercussions. If we don't recognize this, our body doesn't return to a relaxed state, and this stress mode becomes our new baseline. Every new stressor, including trauma, piles onto the stress our body is already bearing. Cortisol levels go up, muscles tighten resulting in knots and inflexibility, and our breathing pattern changes. At a certain point, we hit a threshold. Once we cross that threshold, we can experience whole body crises that stop us in our tracks: chronic pain, adrenal fatigue, chronic fatigue syndrome, panic/anxiety attacks, and more. Help is possible.

We begin by addressing our body position and breathing pattern—both of which can put us in fight or flight mode or relaxation mode. Every time we stick out our chest and straighten our back, we're putting our body in fight or flight mode. This impacts our breathing too. This is great if we're tired or need to be alert for short periods of time, but we're not designed to spend 24 hours a day in this state. We're designed to be in rest mode and act when needed. To encourage this, I ask people to let their belly button go as they exhale because it allows their breastbone, chest, and ribs to drop down and in. This has a very calming influence on their body. Over time, they start to learn what it feels like to relax each part of their body, fight the effects of stress, and control muscle tension and use.

Resilience and Intentional Calm

After only knowing a life where stress was a constant, I've changed my daily habits to ensure calm in my nervous system. The daily body aches are no longer present and mental and emotional stresses no longer have grave impact on my body and well-being.

When I wake up, I sit up in bed in a ball against the wall and spend time breathing. We generally think we're calm during sleep, but we're often very active. If we are in fight or flight mode during the day, our body continues that at night. I correct this by repositioning my body to a relaxed position. I focus on my chest dropping down and in and my belly and lower back releasing during exhalation. From there, I do a little journaling before I get up for a daily run and work out. Lately, I've been spending time gardening to connect with nature.

I am often asked if these new breathing and body position habits last. I share a story of a client and now friend of mine who was scheduled for a total knee replacement and had been doing injections and medications for years. She's a psychologist and had been a psychiatric nurse prior to that. She thought my methods sounded interesting and a little bizarre, so she gave me a chance in 2016. Within two weeks, she canceled her surgery. It has been over four years, and she hasn't had an injection or taken anti-inflammatories since. She's now in her mid-70's and traveling to Antarctica and the Arctic, climbing in and out of Zodiacs pursuing wildlife photography. This client is just one of many who have avoided surgeries for rotator cuff tears, ACL tears, disc herniations, and joint replacements. When our awareness of the state of our body increases and we learn how to relax tension in specific areas of our body while activating new muscles, we own the change we sense. It becomes our new habit. And it lasts.

For more information on Dr. Amy Novotny, founder of the PABR® Institute, her private coaching, virtual sessions, group training, and her techniques, go to www.pabrinstitute.com. Email Dr. Amy for a free 15 minute consultation at amy@pabrinstitute.com.

FREDDY PEREZ
Building on Principles One Person at a Time

Freddy Perez is the founder of The Performance Companies, a corporation comprised of numerous companies centered primarily around real estate. It includes a brokerage, escrow company, property management, investments, insurance, and general contracting. He is a bestselling author, speaker, trainer, and leader in personal development as well as a high-level coach.

It's Not How You Start, It's How You Finish!

I moved from Mexico to this amazing country when I was three years old as the ninth of 10 kids. My dad was in the Bracero program, a seasonal agriculture migrant work program in the US. Wherever the work was, that's where we went. We settled in the Central Valley of California because of the work agriculture provided.

I was in a small gang growing up. I didn't get too far into it. I was one of the few that got out. When I decided that was no longer the life for me, I paid the price by getting my ass kicked a few times. I observed my parents, brothers, and sisters working so hard, and I knew that their sacrifice deserved better from me. So, I dove into sports.

Sports played a huge role in my life and had a big impact on me. I'm a guy who has a million ideas and is always going a hundred miles an hour. I need structure, positive influences, accountability, and to be around like-minded people working on a common goal.

In high school, I was a captain on just about every team I played on. Leadership came naturally to me. I was never the fastest, nor the most talented, but nobody was going to outwork me. That kept me on the field and kept me relevant in every team. I had a few coaches who made a big impact on my life. One in particular, Mr. Munter, made me feel like I was the most important kid in the world with unlimited potential. He was tough on me for sure, but he made me believe I could do anything. That deeply impacted my self-confidence, and once I felt that, I improved in every way.

The Day I Changed My Life

I graduated, and I went to a junior college nearby. I spent most of my days smoking weed and working in the fields and at a restaurant, barely scraping by. I was unhealthy in every way. My father had just had his second heart attack. I asked myself, "What am I doing with my life?"

I was in a small town. Most of my friends who'd had a positive impact on me had left. Some that were still around were from the same gang life I was in when I was a young kid. Some were becoming fathers already, some were starting to get felonies on their records, and some were dead. I realized all my positive influences were gone. Something had to change.

I had been in school two semesters when I told a friend to come over and take whatever furniture he wanted, got in my booger green 1980 Honda Accord, and moved to Bakersfield. I had become disgusted with who I was. Just like that, I made a decision that tremendously changed the trajectory of my life.

That wasn't the last time I've been disgusted with who I was. They say we keep reinventing ourselves as we get older, and I welcome all the improvement possible.

Build the People and They Build the Company

In Bakersfield, I found a job at Costco, and that's where I met my wonderful wife. We have now been together for 23 years and have three beautiful children. After my father died, I decided to leave Costco. Helping my parents was important to me, and so when I finally got the chance to take a risk, I did. I wanted control of my destiny, and I had my eye on real estate. I love helping people, I love being my own boss, and I work hard.

God blessed me with a great start in real estate. I became a Realtor, went to work at a big brokerage, and did well. The market fluctuated for the first 7-8 years, but I always found a way to be a top producer in any market. I started co-leading an office and coaching some agents. They were young, ambitious, and had the student mentality. I found that I loved coaching. They got together and asked me why not start my own company, and that's how The Performance Companies were born. I poured myself into my people, and the results started showing.

I first went to an independent brokerage with my friend and started building it on paper. I had the key people in place, put a plan together, saved enough money, and then built Performance Realtors.

Now in our fifth year, we have turned down more agents than we have ever signed on. We don't recruit much, if at all, which is very unusual for the industry. But that's just not who we are. We call ourselves a personal development company that just so happens to sell real estate. Most of our agents come to us by referral. Individuals in our environment love it so much that they go tell their friends in the business how much they enjoy being with us. If a potential agent doesn't have that mindset, if they don't take their health, finances, education, reading, and overall development seriously, if they're just transactional—they're not going to be a good fit here. They have got to want to get better in every way. If not, they become uncomfortable and leave. And I'm okay with that.

If they think they know it all, and they're not coachable, I don't care how old they are—it's not going to work. If they have the desire to get better and they're coachable and humble, we can work together and do some great things.

There's a philosophy: "You build the people, and they build the company." That has helped make The Performance Companies what they are today. My number one goal is to give my people all I got, to help them build the lives they truly desire. The rest takes care of itself.

I Play Differently

One of my favorite books is *Small Giants*. It's about companies that chose to be great instead of big. In the real estate industry, whoever has the most agents wins. I play differently and get a lot of flack from fellow brokers for that. They say things like, "Why the hell do you care about their development? As long as they're closing deals, who cares what is happening at home or how healthy they are or what they do in their spare time." By focusing on the entire person, I have been able to coach my people to be by far the most productive (per agent) company in the entire county. That is a statistic that I'm extremely proud of.

Some of my agents go home before 3:00 PM because they're so purposeful. They leverage their early morning routine, execute their tasks, and organize their team so that they can go home to enjoy their children. That brings me joy. I don't want workaholics. I want them to enjoy their life.

We're attracting quality people and are not on the path to be the biggest, but we always strive to be the best. That means being true to what we preach and practicing those foundational principles that I've learned from so many in personal development. I'm passionate about what I do and the personal satisfaction I get from watching my people succeed and their families grow.

They say that the number one factor of success is the quality of your relationships. The quality of my relationships is by far the most important thing in my life. And as long as I continue to dedicate myself to that, good things are going to continue to happen.

Always Being a Student

As the master, Jim Rohn said, "A formal education will make you a living; self-education will make you a fortune." That's my parents. They're the two biggest students who have the two biggest hearts. My father was a student of human interaction. He found a way to get along with everyone and always taught me the importance of relationships. If you met my mother, you would think you had just met the happiest person in the world. She raised 10 kids and is now blessed with 50 grandkids and 37 great-grandkids. If that is not true wealth, then I don't know what is. My parents were the true students, and that's why I take such pride in being a student, being humble, and being able to learn from anything and anyone. I believe I learn just as much when I am coaching as my agents do. My parents brought me to this amazing country to not only pursue MY dreams but also to make an impact and leave a legacy. What better way to do it than by always getting better and giving those who believe in me my very best.

Visit founder of Performance Realtors, bestselling author, speaker and trainer, personal development leader, and high-level coach Freddy Perez at www.freddyperez.net.

Email: freddy@freddyperez.net | Instagram: FreddyPerezPerformance Facebook: Freddy Perez

DENIS WAITLEY
Cultivating the Seeds of Greatness

Denis Waitley is a world-renowned speaker and is in the Sales & Marketing Executives' Association's International Speakers' Hall of Fame. Denis has written 16 bestselling books, including classics such as Seeds of Greatness, The Winner's Edge, Empires of the Mind, *and* Safari to the Soul. *His audio album* The Psychology of Winning *is the all-time bestselling program on self-mastery. Denis is the former chairman of psychology for the US Olympic Committee's Sports Medicine Council.*

Overcoming Leaky Self-Esteem

My parents divorced when I was in my teens. They were always arguing about money or my father's drinking, smoking, and socializing. I was always putting my pillow over my head in my bedroom to block out their constant bickering. My little brother was also hiding. He was seven years younger and my sister was three years older. My father joined the Merchant Marines at the onset of World War II and left when I was nine. He came into my room and said goodbye instead of goodnight. He returned briefly after the war, however soon left again, and I only saw him once a year thereafter.

No matter what I did, it wasn't good enough for my mother. She was a very negative person. I developed a very leaky self-esteem dependent on being a straight-A student, student body president, a good baseball player, and popular. One of the greatest mistakes we make is thinking we have to perform to become worthy. Yet, usually, we have to feel worthy before we perform. My mother kept comparing me with my father. *You'll grow up like him. You'll probably be a womanizer. You'll drink like he does. You'll be a "good for nothing" like him.* Unfortunately, I continued to wear some of those labels for years, but finally realized they were not part of a permanent uniform I needed to wear forever.

In her final years, she and I developed a warm and meaningful relationship. She lived to be 97, and I took care of her. She said to me, "I guess I wasn't a very good mother, was I?"

I said, "Actually, you gave me life. You gave me opportunity. You have a great imagination. You can write. You passed on so many things to me, Mom, that you don't even realize. I want you to know I really love you." I understood her better and knew that her life had not been easy. I was holding her when she passed away. I managed to reconcile those years and not carry any bitterness forward. In fact, I don't have any ill feelings toward anyone I've ever met past or present.

The *Seeds of Greatness* Planted in Grandmother's Garden

Growing up, I would go to Grandma's house because Grandma was the positive one in my family. I rode my bike 10 miles every Saturday, mowed her lawn, and got my reward: "Oh, you're such a good boy. You mow such a good lawn. You know, I think we deserve to have a piece of apple pie a la mode or a lemon tart." She just kept teaching me with positive reinforcement.

But the most important thing was the subject of my bestselling book, *Seeds of Greatness*. We planted a victory garden together during WWII. We had these little packets of seeds with a picture of the fruit or vegetable. Holding the cucumber seeds, I said, "Grandma, how do you know this little seed is going to turn into that?"

She said, "Because the seeds of greatness are already planted within the DNA of the cell, and if you cultivate it, water it, and care for it, you'll get out what you put in."

"But be careful. Weeds don't need watering. They blow in on the wind. They come in every day, and we have to pull the weeds out, being mindful of the flowers. The weeds are going to come. Carefully, pull them out, but don't focus on them. Instead of the weeds of failure, we want the seeds of greatness."

I said, "Will we lose the war?"

She said, "No, what goes around, comes around. You harvest what you sow. Here's what you do. Model yourself after people who've been great in their service to others, and you'll be successful and happy."

My grandmother, in addition to my children and grandchildren, have had the most incredible influence on my life.

Values Are More Likely Caught Than Taught

I have four children, many grandchildren, and now great-grandchildren, one of whom is already a teenager. I've learned to be a role model, not a critic. If they shouldn't be doing it, neither should you. Be someone worth emulating to your children. Set the example in your life. By preaching, I never got anywhere. I'm a highly sought-after professional speaker, I give a good lecture, but still, they watched me more than they listened to me talk.

It's much better to walk your talk. If you point out people's shortcomings, they manifest those. It's very hard to come away from what you're being preached not to do. Instead, lead them toward the desired result.

Wisdom and Failures

I have made every mistake you can make as a husband, father, son, friend, brother, you name it. I've lectured throughout the world and, more recently, all over China, and this young Chinese woman said, "You know, you are so perfect. Everything you say is perfect. I'm a failure because my husband divorced me because we had a little girl instead of a boy."

I said to her, "No. Actually, your marriage failed, but you're not a failure. That's an event. I have failed in marriage. I am not married now, but I am not divorced. I'm a single man. I don't continue to be divorced because it is finalized. I'm a flawed person who's not impressed with myself. I made that mistake, but I'm not going to keep living in it."

The older I get, the more I realize the importance of the few we love, our handful of friends, and helping young people by passing on everything we've learned. Knowledge is just like money. It does you no good when you have it, only when you employ it. If you die with it, it does you no good, so you'd better pass it on while you're alive. What you leave your children in values is much more precious than the valuables you leave them in your estate. They will cherish the time you spent with them much more than the money you spent on them.

The Importance of Nature

I wish I would've moved to a natural retreat in my sixties. I said to all my friends and colleagues that I would walk off stage and out of the arena. They said I never could, that I needed the applause. I finally realized that's not what I wanted at all. It never was, but I chased it for a while.

Now, on the family compound, we have bobcats, coyotes, deer, fish, and every kind of tree in the world: walnut, almond, macadamia, peach, plum, apricot, orange, grapefruit, pine, palm, pepper, and even redwood trees. I get to walk around, smell the roses and the fragrance of all the flowers and notice every butterfly and bird that passes by. I'm in charge of the dumpster, weed whacking, leaf blowing, and feeding the koi. It's really great to have something that you want to do, that you enjoy, rather than having to do it or feeding your ego or scoring more points. But I am not retired and never will be. I am engaged in teaching succeeding generations via distance learning. I don't need the money or the social media following. I need to exercise my brain, which like every other part of the body, "If you don't use it, you are bound to lose it."

From age nine, I became extremely interested in wildlife. The most amazing experiences in my life have been taking my entire family almost every year to the middle of Africa on safaris. In fact, I wrote one of my better books, *Safari to the Soul*, on these trips. It wasn't a bestseller because I wrote it for my family. Sitting in the middle of Africa, you're closer to your maker than you are sometimes in a marbled hall. Struck with the awesome creation of the world, I would sit for hours and hours. I'm not trying to record it to show others I was there, I'm engaged in it. We kept going back year after year. I regret not making those pilgrimages earlier in life and feel more at home there than in any other setting. Along the way, I got caught up like we all do in trying to perform and arrive "there." But there's no there. Living successfully is a process, not a status.

Evening Prime Time, Your Time to Create Success

Prime time is 6:00 p.m. to 11:00 p.m. EST. That's when everyone is watching their favorite programs on TV. What are they watching? Other people making money and having fun. Wait a minute. Sure, it gets you out of your mundane daily grind. Okay. Maybe an hour, that's enough. Live in prime time, don't watch it. It's the greatest lesson I learned in my early life. I fell into the routine of coming home after my day in the Navy, relaxing, and watching TV. When I decided to write a book, I had to write it at night and on weekends. That break in my routine allowed me to become involved in my life. I learned that my family and I could play instead of watching other people play. Instead of watching professional athletes, we could play softball or Frisbee, and instead of watching a beach, I could go to the beach. So I got out of my chair and got into life rather than watching it. I don't want to be a spectator.

Chase Your Passion, Not Your Pension

For me, a widow with a rose garden is as important as a politician, rock star, or superstar athlete. Let's say that you're not interested in entering your roses in the local flower show competition and the blue ribbon is not important for you; but you love taking care of flowers. The sheer exhilaration of doing something excellent for its own merit—not to prove it to others, not to get the money, and not to get accolades—is its own reward. We all want to be experts in something. We all want to be competitive and beat somebody to make us feel a little better. We all want material things. But the two greatest motivators of all are the sheer exhilaration of doing something excellent, that feels good, and doing it independently without somebody telling us to do it. Those two motivators drive more people to accomplish great things than all the money in the world.

Every success I've ever known has not been a success because he or she wanted to be rich. It was because each had something inside of them that had to be said or done. Success was then a byproduct because they were filling a need or solving a problem. I have talked to Bill Gates, Steven Spielberg, Jonas Salk, and others. They never really thought they were going to be rich or famous. It happened because what they did was magnificent and solved a problem or filled a need.

Don't let the financial expediency of your first job, paying off your student loans, or starting a family make your life decisions. Many young Gen Z's and Millennials are changing paths more often because they've learned what I learned. Chase your passion, not your pension. If you chase your passion, you're likely to get a bigger pension because you're doing something you love.

44

Don't let your first job determine your career. Keep learning everything you can. Dust off your childhood. Think of the things you did after school and that you loved to do in school. Think of the things you like to do on weekends. Hidden there are latent talents that you can bring out. Maybe your true passions are in an avocation or an after-work activity. Maybe you have a natural gift that will make you more money than your job. Your job does not have to be the major source of your income. Your present job may not be the source of your inspiration either. That may come from a hobby, an avocation. Make sure you're doing things that you love all the time and don't just get caught up in the grind. Don't follow the crowd. Follow your core values. Follow your internal compass. Follow your heart. Live in the moment, not for the moment.

To learn more about Denis Waitley and his speaking, courses, and teachings, please visit www.deniswaitley.com.

MIKE BUFFINGTON

Mentors vs Education, The Path to Building Multiple Companies

Mike Buffington is founder of several real estate management companies and president of One-Stop Communications, central Pennsylvania's leading provider of communication products and services since 1996. His success can be attributed to mentors who have helped him versus a traditional education.

Early Challenges and Opportunities

At an early age, I struggled with school. In grade school, it became apparent I had a learning disability. I see and hear words differently than most do. For many years I struggled with reading and writing, which made most classes extremely difficult.

In fifth grade, the school assigned a special teacher that helped me with some of my classes. At that time, I found it extremely embarrassing to have a teacher assigned to me for one-on-one instruction when others did not appear to need additional help. But today, I would welcome anybody helping me with any of my struggles. I don't agree with the education system that I have a learning disability. I have a learning difference, and this difference does not equal a disability.

My first business partnership started when I was in fourth grade. A landscaper and florist bought the farm across the street from my childhood home. He and his wife were so kind. They did not have kids at the time, and they treated me like their own. I would visit and ask if I could help, and he would always give me something to do. Shortly after we met, he and I started a Christmas business. He made centerpieces and wreaths, and I would sell them and Christmas trees. He bought all the supplies and we split the profits 60/40 after expenses.

We did this two years before my mother and I moved to central Pennsylvania. I remember feeling like the richest kid in town. I had thousands of dollars from this part-time business that we ran a couple months a year. At the time, I didn't realize I was becoming an entrepreneur. I just enjoyed the work, selling, and the fun of running a successful business. Later, I realized this experience sparked an idea in me: There is more than one way to make a living.

Education

I didn't go to college. It was my intention to attend, but after high school, things were not the best at home. My mother was coping with a mental illness, and my brother had taken his own life. He had struggled with substance abuse and most likely mental illness as well. I won't say I was a bad kid, but I am fortunate I graduated high school. I've since apologized to some of my teachers and the principal. I had an attitude and simply did not like being at school.

I wasn't worried about paying for college, but still, my heart wasn't in it. I decided to take a year off from school. That year became the rest of my life.

A mentor took me under his wing and hired me to work in his electrical contracting business. At first, I was organizing inventory and helping with back office tasks. But quickly, he made me an estimator and project manager. He showed me that my education level didn't matter. I could do whatever I wanted to do. He put me in rooms with architects, engineers, attorneys, and bankers and told me, "You know just as much, if not more, than they do about the projects we're working on. Don't worry about their education. You go with what you know."

From Part-Time Janitor to Big Business

I left that company not on the best terms. There were some things going on that I did not care for, but looking back, I was being young and dumb. I should have handled it differently. I do not regret leaving, but I do regret how I left.

I worked several odd jobs. Nothing suited me. I was even doing janitorial work part-time for a while. I started doing electrical contracting and phone system installations on the side. That's when my best friend's father introduced me to a guy in the wireless phone industry. At the time, handheld phones were not common. Most wireless phones were either in a carry bag or installed in your vehicle. He wanted somebody to help him sell wireless phones in central Pennsylvania.

That connection led to my involvement with one of the first wireless phone companies as an authorized retailer in central Pennsylvania that would eventually become part of AT&T. I started selling wireless phones out of my mother's house, and eventually at my uncle's business. I was enjoying selling again and hit the streets, peddling wireless phones, back in 1995.

In 1996, wireless phones sales were just starting to take off. I asked a friend to come work for me. I wasn't sure how I was going to pay him. I wasn't even sure how much we were going to make, if any. I decided he and I would work on commission, which in principle is about profit sharing. If the company did well, we would all do well.

We opened a retail store in my hometown and named it One-Stop Communications. Within a year, wireless phones started gaining real traction with consumers. A year later, things started to explode. After 24 years of adapting to consumer and business needs One-Stop Communications employs over 40 employees with six locations throughout central Pennsylvania and continues to explore new opportunities.

Real Estate

I bought my first rental property when I was 18. I sold it, and after the second property I acquired in my early 20s, I said I would never purchase a rental property again. I made so many mistakes with these first two properties that even though they both ended up being profitable, I could not understand why anyone would want to be a landlord.

As our business grew at One-Stop Communications, I was forced back into real estate to look for business locations. This led to purchase of a couple different commercial properties that took my real estate investing to the next level.

During this journey, I picked up *Rich Dad Poor Dad* by Robert Kiyosaki. His message resonated with me and changed my thinking on business, investing, and real estate. To this day, I refer back to many of the principles Kiyosaki provides in this book. With my first two properties, the problem was not the opportunity, the problem was my poor property management and lack of understanding of the business concepts of real estate investing. Today, I have real estate holdings in commercial, residential, mixed use, and short-term vacation rental properties, and my portfolio continues to grow. Commercial and retail spaces remain my core focus.

Community, The Impact of Relationships

Relationships are key to success in life and business. At one time, I took my relationships for granted and even damaged some. If I look at the areas of my life where I have the greatest success and happiness, I have one or more key people to thank. I feel so fortunate to have crossed paths with so many extraordinary people who have altered the direction of my life.

In my relationships, my aim is to serve without the expectation of anything in return. It's all about creating value for others. The more you develop honest and significant relationships and the more you give within your means, the more the world will create opportunities and reward you. That reward may come from somewhere unexpected, but it will come.

It is equally important to remove toxic relationships from your life. Creating value for others does not mean others have an open door to take advantage of you. If I see someone is just a taker, I am quick to avoid them going forward. There may be reasons I cannot totally remove them from my life, but I can limit our interaction and their negative impact. The most rewarding business relationships I enjoy have always been a fair exchange.

I live in a small rural community in central Pennsylvania filled with so many kind and good people, many of whom have supported me and my businesses over the years. Some of my best relationships can be found in my hometown, and some of my most impactful mentors.

As my community is adapting to meet new consumer and business demands, it is so rewarding to be in a position to contribute to this rebirth. My family and I make it a priority to get involved in projects that make our home a better place to live. I am extremely grateful to live in a community that has supported me for so many years and feel compelled to return that support.

Daily Action Is Success

Inaction equals failure! Every day we must take action! I am always asking myself, what do I need to do to better my life, better my family's life, better my business, and better my real estate investing? And then I take action on those items. For every action, there is an equal and opposite reaction. If we take no action, there will be no reaction and no reward.

Take action only on the items that will provide a worthwhile return. It does no good to take action on anything that produces no return. I always ask myself what the return on investment (ROI) is. ROI is not only about financial return, but also energy, time, and resources.

Wisdom

Attitude is the one thing we have total control of in our lives. You have a choice of how you are going to react to anything in life. The wrong attitude will quickly break any family, business, or organization. I believe life is 10% of what happens to us and 90% how we react to it. We always have three choices. Accept it, ignore it, or change it. Any other action is a waste of energy, time, and resources.

If you want to be truly successful in life, learn to solve problems. Sometimes those problems are our own struggles and disabilities. I find it extremely helpful to look through the eyes of others to understand their perspective and find solutions that are beneficial to everyone. If we put blinders on, we will have tunnel vision, and it will be a small world without many opportunities. The more and the larger the problems you learn to solve, the more successful you will be.

Michael Buffington oversees commercial and residential investment property management companies. He continues to build his portfolio of businesses and real estate investments with partners and help others overcome learning disabilities to develop business and investment strategies.

www.michaelbuffington.com
mike@michaelbuffington.com

MAURICIO RAULD
An Unlikely Blessing

Founder and CEO of Premier Law Group Mauricio Rauld is one of the premier syndication attorneys in the US. Named "Rising Star" by **Super Lawyers** *magazine, Mauricio regularly shares the stage with The Real Estate Guys, Robert Kiyosaki, Ken McElroy, Rod Khleif, Brad Sumrok, and other industry leaders.*

The Rat Race

After graduating law school, I joined a great, family-oriented litigation firm as a first-year associate. I represented big securities firms like JP Morgan, Merrill Lynch, Prudential, and American Express in lawsuits filed against them. This meant I spent quite a bit of time in courtrooms, taking depositions, and attending trials.

Although the firm was amazing, I realized that something was off. I found myself getting up every morning, showering, getting dressed, driving to the office, working all day, working all night, coming home, eating, (maybe) working out, watching a little TV, and going to bed. And the next morning, doing it all over again. I even went to work on the weekends and noticed senior law partners, who I knew were family-oriented, cranking away on Sunday morning. I knew there had to be something better, something more to life. But what?

Big, Defining Moment

My mentor, Jim Rohn, used to say, "and then, good fortune came my way and who can explain good fortune?" Well, for me, good fortune came in the form of a little purple book. In preparation for a five-hour plane ride, while heading home from a birthday trip, I was looking for something to read on the plane. I came across *Rich Dad, Poor Dad* by Robert Kiyosaki. At the time, I hated books with the word "rich" in the title, so I looked for something else to read. Fortunately, I couldn't find anything else and the #1 *New York Times* bestseller sticker convinced me, so begrudgingly, I bought it.

Of course, I devoured it on the plane. It blew me away. I kept saying, "Yes, that's right. There's more to this than what I'm doing now!"

The following week, driving down the streets of LA, I heard Robert Kiyosaki on the radio with a drop-in ad for The Real Estate Guys who were doing a real estate event in Southern California for the first time. Robert said, "If you're serious about investing in real estate, check out The Real Estate Guys, they really know what they're talking about." Had I not read his book the prior week, this call to action would have gone right past me like any other radio ad. Instead, because I was very interested in real estate, I attended the event, and that's how I was introduced to The Real Estate Guys. Months later, I left my law firm and went to work in-house for them.

A Lesson in Single Point Failure

For 30 years, I've lived with Crohn's disease, which is an immune deficiency. Basically, my immune system attacks my gut, causing pain, inflammation, fatigue, and often results in blockages in the intestines. The symptoms are managed with medication.

Following the initial diagnosis and treatment, the disease went dormant for about 15 years, so I was feeling pretty good and I just lived my life and forgot about it. When you're feeling good, you start to think maybe you're okay. I stopped taking my meds and stopped going to the doctor.

A few years ago, I started having some extremely painful flare ups, which led me to get some tests, X-rays, and MRIs done. Tests revealed that portions of my intestines were blocked and surgery was the only option. Typically, it's a routine arthroscopic procedure where surgeons simply cut out the inflamed portion that is causing the blockage. You're in the hospital for five days and then are able to work again after a two to three-week recovery.

Unfortunately for me, three days after my surgery, my intestines were so inflamed that the staples used to reconnect the intestines didn't hold, and my intestines ruptured at the surgical site, causing bacteria and venom to spill inside my body.

They took me for emergency surgery to clean it up. I was septic for a while, which I later found out carries a 30% chance of death. That explains why everybody looked so freaked out when I was being rolled into the operating room. I ended up having 10 procedures in all.

Back to Life

For six months of 2018, I was in and out of the hospital due to infections and other relapses. I lost 60 pounds as my weight dropped to 113 pounds, just bones and skin. It took me a while to gain that back. My body was rejecting food, and I was fed intravenously for a while.

Fittingly, my first event back was The Real Estate Guys syndication seminar eight months after surgery. I was still only 120 pounds, and I wondered if I had enough energy to get through my presentation. I did, and slowly but surely, my system started coming back, and my appetite returned.

Another year, and I was back, having gained back the weight and then some. Fortunately, there was a bit of a syndication boom, and I took on quite a lot of new business.

But while I was recovering, everything came to a halt. My law practice was just me and thus I was a single-point failure. There were no clients coming in. My existing clients were understanding, but at the end of the day, clients have to close on their properties. I learned the hard way that I couldn't keep being a one man show. I made the decision to make some drastic changes to the business.

Being a Syndicator, Benefits and Risks

In real estate, most investors start small, using their own money and credit to buy single-family homes, duplexes, or fourplexes. At some point, real estate investors either run out of money or want to make the jump to buying bigger properties. Their options are either to stop investing (while they save up for the next down payment) or go to friends, family, and other investors to raise the money. That's what a syndication is—simply aggregating other people's money. What many investors don't realize is that when they aggregate and take money from other investors, they are typically selling securities.

You can't just take people's money and put it into a property. This is probably the biggest mistake I see people who are aggregating money make. Because you are selling securities, you've got to follow the rules and regulations from the Securities and Exchange Commission, the SEC. That's what I do. I ensure that when somebody wants to do a syndication they're doing it in full compliance with securities laws. Failure to follow these rules are Federal offenses, so this is serious business.

Securities laws are extremely complex, but my "secret sauce" is that I am able to take complex securities matters and make them easy to understand. This is why I believe clients gravitate towards me and one of the main reasons I try and put out as much educational content on my YouTube channel, social media, and podcast.

If you are not into real estate, it's arguably the greatest wealth creation vehicle of all the time. The tax benefits alone are one of the main reasons people are drawn to this asset class, especially higher income earners with high tax bills. Real estate allows you to shelter and offset much of your income and reduce those tax bills.

Because many high-income earners are busy professionals and don't have time to learn about real estate investing, syndication is a great way for them to write a check and participate passively while accessing the benefit of a multimillion-dollar property.

The syndicator gets rewarded for this. They're adding value to the marketplace by allowing passive investors who don't have the time or the inclination to research and find the right property to still participate in real estate. The syndicator gets rewarded with a piece of the pie without having to put much, if any, of their own money into the deals. The tax benefits for the syndicator are arguably even greater than the tax benefits for passive investors.

Huge Optimist

I'm a huge optimist, a big dreamer, and a big goal setter who lives in the future (almost to a fault). I'm always looking at the great things ahead.

I've never had many obstacles. Everything in life had gone according to plan until my first.

Looking back, it was one of the best things that ever happened to me. Getting sick forced me to create what I have now instead of staying a solopreneur buried with work, unable to scale and a single-point failure. Now, I have mapped out the growth of my company and instituted processes and procedures that ensure that never again will I become the single point failure.

It is a work in progress, but my illness is what finally got me to step away from the day-to-day grind of the business and focus on putting a future plan in place. I feel confident that if the same thing happened again, we wouldn't miss a beat. With my new team in place, if I disappeared off the face of the Earth for three months, everything would be fine.

The biggest lesson I learned from my ordeal is <u>don't put things off</u> until tomorrow. Don't wait to create that living trust and will. Don't wait to make that phone call to your loved ones that you have been avoiding. Don't procrastinate on important things. You never know what's going to happen tomorrow.

Syndication attorney Mauricio Rauld of Premier Law Group can be contacted at www.PremierLawGroup.net. Check out his content on his personal YouTube channel, LinkedIn, and Facebook, including his upcoming YouTube show The Ask Mauricio Show and syndication podcast.

GREG SELF

Escaping the 9-5, Finding My WHY & Building Generational Wealth

Greg Self is a serial entrepreneur focused in real estate investing, private lending, and senior housing developments. He and his wife and business partner Heather co-founded New Hope Senior Living, Self Capital Group, and several other companies. They live near Nashville with their family and enjoy traveling the world.

Getting Started

Growing up in a small town had many benefits, but also a lot of perceived limitations. Everyone seemed to have the same dream; graduate from high school and get a "good job" at the local factory. It was honest work, but watching my parents come home exhausted from a long days' work, day after day, year after year, I knew that I wanted something more.

In 1999, I read *Rich Dad Poor Dad* by Robert Kiyosaki. That book planted a seed that ultimately changed my life. Over the next few years, I spent my spare time reading, going to meetups and focusing on personal development. In 2004, I was invited to a Cashflow game night hosted by our local real estate investors association. This is where I learned about the powerful roles that mentors play.

My first renovation was completed under the guidance of experts. I finished this project on time and on budget all while working a full-time job. Leveraging their knowledge and experience allowed me to collapse timeframes and save a lot of money on unnecessary mistakes.

Soon after I successfully completed that renovation, another deal hit the market. I remember feeling so defeated when I could not get off of work in time to view that property and ultimately lost the deal. A friend of mine purchased the house and made $18,000. Two days later, I negotiated a step-down exit strategy with my employer.

In 2006, on my 30th birthday, I successfully transitioned out of the rat race. Thinking back, missing out on that $18,000 deal ended up making me more money than I ever dreamed possible.

Instant Family

I have learned so many lessons over the years from my parents. Watching how they loved and supported each other throughout my life was incredibly inspiring. They celebrated their 53rd wedding anniversary just before my daddy passed.

I had always wanted to experience that level of love and partnership in my life; however, I was so focused on building my business, it never seemed to be the right time.

Then it happened! In 2009, I met the love of my life. Heather was studying real estate investing and working on building a property management business. I always wanted children and she had four. Overnight it seemed, I had gone from being a single guy to being a husband and a father. People ask me all the time how I handled that transition. Let's face it, I was scared. *What if I wasn't ready? What if it did not work out?* She was everything I had ever wanted in a partner. Heather was an incredible leader, a brilliant thinker, and the most loving, open-hearted, and beautiful woman I had ever met. I knew she was the one! When the day came for me to meet the kids for the first time, I was extremely nervous. After just a few minutes, I knew I was meant to be their dad. Earning that role will always be my biggest success and the greatest honor of my life.

The HUD Niche

Heather and I began working together shortly after meeting. We quickly learned how to leverage each other's strengths and abilities. We were presented with a unique buying opportunity during the aftermath of the 2008 mortgage crisis.

The Housing and Urban Development (HUD) website was a great resource for finding deals at the time. We were making dozens of offers daily and tracking everything on an excel spreadsheet. It was not long before we started seeing a trend in accepted and countered offers. After doing some calculations, we figured out the exact percentage it would take to get an accepted offer.

Soon after learning this, we noticed that many of the new listings were being posted on their website after 5 p.m. This gave us an additional advantage because most people seemed to stop looking for deals after the traditional 9-5 workday. Now, we were able to make acceptable offers before most people even knew the property was available.

With this newfound knowledge, Heather and I started closing 2-3 homes per week for the next few years. Throughout this buying frenzy, we had to become experts in many different exit strategies: we built a substantial rental portfolio, successfully flipped hundreds of houses, and wholesaled countless properties that didn't fit our desired rental specifications. As the market began to heat up, traditional rental properties became more difficult to find, so we pivoted to investing in short-term vacation rentals.

Adjusting to Curve Balls

In 2015 and 2016, life had thrown us many Major League curveballs. After a car accident, Heather had major back surgery that required a long rehabilitation period. My mom's health had declined significantly after my dad passed, and she began needing around the clock care. I was suddenly playing the role of a full-time caregiver, all while trying to keep our fast-paced businesses moving forward. It quickly became clear that what we had been doing before would no longer work. I thought about how my dad would have handled this situation because he always seemed to have the answers. He would have said, "Start where you are, do what you can, and use what you have."

In 2017, we were approached by a California-based hedge fund willing to pay well over market value for a portion of our portfolio. It had always been our strategy to hold our cash flowing assets to fund our retirement; however, our circumstances had changed, and we needed to adapt. Selling those properties allowed us to take some time off and refocus on how we wanted the next chapter of our lives to unfold. During our semi-retirement, we still did the occasional flip and added back a few rentals along the way, but we were more focused on the bigger picture. *How do we continue to transition from success to significance? What problems are we passionate about solving? How do we create a life that will live beyond us?* So, we focused on building our network and attending events across the US with those questions in mind. As my wife Heather says, "Sometimes to grow, you must find people that can introduce you to a new version of yourself."

Anyone who knows me will tell you that I am a very purpose-driven individual. I am a firm believer that once you identify a problem that you can solve, it becomes your duty to solve it.

While researching the best options for my mom's care, we ran into one issue after another. In short, we had options, but none were good. I would have never expected this to be the problem that ignited our passion, but there it was. We are now on a mission to provide our seniors with the best possible solutions to live out their remaining years with grace, dignity, and wellness. In 2018, Heather and I founded New Hope Senior Living. This is a spectacular,

8000 square foot, southern estate on 18 beautiful acres. This home provides all the things we would want in our later years and the lifestyle my mom so very much deserves.

We knew back when we sold those rentals that we would be losing money long-term, but the price of not selling them would have come at a much greater cost.

Giving Back

As a way of teaching our kids gratitude and giving back, Heather and I started an annual charity called Winter Backpacks for the Homeless. Around Christmas in 2018, we put together 50 backpacks filled with hygiene products and winter necessities to donate. In 2019, we decided to do it again, only bigger. We accepted sponsors and were able to serve so many more people in need. This presented a great opportunity to teach the younger generation how to organize, delegate, and set up systems. Our kids recruited friends from school to help organize and fill the bags. It was amazing to watch these teenagers working together to reach a common goal of helping others in need.

During this process, we were surprised to learn about senior citizens who were unable to purchase the basic necessities after paying the high cost of traditional senior care. In addition, we found a large population of college students willing to live in their cars to receive a college education. This charity was originally started because we wanted to teach our children about giving back, but I never dreamed it would solidify our passions for creating a better existence for our senior population and our desire to educate youth on financial freedom.

Final Thoughts

It is important to begin every day, every task, and every business with the end in mind. When I structure a business, I always start with creating a set of systems that my team can run whether I am there or not. I systematize my businesses so that I can manage them from the top deck of a cruise ship from anywhere in the world. To do this, I build teams with strong character and a burning desire to grow, while focusing less on their actual skills, which can be taught.

Integrity and authenticity are qualities I look for when building my network. As Jim Rohn so famously said, "You are the average of the five people you spend the most time with." This idea encourages me to continually evaluate my circle of influence. Adopting this practice gave me the honor of learning from some of the most influential thought leaders in the world. I am honored to call many of them my friends and mentors. When life presents challenges, I ask myself *"What would Bob do?"* Bob Helms, affectionately known as The Godfather of Real Estate, shared so many ideas on life, on business, and on relationships with me. I will forever be grateful for the long conversations and thought-provoking ideas he shared. He made me a better leader, husband, and father. His legacy lives on.

Since becoming an entrepreneur, I have achieved tremendous success, but quickly learned that success means nothing without significance. Always remember, when you get to where you're going, turn around and help the next person in line.

To connect with Greg Self or learn more about investing, email Greg@GregSelf.com or find him on Facebook @GregKSelf. If you would like to receive Heather's Entrepreneurs Guide to Success & Significance, *visit HeatherSelf.com.*

JIM GARDNER
Learning-Challenged Hoodlum to Performance Coach of Elite Athletes and Executives

Jim Gardner is the mental and emotional performance coach of elite athletes and C-suite executives. He was a 30+ year leader and executive with several iconic brands including McKesson, Pizza Hut, Fidelity Investments, and Levi Strauss & Co. Jim is also Board Chairman of The Adaptive Training Foundation.

Tough Times

When I was 10 years old in Wichita, Kansas, my mother decided to divorce my father. She was enamored with a guy who was on the run from prison in North Carolina. The con brought his element with him into my mom's house for four years. My dad remarried, started a new family, and moved to Denver.

After the con, there were a handful of others, including a literal Skid Row alcoholic and sexual predator. Finally, there was a railroader who seemed decent at first, until we found out he used the railroad for interstate cocaine trafficking and lured my youngest sister into the world of drugs.

Because I felt a sense of control, the streets often seemed safer than being in my mom's house during my years from 11 to 17. I was incredibly angry, I lost hope, and I became violent! When my rage got triggered, I didn't care who got hurt or what got destroyed.

Even during the riots of 1968, my friends and I ran the streets. We broke into buildings and blew things up to steal merchandise to resell. I got involved in drugs, more selling than using.

We were diligent about planning things out. It's unbelievable that we never got caught or arrested. That instinct for planning and attention to detail ended up benefiting me in my career down the line.

Every day on the streets there were confrontations and crises. I quickly learned that to survive those situations, I had to connect and communicate, immediately identifying the acknowledgement and love that the other person was desperately seeking. I wouldn't be here to share my story had I not been a skilled connector. If you can figure out that hunger someone is feeling, you can save your life and possibly change theirs in a matter of seconds.

Life Savers

I found out years later that I am dyslexic. If you can't read, it makes everything in school a challenge. I basically just didn't go to school very often, avoiding the agony and additional anger. On a good day, I was a D student through junior and senior high school.

I suffered through to my senior year where, Louis Bourlard, my US Government teacher stepped in. He was kind of a hard-ass, but kids really liked him. Mr. Bourlard actually said to me one day as I was leaving class, "Gardner, you're either gonna die soon or you can change the world." He asked me if I had thought about college. I laughed because that was the last thing I wanted to do. He was relentless with a kid from No Hope, Nowhere, and he changed the trajectory of my life. Mr. Bourlard proved to me that he gave a damn by acknowledging me and giving me hope. Due to his persistence, I graduated with my high school class and then started college that September.

Right Place, Right Time

Serendipitously, I attended Wichita State where the former dean of the business school, Fran Jabara, had consulted for leaders who would become incredible mentors to me. Wichita, Kansas is the original home of Pizza Hut and Rent-A-Center. It is also the home of Learjet, Cessna Aircraft, Beechcraft, and Coleman.

Fran had direct access to all of these business people out of this relatively small Midwestern town and his vision was for them to give back. He started The Center For Entrepreneurship and brought those leaders in along with some others like Dave Thomas, founder of Wendy's, and Jack DeBoer, who conceived the extended stay hotel chain Residence Inn.

Street life prepared me to be fearless in approaching anyone. I quickly learned that the more I sought to learn from these guys, the more they were willing to share with me. I never finished college, but received an invaluable education.

Beyond the Corporate Jungle

Thirty years later, I had grown weary in my global positions. Living in Dallas, it was constant travel for 13 years with Levi Strauss, preceded by commuting for 10 years from Dallas to Boston with Fidelity Investments. I had a family, and I was just tired of the hamster wheel that had become my life. I felt like there was something more.

A few months after I left the corporate jungle, I met a guy named John Maxwell, in my church of all places. John is arguably the world's guru on leadership. I'm blessed to be a Founding Member of the John Maxwell Team.

A few years earlier, my daughter was introduced to the game of golf, ultimately becoming world-ranked. I had the opportunity to observe thousands of hours of different aspects to elite coaching since she had—a swing coach, a short game coach, a physical therapist, a nutritionist, a sports psychologist—and how they all worked together to enable her to be what she became.

It was these two experiences that inspired me to focus on starting the journey of developing my own system to become a full-time professional performance coach.

Elite Performance Coaching

With all new clients, I ask them to explain who they're becoming and why they do what they do. They're so caught off guard with the first question, few have answers. They can quickly and easily explain what they do. It's then readily apparent that we have an identity crisis. Athlete clients get into a sport as kids, excel, enjoy it, and advance. The same is true for my C-suite clients. They were often motivated to excel based on the trophies they received by exceeding the expectations of others.

My clients come to me to learn to optimize their performance to ever-expanding levels. Consistently practicing excellence through relentless, premeditated, meticulous practices, we learn to love the processes in new habits, rituals, and systems that create the best outcomes. My clients soon see who they are becoming through these processes, allowing them to be of significantly greater service in all they do personally and professionally. My clients become masters at practicing excellence in continuing to develop their elite physical, mental, and emotional capabilities, while also developing their capacity for preparation to perform at their best in the most extreme situations.

A More Productive "Day"

One might think that high or elite performers are great stewards of their resources, especially time. Not so much. Second only to fitness, time is our most valuable resource. We can invest it, using it to serve and to create value, we can spend it, using it to take care of routine yet necessary tasks, or we can waste it, the default and usually the largest bucket. So, when I ask my clients how many days are in 24 hours, they look at me strangely and offer the conventional answer of one. But what if you considered that there could be six days in 24 hours, I ask them? And what if you learn how Day 4 is the most critical day of the 6?

Rest, recovery, and fun are investments of your time. These things allow your energy and your focus to be restored. Plan them into your days and weeks. When you think you're too busy, I guarantee you that I can find where you are wasting time and you can convert that time into an investment. Spending time is doing the things we all have to do, such as paying bills, having the oil changed in your vehicle, taking a shower, etc. You guessed it, everything else is wasting time.

The Adaptive Training Foundation (ATF)

I met recently retired NFL linebacker, David Vobora, in 2016 through a common friend, retired U.S. Air Force Pilot, Desert Storm combat Veteran, and nine-year Dallas Cowboy, Chad Hennings.

Following his NFL retirement, David was training professional athletes in Dallas. That is, until Retired Army Staff Sergeant Travis Mills helped David find his true calling. While on patrol, during his third tour of duty in Afghanistan, Travis lost portions of all four limbs from an IED (improvised explosive device).

When David met Travis, he asked what he was doing to get into shape. David then invited Travis to his gym and as they say, the rest is history.

David quickly found that when you create a situation for people to demonstrate to themselves what they're physically capable of, especially when they demonstrate feats that they previously considered to be impossible, it changes their life and the lives of others.

ATF is now where veterans and civilians who were born with or have experienced physical impairment, learn to *Defy Impossible* through physical fitness, mindfulness, and community.

At ATF, people with birth defects, Parkinson's disease, epilepsy, spinal cord injuries, amputations, and other challenges learn to adapt to a new life of health, fitness, and meaning.

Over 200 adaptive athletes, as they become, have graduated the nine-week ATF program. None of the alumni or future athletes pay a dime for their participation in ATF. Everything ATF does is 100% funded by people like you.

I can share with you the incredible stories of these athletes for days, and you can watch the social media videos. However, there is no way to describe the experience of walking through the front doors of the ATF gym. It's an experience you will likely never forget, and you will be compelled, as I was, to become in some way involved with this incredible tribe.

As a performance coach, I'm blessed with the opportunity to work with the staff and trainers on preparation to always present their best for the athletes, donors, and friends of ATF. I'm further blessed to often be asked by the athletes to work with them on personal performance practices.

Journey Checkpoint

I use the tagline *Practicing Excellence* because who we are becoming and what we do is really all about practice for optimum performance in all aspects of life. Being fully prepared to perform is true freedom.

I ask my clients—Are you distracted by focusing on the outcome, the win, or the recognition? Or, are you practicing for the love of always being prepared for "*Go Time*" through your relentless, premeditated, meticulous practice? Are you practicing to become more fit, physically, mentally, and emotionally? My challenge to you today is to take an action step into *Practicing Excellence* for your optimized preparation and elite performance so that you too can begin to experience true freedom.

Develop the mindset and behaviors that enable sustainable, optimized preparation and elite performance. Contact Jim Gardner about coaching, consulting, and speaking. Jim will send you a free signed copy of The Mindset For Practicing Excellence *at Jim@JimGardnerLive.com. JimGardnerLive.com*

ANNA KELLEY
From Girl in the Projects to Apartment Millionaire

Anna Kelley has active ownership in a $60 million rental portfolio and is invested in over 2000 doors. Anna seeks out the best multifamily investments for her partners and investors, is a sought-after speaker and coach, and enjoys helping others overcome fear and minimize risk in real estate.

Humble Beginnings & Big Dreams

Dreams are powerful motivators. Many are convinced only the lucky few with money, skills, intelligence, connections, and looks can achieve their dreams. They give up on the possibility of the extraordinary and resign themselves to pursuing the ordinary. I believe the main thing which separates the successful from the ordinary is a relentless determination to go after dreams despite a lack of resources and despite roadblocks and fears.

For some, it seems the extraordinary happens quickly with little effort. For most, the journey is not a well-paved shortcut. It's a long, bumpy path to a destination, which is but a cloudy vision until the light brings it into view. As I reflect on my bumpy path to financial freedom, the habits which have yielded my success are: dreaming of greater things, mustering the determination to relentlessly pursue those dreams, using time wisely, and "putting on" my armor of hope, faith, grit, and grace.

Growing up in HUD project apartments, I had little given to me. I watched my mother struggle to provide for us, watched my siblings while she worked a second job, and watched as she fought to leave multiple abusive relationships. I watched my schoolmates who seemed to have perfect lives, with successful parents, and nice clothes and homes. I watched and watched. And then I dreamed.

Achieve Extraordinary Success with Extraordinary Effort

From a young age, I perceived that families who made better choices had greater success, wealth, and happiness. To escape the projects, I knew I had to spend my time and effort becoming the best at every opportunity I was given. I practiced my flute and studied for hours hoping for scholarships, and graduated high school early so I could get on with achieving my dreams.

I graduated college early while working full-time and winning two employee of the year awards. I was hired at Bank of America and won the award for top financial relationship manager in Texas my first year, despite being underqualified when they hired me. I credit much of my success to realizing we can only achieve extraordinary success when we push through hurdles and seeming inadequacies to go for what we want, even if it seems impossible.

As life went on, I thought I had made it. I escaped poverty, married a doctor, and had a comfortable life and career at AIG. I was determined to continue up the corporate ladder until I had my first child.

Becoming a Mother Changed Everything

I knew the moment I held my son, I wanted to stay home with him to provide guidance and love. I also needed financial security, as I had worked so hard to escape poverty and give my children a better life. My husband just started his career and had significant school debt, so my job provided our stability. Not inclined to give up on finding a solution, I turned to real estate.

With HGTV convincing us it would be easy, we flipped our first house. We made mistakes, lost money, and gave up flipping. We had another baby, sold our house, moved across the country to start my husband's practice, and bought our first multifamily property in 2007. We bought and moved into a four-plex to save money. I just knew his practice would take off, we could buy more small apartment buildings, and I would be home with my babies in no time!

Developing Grit Through Unforeseen Hurdles

Through a financial crisis in 2008, a job at a company that almost failed, losing most of my 401(k), healthcare changes straining our practice, and banks unwilling to finance more properties, it took years just to stay afloat. My dreams of being a stay-at-home mom were shattered! Having done everything I knew possible to achieve financial stability, nothing went as planned.

Disheartened, working 80 hours a week between my job, rentals, and husband's office, and now raising four children, I was at a crossroads. I knew creating more passive income through real estate was the way forward, but we had to find a way to buy more properties without money or bank financing. In 2014, I developed a five-year plan to buy enough small apartment buildings to allow me to retire. I started structuring deals creatively through seller financing and partnerships, and eventually, banks were willing to lend. I then started purchasing larger apartments with partners.

By the grace of God, I purchased enough rental property to retire in 2019 at age 44. Not only had I replaced my six-figure income, but we went from a negative net worth to a multimillion-dollar net worth. I now have active ownership in over $60M of multifamily apartments. Our hard-fought journey to financial freedom was achieved through blood, sweat, and tears, but I'm grateful I decided to relentlessly pursue this dream for as long as it took! With my children now in school, my dream of being a stay-at-home mom was not realized the way I envisioned. But we have learned valuable lessons and learned to weather the storms of life with strength, determination, faith, and love. I've also discovered habits that lead to success and am now dreaming of and pursuing even greater things through these habits.

Habits That Yield Success

1. Create your dream life by design. You must have a purpose greater than the pain you will experience on the journey! Keep your vision in front of you and a statement on why it is worth relentlessly pursuing! Decide to do something each day toward making your vision a reality!

2. Develop a mindset of faith, hope, and grit. Mindset is a choice! Believe that: it's going to be okay, you have what it takes to solve every problem, and each challenge will make you stronger and wiser. When you fall in the mud, do not wallow in it! Get back up!

3. Give yourself grace! Forgive yourself when you struggle and make mistakes. Allow yourself to slow down or pivot for the sake of joy!

4. Design your work to serve your vision for life. Working from a place of happiness and fulfillment by design will give you greater clarity, energy, creativity, and joy! Watch your business and life thrive because of the happy person at the helm!

   Create a Guiding Principles Document. Answer: Who do you want to become? What are your non-negotiables for a life well lived? What must you do to grow spiritually, relationally, financially, and in health. Then set goals for such growth. My Guiding Principles Document is based on the character traits of the Proverbs 31 woman who balances her household and businesses with wisdom, strength, and grace.

Create a Business Growth Statement. I will share mine as an example: *I will grow my multifamily business as quickly and wisely as possible by working hard and strategically 30 hours a week. This time limit will allow me to focus on my physical and spiritual health and to spend each evening developing strong relationships and memories with my children. If my work regularly causes me to sacrifice my spiritual, physical, and relational health, I will reevaluate, redesign, delegate, or remove those pursuits which no longer serve my vision for a life well lived.*

Filter every goal and opportunity through your Guiding Principles Document and Business Growth Statement. If aligned, consider it. If not, say no!

Implement time-blocking. Block your entire week in 30-60 minute increments. First, block time for non-negotiables from your Guiding Principles Document for physical, spiritual, and relational well-being. Then block time for mandatory family and core business activities. Anything else must fit in your calendar without giving up time dedicated to growth in these areas. For each opportunity, ask: How can I make time for this? Will it bring me joy? What do I have to give up to fit this in my schedule?

Annually reevaluate your goals to see if they're still aligned with your life vision. Ask: Do I have too much on my plate? Am I happy? Am I living financial freedom or am I a slave to its pursuit? Do I need to drop or rework goals not serving me well?

Dreaming New Dreams for Greater Things

Sometimes our dreams are not the full picture of what God has in store for us. Now that my daytime hours are my own, I've started dreaming of greater things for myself, my family, and others.

I've dreamed of helping others create financial stability and real estate wealth that lasts. I started a company, Greater Purpose Capital, focused on bringing strong, passive investment opportunities to investors which also positively impact our world. I've developed a multifamily investing course and have become a sought-after speaker at real estate events across the country.

I'm also a founding board member of Kingdom Minded Investors, a faith-based organization investing in apartments like the one I grew up in, not only for financial returns, but more importantly, for eternal returns in the lives of people in our communities. I feel blessed to be able to encourage little girls and single moms living a life I once lived through proof that with financial education, love, faith, and hope, great things await them. It is something I know I was made to be part of!

There is a beauty that only exists between dreaming a dream and achieving it. In the pursuit, we find who we really are, become who we are made to be, and find a purpose beyond our dreams. Our purpose may evolve, but only in taking the first "leap of faith" do we experience the joy that awaits us. Life is a journey. Success is a journey. I realize now that the journey is not only the path to success, but the reason for it!

To learn more about Anna's multifamily investment opportunities or coaching program, email her at info@reimom.com. Follow her on Facebook at Anna ReiMom Kelley or join the Facebook group Creating Real Estate Wealth that Lasts with ReiMom.

Visit her website at www.ReiMom.com.

PHIL COLLEN
Def Leppard and Living an Adrenalized Life

Phil Collen is a world-class musician and the lead guitarist for the band Def Leppard which has sold over a hundred million albums. In addition to music, Phil is highly committed to fitness, personal development and making a positive impact on the planet.

Learning Guitar and My First Band

I was born in Hackney, a borough of London, and grew up in a place called Waltham Abbey. As a child, I loved music but thought it was completely out of reach until I got a guitar at age 16 and started to play.

I left school and worked in a burglar alarm factory and then as a dispatch rider on a motorcycle while I was in a band called Girl until we got a record deal. We only got about $50 a week, but suddenly, I was a professional musician and I could concentrate on that. I had something I had to get out. My artistic expression was so rewarding and still is today.

Def Leppard, Joe Elliot, and Mutt Lange

On tour with Girl, we played the British clubs and pubs. When I met Def Leppard, they already had two albums out.

Joe Elliot and I became friends. One day, he called me and said, "Pete is not in the band anymore. Do you want to play some guitar solos on this record?" I agreed and ended up on *Pyromania* playing songs like "Photograph", "Rock! Rock! (Till You Drop)", "Rock of Ages", and "Foolin'" and singing backing vocals. That album exploded. It all changed from that point onward.

Robert John '"Mutt" Lange had just come off of an AC/DC album, and our management was fortunately able to hook him into Def Leppard's production. He saw something in the band, that we were malleable and something he could improve on. Unlike some musicians who would let their egos get in the way, we listened to Mutt and his suggestions.

Mutt Lange is, without a doubt, the most influential person in my musical career. He is totally inspiring with the highest intellect of anyone I've ever met. This guy is a giant, but he's humble and modest. We learned so much from him.

Singing, Songwriting, and the Muse

Mutt is the reason I learned how to sing and how to play guitar properly. He had a way of introducing you to concepts so you would excel. It was an amazing way to do things that was almost spiritual.

There's no more complete way to express yourself than through singing. It also improves your confidence. A lot of people pick up a guitar because they're a little intimidated by performing, and guitar is a great way to get out of your shell. When you're singing, it's entirely different, especially if you sing in front of people with no effects or band. If you can get up there, sing with confidence, and not really care what others may be thinking of you, it will improve other areas of your life. If you're a musician, it really takes you somewhere else.

When you add writing, you're not just a songwriter, producer, or singer, you can be all of the above. I have songs going through my head all the time. I can't ignore them. I could sit down and write all day every day. Music can be so many things, and I find inspiration everywhere. It can be a drum beat, the sound of a car going by, or any sound that comes to you out of open windows or on the street when you walk around the city. One sound or phrase makes you sing and think of another phrase, word, or memory. I don't even look for inspiration. It practically comes through the air. When the inspiration hits you, it's fantastic, and you're grateful for the muse, whatever it was.

I just signed with Sony Publishing, and they have been really great, hooking me up with a couple of different songwriters. We've been on a storm, working on stuff I wouldn't normally do. It's very inspiring to get into a different type of music. I'm also always writing Def Leppard stuff and am really excited about where we are going.

"Pour Some Sugar On Me"

The album *Hysteria* was hard work. Rick had lost his arm in a terrible accident. We were moving through different studios in different countries for two and a half years. We went into so much debt that it brought tears to my eyes when I read the breakdown. I thought we would never be able to pay it back to the record company. The album was almost finished, and we had to sell a ridiculous number of albums to break even.

One afternoon, Joe was sitting in the hallway singing with his guitar, "Pour some sugar on me."

Mutt Lange said, "What's that?"

Joe said, "Oh, I don't know."

Mutt said, "Play that again." Over the next 10 days, we wrote and recorded the song "Pour Some Sugar On Me." It was the last thing to go on the record that we had already poured so much into, almost as an afterthought, and it broke the album.

We had three singles out before it and we hadn't broken even by a long shot, and then that one came out. Dancers in strip clubs would request the song, and then it started getting popular by request on local radio. It became this massive song in Florida, and we had no idea. From there, it just exploded.

Rick Allen's Accident

On New Year's Eve, 1984, our band's drummer Rick Allen had a terrible car accident that resulted in him losing an arm. Our band loves and supports each other like a family, so we asked him what he wanted to do. Mutt Lange went to see him in the hospital and said, "There's all this technology, and you've got amazing kick drum bass pedal technique. You can use your foot and keep playing." He would have to change one limb for the other and would do double the work with his feet.

Rick was practicing in bed with his one arm and his foot when Steve Clark and I went to visit him in hospital. The three of us lived in a house together in Donnybrook just outside of Dublin. I remember that it was very frustrating for him. He would practice from eight in the morning till about 10 at night, swearing and cursing. Then one day, there was no cursing, and we heard a cool rhythm that was in time. It just got better from there. He got to that next level and was able to keep taking it to another level until it was second nature.

Playing With Two Other Bands and Touring

I'm always busy creating and am part of two other bands. One is Delta Deep with Robert DeLeo of Stone Temple Pilot, Debbie Blackwell-Cook, Forest Robinson and the other is Manraze with Paul Cook of The Sex Pistols and Simon Laffy. I'm always having fun writing and recording. At some point, I might actually do a solo album.

I did the G3 concert tour with Joe Satriani and John Petrucci from Dream Theater with Delta Deep. Robert DeLeo couldn't make the tour, so Craig Martini stepped in and played bass. Those guys are over the top musicians, yet are so humble.

Touring can be challenging for many musicians, but I love the chance to be a tourist. I get up early in the morning and find somewhere to have a coffee and absorb the local vibe everywhere we go. Traveling can get a bit much, but if I'm on a tour bus, I'm asleep before we leave the parking lot and usually wake up in the next town. I have a wonderful wife and five kids, and I'm grateful that my family comes out at different parts of the tour.

Health and Fitness

Through Def Leppard, I am known for my body and high level of fitness. I'm avid about physical fitness and working out. I believe it is the fountain of youth. I'm 62 now, and I've been doing the 30 Day Workout Fitness Challenge. Moving and keeping the blood flowing keeps you young. I actually still feel like I'm 24, the age I was when I joined the Def Leppard, just with more life experience.

When we're touring, I usually take a trainer out with us. I also love martial arts and have found it to be one of the keys to loosen the hips. I've never have back or leg problems like a lot of people do.

I've been a strict vegetarian for 37 years and have practiced a vegan lifestyle for many years. Becoming a vegetarian was a moral decision because I couldn't eat a dead body. I stopped drinking 33 years ago. I was able to stop, but my best friend Steve Clark wasn't, and it ended up killing him.

Recognizing Addiction and the Benefits of Being Sober

I recognized I had an addiction when I realized I couldn't remember things. There were times I drove blind drunk. I finally understood that I could have hit someone. That really weighed on me, but I couldn't quit cold turkey. I had tried a few times before things like bringing just one glass of wine with me to the social gathering, but I couldn't do it. I'd bring the bottle instead. And then it was Jack Daniels by the end of the week.

On my ex-girlfriend Liz's birthday in April 1987, we were in Paris having a glass of champagne, and I said, "I'm not drinking after this." We went to India the next day, and I quit cold turkey. That was it, actually. It was really easy, and she did it with me.

The benefits were outrageous. I got two extra hours a day that I wasn't spending recovering or just feeling not great. That's when I started working out because I actually had time to burn. I started running, and it inspired me to do more. I'd run along the shoreline just south of Dublin, even in the cold weather. It wasn't the running itself I enjoyed, it was being in nature and the fact that I just felt different because I wasn't nursing a hangover. I was this clear, cleaner version of me.

Adrenalized Life, Def Leppard, and Beyond

Chris Epting encouraged me to write a book because he thought I had some great stories to share. He received some interest from a few book companies and then Simon & Schuster agreed to publish it. I worked back and forth with their editors, and my wife Helen helped me as well. At one point, we sat down and re-edited the whole thing. When you have to write it down, you wonder if it's right, if you are getting the point across, if it sounds too high brow or low brow.

I recently wrote a short story and am planning on writing another. Two short stories would make a great little book. But writing a book, writing a story, or writing a song is a lot more difficult than people think.

Building Confidence by Overcoming Adversity

When I was a kid, I was asthmatic. My doctor had said, "I'm not going to give him an inhaler to rely on. I want him to go swimming." When you're swimming, you're thinking about other things, and after a while, I would forget that I couldn't breathe, and my concentration on swimming would open my lungs up. And when I started playing guitar, I gained confidence in myself and started feeling different, and the asthma more or less went away.

I think every little thing you learn creates confidence, an ability to deal with stuff and not feel embarrassed. When I first became a vegetarian, I felt bad because I felt my dietary restrictions would put people out. At some point, I decided that I wasn't going to please others because I chose to do something else. My vegetarianism became empowering for me. It wasn't ego. It was confidence. You have to accept yourself and your limitations, then make your limitations your strengths. Actually, when you are simply aware of your limitations, they often become your strengths.

Success and Daily Habits

I think consistency is so important. It's so easy to fall off, and when you do, you have to get back into it, and that's a lot harder. If you maintain whatever you're doing and are regularly inspired by it, you achieve more.

One of the hardest things to do is meditate and actually think of nothing, especially if you've got songs running through your head and little boys running around. I struggle with it, but I do it. Meditation is very powerful because it gives you time alone to escape.

I like to have flow in my day and not be rigid. You don't have to fix things, it is what it is. You're on a trajectory. When you're not in that mode, you can overthink things. You can go, *My God, I haven't got any money coming in. I'm not doing this. I'm not doing that. My songwriting is dried up.* You overthink. When you avoid this but keep all the moving parts going in a successful routine, your life actually runs itself.

Phil Collen is the lead guitar player for Def Leppard. For more information on Phil and Def Leppard, go to defleppard.com. To learn more about Phil speaking for your organization, contact info@kylewilson.com.

DUGAN KELLEY

Loving and Serving People Through the Practice of Law

In 20+ years of practicing law, Dugan Kelley has represented transactions of over $3 billion and obtained over $70 million in verdicts and settlements for clients. Dugan is founder and managing partner of Kelley | Clarke, PC with offices in California and Texas. He currently serves clients throughout the country. He specializes in real estate, securities, crisis management, corporate counsel, and litigation services.

Life-Defining Moment

I had just committed the biggest crime of my life. I was busy trying to cover my crime up before being interrogated. I was at a crossroads—a life-defining moment for me where the core of my character would continue to be forged.

All paperboys face the same problem. What happens if your customer pays you the wrong amount for the month? In my case, the check I received from Mr. Cranky Pants (my name for him) was short by 50¢ on his paper check for $9.00. I simply changed the check by 50¢.

My dad (my interrogator, a pastor, and lawyer) caught me. His son would not be completing the crime of check fraud. Instead, I would call Mr. Cranky Pants and confess per my dad. Unfortunately, I only partially confessed. I told Mr. Cranky Pants that "My dad had changed the check," but, I explained, "He wouldn't do it again."

Three hours later, Mr. Cranky Pants called my house to speak with my dad to give him an earful about his supposed crime. My mom answered the phone and handed it to my dad. Any thought I had of escaping personal responsibility for my earlier crime and subsequent cover up was dashed. My dad's face went from normal to red to purple. My full confession came quickly. My punishment included several spankings and personally walking with my dad to Mr. Cranky Pants' front door to fully confess.

At age 11, my life of being an Irish hooligan was over.

Aptitude and Ambition

Not all character is forged through suffering. I was blessed to be born into a family where aptitude, work ethic, and ambition were fostered. As one of four children growing up in Montana, there was never any shortage of opportunities to compete.

My dad was a practicing attorney and pastor. His work and ambition had a tremendous impact on me growing up. He ran for Attorney General of Montana and helped run campaigns for the state legislature and other political races.

In our house, no topic was taboo. We embraced our passion for politics, law, and religion. For our family, they fit together as opposed to being mutually exclusive. Very early on, I took a personality test. I scored high in aptitude to be successful in journalism, politics, law enforcement, or law.

Dad decided we would see how fast and how hard I could run in school. I finished high school at age 16. I got through college with a double major when I was 19 and law school at 21. At that time, I didn't appreciate how fast that was. I didn't have a lot of time to goof off or have the normal college experience. I was busy tapping the limits of my aptitude and ambition, which was fostered by my family.

Building a Practice to Serve

Observing suffering in others, developing empathy, and serving others was instrumental in further forging my character. During law school, my parents moved from Montana to minister in Los Angeles, starting a church and separate sober living facility in South Central. After law school, my wife and I joined them in California.

I was, first and foremost, a litigator. I always thought that justice would be meted out in the courtroom. But after I had been practicing for 10+ years in courtrooms, boardrooms, arbitrations, and administrative courts, I realized that I was wrong. Even when you're fighting a righteous fight, even when you've won, it can still be a significant drain for clients, especially emotionally. In the last 20 years, the practice of law has become much more niche. When you're a generalist, you constantly have to learn new things. So when I approached my litigation partners with the hair brained idea of opening a new office focused on other areas of the law with an office in Texas, all but one of my partners said NO.

However, I couldn't stop thinking about it. There was a better way to practice law. So, even though the country was in a recession at the time, I wanted to open a new office focused on service and empathy over billable hours and litigation.

After months of fear, my partner, my wife, and I took a leap of faith in late 2009 and opened a new firm with an office in the Dallas area while keeping an office in Santa Barbara as well. We started with a simple core principle: *every relationship comes from the Lord.* We look at every relationship as one that needs to be nurtured and cherished because we are only a steward of those relationships. Our practice of law is a ministry to people. Service, empathy, work ethic, and ministry are the bedrock principles that our firm is built upon. Sometimes you end up working for free, but implementing the golden rule of treating others as you would want to be treated has reaped benefits that often cannot be measured by pure financial gain.

During this period, we opened up our transactional real estate and corporate practice groups, which steadily grew over the next 10 years. Serving clients throughout the country in several billion dollars of transactions has shown us that our principles are sound and solid. Now we're serving people starting new endeavors, acquiring real estate assets, forming equity funds to raise private capital, and in the unlikely event that they get sued—handling their litigation needs. On top of that, if there's some sort of crisis in their lives, we help there, too. We're a boutique, full-service law firm with a national footprint. Our mission and our purpose is to serve people.

Giving Back in Service

From those early life-defining moments (like confession to Mr. Cranky Pants), gratitude is what I feel now. I'll be forever grateful for everyone that helped shape my character and all the opportunities that my parents provided me to help me excel.

Growing up in a family of lawyers and pastors, helping nonprofits and public speaking was in my DNA. I have learned to use my gifts to benefit organizations, churches, and clients by speaking at a number of conferences and events on different areas of the law, most frequently about real estate, real estate syndications, and how to raise money for new acquisitions. I also speak on behalf of nonprofit boards that I sit on, one of which has the goal of ending human sex trafficking. I'm happy to do so, because it's one way I can maximize the talents that I have for the areas in which I can actually serve and give back to both my local community and my church.

Success Habits

Over the last 20 years of my professional life, I've had time to reflect on what works and doesn't work—what contributes to continued growth. There are certain characteristics that have greatly aided me in gaining the success I have achieved.

Listening. I want to be at the core a great listener before I say what I think or believe. If you do not listen, you become one person with a bullhorn in a gaggle of other people with bullhorns. Nothing's ever going to get done. Listen first, speak last, and be slow to get angry.

Faith. What's important to me first and foremost is my faith. That is one of the cornerstones of who I am. I believe my faith is essential to how I practice law and how I serve people.

Empathy. I am probably overly empathetic with clients. But I find that I am my best when I really understand the client's problem. I put myself in their shoes.

Pursue your passion and let go of fear. Learn to manage your fear and press through it. Very young in life, I resolved, if something makes me afraid (speaking, starting a new business, trying a case, etc.) DO IT! Do the thing that you fear to reveal the fallacy of fear!

Work Hard. Nothing is given for free. Success doesn't happen overnight. It requires grit, sacrifice, and tenacity in everything.

Loyalty. As lawyers, we are trained to be fiercely loyal to clients. With me, that extends to my family and my inner circle. I believe loyalty is critically important.

Positive mindset. Positivity, to a far greater degree than sheer will, has the power to make things happen for you. There are going to be challenges. How you deal with your stress will largely determine your level of success.

To contact Dugan Kelley about legal advice, speaking, or any other questions, send an email to dugan@kelleyclarke.com.

MARCO SANTARELLI
From Dot-Com Failure to Passive Real Estate Investing Expert

Marco Santarelli is the founder and CEO of Norada Real Estate Investments, a national real estate investment firm offering turnkey investment properties in growth markets nationwide. Marco is also a serial entrepreneur and host of the Passive Real Estate Investing podcast.

Big Dreams and Self-Taught Skills

I knew I was an entrepreneur at age 13. I taught myself computer programming and started coding a game on an old Radio Shack computer with a minuscule 4K of memory, which was a lot at that time. At 15, I started ordering programs to teach myself about business, entrepreneurship, and real estate investing, as well as personal development from people like Tony Robbins, Zig Ziglar, Brian Tracy, and Jim Rohn.

I invested in myself first and then applied what I learned in the real world when I had the opportunity. I went on to buy my first rental property when I turned 18.

I've achieved what I have because of the organization, focus, and discipline I developed over the years. Often, we don't have a clear path. Persistence is such a critical part of being a successful entrepreneur. Most people quit too early, not realizing that their breakthrough and success was right around the corner.

The thing about entrepreneurship is you keep trying, learning, and doing what you think you need to do to create a successful venture. But you will fail more often than you succeed, and when you fall down or get kicked in the gut, the important thing is to get back up, dust yourself off, and look at it as another lesson learned.

Dot-Com Startup

In 1998, I joined my cousin in launching a new dot-com business. I moved to California from Canada as a co-founder and chief technology officer of our new venture. We then raised $9.5 million from venture capital investors and worked to grow the business. We had a good two and a half year run until the stock market crashed. After the NASDAQ crash, all VC funding around the country dried up. Unless you were cash flow positive, which 99% of dot-com businesses were not, you basically had to close your doors. We were now another dot-com failure. Sadly, with over 105 employees, we had to lay off every one of them.

Bouncing Back From Failure

With the dot-com business behind me in 2003, I took some time away from work to reflect on what I had learned and think about what I really wanted to do. The last thing I wanted was to go back to corporate America.

But every time a door closes, another one opens. Even if you don't know what you're looking for, if you stay alert, something good will come up that resonates with you.

That summer, I received an email from a real estate author named Robert G. Allen saying that there was an upcoming, free, three-day boot camp in Orange, California. I had a passion for real estate, so I decided to go.

The event was great, and the speaker had you riveted to your seat. Of course, being a free seminar, they were selling five-day boot camps in different cities around the country. And like the hundreds of people going to the back of the room, credit card in hand, paying up to $35,000 for the education, I too pulled out my credit card and made the investment in myself.

I've always loved real estate and the idea of creating wealth and financial independence. I was on the path, but I wasn't there yet. That event was a major turning point and began the next chapter in my life in 2004. It gave me the additional education and a kick in the butt to launch my real estate investing to the next level.

The Magic of Real Estate Investing

In 2004, I purchased 84 units of rental property within a nine-month period. These were all over 2000 miles away from my home in Orange County, California in markets such as Florida, Georgia, and Michigan.

People were coming to me saying, *"Hey Marco, I see what you're doing. It's great. How are you doing it? Can you coach or mentor me?"*

My answer was always, *"Sorry. It's not that I don't want to, I just don't have the time."* I then realized there were a lot of people spending tons of money in an effort to be successful real estate investors, but they still needed help. They were paying to get the education, but they weren't pulling the trigger to find and purchase good deals.

Since I was already doing the work of picking markets and finding and analyzing properties, and most importantly, I had teams in place in each location, I decided to become a deal source for other people. That's how *Norada Real Estate Investments* was born—a national real estate investment firm offering investors turnkey investment properties in growth markets nationwide.

How to Create Lasting Wealth

I like to say there are five benefits to real estate. First is cash flow, which is great, especially as you start to build a larger portfolio. That's when you start to see your financial independence kick in. Second, you have equity growth through the amortization of the loan as your tenant pays the property mortgage off for you. Third, you gain equity over time as your property appreciates.

Fourth and fifth are two magical things called depreciation and leverage. Where else can you put 20% into an investment, borrow the other 80% using other people's money, and still retain 100% ownership, 100% of the cash flow, 100% of the appreciation and equity, and 100% of the tax benefits of the investment?

My advice to aspiring investors who make their money at their day job is to make as much as you can, as fast as you can, and then deploy that money into income-producing investments. That's the secret: *turn your active income into passive and portfolio income.*

I personally like to invest where I see high upside potential as well as cash flow. I will always be a direct investor because I want to have control. If you are going to invest with partners or in a syndication, make sure you know and trust the people you're investing with.

Seven Philosophies for Success

1. Write S.M.A.R.T. Goals. We may have heard this to the point of getting tired of it, but I can't emphasize how important it is to write S.M.A.R.T. goals. That's an acronym meaning Specific, Measurable, Achievable, Realistic, and Time-bound. You have to have a start and end date so your subconscious mind will work on it. I have a spreadsheet with a tab for every year. Each year I review, rewrite, and recreate my goals. I have goals for family, finance, business, health, and fun. I turn that into a PDF and put it on my iPhone so I can review it often.

2. Stay Organized. I naturally like to keep things in their place. I believe if you stay organized with your emails, your desk, your files, and folders, even your pens and pencils, a burden lifts off your shoulders. Order and organization increase your ability to think clearly and act with clarity.

3. Use Time Blocking. I've become greedy with my time. Every minute is precious. I block activities by the hour, the half-hour, and sometimes quarter-hour. Whatever is on my calendar in that slot is what I focus on. You have to manage your time like it's sacred. It's the most valuable asset you have because it's the only thing you can spend and never get back. I used to think I could multitask, but it doesn't really work.

4. Educate Yourself. This is also the first rule of my *10 Rules of Successful Real Estate Investing* available on our website. Don't go out and invest in real estate, or anything else for that matter, until you've invested in yourself. If you only have $1,000 to invest, don't go looking to purchase stocks. Invest that money in yourself. Think about how many books, audio programs, and other education you can get to build your knowledge, your confidence, and your competence.

5. Learn to Say NO. Sometimes we fall into the trap of feeling bad for saying no. Every time you say yes to something, you're saying no to 10 or more opportunities, whether it's time with your family, a business opportunity, an investment, or whatever else. So, you have to get comfortable with saying no.

6. Focus on Your Top Line, Not Your Bottom Line. A lot of people seem to think they need to budget to save enough money to invest. There's some truth in that, but that's a philosophy I dislike. You can't save your way to wealth. The way to maximize the amount you save and invest as quickly as you can, is to focus on your top line (income).

7. Take Action. Confucius said, "It doesn't matter how slowly you go as long as you do not stop." So if you take action in the direction of your desired goal, you'll start to build momentum. The hardest part is getting started. Once you get started, you start to realize that you can manifest whatever you set out to achieve.

Visit Norada Real Estate Investments to download your free copy of the Passive Real Estate Investing book and other free resources at https://www.NoradaRealEstate.com. Find the Passive Real Estate Investing podcast on iTunes and iHeartRadio or at https://www.PassiveRealEstateInvesting.com.

NEELU AND ROBERT GIBSON
Taking Leaps of Faith and Sticking the Landing

Global corporate executives Neelu and Robert Gibson founded Seaglass RQA, a boutique regulatory and quality consulting firm that helps companies bring innovative medical technologies to market, and mentor regulatory and quality professionals. Neelu is also the worldwide vice president of regulatory affairs for a Fortune 500 medical device company.

Cut to the hero of a movie standing in front of a deep and wide chasm, trying to figure out how to get to the other side. He mutters "Leap of faith. Take a leap of faith." He stops, exhales, closes his eyes, and steps into the abyss...and...there is a bridge. This is my visual each time I make a life-changing decision.

My first leap of faith after becoming a single parent was, in hindsight, my first step towards becoming the person I am today. My choices: go back to the UK, to family and friends who would welcome me home, or take the path less traveled—stay in the US and face a world of unknown possibilities.

I decided to stay in California with my little son, truly believing that I made the best decision I could make, trusting that life would work out for the best, and that there was a bridge taking me to the next chapter of my life.

Being single, I had to learn to be my own hero and overcome societal norms for simple things like going to the movies alone or buying flowers. Sympathetic voices often said, "I'm sorry you had to go see that movie alone" or "you will meet someone one day to buy you flowers" when, in fact, I was just fine. I learned that empowerment comes from within. While there are people willing to share the light of their experiences when we need them, there are times we need to be our own light.

As I explored transitioning from working a job to pursuing a long-term career, I thought about what was important to me and wrote it down on a piece of paper. I later came to realize I had created my personal mission statement.

I wanted a career that excited and challenged me, helping people and/or the environment. A career that would show me the world while enabling me to spend quality time with my son, family, and friends.

"That's a TALL order," I hear you say. Yes, it was, and yet, I lived into every element, thanks to my career at a major medical device company.

As I navigated the highs and lows of balancing a career and family life, a friend sent me a copy of *The Journey* by Mary Oliver during a particular time of self-doubt. It begins,

> *"One day you finally knew*
> *what you had to do, and*
> *began,*
> *though the voices around you*
> *kept shouting*
> *their bad advice—*
> *though the whole house*
> *began to tremble*
> *and you felt the old tug*

at your ankles.
"Mend my life!"
each voice cried.
But you didn't stop.
You knew what you had to
do..."

This poem has been a powerful light during challenging times, as it refocuses me and reminds me to trust in myself.

Robert, my husband, has experienced a similar life journey. One of the things that drew us together was the commonality of our stories, going through game-changing events in our lives, tackling—and finally quelling—the voices of dissent, and learning to trust our own inner voices. I had recognized early on the importance of having a "Plan B," which enabled me to pivot if needed, as I moved forward in getting my life together.

Unfortunately, Robert did not have a back-up plan when his life-long dream of becoming a fighter pilot was taken from him just as he reached adulthood. The culprit: poor eyesight, for which (in those days) there was no remedy. Robert had gone through his pre-adolescence and adolescence without contemplating that something beyond his control would interfere with his career ambition.

For a brief time, Robert decided to pursue a military commission and become a navigator, which would have enabled him to fly, but his inner voice was drowned out by the misguided direction of others whose interests he placed above his own.

A hard lesson Robert learned was the importance of being mindful of the people you associate with on your journey through life. In addition to identifying the people who are important to you and never letting them down, you need to recognize that not everyone has your best interest at heart or wants you to succeed. Either unintentionally or purposely, well-meaning people may place their interests above yours or convince themselves they know what is best for you.

In either situation, it is essential for us to learn to be our authentic selves and not lose sight of being true to our character. Otherwise, we risk the real danger of living the life someone else wants for us, not the one we want or deserve.

Although Robert did not find his inner voice until much later in life, he developed several key traits: perseverance, self-reliance, and adaptability—among others—to enable him to excel in his career. However, as he once told me, "being passionate about something and being successful at something are not necessarily the same thing." It is possible to have one without the other, but without passion, success can be meaningless.

As we managed the ups and downs of work/life balance, two key events brought our mortality into sharp focus and held a harsh mirror to our priorities. Our maid of honor passed away unexpectedly, and shortly thereafter, my best friend was diagnosed with breast cancer. I was completely unavailable to support my friend, as I believed I couldn't step away from work. Without realizing it, I had lost myself in my career and had strayed away from a core element of my mission statement, "...*enabling me to spend quality time with my son, family, and friends.*"

I made the decision to step into the abyss of the unknown once again by resigning without the safety net of another job. Leaving a company where I had worked for over 22 years was more difficult than I imagined. I loved being a part of the organization but hadn't realized that it had become my comfort zone. After conquering my fear monster, I left without any regrets.

I happily focused on being available to my friend during her cancer treatment journey (successfully completed). I kept myself open to all opportunities that life presented. I co-authored the first of three books, we traveled to eight countries, and we were extended an invitation to attend our first Kyle Wilson's Inner Circle Mastermind. This chance meeting has opened up a new world of positivity, encouragement, entrepreneurship, and growth for both of us. We are surrounded by wonderful people with amazing stories and continue to learn so much from each interaction.

Perhaps not surprisingly, I returned to the corporate world, accepting an executive position with a major medical device company. I believe that I would not have found my new home, both professional and personal, had I not made the decisions I did and took the time to focus on what was important to me. The time spent living the core elements of my mission statement and being available to the people who mean so much to me has been invaluable. It has renewed my energy and focus and enabled me to continue actively living my mission statement and so much more.

The simple moral of our story is *plan, trust, and execute*…and believe there is a bridge waiting for you.

To contact Neelu and Robert Gibson about their story, medical device requirements, leadership, and mentoring or coaching, please email

neelu@seaglassrqa.com

robert@seaglassrqa.com

www.seaglassrqa.com

BEN SUTTLES
It's Our Defeats That Shape Us

Ben Suttles has been an entrepreneur for 15 years. He now owns ten companies with 50+ employees and revenues near $20MM. A management and sales background helped him propel into commercial real estate in 2013, and along with his partners he has acquired and managed ten multifamily properties, totaling over $100MM in current assets.

Entrepreneurial Parents

I got the entrepreneurial bug from my parents. They are entrepreneurs and were my first mentors. Everything that goes along with creating and building a business, I learned from them. They instilled in me the spirit of seeking out challenges and finding creative ways to start businesses to solve those issues. To this day, along with my wife and daughter, they continue to inspire me to be better and push myself to solve bigger and more important challenges, and for that, I'll be forever grateful.

I have dealt with a lot of corporate clients, especially at our IT firm, but I've never really been in corporate America. The rigidity that comes along with most corporations is stifling, so instead, I chose to blaze my own trail and find ways to add value to people as a problem solver. The harder and more complex the problems I solve, the more value I'm ultimately adding. Today, I'm the proud co-owner of ten different companies that all provide solutions in the market, and I'm forever blessed to love what I do.

Hollywood Dreams

I caught the acting bug after dropping out of college, so I moved from Austin to LA in the early 2000s. For seven years, I wrote scripts, directed, and even got the courage to get in front of the screen as an actor. I wasn't a part of anything you would know, but I was having a lot of fun doing what I was passionate about.

I still love writing. I write a lot of poetry, mainly to my wife. I'm still not 100% extroverted, but getting in front of the camera really got me out of my shell. When you have the lights blaring and 20 people looking at you who don't want to do 20 takes, you've got to get your lines right, and that forces you to come out of your shell very quickly.

I have learned that everything you endure leads to something else. Just because the path you ultimately went down doesn't pan out, that does not mean that you can't learn a lot of great lessons and meet a lot of great people along the way. So, although I never made it to the big screen, I learned a lot about life and myself during my time in California, and a lot of those lessons have shaped the entrepreneur I am today.

In 2009 though, I had to get back to reality. I moved back to Houston and found an opportunity to prove myself by helping manage my family's IT company, OmniData. Coming from an entrepreneurial family, I didn't mind stepping into the management role, and my personality gravitated towards sales, so I followed that path and continued my journey of becoming more comfortable in my own skin.

The Appeal of Real Estate

When Laura, my wife, was pregnant with our daughter Lillian, I had a ton of time to read books and listen to podcasts. I was always interested in real estate, so one day I stumbled across *Rich Dad Poor Dad*. It's light on how real estate works, but heavy on all things mindset. At that point in my life, I was looking for a bigger challenge to take on, and that book was my light bulb moment. Once I put that book down, I knew I'd be going into real estate.

Real estate spoke to me because it has both an analytical and a relationship side—numbers and people, two things I loved to have in my life. You have to have relationships to find deals in this business, but you have to know your numbers will work to convince investors to partner with you, so the duality of the business is one of its most interesting aspects. Looking for an even bigger challenge than just buying homes, I found out about multifamily.

Multifamily syndication is like project management on steroids. I'm constantly moving pieces around and keeping the ball rolling forward. I'm juggling between lenders, lawyers, CPAs, title companies, investors, my team, and my partners on a daily basis. As a syndicator, I'm an active investor. I am in the weeds daily. You have to be organized and willing to step in, roll up your sleeves, and get things done, even in stressful times. If you're not comfortable in a role like that, I would take a more passive approach to investing because while you may have a slightly lesser degree of control, you have much less worry, and you can achieve much of the same benefits.

As Disrupt Equity, our commercial real estate firm, has grown, we have been able to hire on and delegate out, but you still have to be comfortable with getting into the weeds from time to time. To get to the point where I am introducing a project to my investors, we've done a minimum of three to six months of legwork, put up our own money, and done a ton of due diligence, so these projects do not come easily. When I say "raise the money," people tend to think it's some kind of Wall Street lingo. But, that's not who we deal with. Our investors are high net worth individuals—friends, family, and people that we meet through networking. Each investor is putting in fifty to one hundred thousand dollars each. When you're talking about multimillion-dollar projects, that's a lot of phone calls, dinners, lunches, and meetings to get the raise across the finish line. But I enjoy it. I think I enjoy the challenge of it all. It's like sales, but in this case, we're trying to buy something. Same thrill, but slightly different end results.

Abundance Mindset

In 2017, Hurricane Harvey hit me, my family, and my real estate business like a ton of bricks. From flooded houses, to flooded apartments, to almost losing my life, it was a tough time in my life. But as is the case with every challenge, you can use it as an opportunity to learn and thrive from the adversity. After the storm passed, I used the time to reflect and assess the things that were most important around me. I decided to switch my mindset from one of mostly scarcity to one of abundance. It sounds so simple, "to be helpful" and "to be a good person," but in reality, it takes work. I don't mean helpful where you let people take advantage of you, but the kind of helpful where you constantly strive to do the right thing, take care of the people around you, and do it all without the expectation of reciprocation. Life doesn't always have to be a one for one transaction. The universe has a way of reciprocating in totally unexpected ways, and as long as you don't expect an immediate payback, sometimes the reward of just being a good person to people is reward in itself. I think the universe has rewarded that behavior through the success I've had, and that success has helped me inspire other folks to push themselves to be better. And that's always a good thing.

People quickly assume that "being a good person" is about giving to charities or giving a dollar to the guy on the street corner, but I look at it more holistically. You can also give your time, knowledge, or experience, especially in real estate. There's a lot of bad information out there in our business, but I think my business partner and I are trying to put good information out into the world to genuinely help people be successful in the real estate space. People gravitate to us because of that approach. If you go into every situation with an abundance mindset where you are open, transparent, honest, and just a good person that's there trying to help, the universe will take care of you.

The Takeaway

I wouldn't be where I am today without the support of my wife, my daughter, my parents, my business partner at Disrupt Equity, and our whole team. Without my family, friends, and team behind me, I'd be lost, so I'm truly grateful to have them in my life.

So what have I learned along the way? Knowing your why and looking at everything you do through that lens will propel you to places you wouldn't normally go. I've learned that having a smaller piece of a bigger pie is a good thing. I know that I'll learn more from my failures than I ever will from my successes. I've learned that if you're comfortable, you're not pushing yourself enough. I've learned to love and respect my wife and daughter more than I could ever show them and having that love in your life will be your biggest motivator. But the biggest thing I've learned along the way is to never discount yourself. We're all capable of incredible things, so believe in yourself, push yourself, keep focused on your goals, and don't let the world distract you. Because, ultimately, as the old Roman proverb goes, "Fortune favors the bold."

As the co-founder of Disrupt Equity and the VP of Business Development at Omni Data, Ben Suttles is a husband, father, seasoned entrepreneur, and real estate investor who values kindness and generosity above all else.

Contact at www.disruptequity.com ben@disruptequity.com.

MIKE MUHNEY
Finding and Nurturing Your Authentic Soul

*Mike Muhney is the co-inventor of **ACT!**, which created the relationship management software global industry known as CRM. **ACT!** has been bought by over 40 million people. As a professional speaker, Mike uses his S.T.A.R. program to help businesses achieve greater relationships, reputations, and success.*

The Top Gun of Software Sales Training

Just out of university, I was fortunate to be hired by IBM as a salesman in the pre-PC, mainframe-only era. Little did I know, the first 15 minutes of my sales career would change my life forever.

In those first 15 minutes, IBM taught us a life-changing principle. Many other principles followed, but they all depended on this first one.

These were their words: "There are only two types of salespeople in the world. The first are jackasses—they can carry a heavy workload, but you constantly have to kick their butts. IBM doesn't hire that type, period. The second is what you all are right now, and that's wild stallions. We only hire wild stallions!"

I can assure you that I never would have pictured myself as a wild stallion! It conjures an image of power, independence, and conquering.

Without skipping a beat, the instructor said, "But…by the time we're done with you in six months, you're no longer going to be wild stallions, you're going to be thoroughbred racehorses!" Thoroughbreds are an elite class distinguished by pure athleticism and used for high stakes racing and equestrian sports and their value can be astronomical!

I have come to see that I did not go to sales school, nor was their goal to teach us how to sell. Make no mistake, they did teach us selling techniques, but they knew there was something more powerful to distinguish us from our competition. They sought to teach us to be better humans and true leaders. Principles trumped technique. My career, and my being, has stood on those principles ever since.

From that moment, I looked up towards the infinite possibilities of my future. But if there are times when we are looking up, there must also be times when we are looking down. Those are the times when you confront who you really are. And that time would come.

Start Ups, Angel Investors, Mentors, and FAILURE

Ten years after joining IBM and living those great principles, I began a new phase of my career. My best friend, another sales guy, and I became software entrepreneurs. We believed we had the required passion, determination, risk-accepting qualities, (and naivety) required to start a business and persevere through building it.

After spending $85,000 of our angel investor's original $100,000 investment, my business partner and I came to the conclusion that our first software product was a failure. We were going to have to confess failure and loss of our investor's capital.

I had earlier befriended the CEO of a company that could use our product. I had no business calling on the CEO, but this practice was a part of me from my IBM days. With our investor's visit looming, we sought out his advice. The only option my business partner and I could see was to close down the business and return the remaining $15,000 to the investor. In our minds, we had hit a brick wall, and we couldn't see beyond it. Believe me, we had tried.

After telling the CEO why the product was never going to succeed as it appeared, his wise response was simple, profound, and prescient. It also followed the principles we held. You must see yourself higher than you think you can go if you are to survive and succeed. If you embrace those moments and set your fears aside, you can truly change your life, even against a backdrop of darkness.

His advice shattered our limited vision. He said, "You two are smart guys, why don't you have a brainstorm session from 8:00 a.m. till noon on July 4th." This was only a couple days away. We hadn't thought of that, and we could still afford coffee and toast, so why not?

Brainstorm

What we conceived at that brainstorm breakfast was going to change the world.

We had lunch with our angel investor and presented our new ideas. He was not offended by the failure of our previous effort or that we had spent nearly all of his money. Rather, in support, he pledged another $50,000. He said he didn't invest in our product, he invested in us. Hearing this, the CEO who suggested that we not give up invested $400,000.

Creating the CRM Industry, Stratospheric Global Success

Nine months later, on April 1st, 1987, we launched **ACT!**. I could write an entire book regarding that entrepreneurial journey and all of the twists and turns. Since there was no appropriate category in which to place **ACT!**, we also had to create a new category of software: Contact Management/Relationship Management software.

We had no idea we had also created what would be an annual $100 billion software category and global industry today known as CRM. **ACT!** today is into its fourth decade, and still on the market, nearly unheard of in software, with over 40 million users.

I experienced stratospheric success on the global stage, speaking all over the world, impacting people's lives and incomes, and creating a cottage industry of consultants and service providers, and inevitably, major competition. The success and my impacting tens of millions of lives through co-inventing **ACT!** validated the vision I had of myself at a level beyond my ability that IBM instilled in me. I am, and always will be, grateful for that accomplishment and all that I learned about business and myself in that process.

From the Highest High to the Lowest Low

Success doesn't reveal as much about who you are as failure does.

I've learned on my journey that wherever you look, there are corresponding opposites, and those opposites are ultimately inseparable. We need them both—the success **and** the tragedy. We cannot fully know one without the other. In my lowest low, I discovered my authentic soul.

We created a product and category completely focused on relationships and stronger connections. But my efforts to build and grow our company and a major industry caused me to lose two of my most valuable relationships—my spouse and my best friend.

The global success of **ACT!** was blinding, so much so that I was blinded to just about everything outside of **ACT!**

ACT! became my mistress and consumed my every thought. It took me to 27 countries to give keynote speeches at major corporate and industry events, to work with our distribution and retail partners, and to open up international offices and hire staff. It got to the point that I was rarely home. I let **ACT!** become my identity at the expense of everything else.

Three years before we sold the company, I lost a 19-year marriage that had produced three great kids. I didn't even see it coming.

Around the same time, the stupendous success of **ACT!** began to create a fracture between my business partner and me on numerous product and company issues, complicated by ballooning egos. I often say that parents don't always agree on how to raise the child, and **ACT!** was our child. My business partner, my very best friend for over 10 years, and I were civil with each other, but we never regained our close friendship.

The Abyss of Despair

ACT! enabled me to keep going despite it being the very thing that destroyed those relationships. To this day, where others see my "success," I see myself differently. Let's call it the difference between their gross versus my net perception of success. I had to cope with the tragic price I paid to succeed.

In June 1993, we sold our company to Symantec in Silicon Valley. As usually happens in this type of deal, they signed my business partner and me as the visionaries and inventors of **ACT!** to a two-year employment contract. We thought they genuinely wanted our input, but in fact, they resented us and preferred we showed up to meetings for optics but kept our mouths shut. When we disregarded the CEOs warnings to butt out or else, we were fired four months into the acquisition. Instantly, I was without any day to day attachment to **ACT!**.

Revelation: Finding Inherent Value in My Life

Without **ACT!**, I had no identity. What was I without the company and product I had been laser-focused on for the last seven years?

For the next two years, I wandered, filling my time with many things but feeling empty. Every day, I was seeking to answer what I was.

Then, serendipitously, I found it. I bought the videocassette of *Indecent Proposal* starring Robert Redford, Demi Moore, and Woody Harrelson. I related to the character Woody portrayed: a brilliant and acclaimed architect with a seemingly happy marriage who lost his job, his wife, and their dream home in a severe economic recession.

Sitting in my family room by myself, mid-week, in my robe, I was absorbed in this scene.

Woody's classroom was standing room only. The students knew they were in the presence of greatness and were mesmerized by his words. Woody pulled out a brick from his desk and asked the students what he was holding. One student stated it was a brick. Another student said it was a weapon (and some other students laughed nervously). Woody smiled as the projector screen behind him began to display architectural icons of the world, then he raised the brick into the air. Then he told the class, "The famous architect Louis Kahn said, "Even a brick wants to be something!" As the camera panned from the iconic buildings on the projector to the students' faces, they and I felt like we had been hit over the head with a brick of knowledge.

I broke down in tears. I knew I was that brick. I wanted to be something at the baseline of my existence, despite what I had achieved in life. Despite my successes and failures, at my core there remained a desire to lift the human spirit. But the only way to do it authentically was to see myself as an ordinary brick. In those tears, I let **ACT!** go and turned forward, thinking, *If I could create* **ACT!**, *what more could I do?*

I recognized and embraced the real me that I had for years departed from. I was back to my authentic self, stripped of ego and my habit of elevating myself compared to others. What I had done and what I would do was separate from what I was. And seeing myself for what I am was more important than anything I had done or would do. Until that moment, I had based my worth solely on what I had accomplished. Now, I was free.

Living for Others

The brick revelation was a whole new beginning and blessing. To this day, not only in quiet moments alone but also in every encounter I have, this moment stays with me. It has made me a better person.

My journey has been long and circuitous. I have learned the immense value of humility, come to appreciate the worth of every human being, and found the joy in interactions that leave people with a smile. I seek every opportunity to practice genuine interest and appreciation toward others, no matter how brief the encounter.

Attendees to my speeches have regularly shared the impact my principled lessons, experiences, and personal revelations have had on them. Making a positive difference in others' lives fulfills my desire to lift the human spirit in myself and others.

I can't think of a better daily habit. It's born out of how I see my authentic self, finally knowing what I am, and daily working to fulfill my destiny.

Mike can be reached at Mike@MikeMuhney.com. You can visit his website at www.MikeMuhney.com and request his response to a speaking appearance at your next corporate or association event in the Contact section. Mike also conducts sales workshops over half-day, day, and customized extended timeframes.

STEPHANIE WANKEL
Fighting Fears and Finding Freedom

Stephanie Wankel is a change agent, coach, and product development leader who has led groups to solve problems and bring products to market for over two decades. In real estate investing, she and her partners have over 2,200 units (over $230M).

Fighting Fear with Action

I followed the rules by doing well in school, going to college, and getting a corporate job. Fresh out of graduate school, I started my career and thought that I was on top of the world. Being an entrepreneur at heart, I was lucky to have the opportunity to use my communications degree to create new products and find solutions to complex customer problems. However, bit by bit, my world started to buckle under me. As I sat with my head in my hands, sobbing in the bathroom stall at my new, amazing job, all I knew was that this was not my plan. As I tried to pull myself together to get back to work, I looked in the mirror and saw someone I don't even recognize…. I was a single mom raising two young children by myself, feeling overwhelmed by the uncertainty of how to pay bills, how to parent alone, how to survive. The responsibility and guilt swept over my whole body. As fear welled up and began to take over, I knew my only response could be action. I had to fight the fear. I didn't know how, but I did know one thing for sure, and that was that my trajectory had just changed. It was time to put my career moves on the back burner and make my kids the top priority. That meant the requirements for my new dream would have to be close to home and school, no commute, no travel, no excessive hours, no upward climb. During these times of struggle, the one thing we could count on was our habits. As a family, we stuck to our morning routines and evening dinners together. This brought stability and actions that we could control.

Succumbing to Shame and Sabotage

"Whether you think you can, or you think you can't—you're right."

– Henry Ford

Nobody enters marriage expecting it to end. Personally, I believed that divorce was bad, and this core value caused me immense shame and judgment. The days leading up to the traumatic events that ended my marriage were brutal. I knew things were spiraling out of control, but I didn't know how to stop it. I was in such a dark place, I really considered ending it. I did not know how the sun was going to shine any longer. As things were falling apart, it went from bad to worse as there seemed no hope of fixing it.

Although my marriage was struggling, it ended abruptly and dramatically. One night my kids had two parents living at home, and the next morning, their dad never came back. My daughter was five and my son was eight. Emotionally, I was shattered. My kids were confused and hurt, and I felt like a failure as a parent.

Because my ex-husband was dealing with emotional challenges and anxiety, my kids lived with me full time. As the divorce unfolded, my son began to struggle with behavioral issues and challenges in school. This was a challenge because I had to learn how to help him on my own, without a partner. I felt very alone.

Believe and Know, It Will Get Better

Being raised by a Marine Corps mother meant pulling yourself up by the boot straps. No whining, no crying. It was a "lemonade out of lemons" kind of upbringing, which served me so many times throughout my life. At the core, even in my worst moments, I knew things would get better, and I learned to be resilient and adept at dealing with change.

"The oak fought the wind and was broken, the willow bent when it must survive."

– Robert Jordan, *The Fires of Heaven*

Whether it be dealing with divorce, struggling children, or any of the challenges in life, bending with change is better than fighting it head on. As the winds of change were blowing me up, down, and all around, my faith and deep down belief still stood strong. I found this to be true through my real estate investing too. Early on, I learned that even if your tenant destroys your rental property, anything can be fixed. Every circumstance is temporary—even after a decade of seemingly never-ending darkness after my divorce, I eventually saw the light again, and ultimately became stronger in the process.

Even still, I accomplished a lot, and was successful, but emotionally I shut down. My only focus was on raising my kids and getting us through the drama. So, the sun doesn't necessarily shine the next day, but it shines, and it's worth sticking it out.

I'm truly grateful for everything I've been through, the gift of learning and becoming has brought me to a place of fulfillment and joy. The things I learned about myself, and the opportunity to be better, that's the silver lining. Hard times are the great teacher, and I believe that my kids also learned to persevere through their hard times because they know they can make it through too. I learned the valuable habit of gratitude. Every morning, I wrote at least three things I was grateful for. This practice helped me keep my eyes open throughout the day. I do this practice every morning to this day.

Surrender and Have Faith

Surrender brings peace. As a mom with no control to help my daughter's battle with a chronic, debilitating illness, all I could really do is have faith and believe.

As part of my disappointment and shame from my divorce, I had a faith crisis and fell away from consistently praying, meditating, and believing. When my daughter became ill, I realized that I had zero control over the situation, but I could control my daily habits that would help support us both. Daily prayer and meditation were key to reducing my stress and helping me deal with the changes in our daily life. As my daughter had to drop out of school and endure countless doctor appointments, my daily practice kept me grounded and positive.

After over a year of endless specialists and tests, we finally found a cardiologist who was able to diagnose my daughter with postural orthostatic tachycardia syndrome (POTS). Over time, she has learned to manage symptoms and challenges. She continues to persevere, and surrender and faith remain.

Freedom Through Real Estate Investing

Growing up, I spent a lot of time with my grandmother who owned and managed several duplexes. Through osmosis, I learned the power of investing in real estate, and somewhere along the line, I knew that I was going to be a real estate investor. I didn't have a plan, I just knew that it was going to happen. I got divorced in 2006, and then the economic collapse of

2008 happened. The real estate world was turned upside down, and people were unloading houses. An opportunity came my way.

I knew enough to evaluate a deal, but I did not know anything about being a landlord. Having decreased my household assets and income with my recent divorce, this was not an ideal time to jump into real estate, but I knew it was right. I took the tenant that came with the house, and six months later bought two more properties in a challenging neighborhood. Managing these properties was difficult. Tenants wouldn't pay, turnovers were often, and there were a lot of issues. Sometimes, it was downright scary. But, what an amazing education.

After managing those properties for many years, I 1031-exchanged into better neighborhoods, then dabbled in corporate housing and vacation rentals. While my kids were growing up, we had a ski vacation home that also provided cash flow—nothing's better than that. Over time, I purchased turnkey properties in emerging markets where I could significantly increase my cash flow. Then, I decided to scale bigger, learned about apartment investing, and jumped into multifamily where my partners and I have over $230 million in investments.

Real estate investing has created so much opportunity for my family that I feel committed to share what I've learned. I love connecting people with great opportunities to invest in real estate, and am especially passionate about helping other women experience its power so that they can create options in their lives.

Adaptive Resilience Is a Super Power

For me, adapting well to all the change that comes with life comes from resilience and gratitude, which are practiced and developed through my daily habits. I am most successful when I am consistent with my morning rituals that set my intentions for the day. The highlights of my daily practice are prayer and meditation, journaling, and being grateful. It's very hard to be stressed and upset while you are feeling grateful.

If interested in creating transformation and innovation, visit stephaniewankel.com.

To partner in real estate opportunities, email stephanie@newheightsinvestmentgroup.com and check out Stephanie's Frenzied To Financial Freedom Podcast.

ADAM BUTTORFF
Success Is Not About ME!

Adam Buttorff is the entrepreneur founder of Renown Roofing, an INC 5000 fastest-growing company two years in a row. He's an amazing speaker, coach, and sales trainer with his company TodaysChangeAgent.com and he is passionate about building sustainable businesses and growing people.

Losing a Father

I grew up one of seven kids in Dallas. Losing my dad when I was 11 years old was tragic to my entire family. I got my first job at 11. All of us got jobs and pitched in. I quickly and painfully learned a strong work ethic. My mom was resilient. She got three jobs and we moved into a little bitty three bedroom house. We had four boys packed in one little room. I remember from 11 to 15 not having any new clothes. Everything was used. Overall, it defined us as a family and brought us closer.

The Young Entrepreneur

In fifth grade, I started selling bandanas and did very well. In contrast, I struggled in school. Everybody liked me. Teachers loved me. I was very entertaining, but not your typical student. I went to college because that's what I was supposed to do. After seven "short" years, working full-time plus side jobs and studying, I got that degree.

I thought my problems would be solved once I had my degree. Then my boss said, "Don't expect a raise just because you have a degree now." What a reality check. I began trying all kinds of jobs. Failure is a great teacher. The success I have today is built on those failures. I love the saying *you don't know what you don't know*. I didn't know a lot. I went through 10 different businesses, network marketing, self-startup, parking lot striping, door to door sales... before I launched an in-home personal training business with a business partner and at the same time I was flipping houses.

Boom, The Crash

I'm an avid reader. I didn't have real mentors growing up, but I had books: Jim Rohn, Zig Ziglar, and Robert Kiyosaki. I was looking for the vehicle to prosperity that made sense. I had the personal training business and real estate and found I was doing great in both.

Then, boom, the market crashed. I was leveraged to the hilt with all my money in remodels. At the same time, my business partner pushed me out of the fitness business. I went from a successful entrepreneur to broken, no job, and married with two little kids. It was very humbling.

My late wife connected me with her brother who sold roofing. I was not excited at the prospect, but God had humbled me to do whatever it took. I got into the roofing industry, started selling roofs, and figured out that I love it. I launched my own company about a year and a half later. It has been a crazy trajectory ever since and the best thing I've ever done.

INC 5000 Fastest-Growing Company by Building a Team

Five years into the business, we hit the INC 5000 fastest growing companies in America. My team made it happen. I'm a big believer in development and investment in teams. Life is about people.

Initially, by inclination, I was very results oriented. I thought it was logical. If we got results and moved the bottom line, everybody's happy. Well, that's actually not true. As a matter of fact, my team was very frustrated with me early on. I was baffled. I found out I didn't know their dreams. I didn't know their likes and dislikes. I didn't really know anything about them other than their performance. We got results and they got paid. But, if you do your research, you'll see money is not the number one motivator. It's not even the top five.

The most successful companies build a culture. We so easily forget culture is the engine of the vehicle that drives the metrics. The truth is doing anything of significance is a team effort. Because behind every great leader is great team members.

Losing My Wife

You see it in movies and think *that will never happen to me*. You just don't know what life is going to hold. One day my wife was happy and super healthy. The next she fell down in a seizure. We went to the doctor, brain cancer. "There's nothing we can do. You have four to six months to live." That really rocks your faith...every aspect of who you are.

It was a very hard time. I'm thankful for the people in my life that were there to help support me.

Most people don't know what to say to you. I always say, don't ask what you can do for someone grieving. Because they just don't know. Find something and do it for them.

My favorite messages are usually, "You're on my heart, I'm praying for you." or "I just want you to know I love you." I would tell friends, all I need to hear is that this sucks and I love you.

Advice for Entrepreneur Single Parents

Build a great team. When you invest in your people, understand their strengths, and put them in their sweet spot, your systems will run really well. Then you have a company that's not 100% dependent on you so you can really be the parent you need to be. I'm home when the kids get home from school so I can invest in them. I structured my life around my kids because kids spell love T-I-M-E. You can say it all day long, but you're missing out if you don't show it by spending time with them. Looking back to my loss at 11, time with my father is the one thing I wish I had more of.

You also have to schedule time for you. It's the old adage, how are you going to pour out of an empty cup? I had to block out time for me, and I had to figure out what really resonates with me. For some people it's alone time or it's time with friends. Figure out what feeds you.

Things I Had to Quit for Success

Watching the news – Have you ever heard anything positive on the news? I'm not starting or ending my day like that. If it's that important, I'll find out. Instead, I feed myself with good things.

Victim mentality – I cut out a lot of TV. In some ways TV represented my mentality that I wanted life to be comfortable and easy. When I cut out that negative mentality, I could actually live. That expectation was hindering me. I was thinking, "I deserve XYZ, and I'm not getting it. Because life is tough." I realized that had to go. Instead, I focus on the benefits of my life. I get to be a dad. How awesome is that? There's a lot of people struggling to have kids. I get to run a successful company with a great team. That's amazing. The positives drive me and made a big difference in me going through the really tough times. God is good and life is still good. Circumstances aren't always good, but life is still very good.

Avoiding problems – I tend to be aggressive. If there's a problem, I want to dive into it. The more we avoid problems, the bigger they grow. However, we can't go around attacking every small little issue. Most things are better to let go. If it lingers with you, then it's time to start an open dialog. This makes a huge difference with people, and I make sure I am always open to their feedback as well. If I offend somebody or hurt somebody's feelings, I am vigilant to work that out. I humble myself before them. Let me tell you, that will unify relationships and deepen into unbelievable respect. I have gotten more respect from people from my being humbled than I have ever gotten from being arrogant.

Success Habits

So many people think that success habits are if I do these three things, life will be amazing and perfect. I've realized it's actually consistently doing the little things. For example, the most important part of my day is my quiet time to center myself in the morning. When I'm consistent with that, everything else falls in place. Not to say it's always going to go perfect, but it makes a huge difference. *Jim Rohn said success is nothing more than a few simple disciplines practiced every day, while failure is nothing more than a few errors in judgment repeated every day.*

Everyone needs a mentor or coach. Always be a student. Learn, learn, learn, from books and by being around others that challenge you and make you better. All results come from growth, even if we don't necessarily like going through it. If people are dragging you down and they're negative, cut them out of your life. This can be hard, but just get around people who want the best for you and encourage you because it'll transform your life.

Broken Belief Systems

I often speak about belief systems. Our belief system affects every aspect of who we are. What are your self-limiting beliefs? We all have them. What do you really believe about yourself and what you can and can't do? We believe ourselves more than we believe any outside source, and we're talking to ourselves nonstop. An average person has about 50,000 thoughts per day. Of those, 80% are negative and 95% are repetitive thoughts. If we repeat those negative thoughts, we think in a negative way more than we think positive.

We have to focus on what comes in the brain. If you eat Twinkies and Ding Dongs all day long your body will not function well. If we read and listen to junk all day long, our mind is not going to do well. You've got to feed yourself positive things because this builds your belief about who you are and what you're going to accomplish. I learned that from Zig Ziglar, Jim Rohn, and honestly, Jesus in the Bible. As a man thinketh in his heart, so is he. So, be careful of your thought life.

Keeping a journal is a key part of the process to find the roots of your belief system. Sometimes, we won't do something because we don't believe we deserve it. If we get down to the root of where this is coming from, you will be released from sabotaging your success. By writing in your journal about what you're feeling or what you're trying to avoid feeling, you'll start getting down to healing. Eventually, your increased awareness will actually change your belief system. And you will be able to do so much more than you thought possible.

Connect with Adam Buttorff about coaching, speaking, and sales training for sustainable businesses at TodaysChangeAgent.com, Adam@TodaysChangeAgent.com, or LinkedIn.

TYLER GUNTER

My Why to Retire Before 30 and Become a Disruptive Financial Educator

Tyler Gunter is an award-winning financial advisor, investor, and serial entrepreneur helping others live full lives through financial investing for now and the future. Tyler retired before 30 and is now founder of Priority Plus Insurance and Financial Group and CEO at Park Place Communities.

Blessed With Twins

I married a wonderful, amazing woman, Tamra, in my early twenties and worked as a commissioned salesperson for heating and air conditioning equipment. I was nearly 27 when we found out we were expecting and I was very excited to be a father.

Eight weeks into Tamra's pregnancy, we found out we were having twins! We realized daycare for one kid made sense, but for two, it made more sense for my wife to stay home and leave her job in the insurance industry. We were going from a dual-income family of two to a single-income family of four. It was time to figure some things out. So, we hired a real estate coach. I always knew I wanted to get into investing and thought this could be our answer.

Our timeline was shortened when Tamra was put on extreme bed rest a couple of weeks later. We were given a very grim prognosis on whether our kids would make it through the pregnancy. My wife has a protein C deficiency, which means she is prone to blood clotting, so there were some extreme risks that come with that. I don't think I truly understood how serious those risks were at the time and how close I was to losing all three of them until several months later when the pregnancy was 31 weeks five days.

Some Things We Can't Control

That night, we were playing Cashflow and having fun. Tamra was able to move a little bit. Up until then, she wasn't allowed to be out of bed for more than five minutes at a time and no more than maybe twice a day. She started having contractions. We still had two months to go. I thought they had to be Braxton Hicks, but they became regular to the point I could time them to the second, so we went to the hospital.

Our rural community hospital was not set up to handle a two-month premature child let alone two. When we got there, they confirmed Tamra was in labor and did everything they could to delay delivery. In the meantime, they called Salt Lake City's University of Utah Hospital to have one of their helicopters come pick up my wife.

The helicopter was full: Tamra, the pilot, and two neonatal nurses in case the babies came mid-flight. So I would have to drive the four hours to Salt Lake City.

Tamra was in active labor for five days. Eventually, they couldn't stop it anymore, and they called for an emergency C-section. Still oblivious to the danger my family was in, I was a giddy, happy dad. God bless my wife. She knew the risk she was taking.

In the Operating Room

There was a drape shielding us from the operation. Tamra was hooked up to all kinds of monitors. There were a lot of noises and people. Then I heard, "Okay, Dad. Get your camera." I turned around, and the doctor held up my crying son. It was incredible. I got a photo, then the doctor passed my son through a window, and I couldn't see him anymore. I was showing my wife the photo when my daughter came out.

She wasn't crying.

"Dad, get your photo hurry." I took my photo, and she was passed through the window. I couldn't see what was happening. But when she started crying, I felt so much relief.

But then, the alarms on my wife's monitors started going off. My wife looked at me panicked and said, "I can't breathe." I was completely helpless. I looked at the monitors, and her heart rate was dropping. Her body was going through major trauma.

Everything was such a blur: the alarms, the screaming back and forth between the doctors and medical students, the phone calls for further advice, and me being told to get out of the way for a minute. But they got Tamra into recovery.

Trust Your Team, Trust in God

My wife and kids were in the hospital for two months. Our babies were in one-on-one care in the neonatal intensive care unit. Slowly, they grew and learned how to breathe and live on their own. Throughout the process, I was mostly helpless. There was so little I could control.

I learned about faith. When there is something I can do, I do it. But when things are out of my control, I learned to trust that God has a plan. I trusted that God had a reason for my children to live. And then I learned to trust in my team. The nurses in the NICU were incredible.

The day of the delivery, my wife spent 10 hours convincing her nurses to let her see the babies. They weren't going to let her because of everything she had been through. She was heavily sedated and in extreme pain. When they finally agreed, we put her in a wheelchair and prepared to do kangaroo care, skin to skin contact.

My babies had ventilators on, IVs taped to their heads, wires all over their bodies, and the tiniest diapers you could ever imagine that they were swimming in. When it was my turn to hold my daughter, I got her tucked inside my gown, and she suddenly stopped breathing. I was in panic again. I hate those alarms. Sometimes I wake up at night hearing them. But, what happened next was amazing. A nurse came up, and he started rubbing my daughter's back saying, "Come on baby, breathe. Breathe, baby." I could do nothing, but this nurse, seeing what he saw every day was calm.

That wasn't the only time she stopped breathing. It was an ongoing thing up until about five days before we left the NICU. That nurse brought such a calming presence the first time it happened. Even with the high stakes, he was so relaxed and peaceful. There was not much I could do in that situation. So, I trusted there was a greater plan.

Business and Real Estate

All the while, we were working with our real estate coach. We were two weeks away from closing on our first rental when Tamra went into labor. Once things settled a bit, we closed on the little three bedroom, two bath home.

After that, we realized we could go bigger, faster, and it took the same amount of energy. So, we bought 25 homes and a 33-space mobile home community all at the same time. That put us over the top. We were earning more passive income than our personal expenses. I wasn't yet 30. If you keep your feet in the fire and remain calm, there's nothing you can't overcome and nothing you can't achieve. The calmer you can stay while standing in the fire, the more you will grow.

I continued to work because I loved the job and the people I worked with, especially the people I worked for. But, I was all in. When I find something that works, I figure why not do that in every area of my life. We created a start-up company in property maintenance doing window cleaning, power washing, and handyman services. And at the same time, I bought an insurance company from a man who had been an incredible mentor to me when I was just getting started.

My biggest investment was in myself and my education, hiring coaches and getting around people doing it bigger and faster at a level where I wanted to be. Today, I don't surround myself with people that are at my level or below because you can't grow. Getting in a room with people that are doing what I want to be doing has been very important, and I do that regularly.

Mentorship

There was a gentleman in Elko, NV, where I grew up, who was extremely successful. At the time, I was determined to become a successful entrepreneur and real estate investor. I got word that this man might be interested in selling his portfolio, and though I had no experience at barely over 20 years old, I wanted to buy it.

I wrote out a very nice letter of admiration and an offer to talk to him about selling his portfolio. He responded with so much tact. He saw where I was at in life and invited me to his office. When I visited, he told me he wasn't quite ready to sell, but he wanted to tell me how he got his start. We went into his conference room where he had white boards across all of the walls, and he told me in incredible detail the process of exactly how he built his vast portfolio.

Time is valuable. This man spent probably three hours with me that day. He understood where I was in a way I didn't. He showed me how I could get where I wanted to go in life. Then he told me any time I needed guidance, I could call him.

I did reach out to him when Tamra and I bought our portfolio for a second set of eyes to see if there was anything I was missing. He was always so supportive. Fast forward 10 more years—he is the man I bought our insurance company from.

Why Insurance?

After we had the twins, we had $750,000 in medical bills. I saw the good and the bad of the insurance industry. There are a lot of options in insurance that aren't widely talked about because they're not as lucrative for insurance providers, but my wife was fortunate. She had these options because it was part of her employment package in her insurance job, and I'm so glad she did. And these options are available to everybody.

After our deductible, not only were we covered for our bill, we actually came out ahead thanks in large part to the disability coverage and hospital income coverage we had. We also had life insurance policies that we were able to pull cash value from if necessary.

I can remember the day I opened up an envelope to find a $21,000 check for my daughter. It was written to our trust. I opened another one, and there was another $21,000 check in there for my son. I opened up the third and there was a $12,000 check for my wife and I.

There are resources out there that we don't always know about that are available to everyone. These resources made a huge difference for my family and can pay dividends in your life.

There are ways to to structure life insurance policies for cash and investment advantage and life advantage. In the traditional way, you create a legacy you can pass on to your children, loved ones, or business. Alternatively, there's an avenue where you can leverage the tax advantages and security of insurance companies to build wealth faster in a banking-style system that you can borrow from and utilize for physical investments that fit your portfolio while still preserving your monetary legacy like a traditional policy.

Most of us accept you need money to earn money. An amazing book, *The Richest Man in Babylon*, talks about sending your gold out and having it returned with friends. This is the same concept. You can put your money in a place where it's generating income, and you can take money from that to invest, and all the while, it still continues to grow as if you never took it out. The cash you put in is actually a basis for the insurance company to lend you money. By using this practice, you become your own bank.

I dedicate my time to teaching others how to take advantage of these incredible, barely known opportunities because I know what a blessing they have been for my family, and I want to share that with others through our services and financial education.

Contact Tyler Gunter, founder of Priority Plus Insurance and Financial Group, about creating your own personal bank to invest in your financial freedom at disruptivefinancialeducation.com.

tyler@disruptivefinancialeducation.com

Facebook: https://www.facebook.com/trgunter

Instagram: @thetylergunter

SETH MOSLEY
How a Three-Time Grammy Winner Lives Full Circle

Seth Mosley is a three-time Grammy winner and one of the most awarded songwriters and producers in Christian music. He was Songwriter of the Year 2015 and has 29 #1 songs. He is the founder of Full Circle Music, creator of The Song Chasers Commercial Songwriting Course, and a real estate investor.

Full Circle

Our company is called Full Circle Music for a reason. When I was a kid, my first CD was *Take Me To Your Leader* from the band Newsboys. In 2009, the first label record I got to work on in Nashville as a producer and co-writer was Newsboys' *Born Again.*

My whole life has been this big series of full circle moments, working with people that I grew up listening to and loving—incredible artists like TobyMac, King & Country, Unspoken, High Valley, Jeremy Camp, and Matt Kearney. That's one of the big reasons I wanted to start The Full Circle Music Academy and our publishing company. I want to help other musicians along their journey.

10,000 Hours and The World Tour

I've been a music fan as far back as I can remember. When I got home from school every day, I would go down to the basement, turn up records, and jam on a plastic hockey stick. It was the thing I always wanted to do. I had no plan B. I had to make it work. Thankfully, I've had great mentors that have helped me on my way. One thing leads to the next, and I've built my career a little bit at a time.

I started out as an artist. Most people do when they're passionate about music. I taught myself piano and guitar. When I got into my teenage years, I started leading on stage at church.

Eventually, I figured out a way to record my bad songs on my parents' computer. When you're from a small town, there are no recording studios. You've just got to figure it out. I saved money from mowing grass and teaching guitar lessons to buy basic gear and start a recording studio in our basement. I would only come up for air, food, and water. I released some things on my own in high school, and then some friends asked me to record them too. That was where I found my calling as a music producer and songwriter. I learned the art of the creative process by doing it over and over again.

After I graduated high school, I was hired straight into a little recording studio in Columbus. I was being paid full-time to do something I had planned to go to college to learn! That is where I got my 10,000 hours.

Wanting to start my own thing, I then toured around the world with my band Me In Motion for more than five years.

Initially, we would make a list of cities we wanted to tour, and since we were a Christian band, we would look up local churches and cold call 40 or 50 of them a day. If we got one or two yeses, that was a big win for us. When we were starting out, we would book the whole tour just by getting on the phones and building relationships with promoters and local pastors. I believe you need to start doing it on your own before you bring in a booking agent or manager. You've got to learn how it works, and you've got to have something worth booking first.

From our very first tour, we brought opening bands with us, bands that I had worked with as a producer. We always felt like everything was a lot more fun as a team. It wasn't always the most fun thing: we were piled in a van together, driving around through the middle of the night all around the country, setting up our own PA system, and doing it all. But it was definitely a learning experience.

We ended up touring 10 different countries and played a thousand shows.

Making the Leap and Moving to Nashville

Eventually, I decided to move to the center of country and Christian music in Nashville, TN. If you want to be a part of country or Christian music, Nashville is the place to be.

I was young, and I wanted to go all in. I had no reason not to. I thought of it as an experiment. I figured even though I might fail, I thought I could always move back to Ohio, go to college, and get what I considered "a regular job" if I needed to.

Get Ahead with a Servant's Heart

I've always maintained the habit of looking for ways to serve people. That's how we look at everything in business. It's always give first, not ask, not take. As Zig Ziglar said, "You can have everything in life you want, if you will just help other people get what they want."

For me, much more important than being the guy on stage is helping other dreamers get there. That realization launched me into my incredibly successful role behind the scenes as a songwriter and Grammy-winning producer, which in turn, has given me the platform to mentor up-and-coming musicians on their journeys. The irony is that serving led me to success.

Full Circle Music Academy

After writing 29 Billboard #1 songs, I created The Song Chasers Commercial Songwriting Course to share all I know about songwriting. I always tell people, songwriting is 90% perspiration and 10% inspiration, *but* you've got to do the 90% to be there for that 10% when it happens. Those are the moments that you live for. The songs are out there, and I believe they come from a place outside of us. It's our job to show up to grab them and steward them well.

Recently, we developed something that has not existed until now: a music industry baby step plan. We take you step by step from the groundwork of deciding what you want to do, setting goals, creating a personal budget, and building your network all the way through developing your skills and knowledge to eventually charging a premium for your services.

Most people aren't working a job where they can see the direct fruit of their labors. But when you write a song, you have it right there. That's an amazing thing. I can't really describe it any other way than as a God thing. God is a creator, and we get to co-create with him. I think when people realize the power of that, they're hooked on it.

Mentors Along the Way

I have many mentors to thank who showed me the way. The guy that first hired me when I graduated from high school in 2005 used to run a studio, and he mentored me by showing me how to work in a room with other artists. Ian Eskelin was the first producer that brought me to town. I sent him a demo when I was 19. I still see him at the gym, and we have a good relationship. Outside of music, Kyle Wilson is a mentor from whom I've learned so much about marketing and doing it in a way that's authentic, real, and from the heart. I don't know if we'd have our podcast, *Made It in Music*, if it weren't for Kyle Wilson's encouragement. I also have to give a shout out to Craig Ballantyne, a great author, speaker, and high-performance coach.

There are many more mentors some of which probably don't even know they're my mentors. But I am grateful for every one of them.

Habits for Success

Healthy family balance. Time with family is so important for me, and I also encourage it for each of our team members. Having a life outside of work is important because it makes your work better. I thank my wife for drilling that into my head because that wasn't always my natural way. I learned it through lots of marriage counseling, lots of hard conversations, and lots of apologies on my part. In the beginning of your career, you've got to burn the candle at both ends sometimes, but there comes a point where doing that is not worth the sacrifice.

Personal development is one of my passions because if you're not growing, you're going backward.

Take action. If you learn about something that you believe will positively impact your business or personal life, implement it. Until you put the philosophies you read about into practice, they will do you no good. Only through taking steps forward will you see massive shifts in your life and success.

To connect with Seth Mosley about The Full Circle Music Academy or the Song Chasers Commercial Songwriting Course, visit fullcirclemusic. com/pro or follow him on Youtube @officialFCmusic and Instagram @theSethMosley. Check out the podcast Made It in Music *at madeitinmusic.com.*

JERRY HORST
The Road Less Traveled

Real estate developer, investor, syndicator, and philanthropist Jerry Horst is CEO of Vanguard Development Group, providing investment class real estate assets. Jerry and his wife Sue have seven children and six grandchildren. They travel the world speaking on success, marriage, family, and living your fullest.

How Would You Describe Your Life?

Would you use words like, *miraculous, amazing, adventurous, thriving, passionate, exciting, satisfying*? Do you wake up every morning ready to face the day? Do you feel engaged and excited to live your life? Or would you say, "Each passing day I'm just trying to get through it. I'm exhausted, frustrated, resentful, stressed out, stuck, slipping, surviving....?" I know you want to say some days are good and some days are tough, but what is consistent in your life? We think and hope that this roller coaster ride will stop at some point when certain conditions are met and things magically get better, but without effort on our part, that's not realistic. Every day is an invitation to practice living an intentional life with a sense of destiny.

My First Business

My father was superintendent for a large commercial construction company. When I was in high school, he asked me what I wanted to do when I grew up. I loved gadgets, so I wanted to do something with electronics. He asked me to work for him until I figured it out. I agreed. At 18, I went into business for myself, and my dad came and worked for me. I am in construction and development still today.

I grew up in a very conservative community. Even when people are uber-wealthy, you would never guess because it's a sign of humility to look poor. It's just the culture here. When I was young, that's not how I wanted to live, so I read books like *How to Win Friends and Influence People* and *Think and Grow Rich*—all the books that everybody reads now, but back then, nobody had ever heard of them and couldn't understand why I found them compelling. Thanks in part to those books, I had unreasonable success from the moment I was out of high school. I think I made about $80,000 that first year, which would be around $375,000 in purchasing power today.

It didn't take me long to become an arrogant jerk. That's kind of how life works when most everything goes right for you.

Life-Defining Moment

I've had many completely outrageous life-defining situations. Once I stumbled into a Bible study led by a local chicken farmer. Like many during that era, he seemed to believe that poverty was next to godliness. My goal was to be a millionaire by the time I was 30. He was the opposite of what I was looking for, and to him, I was a personification of everything wrong with the current culture. I was an arrogant jerk who drove up in his brand new white Corvette dressed in designer clothes to a meeting of 12 people from a local trailer park. A crazy picture, and yet within a few weeks, he became my best friend.

That night my life changed forever. Like me, this man had grown up in church, except that he talked like he knew God personally. I never knew God, and more importantly, I never knew that He could be, or wanted to be, known. This short-circuited my brain. I remember saying to myself, *My whole life is a waste. I've missed the entire point. No matter what it cost me, I must know God like this guy does.*

95

Miracles

Years ago, I accepted an invitation to go on a mission trip to India. It sounded exciting, and I thought it would be gratifying to help people.

Clearly, I was not prepared for the shock I was about to encounter. As we arrived in the smelly, hot Bombay airport, the man who invited me showed me articles he had placed in seven of the major newspapers with the headline, "Evangelist Comes from America, The Lame Will Walk, The Blind Will See, The Deaf Will Hear." That headline was directly above a 5x7 photo of my face!

I didn't believe in faith healing, and I certainly wasn't going to be healing people. But he said, "No, you are going to heal people. People are going to come 100 miles on an ox cart, and you're going to heal them."

I said, "Okay, so what if I do this, I pray for people, and then they're not healed?" There was no question in my mind… no one would be healed.

He looked at me very seriously and said, "Well, Jerry, they'll most likely stone us. But don't worry. They'll be healed."

That was my introduction to foreign missions work and healing.

In the next three weeks, I saw miracles. Every person I prayed for was healed, most of them instantly. The only person who didn't believe what they were seeing was me. It was the most incredible thing I had ever seen. I realized then that the whole Bible is true, and the Lord actually invites us to live like that.

It was fairly difficult to focus on business from then on. It just seemed a bit less real than what had left a permanent mark on my reality. Nevertheless, business success came easily, and any missions work we wanted to do, we simply had the resources. It became captivating to see money being used to change the world. I began to realize that as I focused on people and asked how we could impact their world, God would give us ideas, strategies, and favor to create products that would give us an abundant supply of money.

Why Not Retire

For many years, I was semi-retired, traveling the world doing mission work. Today, I enjoy my life in business, making the world a better place for people, while remaining active in missions.

I'm more in love with my wife than ever before. I have never seen any movie or read any book that comes close to the joy I have had in my marriage for these past 40 years. We have intentionally lived with small habits that have given us huge returns from things like, praying together every morning, making God the center of our marriage, journaling, keep our physical health a priority, committing to grow by reading, and taking time off every year to just hear God so we can plan according to what He speaks to us.

Secondly, we endeavor to create children who are capable and worthy of stewarding vast sums of wealth and impacting nations. We want our efforts to have an exponential impact. For us, mentoring our children has the highest capacity to have exponential impact on the world.

Parenting and Mentoring

All of us become experts at presenting who we want people to think we are, which is, hopefully, close to who we actually are. But children see right through any act. The most important thing is to be real and who you are. If we act like life's a breeze, they never see us struggle. When they hit those walls, they're going to think this isn't right, it's not how life is supposed to be, and they'll fall apart because they don't know what to do. I try to be honest with my kids without dragging them into whatever I might be experiencing, but still letting them know how I process pain and disappointment.

In our relationships, we always focus on people with the potential for great impact. We've learned you can push very hard for minimal results, or if you're selective, you can have an exponential effect. We want to pour our energies into people and projects that will have the greatest exponential impact. Then, daily and weekly, my wife and I sit down and ask, what's working? And what do we need to move on from that isn't helping? It's simply about being intentional.

When I was young, I realized that every interaction we have with a person is an opportunity to lighten their lives or make them heavier. I've adjusted my public personal presence to work to lift and encourage people. Just smiling is a simple habit, and it actually releases endorphins in other people. It makes their whole day better, and it costs nothing.

Building Communities

Early in my construction career, I was buying housing developments, building houses, and then selling them. I was involved in every part of the process. I've always held the opinion that you're more empowered if you have firsthand experience of how everything works.

It didn't take me long, however, to realize that tasks like installing kitchens were below my desired pay grade. Doing that work, I was worth the same $20 an hour I paid any kitchen installer. At nearly 20 years old, I realized that when I was on the phone negotiating deals, I was often making $5,000 an hour. I needed to spend a lot more time on the phone and a lot less time installing kitchens. It was simple math.

Today, development is one of our core businesses. We take land and create great communities and cash flowing assets for high net worth investors. We started out in construction, later building a few hundred homes a year, most of which I designed myself, then grew into multifamily and communities. We also create a variety of commercial real estate assets.

We really enjoy multifamily projects because we get to design spaces that we'd want to live in which elevate lifestyle and community. It is exciting. We usually bring in multiple investors to create a multifamily asset. Ideally, we refinance out all the investment capital once it's stabilized, returning all the original capital to the investors (tax-free), while they retain their equity in the project. That investment magic is called infinite returns. Investors get all their capital back but still own the asset.

My son in law, Michael Manthei, and I created a monthly local real estate Meetup which has been quite successful. We have about 200 people attending regularly, and we talk about everything real estate, how to find property, creating pro formas, how to recognize and vet a deal, raising money, everything. Then we take it to another level by helping people connect to purpose by improving their lives and making an impact on others.

How do you become the person that you're glad you are? The small intentional decisions that we make today, tomorrow, and the day after that, stack up, and after a while, when we look back, we will realize that they made all the difference in creating the life we imagined for ourselves. The worst thing we could ever waste is our life. Instead, commit to live intentionally and on purpose.

Be intentional about life. Ask yourself, Am I in the driver seat, or is my life on autopilot? Is the direction I'm going taking me where I want to go? Is there more to life than what I have experienced? Have I settled too quickly because of pseudo success or intimidation?

Life is experienced and measured in time. Actions are exponential, so whatever you are going to do, the sooner you do it, the greater the impact. What is one thing you can change today that will have the greatest return in your life?

Jerry Horst can be reached at Jerry@VanguardDG.com

VanguardDG.com | Investelevate.com

Facebook ELEVATE Investing Group

DR. JOHN R. OBENCHAIN
Samantha's Eyes

Dr. John R. Obenchain is a professor and corporate trainer who designs and teaches coursework for Big-10 universities and Fortune 500 corporations. He is a man of huge heart, and what follows is his story in his own words.

"Hello? Johnny," Mom called out on the other end of the line. "Johnny? Is everything okay? Johnny!?"

I tried, but I couldn't. I'd never experienced anything like it—being so overwhelmed with emotion that I was unable to speak.

I looked helplessly at my wife, lying in her hospital bed. She knew I was having trouble, so she nodded, and I handed her the telephone.

"Hi. No, he's okay. It's the baby. It's her heart. Well, they say it's two things. Her aorta is too small to carry enough blood to the rest of her body. Um-hmm. Yes, and there's something else. The doctors say that she's got holes in the wall separating her ventricles. This means that the blood coming from her body is getting mixed in with the blood coming from her lungs. Yes. Yes, it's very serious. Uh-huh. They're taking her to the Children's Hospital of Philadelphia in a few minutes. Yes. Yes, John's going to ride down in the ambulance with her. We don't know yet, but..."

She looked up at me, and I nodded.

"We'll call you as soon as we know more."

I woke up and didn't know where I was. Looking around the tiny room, seeing just a door and soundproofed walls, it all suddenly came back to me: the birth of my daughter. The confirmation that she had a bad heart. The doctors placing her in an incubator, on life support. The midnight ride in an ambulance across the state line to The Children's Hospital of Philadelphia.

And now, here I was.

I decided that the first order of business would be visiting my baby.

As I left the small bedroom the hospital had kindly provided, part of me wondered if I would see her again... Or if she'd died while I'd slept.

My heart beat nervously, and my mouth went dry as I made my way into the critical care unit. Turning the last corner, however, I saw her there, right where I'd left her the night before. She lay helpless in an infant hospital bed, plugged into various machines via numerous wires and tubes.

My baby...

My baby girl...

I hated seeing her like that.

Reaching down, I gently stroked her cheek. She opened her eyes. Though she couldn't focus, not yet, she did look about. Her arms reached upward and outward as if searching blindly for me.

I stopped stroking her cheek and placed my index finger on the palm of her tiny left hand. She clutched my finger tightly, instinctively holding onto me.

My baby girl...

She didn't even have a name. This was intentional. If we had to lose her, it was best not to get too attached.

I began singing to her. This was instinctual on my part. I hadn't planned on singing, and the song I sang was one I'd never heard before. It probably never existed until that moment. But suddenly, it was there for me—for us—in a rush of emotional creativity.

> *Whirly-girly-girly-girl*
> *She's as precious as a pearl*
> *Hold her tight*
> *And treat her right*
> *'Cause she's my Whirly-girly-girl*
>
> *Whirly-girly-girly-girl*
> *Wind her up and watch her twirl*
> *Hold her tight*
> *And treat her right*
> *'Cause she' my Whirly-girly-girl*
>
> *Whirly-girly-girly-girl*
> *She's the best-est in the world...*

I stopped singing because I heard soft giggling behind me.

Turning, I saw that three student nurses had been watching. They were smiling, their faces all aglow, as if enchanted.

My face glowed too. It glowed bright red with embarrassment. I sought to apologize—for what, I do not know. Before opening my mouth, however, the nurses told me that my baby girl had to be taken downstairs for testing.

I walked around the critical care unit while my baby girl was away, and I saw many things—infants who were dying before they'd had a chance to live, babies whose insides were on the outside, newborns who had been born incomplete. I saw babies connected to so many tubes and wires they looked more like science experiments than newborn children.

In a way, this made me feel worse, yet better. Worse, because I saw just how bad it could really get. Better, because I didn't think my baby girl was as bad off as some. At least, this is what I hoped.

As I walked, I also saw the shadows...

They drifted much like I was drifting. They were hunched over and slow-moving. Their faces were ancient scrolls upon which the saddest stories were written. These shadows had once been human, but their humanness was being drained away by tragedy. They drifted here and there, aimlessly. When they stopped drifting, they sat down, close to their dying babies. There, they watched, waited, prayed....

Is this what I look like, I wondered.

Catching my reflection in a mirror, I realized that I not only looked like one of those shadows, indeed, I had become one.

When my baby girl had been brought back from testing, I learned that she'd been scheduled for open-heart surgery later that week.

I was sitting by her side, watching her eyelids get heavy, watching her breathing settle into a soft rhythm.

As soon as she was asleep, I decided then that I needed to call some people.

I called my wife to ask how she was doing. Honestly, she wasn't doing very well.

I called my mom to let her know about the open-heart surgery. I asked her to tell the rest of the family for me so that I could focus on my baby girl.

Then, I called the office.

They'd known this was coming. I'd advised them that my wife's pregnancy was considered high risk. Nonetheless, their reactions caught me by surprise.

I told them about my baby girl; they told me about the critical deadlines I was letting slip by. I told them about her scheduled open-heart surgery; they told me about the work that was piling up in my absence. I told them that I'd have to be out a few more days; they asked me why. After all, I wouldn't be doing the surgery myself. I wasn't doing any good just sitting there. No, where I needed to be was back at the office, doing the job I was being paid to do.

Realistically, they were right. There was nothing I could do in the critical care unit, but there was plenty for me to do at the office. My baby girl would never know if I'd been there or not, but my boss would know. My clients would know. My stakeholders would know.

I would know too. But what, specifically, would I know...

I knew this: If I returned to work, as I was being pressured to do, then as long as I lived, I'd know that I'd abandoned my dying baby girl. I'd abandoned her when I was the only family that could be by her side. I'd abandoned her to meet other peoples' deadlines.

No, I couldn't live with myself if I did that.

So, I told the office that I would keep them posted.

Thirteen years ago, I made the decision to stay with my baby girl and ignore the pressures and deadlines of work.

What's happened since?

The work got done, before it got undone. Entirely undone.

You see, our company ended up merging with another. Through no fault of our own, our department fell directly into the crosshairs of the corporate reorganization. First, our director was let go, then our vice president, then my manager, then me. All of the work I'd done for the company, all of the deadlines I'd met, all of the crises I'd faced... in the end, none of that mattered. The company let me go, and after a difficult adjustment, I let the company go.

But my baby girl...

She's grown into a brilliant and active 13-year-old. In fact, other than a faint scar down the center of her chest, there's not a hint that there was anything ever wrong with her. She has recovered completely.

And her name is Samantha.

So, what's my success habit? Warning: It's not for the faint of heart.

You have to face disaster head-on. You have to find yourself in the middle of a situation so bad that a happy ending is unlikely. Why? Because once you've overcome the impossible, doing something hard is comparatively easy. Trust me. I see this every time I look into Samantha's eyes.

So, what's next for me?

I've designed and taught coursework for universities and corporations, but now I'm expanding my classroom beyond these limits by creating my own business. Through public speaking, carefully researched books, online coursework, coaching, and consulting, I'm enabling corporate professionals to communicate their message by helping them engage and empower others to remember and apply their ideas.

Dr. John R. Obenchain can be reached at jobench18@gmail.com

JEFF E. THORNTON
Putting Family First Makes Success Even More Rewarding

Entrepreneur and investor Jeff Thornton leads Velox Capital, LLC, a leading investment company in industrial and multifamily buildings. He's run multimillion-dollar companies, has been in real estate for decades, and also operates in private lending.

Growing Up All Over

I grew up everywhere. My dad worked in the corporate world, and we were always moving. I was in 13 schools from first grade through high school. We would move, stay in a rental for six months, and then my parents would buy a house. We would be there for a year and a half, and then we would move again.

I had to learn how to make friends quickly. It was tough, especially as I got older. The hardest year, I was a sophomore in high school. That's a tough time to move because by then you're coming into your identity, you know who you are, and have started building solid relationships. I had a hard time adjusting for my first year there, but then it got better. I made some good friends and loved it in the end.

Finding Inspiration

Once I graduated, I went to college for one year. I was one of those guys that did not always have the best grades. Like so many future entrepreneurs, I got bored easily. I think that's how entrepreneurs get started. They get bored and start thinking, and more importantly, *taking action*. I decided I was going to quit college and go make my first million.

Looking back, it was inspiration from Dr. Denis Waitley, Jim Rohn, and Zig Ziglar that set me on the path of success. My high school best friend, who never went to college and has gone on to do very, very well for himself as an entrepreneur, picked me up one night to go out. We were about 19 years old. I got in the car, and I was waiting for Bad Company on the radio. There was no Bad Company, but there was Zig Ziglar. We listened to him all the way to the dance club, and I was hooked.

I think their lessons helped me stay positive. Over time, I've learned you're not always going to be able to maintain that mindset. There are things that are going to happen in business, but I learned to work around them. I'm a sales guy when you get down to it, and I experience that salesman's high—when things are going great, you're unstoppable. But when things are not going well, you have a tendency to get really down. I have to be careful to get myself out of that quickly. Without what I learned from those cassettes, I may have let it just walk all over me.

Economic Uncertainty Launched My First Career

The late 80s were some scary times economically. Interest rates were hitting 18-20%, and there was a lot of uncertainty. The S & L crisis that began in 1985 threw us into a full-blown recession in 1990.

By 1988, I was the seasoned Director of National Used Equipment for a semi-trailer manufacturing company. We had accumulated a lot of used trailers, and unfortunately, the company was not basing the book values on my appraised value. Ultimately, a combination of overvalued trailers and government tax subsidies on the trailers caused that company to go bankrupt.

They were owned by a great company out of Minnesota that was very strong financially, so they kept me around.

They now had all this inventory from the bankrupt company they no longer needed, and they asked me to put together a list of appraisals, retail, wholesale, and fire-sale prices. I ran around the country to give them quick and accurate numbers, and to my great fortune, they offered me the task of getting rid of everything. I was to use the fire-sale price as my cost, and I could keep all the profits!

I had an instant two million dollar inventory. And I took off with it.

It probably took me four months to sell it all, but that fire-sale inventory put me in business. I took over the lease on the office and the equipment yard, and I never even had to move my office. It was truly a "right-time-right-place" scenario. At the same time, I recognized what I did to earn that opportunity. I worked hard and fast, traveling around the country to get them what I could during their difficult time. I jumped at the chance to help, which I like to do, and that built trust. In the end, I want to help people. It makes me feel good.

A Lucrative, Easy Business

I was with that company for two years, and that jump-start allowed me to start my own company.

From that point on, the business grew and changed. In the 90s, bigger trucking companies made it very difficult for owner-operators, the guys who had one or two trailers, to make a living. So, in 1992, two years after I'd started the company and incorporated, I repositioned into wholesaling and rentals. For ten years, that became my main business. It was very lucrative and easy. I wasn't renting for road use, but instead strictly for storage purposes. I'd send trailers to a warehouse because they'd run out of room in their building. The trailer would sit there at the dock, and if it was eventually forgotten, the checks would still keep coming. It was a very good business until the great recession.

Back-Up Income Launched My Second Career

In 2009, 70 percent of my fleet of 185 trailers was sitting. Suddenly, my main income went away. My W-2 in 2010 was a goose egg from my trailer company. Though I kept the trailer company going, I didn't take any money.

Fortunately, I had started investing in real estate back in 2001, and our portfolio survived. I lived off real estate investments, and that was HUGE for me. It was a paradigm shift to realize just how powerful it is to have income from multiple sources.

We started investing in real estate with partners in 2007 with our first multifamily property. We purchased another in 2008, then another in 2012, and another in 2014 just before the market got hot for multifamily.

I knew about warehousing and industrial properties. I thought industrial real estate might be the best fit for me, but multifamily was where the action was. Since then, we've made a pivot to any type of multi-tenant property to reduce risk for our investors. The private lending I do is a bit riskier, but I am very picky about who I do lending with. Generally, we have to have a good relationship for years. Excellent due diligence is a must for private lending.

My First Deal

I did my first real estate deal in 1984. The owner of the company I was working for wanted to purchase one of four acres of land next to the business. He only wanted the one-acre on the road, and he wanted me to purchase the other three acres from him. I didn't think I could afford it, but he offered the additional acreage to me for next to nothing.

I ended up selling that property and then invested in another project with someone I didn't know well. That's when I learned a hard lesson. I didn't do my due diligence, and I made a horribly bad mistake. My partner was using the deal to buy drugs. People lost money, so I shied away from real estate for a while.

In 2001, I bought a couple of acres of property in Arlington, TX for my trailer company. The area was a little run down, and the view from my office window was railcars and a few older office warehouses. Guess what's there now? AT&T Stadium, home of the Dallas Cowboys and a new baseball stadium for the Texas Rangers. The new baseball stadium is less than a block away. It's so massive that I have to look up to see it. It feels like it's in my backyard! What an awesome feeling.

Some other events in my life really got me motivated to help others in real estate investing, and I share that in the book *Don't Quit, Stories of Persistence, Courage and Faith.*

Family Is Everything

My family is very important to me. My dad worked very hard to provide us with a living as he worked his way up to the corporate ladder, but he wasn't home much. He was there when he could be there, but he was not there like I would have liked him to be. So, one of my goals was to figure out a way to make a very good living without having to give up family. I made up my mind when my wife and I had kids that I would be there…always.

When I created the trailer company in 1990, my kids were three and almost five. I arranged my schedule so I never missed anything. Literally, from the time that my daughter started school until my son graduated high school, I didn't miss an event. And I love that. It was great because we were able to build a really close family relationship. I was always there and able to put my family first. Our first grandchild was born last year and being able to spend time with her is pure joy!

Honestly, I think this helps me in business because I put my investors first as well. I consider each investor a true partner, and I couldn't have learned to do that if I hadn't put my family first.

To connect with Jeff Thornton about real estate investing, private lending, or other alternative investments, email jeff@veloxwealth.com. To learn about Invest S.M.A.R.T. and receive valuable free resources, visit veloxwealth.com.

SOPHIA STAVRON

Live Your Light

Sophia Stavron is an intuitive coach and advisor, international speaker, #1 bestselling author, an executive producer of multiple Emmy and Telly award-winning films, and music producer. She's an authority on the ancient Greek, Philotimo Lifestyle™, and a funding manager of the nonprofit HopeSeed Foundation.

Growing Up with Knowingness

I have strong memories of feeling I was different. I could manifest things to happen. If I wanted something, I had it. If I wanted relaxation, I got it immediately. It was like I knew how to work my body-mind connection, and I was able to speak to others on that soul level. It seemed consistent that I would say something to an adult and he or she would reply, "How did you know that?" or "I was just going to say that."

I got some feedback that caused me to wonder if there was something wrong with me, but the positive feedback I kept getting allowed me to not shut down. If I were so wrong, why did it feel so right? During my prayer time, I would say, "Show me if I'm wrong. Show me if I'm crazy." That was a conflict throughout my childhood and all the way to age 25.

Today, I help others through teaching the ancient Greek philosophy of my ancestors, Philotimo Lifestyle™. Very simply, Philotimo Lifestyle™ is focused on the benefit of others. It's like the honor of being in service of others. I teach the modern day version because when you are living your light and you are really in that space, it's easy for you to see what another person needs or wants, because it's when you're living that lifestyle that you are of service. It's natural…that's being philotimo.

For me, I came into this life conscious at a very young age. Living philotimo was just a natural thing. When you see your role models, your mother and your father, being philotimo, and you see it's who they are both in public and in private, you manifest that. And as you grow, you just notice more, learn more, practice more, and experience more.

Discovering My Creative Genius

Very early in life, I found a consciousness that most people are searching for. I felt that music was in my blood. At age two, I was the inventor looking for instruments. I would invent things to play. I knew I had to have music and I could use it to change anything. At three years old, I demanded a violin. Any music teacher will tell you violin is one of the most difficult instruments to learn, even to hold. So the fact that at age three, I intuitively knew how to hold a violin properly was something to notice.

Throughout school, I was first chair violinist. Thankfully, in junior high, Mr. Miller, the music director, allowed me to also come into band practice if I came in early enough in the morning before school. He gave me freedom to play percussion when there were no girl percussionists at that time, so long as I didn't distract the boys. Ha! I provided value to the band by adding more sound flavor. Mr. Miller was an impactful mentor.

The easiest way to the soul is through the universal language of music. I'm bringing that to the forefront now in my life. I had left music as a priority behind, and I've felt the consequence. What I experience in life when I'm not working with music is that I'm not fully on and in my full joy state. As a Hollywood executive producer, I am able to make the most of my creative genius to benefit others by sharing positive messages. Every project I choose to participate in brings me joy!

Education and Becoming an Entrepreneur

I graduated from high school in 1988, and at that time, the outlook of making a living was a bit different. I was taught making a living was going to be harder for me as a woman. I was also going to be the first one in our family to go to college, so I had that pressure. Still, I was looking for something that would inspire and uplift me. There was no existing career for me to make a living off of my knowingness from childhood, and I had no model for how to do business with my unique gifts.

I pushed through that by going on to college to study what I loved and what came easy to me, music, health, and sociology.

I started a daycare at age 25 because I wanted to teach. I've always been a teacher with a desire to lead, especially in church. For a while, I wanted to be a priest so I could speak to the congregation and show them how to relieve anxiety and live their light.

If you have great teachers, you excel. I knew that children who excelled had teachers that allowed each of them to be thriving children. In my daycare, every child knew he or she was seen. At age 25 with no children, I had the opportunity to help parents become better parents to their children. After that season, I knew I was not really being fully myself and wanted to explore even a higher level of teaching people intuition, the mind, body, and spirit connection. That's why I went professionally into teaching and educating people about themselves and their untapped human potential.

I have an entrepreneurial spirit and knew that if I used my gifts and lived a philotimo lifestyle™, I would make money. I didn't need college because a college degree wouldn't get me where I want to go. I would get me where I wanted to go. And I was right! My college education did not open doors for me...using my intuition and connecting soulfully to people did!

Live Your Light

That has always been my message: live your light. It's my theme in speeches and when I write. I knew that unconditional love was the path to healing and to getting to your goals in life. So, I thought, why not teach? I'm not sure that teaching was my gift, but I thought that was my gift. Then again, when you're young, you don't really know your real purpose.

When you are not working on your intuition and you're being everything that everybody else wants you to be, you're not living your light. That's why you can't hear the messages that are coming to you. More often than I can count, I say to my clients, "Messages are coming. You're not listening." If you're not in practice, that's when it gets a little messy. You start getting into things that are not about you. When you start getting into somebody else's idea of you, you're off your path. When people say they're stuck, it's not that they're stuck and can't hear something. They're stuck in a brain loop and don't have the practice to clear themselves. You are stuck wanting to hear what you want to hear. The truth is usually something you might not want to hear. They say the truth hurts, but truth is freedom. When you hear and understand the truth, you are awakened and can let go.

Coaching and Sharing My Unique Gifts

I have a gift, and with my gift, I'm in service to others. It is my purpose to ignite and help others shine! That's my superpower! By my being philotimo, helping, and serving you, you get to be a bright light in this life, and you get to share your own gifts with the world.

The biggest challenge clients come to me with is their belief system. No matter what they present to me, I find that, for the most part, the underlying question is: Am I doing the right thing? The majority of my clients are not aware that their inner spirit, the trueness of who they are, wants them to go one way, while everybody else wants them to go the other. I had a whole group of MBA university students, each of whom had that conflict. They knew they had these dreams and wanted to do big things in life, but their parents, who were paying for their expensive education, wanted something else for their future. Because of the inner struggle and feelings of guilt, the students felt they were on the wrong path. Usually, this also presents as anxiety. It's knowing there's something more to who you are but not quite being able to put a finger on it.

When someone comes to me with an issue, it could be with a relationship or within their career, there's always an internal toggle that they have going on, back and forth, restless and anxious. In the first 10 minutes, I show them that I see them and share with them that what they've just explained and what they think is the issue is actually not the issue. That's when I feel them relax and wonder, "Oh, how does she know?" For the first time and suddenly, they find peace and can be themselves. My clients are not judged. I take over and help them find the answer. It's the same theme over and over. They are not aware that the mind is running itself. In many cases, my clients have not established positive habits to train the brain and be in control of their thoughts. When you allow your mind to run loose, your body runs loose and you experience the physical symptoms of those thoughts. You are in conflict because you have forgotten who you are, and that's why you have anxiety and why you may develop other health issues.

Most of my tools just come from experience. I ask people to be open-minded to receiving the solution that they need. A lot of the time, when people are in a struggle, they are stuck in their belief system. This is the most powerful prayer I can send to them. Open up your mind and surrender for a moment so you can hear the solution. Because you have the answer! When I say this out loud to people, it's almost like in that moment, the solution appears and the problem goes away. When my clients practice this, every single one comes back to me saying they could feel my presence, could feel me sending them that path (like I am in their ear), and letting them know it's okay.

Being Highly Intuitive

I'm a high level intuitive. So I'm operating from a whole different space above what most people know as intuitive. It's not that I'm a weirdo, even though some people might label me as such. Highly intuitive, in my case, means that I catch and pick up on energy that is passing by me from people and things. Recently, there is scientific evidence to support my understanding of the universe. Science is catching up to understanding me and who I am.

People have an energy before they even speak, so I just catch that energy. Sometimes this occurs for people I'm not even talking to or near. Multiple times, especially with my sister, even when she's in a whole different country, I have felt exactly what's going on with her in a bad moment. I'll call her and ask if she's feeling okay, and she asks how I know. I firmly believe we all have this ability in us because everything is energy. Have you ever been thinking of someone, maybe even someone who you haven't talked to in a long time, and they call or send you a text right then? This is no surprise to me. They feel your presence. Love is such a strong energy.

First I Connect to the Light

Getting connected to my light moves me morning and night. I don't know how to serve others until I complete my practice of visualization, meditation, breathing, and being with my spirit. It's a ritual morning and night that is non-negotiable because that ritual is how I create my future and how I am able to serve others.

When I'm in that space, I am able to determine which movies to work on or what song lyrics to write that will allow me to serve others within that spirit. A movie I have worked on that is premiering and being distributed shortly, titled *Dreamers*, is all about people just like me: out of the box thinkers who don't "fit in," and use their light to pursue their moon-shot dreams. I am all about projects that create massive positive impact. I make movies or create music which inspire others and reinforce the messages that the mind is so powerful and the way to your true self is to refuse to let other people define you.

You need to find your personal definition and then run with it. I believe there are no mistakes in life. Maybe your experience didn't unfold in the manner you expected, but it unfolded in a way that allowed you to learn more. When you learn that it doesn't work, then do something different.

I constantly look forward to helping others with the power of being seen through music and film. When people are seen, they can be guided to their light. They can receive the message that they do have a purpose. When you're living in that place, everything seems easy, your intuition gets easier to connect to, and you hear the messages coming to you. One of my biggest gifts is teaching people how to be intuitive for themselves.

For more information about coaching with Sophia Stavron on unlocking, developing, or elevating your own intuition and living a Philotimo Lifestyle™ or to engage her for speaking, visit www.sophiastavron.com or email questions to sophia@sophiastavron.com.

LES BROWN
The Deck Is Stacked Against You, So What!

Les Brown is known as one of the world's greatest speakers, motivators, inspirers, and authors. He is the #1 bestselling author of multiple books, including You've Gotta Be Hungry *and* Live Your Dreams.

Two Mothers

After giving birth to me and my twin brother Wes on the floor of an abandoned building, my biological mother gave us up for adoption when we were six weeks old to Mrs. Mamie Brown.

I always say to audiences that I'm on stage because of two women. One gave me life, the other gave me love. God took me out of my biological mother's womb and placed me in the heart of my adopted mother. I feel like Abraham Lincoln who said all that I am and all that I ever hope to be I owe to my mother.

My adopted mother was such an incredible force of goodness and love in my life. She is my reason for being, and she has inspired me to do so many things that I had no idea I could do. I wanted to do things for her, and that took me outside of my comfort zone. I believe to do something you've never done, you have to become someone you've never been. She has been the driving force for my success.

Labeled Educable Mentally Retarded

When I was in fifth grade, I was forced back a grade by the school's principal after being disruptive in class.

I was labeled educable mentally retarded. Later, I failed the eighth grade.

My mom taught me that sticks and stones can break your bones and words can never hurt you, but words can hurt you very deeply. Being labeled by others did hurt me.

I had a defining moment when I was a junior in high school when I met Mr. Leroy Washington. I went into his classroom looking for a good friend of mine, and he said, "Young man, come. I want you to work this problem out for us before the class."

He wanted me to read a script, and I said, "I can't do that, sir." He asked why. I said, "I'm not one of your students."

He said, "Do it anyhow." I told him I couldn't, and the other students started laughing. They told him I was Leslie, the DT...the dumb twin compared to my brother Wesley. I told Mr. Washington it was true.

He came from behind his desk, looked at me, and said, "Don't you ever say that again. Someone's opinion of you does not have to become your reality." That was a turning point in my life. On one hand, I was humiliated, but on the other hand, I was liberated. He looked at me with the eyes of Goethe, who said, "Look at a man the way that he is, he only becomes worse. But look at him as if he were what he could be, then he becomes what he should be."

I adopted him as my spiritual father. I wanted to be like him. He was a great orator and instructor, and I admired his style. I watched and studied him for the year in school. I was never one of his students, but I feel I learned more from him than all the thousands of students he taught.

Speaking and Impacting Others

I've been speaking 51 years now. I believe you were not born to work for a living, but to live your making, and by living your making you will make your living. And I believe I was born to speak. I love it. That's what I do best. I also train speakers.

Most people don't realize speakers get more out of it than the audience does. As Mr. Washington told me, love, hope, and inspiration are perfumes you can't sprinkle on others without getting a few drops on yourself. I always feel when I speak that I leave stronger, better, and more powerful because I was sharing with people a message that I needed to hear. We give a message out of our mess. They say a calling is something that you love so much you would do it for nothing, but you do it so well that people pay you to do it.

How people live their lives is a result of the story they believe about themselves. When we speak, we distract, dispute, and inspire. We distract people from their current story through the presentation of our knowledge, which we gained from what we've experienced. We dismantle their current belief system and inspire them to become, as Mother Teresa would say, "a pencil in the hand of God" and start writing a new chapter with their lives.

Many speakers give information. If information could change people, everybody would be skinny, rich, and happy. So I come with stories, my story, a story about me, about my mother. A story has a human face, and it touches a person's heart. I use stories to expand a person's mind, to touch their heart, and to ignite their spirit. And that has been my success.

Being Transparent and Authentic

I had a period when life knocked me senseless. When I was going through a divorce, I was diagnosed with prostate cancer, my best friend died waiting on a liver transplant, and my mother died.

My son John Leslie was 10 years old. He came into my room and said, "Are you going to die?"

I said, "We're all going to die one day."

He said, "No, I need to know. Are you dying soon from this cancer?"

I said, "Why would you ask me that question?"

He said, "I don't hear any words coming through the doors, any motivational messages, the room is dark, the shade is down. Where's my daddy? I just want to know where he is. Is he still here, or is he in a slow process of dying? Will you fight?"

I said, "Yes, I will fight. I'm so glad you asked me that. I'm going to fight."

He let the shade up and said, "Who do you want to listen to?"

I said, "I think I need to listen to my own words right now. Put on Les Brown speaking in the Georgia Dome." He left me with the tape, and I got back into the fight. But sometimes life can knock you so so silly you can't think. I teach that life is a fight for territory. And once you stop fighting for what you want, what you don't want will automatically take over.

Once when I spoke on stage in San Francisco, I talked about the fact that when I went through a divorce, for a while, I couldn't get on stage. I was ashamed. I wondered how I could talk about success when I had failed. Success is more than just earning money or acquiring materialistic things. It's about being a good father, being a good husband, and making a growing family work. And I failed at that. But I told them I had failed, but I wasn't a failure.

There was a lady who had been a marriage counselor for like 20 years, and she stopped because she went through a divorce. She said she loved providing counseling for couples, but she felt that she couldn't do it anymore because she couldn't make her marriage successful. Because of my transparency, she went back to work. She realized that her career was not over. She failed in that marriage, but she was not a failure, and she still had something of value that she could provide people.

Battling Cancer and Staying Positive

I'm a 27-year prostate cancer conqueror. I'm dealing with stage four cancer. As I talk to you, I'm under the auspices of the Cancer Centers of America and Dr. Taha. When Dr. Taha told me the cancer metastasized to seven areas of my body. I smiled. Seven is my lucky number. I'm one of seven children. I was born February 17th. Joshua marched around the Wall of Jericho seven times and dipped himself in the river seven times.

I practice meditation, prayer, upgrading my relationships, and having a mindset that whatever I'm dealing with has not come to stay. I ask what's the good in it? What is it that I can discover about myself?

I think there are four main questions that we have to answer.

1. Who am I?

2. Why am I here?

3. Where am I going?

4. Who's going with me?

When you answer those questions, it allows you to handle the storms of life.

Storms are going to come. Viktor Frankl calls it unavoidable suffering. The Book of Life says, think it not strange that you face the fiery furnaces of this world, you will. Not you *might*, you *will* have tribulations. Those things are there to test you. They'll bring a strength out of you. They introduce you to a part of yourself that you don't know. And I think that's why Victor Frankl said that adversity introduces a man to himself.

It's part of the human experience. Everybody's going to get their butts kicked. I don't care who you are. As Forrest Gump said, "Life is like a box of chocolates. You never know what you're going to get."

I'll never forget when Dr. Goldson, a top oncologist in Washington, DC, diagnosed me with prostate cancer. He told me my PSA was 2400, and four is normal. But then he stopped and said, "But you got this. We determine the diagnosis. God determines the prognosis."

The Key to Influence

The number one key to having more influence is your ability to communicate—to expand a person's vision beyond their mental conditioning, touch their hearts, and ignite their spirits. When you're able to communicate, you can take a person to a place within themselves that they can't go on their own.

I work first on the messenger and then on the message. There are a lot of people speaking, but they haven't done anything. They have not lived an achievement-driven life. I think it's very important that you not just practice what you preach, but you also preach what you practice. Who you are behind the words is far more important than the words you speak.

LES BROWN

You Have to Be Hungry

The deck is stacked against you. There's no question about it. And to get out of where you are, you gotta be hungry! Jackie Robinson said, don't level the playing field. Just let me on the field, and I'll level it myself. People that are hungry level the field, all they want is access in the game. When you are hungry, your gifts will make room for you. Bring what you have, do the best that you can, and God will do what you can't do.

Accomplishments

Les Brown has been inducted into the National Speakers Hall of Fame and is the recipient of its highest honor: The Council of Peers Award of Excellence (CPAE).

Les has received the highest award from Toastmasters International, the Golden Gavel award.

In 1992, Les was selected as one of the top five speakers in the world alongside Gen. Norman Schwarzkopf, Lee Iacocca, Robert Schuller, and Paul Harvey, receiving more votes than all combined.

To contact Les Brown about mentorship and speaking, send an email to LesBrown77@gmail.com. You can get Les' newest book You've Got to Be Hungry: The GREATNESS Within to Win *through Amazon and all major bookstores.*

RAVIN S. PAPIAH
After the Rain, The Sunshine

Ravin Papiah is highly decorated in professional speaking and direct selling in the country of Mauritius. He's a founding partner and certified coach, speaker, trainer, and executive director of the John Maxwell Team and a Jeffrey Gitomer Licensed Trainer as well as the Managing Director of the Mighty Champs Marketing Co. Ltd. and the Professional Leadership Centre Ltd. and a Soaring Eagle Manager with Forever Living Products, USA. He has received the highest decoration of Toastmasters.

My Mum Gave Me Strength

When I was born, the doctor told my mom I wasn't going to survive long, that I was too weak. This was 50 years ago in Mauritius, so health care was not what it is today. My mum didn't believe the doctors and took great care of me.

She also didn't want me to have the thought that I was weak, so she pushed me towards growing myself. When I was old enough, my mum took me with her to work in the sugar cane fields. At that time, I was thinking my mum was breaking me. I would spend all of my holidays in the sugar cane fields helping in the hard work. Because of my precarious health, I was bullied at school. Two or three days in the week, I would fall unconscious during the morning assembly at school. It became routine. I was not able to play. Still, working hard under a hot sun in the sugar cane fields later on, gave me belief in my strength.

My Life-Defining Moment

Because I was not allowed to play, my teacher, Ms. Chantal, looked after me in the classroom during recreation time. I was six years old at that time. One day, she became bored just sitting and watching me. She asked me, "Can you read?" I was confused and didn't know what to say. So, she said, "Take your chair and come here." I did, and she took a book out of her bag and started teaching me how to read.

At the age of seven, I was reading three to four books every week. Reading became my escape and my world. While I was reading, I saw myself as the hero of my stories. I saw myself succeeding in life and becoming someone big. That pushed me. I knew that if I studied hard, I would be able to go further in my life. Going far as quickly as possible seemed so important to me, as I had the thought that I may not survive long because of my illness. I didn't have friends, so I was left alone with my books. I'm still a bookworm.

I will be forever grateful to Ms. Chantal who taught me. She opened up the reading world for me, and it completely changed my life. I'm hoping to see her again and thank her for this gift one day.

Taking The Next Step

I did quite well in school despite missing a couple of days a week by falling unconscious. During the holidays, after working in the sugar cane fields, we would take a bath in the river. We didn't have the beautiful bathrooms that we now have. The sugarcane leaves had cut the skin on my face, and as I washed, I would feel each one of the cuts and think to myself, "No way. I'm not going to come back. This is not going to be my future." So, I studied very hard. We didn't have electricity at home at that time, so I studied burning a small oil lamp at night.

Because I studied hard, I was the first scholarship winner in my primary school. I had great high school certificates as well, but you had to pay to go to university at that time, and we just couldn't afford it. I had to start working at the age of 18. I got a position at the bank and worked there for nearly 10 years. Two years in, I got an opportunity to work part-time in direct selling with the AMC cookware pots.

I was very shy, so when a friend came to my place to sell the pots to me and then tried to recruit me, I was not interested. I didn't think I was qualified because I didn't have a certificate in cooking. He said, "You don't need one." As I was eager to do something more because my salary was low at the bank and I wanted to help my parents, I joined in.

Being shy, it was difficult for me to communicate with strangers, but I loved what I learned at my first meeting. I didn't have any diploma in cooking, but I had learned much from my mom and my sisters. My first demonstration was for my family, and I was excited. It didn't go very well but, maybe because my uncle loved me so much and wanted to support my endeavor, he bought a set of pots from me.

My Entrepreneur's Journey

When I started selling, I realized that I am a fast learner with a talent for explaining things to people. When I was working at the bank, I had many customers who were very close to me, and they would always ask me when I would come around for tea. I took that for a joke and just smiled back. When I started in direct selling, I seized the opportunity by asking them, "Hey, today I'm coming in the direction of where you live, so I was thinking about dropping by and having that cup of tea. Does that invitation still stand?" The responses were positive and inviting. That started my entrepreneurship journey. That taught me something important: If you ASK, you GET!

I was very hesitant to become a salesperson at the start. But when I sold the first set of pots to my uncle, the commission paid to me triggered me! I had spent about an hour at my uncle's place, didn't know anything about selling or much about the pots, and had earned a commission of above 1000 rupees, which represented 50% of my monthly salary at that time! A 1000 rupees an hour compared to 7 rupees an hour at work! That clicked my mind and created a shift in my thinking. Later on, the words of my mentor, Jim Rohn, made sense: "Profits are better than wages."

Developing Relationships

I was not prepared for the opportunity, but I took it. I didn't have any sales skills, so instead, I had conversations with my customers.

Every day after work, I would go to a customer's place to do a presentation. I didn't have a car or a driving license, so on Saturdays, I went to the office, took boxes of products, and carried them on my shoulders to the bus to ride an hour and a half to where I was working, in a village in the South of the island, to meet my customers.

My second sale taught me yet another lesson. I told my prospect, "I'm doing a part-time job. Maybe you've heard about the pots I am selling?"

And he said, "Oh yeah, I know those pots are very expensive."

That was the first objection I got, and I didn't know about objections or how to overcome them. So I said, "It's okay. I'm not here for you to buy. I'm just here for you to help me. I need to do some presentations, and I just need you to listen to me. And then if you want to buy it's okay. But if you can't buy, it's not a problem. I'm not here to sell you the products."

So he called his wife and his family, and I started the presentation. I didn't cook that day, but I gave a presentation highlighting the features and benefits. I told them they could save on oil and save on gas and those were two big costs to every family. And, when you use less oil, it's healthy, isn't it? So, really the product offered better health and savings.

My prospect turned to his wife and asked her what she thought. She said, "We didn't know about all of these things! People try to sell us, but they've never told us how it works and how we can benefit." Thus, I sold my second set without doing any cooking! Although I did go back and do the cooking when I delivered! That's how it started. I connected. It was all about developing relationships and trust with my prospects, who became my customers for life and better, my advocates.

So, the lesson learned? Give your customers what **they** need, not what *you* are selling.

Finding Personal Development

I started direct selling in 1988. I was introduced to Jim Rohn and the personal development industry 10 years after, in 1998 by a friend from South Africa, Val Leech. When Jim was talking about network marketing, he was talking about relationship building and selling by relationship building, and it made me smile because I had discovered that on my own through trial and error.

When I was introduced to Jim Rohn and the personal development industry, my reading rose to a completely new level. I read everything about becoming a better version of myself, and still haven't stopped.

Because I was a sick child, taking care of myself and eating the right food became important to me. I've never smoked and I'm not a heavy drinker. My mother was very careful about what I ate, so I grew up with good eating habits. I've also been in my network marketing company, Forever Living Products for the last 10 years. I take my products, especially food supplements and aloe drinks, daily. I'm slimmer and building more muscles, and it has gotten easier. I sleep seven to eight hours now every day as well. Those major **habits** give me more energy and have brought me closer to success.

I've had a lot of hard moments in my life, and prayer has been instrumental in helping me through. Have faith that things are going to change, because it doesn't rain all the time, and after the rain, there is sunshine. Mentors and coaches like Jim Rohn have had a very big impact on my life, and I will be forever grateful to my friend for introducing me to Jim. He taught me that when you're going through some rough times, it's rough. You're human, and you are going to cry. If you feel like crying, cry. Let your emotions come, and go through it. But after the rain, there's a rainbow, a beautiful and life-changing, colourful rainbow.

Through Jim Rohn and especially my mentor Kyle Wilson, I have had the opportunity of connecting with all the other greats, all my other mentors, Les Brown, Brian Tracy, Jeffrey Gitomer, and John Maxwell. I think mentors and coaches are very important to discover your true self, and I believe that everyone, at whatever level you are, needs a coach and a mentor. A coach is that "someone" you need to whom you can open your heart to and can trust. Kyle Wilson has been that someone for me, and I am forever grateful to him.

The challenges are still there in my life, but I'm stronger and seeing greater results. I stay positive because I believe that things are going to turn around. It's important to look forward. As John Maxwell would say, "Fail forward." It's okay to go through a rough time because on the other side, the sunshine is waiting. The sunshine of the life you have always dreamed of living—and it is all within your power. Just emulate the great habits of super successful people, and success will be just a few dreams and dares away.

Connect with Ravin S. Papiah, professional speaker and trainer, in The Life Defining Leadership group on Facebook, on LinkedIn, on his website www.plcleadership.com, or by email at plcjmleadership@gmail.com

BRAD NIEBUHR
Road to Becoming an Entrepreneur and Investor

Brad Niebuhr is an entrepreneur and investor in central Washington. He owns an electrical contracting business that has had over 50 employees. With his wife Emily they personally have a multimillion-dollar portfolio of investment real estate and run a private investment company, Full Circle Investments, with syndications in the US and abroad.

Creating My Future

I grew up with my mom, dad, and brother in a small town called Lake Forest Park 10 minutes north of Seattle. Both of my parents worked standard jobs. Our house was a small 1920, two-bedroom log home. In high school years, I lived in the garden shed out back.

After high school, I decided to go to college along with all my friends, but I had to pay for mine. I went to community college for about a year and a half while also working at a sign shop until I felt I was wasting my money and decided to go to work full-time instead.

At 20 years old, I was working at the sign shop and hardly making any money. One day, my boss pulled me aside and said, "Brad, you're one of our best workers. We'll never be able to pay you what you're worth. My brother's an electrician and makes pretty good money. Why don't you go check it out?"

Two weeks later, I was an electrician's apprentice working out of Seattle Union Hall. I did my five years there and had moved to central Washington during my apprenticeship. I was commuting over the pass with a treacherous, snowy, hour and a half drive in the winter to Seattle. When I was laid off, I decided I could do better on my own, and I would not have to rely on somebody else to create my future for me. So, I started an electrical contracting business 15 years ago.

Mentors in Real Estate Investing

When I first started the electrical business, I also worked for Medic One driving an ambulance. I rode on a medic unit for 10 years while owning the electrical business. I met my future mentor Jodi in our EMT class. Later, we both ended up working at Medic One.

Jodi and her husband Andy, a firefighter over in the Seattle area, read *Rich Dad Poor Dad* and started quietly buying real estate. When I asked more about what they were doing, they were eager to explain. But for years, I was juggling my time between two jobs and employees. I thought I was just too busy to think ahead.

Finally, it was time for me to think about my future. I sat down to talk about what they were doing. I started reading books and becoming financially educated. My wife Emily and I bought our first property, a multi-tenant commercial property, a little strip mall, which we still have. If it weren't for Jodi and Andy who had been in the trenches educating me, allowing me to watch and learn from them, we probably wouldn't have grown as quickly.

Construction Background Advantage

Since I've been in commercial construction for 20 plus years, I gravitate towards commercial real estate. I've been accused of having too much vision, when I look at something, I can see a finished product when everybody else just sees a rundown building or something that needs too much work. I can see the end result, know what really needs to be done, and get it done. I love crunching numbers on projects, coming up with budgets, and figuring out how to do things. The deal is something I really enjoy doing.

Understanding the process with development, construction, and permitting is really helpful. You can hire somebody to do it for you though. I've hired people to inspect our buildings, even though I felt like I was qualified, but if it's something we're going to put out for investors, I'd rather have a third party come in to avoid any conflict of interest.

One of the best lessons we have learned in real estate investing after self-managing and going through different property managers is we always find the best property management company with the highest-rated property manager in your city. Don't skimp when it comes to property management because even though it may cost you a little more on the front side they will save you money in the end.

Our top criteria when looking at an investment property are cash flow and location. When we got started the tax advantages weren't even on my radar, but now that I've been educated, they are very advantageous as well.

Sharing Benefits with Others

Emily and I live on seven acres in central Washington with lots of pets: horses, goats, donkeys, dogs, birds, cats, all sorts. I also have a Cessna 206, a single-engine six-seater airplane, which I enjoy flying. I've been a pilot for almost 10 years. Last year, we purchased an 1800s farmhouse, which we completely gutted and renovated.

Finding true success means taking responsibility for your own actions, not blaming people, and learning from your mistakes. Mistakes are a good thing. Don't get down about a mistake. It might have cost you a lot of money, but you're going to remember that next time. If you flip that around and say, "Wow, that was a good learning experience," it changes your perspective on life. That's what an entrepreneur does, solve problems. Sometimes the universe will give you something that doesn't look nice, but you needed it for some reason to learn from.

We invest because we want to give back. They don't teach financial education in school. I feel the world would be a better place if everybody could learn how to take care of their financial futures. I teach by sharing the wisdom I have gained from my mistakes and the wisdom of others. Emily and I started a Meetup. We bring experienced people in real estate and other forms of investing from all over to speak. It is an opportunity for us to help out entrepreneurs who, like I was in my early entrepreneur years, go, go, go and not thinking about the future.

If I could help other entrepreneurs sooner to realize what they should be thinking about instead of just working, working, working, I think it'd be a benefit to the community. We live in a large farm community, and the farmers around here work so hard and so long, sometimes 20 hours or more a day. I want to offer them something else to help them meet their goals. Our driving factor has been to help other people be financially free.

I wholeheartedly believe that every business is all about relationships. I have seen it in my electrical and real estate businesses. If you're in business and you're not focused on building relationships, you shouldn't be in business. Everybody should work together for the better. Zig Ziglar said, "If you help enough people get what they want, you'll get what you want."

To learn more about Brad's Meetup group, any contracting questions, or being part of his syndication opportunities, contact Brad Niebuhr at brad@cabincreekelectric.com or brad@fcinvestllc.com.

DANA SAMUELSON

My Own Yellow Brick Road – 40 Years Trading Precious Metals

Dana Samuelson is a nationally recognized US rare coin dealer specializing in pre-1933 US gold coins and founder of American Gold Exchange. With more experience and technical knowledge than almost anyone in the field, Dana helps individuals balance their portfolios with gold and silver and serves rare coin collectors with advice on building real generational wealth.

Getting Started in Gold

I graduated from a small college in Virginia called Washington and Lee with a German degree in 1980, which was like graduating college in 2009 with a German degree. I was unmarketable and nobody was hiring. However, gold and silver prices had taken off like crazy in 1979. My brother Clark was working for a high-volume company in Houston, Texas. They hired me to work in their vault counting, shipping, and weighing literally tons of silver and pounds of gold because I was completely trustworthy. If this was a restaurant, I started at the kitchen sink.

Learning from Jim Blanchard

In 1983, I got the opportunity of a lifetime. I was hired by James U. Blanchard, III who had the biggest gold company in the country. This is where I learned my trade. Jim was the individual most responsible for the re-legalization of private gold ownership in 1974 (gold was illegal to own in the US from 1933 to 1974). I went to work for Jim as a coin appraiser trainee and learned over the next two years how to expertly appraise vintage, pre-1933 U.S. gold and silver coins.

In 1985, I was promoted up to the trading desk where I spent over $50 million of Jim's money every year buying inventory from the industry. In the process, I got to know almost everyone of significance in the industry. My career took off. Deep in my soul, though, I longed for something of my own.

Entrepreneurship and Founding American Gold Exchange

When I decided to start my own business, American Gold Exchange, in 1998, I had some luck. I was well-known, and more importantly, well-trusted in the trade. My colleagues gave me friendlier financial terms than I deserved at the time. After two years, our business was up and running, and I've never looked back. It's been wonderful to be my own boss.

Today we buy and sell $100 million in business annually in physical precious metals, including modern bullion coins, classic pre-1933 US gold coins and silver coins, and vintage European gold coins as well.

Historically, gold has always been money, used as currency and traded in daily life worldwide until the depression of 1933 forced the gold out of the currency. The U.S. dollar was backed by gold until the US went off the gold standard in 1971. Between 1935 and 1971 the gold price was fixed internationally. Since 1971 gold has been free to trade in open markets and we've seen major periods of gold and silver price expansion and contraction over the last 50 years. It's an exciting market affected by economics, politics, even the daily news. For the most part, precious metals trade countercyclical to the economy. When stocks, bonds, and real estate are doing well, gold is usually a little weaker and vice versa.

I've never had a boring day in the last 40 years. Plus, I get to see and buy and sell heirlooms of our monetary history, incredible US gold and silver coins dating back to 1793. When I hold a coin minted in 1799, I love to imagine what kind of life this coin has had over that incredible period!

The Business of Gold

We help our clients in the physical precious metals marketplace. We help them identify their goals and desires, then we make appropriate recommendations to fill those needs, depending upon what makes the most sense for each particular individual. We maintain a large inventory of pre-1933 US gold and silver coins. Over 40-years, I've developed a very discerning eye for vintage coins. If I've screened a coin and put it into our inventory, I've satisfied myself and my customers are usually going to be happy with that coin as well. The benefit to our clients is since I know its quality, I'll buy it back sight unseen in the future, even 20 years from now. That gives our clients instant liquidity that they simply don't have elsewhere.

My expertise is primarily gold and silver. I'm what I call a bread and butter dealer, dealing in mainstream items that are widely traded and immediately liquid, that people can sell anywhere easily. If my clients need to be liquid fast, their holdings are easily sellable anywhere there is a reputable dealer. We want you to come back to us, but if you don't have the luxury, or the time, you have the option to easily sell elsewhere. We don't deal in esoteric, thinly traded and illiquid coins. There is no benefit to that.

Since modern bullion coins are all virtually perfect and easily replaceable from the various mints around the world, the coins that require my expertise are the classic, pre-1933 vintage coins. We source these from other dealers, usually at trade shows. There's a major coin show somewhere in the country about once a month. I've become adept at finding above quality coins at the right price.

The Philosophy of Serving the Customer

What used to be an in-person and mail order business has become an online business today. Most of our available inventory is listed on our information rich web site with high definition pictures. While online listings streamlines the buying process, to fully appreciate the heirlooms we deal in you must see and hold them in person.

If you are interested in allocating a significant portion of your assets into precious metals or vintage coins, it's best to call us to talk to one of our account managers. I have four account managers I've personally trained who help our clients make intelligent and informed buying or selling decisions based on their goals and needs.

We produce a newsletter that is unique to the marketplace. We try to help people who don't follow these markets understand what's happening in the gold and silver world, why it's happening, and what might happen next. By being vigilant and experienced, we've been able to see trends forming in advance and get ahead of some of the biggest moves in the marketplace, which is very difficult to do. We're not perfect. We don't always get it right, but we've been very good at understanding shifting markets and how that is going to affect gold and silver.

We respect that buyers and sellers have choices. We treat our clients with courtesy and respect. Sadly, our industry is unregulated, and we have our share of unscrupulous operators. By being transparent, straight forward, and honest, we usually stand head and shoulders above most others. We put our customer's interests first, period. We like to build good, long-term relationships. As those relationships strengthen, some customers will refer others to us, and our efforts will compound over time. This has served us well because it serves our clients well.

I learned from the best. Jim Blanchard was an amazing guy. He was brilliant and was an incredible creative thinker. I watched his business grow from 35 employees to 140 when he sold it to General Electric in 1988. I also saw a few of the mistakes Jim made. When I went into business for myself, I vowed to do what was right by following his philosophy. That's what we've done for 23 years now.

121

Avoid Counterfeiting

There are many sovereign minted gold and silver coins available today, and their authenticity is unquestionable. We do, however, have a minor but growing problem with Chinese counterfeit coins and bars, mostly bars. Their designs are easier to replicate. Counterfeiters can take tungsten, which has almost the same density as gold, and plate it with gold, making it look like a good gold bar. While these won't fool most professionals, they can fool the public.

I'm a long-standing member of the Professional Numismatists Guild (PNG), the leading organization of rare coin dealers in the country. I served on their board for 12 years and was president for two years. During my presidency, I helped to establish the industry anti-counterfeiting taskforce, which today works with the Secret Service and Homeland Security to intercept counterfeit Chinese shipments coming into the country. It has been a big success. In fact, at PNG's urging, the US mint will incorporate anti-counterfeiting technology into their gold and silver Eagles in 2021, something the Canadian mint has already been doing for four years. It gives the public one more level of security. Helping to conceive of and develop the task force during my PNG presidency will probably prove to be my greatest industry accomplishment. It's my way of giving back to the community.

Gold in Global Crisis

There have been long-term studies done for years now that prove by having 6% to 10% of your assets in gold and silver, you'll insulate your portfolio from economic shocks like the 2008 financial crisis. This is the portfolio sweet spot for a financial insurance policy that offers an excellent counterbalance to traditional stocks and bonds. It's recommended that everyone has a small percentage of their portfolio in precious metals as a hedge.

Invaluable Heirlooms

Sadly, the heirs of most coin collectors who build a serious collection are not collectors themselves. It's always important that you train your heirs with basic knowledge of their inheritance, so they know how to liquidate it properly. We get collections brought to us on a regular basis, and we've purchased some big ones over the years.

When it comes to passing on value to the next generation, gold is hard to beat. It's private, and it has intrinsic value that can never be second-guessed. And people always remember who gave them a special coin, especially gold and silver coins. It's a tangible reminder of a gift from mom, dad, grandma, or grandpa.

Today we're four generations away from gold and silver being used as currency, and we're two generations away from gold and silver backing our currency. Unfortunately, most kids today don't understand what sound money is. We want to help educate people about what sound money really is. Governments today are printing money at will, but you can't easily print more gold. Gold and silver are the ultimate currencies of last resort.

Reach out to Dana Samuelson and American Gold Exchange at info@amergold.com | amergold.com | (800) 613-9323

JO HAUSMAN
Unanswered Miracles: All Women Need a Plan B

Real estate investor Jo Hausman is a passionate speaker, bestselling author of Go For It! A Woman's Guide to Perseverance, *and host of* Go For It! *live radio show. She loves teaching and coaching women on entrepreneurship. She served eight years on city council ending as vice president.*

I Knew I Had to Be the Boss

When I was in my early 20s and pregnant, I went through a divorce and had to figure out how I was going to raise a child as a single mom. In the back of my mind, I knew I had to have passive income coming in. I had to be my own boss someday.

I moved a couple of places, but it was my dream to live in Colorado. My son Cody and I moved there in 1997 and met Jim in 2000. He was a gift to us. He was very low key, just a great guy. Jim had been diagnosed with a chronic illness before we met, but he was in remission. We married September 2001 and in 2004 moved to South Dakota.

After reading Robert Kiyosaki's book *Rich Dad Poor Dad* in 2004, Jim and I started investing in real estate. We started with a single-family home and eventually built up to several single-family homes.

Roller Coaster

Unfortunately, my wonderful husband's illness returned, and he was diagnosed with liver failure due to Hepatitis C in November 2007.

By 2009, his infection had progressed to the point where he was in and out of the hospital at least a week out of every month. The doctors told us Jim needed a liver transplant. Without it, his death was imminent. He often said he wanted to go home, which for him meant Heaven.

At that time, I had been running my virtual assistant business successfully for two years. All of a sudden, my personal life was upside down. I'm so thankful for that business now because my clients were absolutely wonderful. I brought on 10-12 virtual assistants to help me, and I was able to go to all Jim's doctor's appointments and keep up with my son and all his activities and sports.

Unfortunately, with Jim's illness along with the financial crisis of 2007, we ended up selling our investment properties.

Unanswered Miracles

Jim was slowly slipping away, and I was desperately holding on. I give Jim so much credit for fighting as long as he did. It couldn't have been easy for him.

We had so many doctors that it was hard for them to get to know Jim. My prayer was answered when we were assigned a wonderful doctor who was communicative and honest with us. He said, "Most people who need liver transplants only live two and a half years."

The eternal optimist, I said, "We're going to fight this." I was convinced Jim would get a liver. But, I had no idea that a liver was the most difficult transplant organ to receive. It would take a miracle.

Coping with Death

When my husband and I met, he told me he didn't want anyone to know about his illness. So, I honored his wishes and kept a smile on my face. In reality, I was dying inside.

While Jim was suffering, I was suffering too. As Jim got sicker, people asked if they could help me, but I wouldn't let them. I thought that if no one saw the depth of our pain, it would go away.

Jim considered me his nurse. I was grateful to be there for him. But I also missed being his wife and wished I had the Jim—wonderful husband, loving father, and brave veteran—I had married.

Cody graduated high school in May 2010. Jim came home from the hospital for the ceremony but was too sick to attend. The next Monday, Jim was so sick that I had to take him back to the hospital. As I wheeled him in, I had the heartbreaking feeling that he wasn't coming home again.

Several doctors told me you practically have to be dead before you will receive a liver transplant. Now I believed them.

Jim was transferred to a hospital in Pittsburgh. When Jim was first flown out, he could talk a little. When I got there, he wouldn't say a word. I knew something drastic was wrong, and the doctors didn't have any answers.

A few days later, the doctors ordered an MRI. I took a walk, and they called me on my cell phone with the results: "We're so sorry, but the MRI showed there is no brainwave activity. He's not going to get his transplant, and he is going to die soon." Then he asked the worst question I believe anyone could have asked me, "Do you want him to die here in Pittsburgh or home in South Dakota?"

With a brave face, I said, "He won't die here. I want him home in South Dakota so friends and family can say goodbye."

When Is It Time?

After we flew Jim home to South Dakota, the doctor called me into Jim's hospital room. She informed me it was time to unhook Jim from life support. I wanted to wait for Jim's mom to arrive, but they said it was time. A nurse spoke gently to me, "Your husband is with the angels now, and they are just waiting for their cue to take him home to Heaven."

With his words, a peace came over me. I remembered how Jim used to say, "I just want to go home to Heaven."

They unhooked him from life support around 12:30 PM, and he kept holding on! After a few minutes, I leaned in and said, "Please hold on because your mom is coming and she wants to see you. Then you can let go."

When Jim's mom arrived, I tried to prepare her for what she would see. But nothing could prepare for this. When she got to the hospital room, she screamed, "My baby boy, oh my God!" crawled in bed with him, and placed her hands on his chest, above the butterfly tattoo that gave him Hepatitis C, causing all this pain.

Jim passed away the next morning, July 17, 2010, at 9 AM. Our hearts were broken.

Isolation

Five weeks after Jim passed, Cody left for college, and I was alone for the first time in 18 years. I dub the summer of 2010 my summer of hell: Cody had major surgery, and after Jim's death, my garage was broken into, my computer crashed, my washing machine broke, and my air conditioner quit and had to be replaced. I believe God doesn't give us more than we can handle, but that was a lot. Every time something happened, I repeated with a smile, "Bring it on, bring it on. The more you bring on, the more I can handle." That statement kept me going through the good times and bad.

As much as it was a gut-wrenching roller coaster ride, I consider that experience a blessing. It made me stronger and more willing to go after what I want in life. I would not be where I am today without the trials life has put me through.

The Power of Connection

Six months after Jim passed, I decided to return to graduate school and achieve my dream of getting an MBA. Ten months after he passed, I was elected to my local city council as an alderwoman for Ward 2. I received my MBA in May 2014 and sat successfully on city council for eight years, leaving as vice president.

In 2012, I started investing in real estate again. It was a dream Jim and I had together, and I was ready to pursue it. I now have bought and sold more properties than Jim and I had together, including commercial, residential, agricultural, and bare land. In 2016, I published my first book *Go For It! A Woman's Guide to Perseverance*. The book looks at life before, during, and after Jim's sickness and untimely death. I thank my son Cody for putting a dream of writing my book in my heart and for co-authoring the book.

I closed my virtual assistant business in 2015. Since then, I've focused on coaching women on how to start businesses. I am proud of my client's successes, each achieved while I have pursued my absolute love, real estate investing. I'm shifting now from business coaching to full-time real estate investing and teaching women how to invest in real estate and achieve financial freedom.

You never know what's going to happen in life. I didn't know divorce or becoming a widow were in the cards for me, and I want every woman to be prepared in case these challenges happen to her. Have a plan B and passive income coming in.

What Now

There were so many times I felt worthless and like a failure. I wanted a normal business, a normal husband, normal everything, when in reality, nothing in our life was normal. You make your own normal; you take what God has given you and you make that your normal.

Through all the hard days, my faith never wavered. I knew my faith was a priceless treasure from God. What we can't see or don't know are sometimes blessings in disguise.

Learning perseverance to survive and thrive through the hard times has brought me to the good times.

My mantra I live by and tell others is, "You are stronger than you give yourself credit for."

Always remember to Go For It!

Jo Hausman offers a 30-day real estate education training for women to get into the real estate investing world. Sign up and receive a special download at www.johausman.com or contact her jo@johausman.com, 605-941-7969. Also on Facebook (facebook.com/coachingwithjo1), Twitter, LinkedIn, and Instagram.

ROBERT HELMS
It's Always Who You Know

Robert Helms is a professional real estate investor with investment and development experience in nine states and six countries. As a former top-producing real estate agent, Robert ranked in the top 1% of sales in the world's largest real estate organization. Robert's investment and development companies have past and current projects valued at over $800 million. He is the host of the nationally syndicated radio show The Real Estate Guys™, *now in its 23rd year of broadcast. The podcast version of the show is one of the most downloaded podcasts on real estate and is heard in more than 190 countries.*

It's Nearly Impossible to Do It Alone

Is there anyone who wants less success? Fewer wins? Lower self-esteem? Diminished lifestyle? Lackluster motivation? Limited opportunity?

It's hard to imagine. Yet we all know plenty of folks who accomplish far less than they could. You see, potential is not the same as achievement.

In reality, success is not all that difficult. But it does take effort.

And it's nearly impossible to do it alone.

Which is why one of my greatest personal success secrets is forming, developing, and nurturing fantastic, productive, authentic, win-win relationships.

My First Mentor

Brian Tracy teaches that whatever you were interested in between the ages of 7 and 14 might hold the keys to discovering your ideal career. When I look back at that time in my life, one of my favorite things to do was play the board game Monopoly.

It also helped that my Dad was a seasoned real estate investor by then. We went on to work together as real estate agents representing mostly investors for nearly 20 years.

Dad was great with people and a patient teacher. He had a genuine interest in and love for people. Much of our success in real estate came from our ability to focus on the relationship over the transaction. My father taught me that focusing on the transaction might get you a sale, but focusing on the relationship would cultivate a client, and a client would provide many transactions.

He also taught me—as much through his actions as his words—that real estate is a people business. Given a choice, people do business with people they like and trust.

Seeing the Possibilities

The week I got my real estate license, my Dad took me to see legendary sales trainer Tom Hopkins who was speaking to our local Board of Realtors®. While getting my copy of his book signed, Tom told me, "You will make a living selling real estate to other people. You will become wealthy if you become your own best customer."

My first commission check became the down payment on my first rental property.

Tom was also great at building relationships. He taught me to send hand-written thank you notes to every prospect. After an evening listing appointment, we made it a habit to drive directly to the post office where we would write a thank you note in the parking lot and drop it in the mailbox. Often the note would arrive the next day. This was long before email, so it really made a strong impression.

Nearly ten years ago, we reconnected with Tom by inviting him on our radio show, and we got talking about the importance of setting goals. By the end of the conversation, he agreed to attend our annual Goals Retreat a few months later.

Just as the event concluded and we began striking the set, I noticed an envelope with my name near my work area. It was a hand-written thank you note from Tom.

Today—more than 30 years after first meeting Tom Hopkins—Tom and his wife Michele have become good friends, and they join us every year for our annual Investor Summit. And Tom wrote the foreword to my Dad's great book *Be in the Top 1%: A Real Estate Agent's Guide to Getting Rich in the Investment Property Niche*.

Solid Relationships Take Time

The Real Estate Guys™ Radio Show was launched in San Francisco in 1997 and has gone from a fledgling local talk program to one of the most downloaded shows of its kind. We think much of that is due to the extraordinary caliber of our guests, who are not only real estate experts, but also folks who look at the broader economic picture.

One of our early guests (and to date the guest that has appeared on our show the most) was Robert Kiyosaki.

Robert's pivotal book *Rich Dad Poor Dad* has had a profound impact on millions of people. When we first met, it was only beginning to be discovered. He was not yet the bestselling personal finance author in history.

I met Robert at an early live Rich Dad® event and invited him on the show, to which he gladly agreed. We set the date around his next scheduled event in San Francisco and assumed he would be a phone-in guest. To our pleasant surprise, he showed up live at the studio which gave us a chance to spend some time with him after the broadcast.

While we certainly did hit it off, we did not become fast friends. But the power of his message resonated with us and our audience, and each time he wrote a new book, we would reach out and offer him the opportunity to come on the show and talk about it. We also sponsored and showed up any time he did a live event anywhere near us.

Each time, we made the focus promoting Robert and the Rich Dad message. While it was tempting to try and figure out an "angle" that would serve us, we waited. We never asked for anything in return.

When his book *The Real Book of Real Estate* was nearing release, for the first time, his team reached out to us (as opposed to us reaching out to them) and invited us to the book launch event, followed by the opportunity to meet and interview most of the other contributing authors.

At the end of the evening, Robert called my co-host Russell Gray and I over to his table and sincerely thanked us for always supporting his message. He then asked, "How can I help you guys?"

Russ and I told Robert that we had some ideas of a few ways we might work together, and he invited us to come to his office the next day to discuss them. That conversation led to Robert and his wife Kim joining us for the 2012 Investor Summit, along with most of their Rich Dad Advisors. Spending a week with them changed everything, and we transitioned from acquaintances to friends.

Robert's 70th birthday party (and the 20th Anniversary of *Rich Dad Poor Dad*) took place on one of the seven The Real Estate Guys Investor Summits he's attended, and he is more supportive of us than anyone else in our space.

Learning a Valuable Lesson

While my partners and I have certainly enjoyed our fair share of success in real estate, we're also the first to admit that we got our butts kicked in the downturn of 2008.

It was somewhat of a consolation that lots of folks bigger and smarter than us never saw it coming and lost billions compared to our meager millions. But we humbly looked around to see who had seen the crash coming. And that's when we learned of Peter Schiff.

Today, lots more people claim to have seen the crash coming, but when pressed, they have a hard time pointing to any supportive facts. Peter, on the other hand, published his book *Crash Proof* in February 2007, where he predicted the mortgage meltdown with eerie accuracy. While the pundits ridiculed him, in the light of day, he was exactly correct.

After reading his book, Russ and I made it our mission to learn from Peter and before long, we had the opportunity to have him on the show. While he's not a real estate guy (although I have spent time in both of his incredible homes), he has excellent insight into the inner workings of monetary policy, the Federal Reserve, international equities, and precious metals.

Since 2013, Peter has never missed our Investor Summit, and he and his wife Lauren have become our close friends.

Great Relationships Lead to Great Relationships

My friend and international real estate developer Beth Clifford taught me that hiring the best doesn't cost you money…it makes you money. This shattered a paradigm for me, as like many people, I often assumed that getting the lowest price was the smartest strategy.

When it came time to hire architects for one of our development projects, we decided on a team with incredible background, portfolio, and experience over reputable, but less expensive options. And it paid off.

With a degree in art history and a master's in architecture, Julia Sanford headed up our interior design team. Her diverse background working with libraries, museums, and private galleries as well as designing feature film sets for Twentieth Century Fox, Universal, MGM, and Walt Disney Pictures gave her not only great experience, but also incredible connections.

As our project progressed, Julia offered to introduce us to a friend of hers, the editor of *Coastal Living™* magazine, one of the top magazines by income per reader. To make a long story short, today, our development is one of a small handful of COASTAL LIVING™ Communities.

At the time we were developing our relationship, *Coastal Living* was one of more than a hundred magazines published by Time Inc. (Time was acquired by Meredith Inc. in 2018.) This led to branding opportunities with other magazines including several (no cost to us) full page ads in *People* magazine, and participation in the 2018 *Sports Illustrated Swimsuit Issue* with a 12-page section photographed at our resort. Page 12 was a full-page ad for our project which still provides guest and investor inquiries today.

Become Valuable to Valuable People

The New Orleans Investment Conference is the longest-running investment conference in the United States. Past speakers include Margaret Thatcher, Milton Friedman, F.A. Hayek, Ayn Rand, Alan Greenspan; Steve Forbes, Henry Kissinger, Ron Paul, Stephen Moore, Doug

Casey, Danielle DiMartino Booth, Robert Kiyosaki, Dennis Gartman, Peter Schiff...and The Real Estate Guys. For the past several years, I have been honored to MC part of the event.

How did that happen?!

Simple. We found a way to add value and support the promoter of the event, and editor of the Gold Newsletter, Brien Lundin.

We first attended the event as press, since after 2008, we realized we need to attend more than just real estate events. It was a well-run event, filled with accredited investors and investment thought leaders. As primarily a resource conference, most of the emphasis was on precious metal, mining, and oil & gas. There wasn't much on real estate, and we saw an opportunity.

Not an opportunity to forcibly insert real estate into the mix and drive our agenda, rather a chance to enhance what Brien was already doing with an educational perspective that included real estate as part of a portfolio. Year after year we've increased our presence and support, which has created lots of great synergy and many memorable moments with our listeners.

Attending each year has also increased my own knowledge of the investment world beyond real estate, which has served me well.

We continue to focus on Brien's needs as a promoter. We promote the event to our audience (because it's awesome), invite several of his speakers on our radio show, and even help find additional speakers and sponsors (including inviting Robert Kiyosaki to speak). After all, when the event gets better, everyone wins.

Brien has also become a regular faculty member of our Investor Summit and has helped introduce plenty of our listeners to the world of gold and silver and lots of his readers to *The Real Estate Guys*.

Real Relationships Create Lasting Value

It's been said that people come into your life for a reason, a season, or a lifetime. I first came into Kyle Wilson's life for a reason and am now happy to call him one of my most cherished friends.

Kyle is a connector of dots...and he always looks for ways to introduce achievers he knows to each other. For me personally, that has resulted in many treasured relationships, and vice versa I'd like to think.

Part of the magic is that Kyle calls it like he sees it and doesn't get attached to the outcome. If he sees potential synergism between folks, he makes an edifying introduction and lets the cards fall where they may.

He also provides a great sounding board and will tell you where he sees the issues in your grand idea, which is often more helpful than simple encouragement. And there is no one better on Earth to introduce you to an audience!

Kyle's 18-year partnership with Jim Rohn and impressive list of long-time thought leaders, authors, and speakers is a testament to his relationship philosophy.

Robert's Rules for Successful Relationships

So what are the keys to finding and forging world-class relationships? I'll leave you with a few.

Be Thankful. Express genuine gratitude for what you have and who you know.

Add Value. Look for ways you can help people and focus on their needs, not yours.

Give First, Give More. You can almost always rely on the law of reciprocity.

SUCCESS HABITS OF SUPER ACHIEVERS

Welcome Challenge. Be challenged by the greatness of others, not intimidated, skeptical, or resentful.

Celebrate the Success of Others. As their star rises, so will those associated with them.

Step Up. Become worthy of association with great people.

Embrace Abundance over Scarcity. There is always more than enough to go around.

Be Yourself. Authenticity is at the core of the best relationships.

Play the Long Game. Treat everyone you meet as though they will be part of your life for a long, long time.

You are one relationship away from massive success in your business and life. Here's wishing you more rich, meaningful, and prosperous relationships!

Robert Helms is the co-author of Equity Happens – Building Lifelong Wealth with Real Estate. *Robert's annual Goals Retreat helps people unlock their potential and provides a blueprint for achievement in all areas of life. Listen to* The Real Estate Guys™ Radio Show *at www.RealEstateGuysRadio.com To learn more about The Real Estate Guys™ programs and events, send an email to SuccessHabits@realestateguysradio.com.*

DAVE ZOOK
Wholly Successful – Family, Investments, and Personal Growth

Dave Zook is a successful business owner, entrepreneur, and investor in multifamily apartments, self-storage, and ATMs. Dave and partners have acquired $150+ million in real estate since 2010. His team is one of the top five ATM operators in the US. Dave is a sought-after speaker and loves teaching about tax and investment strategies.

The Family Businesses

I was fortunate to grow up in an entrepreneurial family. My dad is a very successful businessman, and he started the family business the year I was born. I started working in the family business on Saturdays and after school when I was six years old and branched out from there. Today, my three brothers and I run the family business with our dad.

We built a 65,000-square-foot manufacturing facility on 35 acres of land and we build modular garages and storage sheds and ship them directly to our customers.

Marketing Online

Shortly after the internet became a reality, several of our wholesale dealers put some of our modular buildings online, and back in those days when you posted your product, often you would be on the first page of Google with very little or no effort.

I said to my dad, "I think we have an opportunity here. Let's see what we can do on the internet." He looked at me like I was crazy, since our lead times were at 2-3 months, and we couldn't move fast enough. He asked me how busy I would like to be.

So, I went in a different direction and I started another business marketing modular buildings mostly in the horse barn and equine space. Today, Horizon Structures is one of the lead modular horse barn companies on the East Coast, and we've delivered buildings to thousands of customers in all 50 states.

With a lot of strategy and effort, we are organically number one on Google for several hundred keywords in our industry.

In 2017, I sold each one of my three brothers a 20% stake in the company, and just a few months ago, I sold my oldest son 20% of the company. So, there are now five owners, and we are growing aggressively.

One of my strengths, and maybe a weakness too, is I'm not afraid to take calculated risks. I like to try new things. From a marketing perspective, for every 10 things we try, there may be five that fail miserably, another two that get us some results but not enough to get us excited, another two that stick, and finally one or two that really move the needle. We have been trying and evaluating strategies for 20-plus years now, finding what works and building off of that.

Life-Changing Tax Strategy

Over the last two decades, I've founded or partnered with folks in several different businesses. Some of them started to do really well, and I got to the point where I was making a lot of money, but the problem was I was paying a lot of tax too.

After paying more than $500,000 in tax in a year almost a decade ago, I started reading, studying, and getting around folks who could help me be much more efficient from a tax perspective, and I figured out how to make a lot more money and pay very little or no tax legally.

Tom Wheelwright said, "If you want to change your tax, you have to change your facts."

I realized I was being taxed based on the way I was doing business, investing, and behaving.

Investor at Heart

Although I'm an entrepreneur, I have been an investor at heart since my early teens.

And while I'm a syndicator, today having raised almost $200,000,000 for real estate deals, ATMs, and energy projects, I never started out as an investor thinking I was going to be a syndicator.

I started investing in real estate because I had a big tax liability and I needed protection. Turns out, I wasn't the only one with that problem, and I started helping other people navigate through their tax liabilities.

I started doing business differently. I started investing in multifamily apartments in 2010. It turns out that was pretty good timing. Not only was multifamily investing a good way to build additional streams of income, but it also gave me the tax benefits I desperately needed.

I bought several hundred apartment units and eventually ran out of cash. I was invited to sit on the planning board of a local startup bank, and there, people who I respected, who I knew could write seven-figure checks, were having conversations like:

> You think we should invest in a bank? We may not see a return on our investment for five to seven years, but I guess that's better than keeping our money in a CD.

At the time, CDs paid less than half a percent interest. I was shocked, and I decided I would give these folks access to investments that would produce a good ROI for them.

The next multifamily apartment building that we put under contract looked like a great deal, and I took it to some of those guys and raised the money for it. That was my first step into the apartment building syndication space, and we have been going strong in syndications ever since.

Since then, I've pivoted a few times into some other asset classes that I like and that have fulfilled a specific purpose for me. And it just turns out that a lot of the times when I have a need, there are many others with the same need. It has been very rewarding to help people build their wealth and keep it, and I can see myself doing that for a very long time.

Do the Right Things with the Right People

A shortcut to financial success is getting around the right people and doing business with the right people.

When you get introduced to a new group, there's two things you don't want to be: the person who nobody's ever heard of, and the person who's got a bad reputation in the market.

I've pivoted several times because of the opportunity to work with a team with a great reputation.

The 10,000 Hour Rule

Normally when I do business with a new team, they come highly recommended from several folks who I trust, which gets my attention.

A few years ago, I kept hearing a lot of good things about this certain self-storage team, and since I was already interested in the self-storage business, I became interested in what they were doing and learned about their business model.

I talked to several of their investors, including some who were invested with me who had done business with them for a decade. They couldn't say enough good things about them, and so I wanted to invest my own money with this team.

I connected with them and did a deep dive due diligence including having one of the principles travel over to meet with me and my advisors.

Just a few months ago, we finished a $47 million equity raise on a fund with 11 institutional-grade self-storage facilities, and we look forward to doing a lot more business with them. They are a solid group of true professionals in the self-storage space. I believe one of the reasons for this is because self-storage is their one thing.

One of my questions to the principal was, "What else are you invested in?"

He said he had only ever invested in self-storage, and he'd been in the space for more than 35 years. He has his 10,000 hours, as author Malcolm Gladwell would say. Being able to tap into a true professional like that is a huge advantage.

When I'm getting into a new asset class that I'm not proficient in or that I don't know everything about, it's really important to have somebody on the team who has put in the 10,000 hours. Rather than me putting in the 10,000 hours in every area of my interest, I team up with people who have.

How to Treat Fear

Years ago, I started sharing my knowledge and experience on stage, on podcasts, and other platforms. In the beginning, it was very uncomfortable, and I was scared.

The last couple of years, I have begun to embrace the fact that pushing through that fear to get to the other side is very rewarding.

I started small, at a local real estate event with 15-20 people, then eventually, educated crowds of more than 500 investors.

I was still scared out of my mind, but I realized that to get to the next level, I had to face my fears. Today, I actually enjoy speaking and educating, and I now realize that when you embrace your fears and fight through them, you get to the point where you enjoy it.

As difficult as it is to fight through obstacles and challenges, you have to go through it if you want to get to the next level. Darren Hardy says you're going to hit a wall. Everybody hits a wall at some point, but it's the few that break through or climb over the wall who reach the other side and find success. On the other side of that wall, there is much less competition because it takes effort and discipline to face your fears and get to where you want to go.

Habits Count

I travel quite a bit to speak and attend events to develop myself and spend time with experts and peers, but I always try to be conscious about balancing time away with time with my family. I only commit to select events, like The Real Estate Guys Secrets of Successful Syndication twice a year.

I receive invitations all the time, but I always try to be home for the weekends. Sometimes I'll get an early flight in for an event that starts Friday morning and the last flight out for Saturday night.

Sometimes I'm able to bundle events and other agendas together into a two-day trip rather than a four-day or multiple trips. It's taken some navigation to get to this point, and my children are getting older, so it's becoming more possible for my wife and I to travel together.

I'm always reading, and I'm part of a local book club with a group of entrepreneurs and business owners. We read a book every month. That holds me accountable and encourages me to read outside of my norm of reading about asset classes or market and economic data.

Wholly Successful

When people talk about success, most tend to focus on the financial part. But if you're a billionaire about to end your third marriage, you have poor relationships with your family, and your health is failing you due to several decades of not taking care of yourself, you're not successful.

I believe to be wholly successful, you are successful spiritually, physically, financially, mentally, and relationally.

Last year at our annual investor event, we were sitting around the campfire with good friends, just having a great time cooking steaks over the fire and enjoying a glass of wine, and I remember making the statement, "You know what? I feel pretty rich right now." And it had very little to do with money. I was grateful to be in that moment with people I cared about in a wonderful environment.

That's part of true wealth.

To contact Dave Zook the founder and CEO of The Real Asset Investor, investment and tax strategist, syndicator, and business owner,

TheRealAssetInvestor.com | info@TheRealAssetInvestor.com

JENNIFER MORAN
Starting a Health and Wellness Movement from Within

Jennifer Moran is a sought-after coach, leader, and mentor in her industry. She's a top, seven-figure earner in network marketing, a bestselling author, internationally certified John C. Maxwell speaker, trainer, and leadership coach as well as an NPC Masters Bikini Bodybuilding Champion.

The Entrepreneur

I grew up in a very degreed professional family. It was your typical go to school, get a good job, work 40 years, and get-a-gold-watch-when-you-retire mindset. However, my father was very entrepreneurial, and outside of his profession as a physician and Colonel in the Army Medical Corps, he also invested heavily in stocks and real estate. I think he instilled in me a curiosity about being an entrepreneur.

My first job out of college was in customer service for a large corporation. Eventually, my boss talked me into moving from customer service into sales. Reluctant at first, I quickly became one of their top sales performers, but after four and a half years, I was recruited into medical sales for a for-profit hospice company. Since my father had passed away when I was 16 and my mother had passed away when I was 22 and no one offered us hospice, it quickly became a passion of mine to educate physicians and families about the benefits of palliative care.

After becoming a top rep with hospice, I was recruited away once more to sell medical equipment for a very large medical equipment and disposables manufacturer. I was traveling a lot, but then I met my future husband, Sean. When he jokingly told me that he'd like to see me more than one week out of every month, I decided to transition into pharmaceutical sales. For the next 11 years, I was a cardiovascular specialty rep and a district trainer for various big pharmaceutical companies in the Texas Medical Center, the largest medical center in the world. This allowed me to do a lot of sales and clinical training in both one-on-one and group settings as well as gain invaluable experience as a sales coach and public speaker. I loved it, but when I was offered a more lucrative position with a start-up cardiovascular biotech company, I took it.

The move into biotech was going to be my ticket out. I was earning more money than I'd ever made in my life with stock options and a Lexus as a company car. I thought I had finally arrived career-wise and that I would be able to retire in four or five years as a millionaire.

During that time, Sean and I got married and had three beautiful children, but when each child was only eight weeks old, I was having to drop them off at a daycare to return to work. With my last one, I had a nanny, but due to the amount of income I was making, I couldn't just walk away from my career to stay home with my kids. I was constantly paying other people to raise my children, and it was really starting to wear on me.

Network Marketing Was Never on My Radar

I had always had a very low opinion of network marketing despite being uneducated about it. If it hadn't been for someone with huge credibility approaching me, persevering with answering my questions, and most importantly, getting to the root of where I was dissatisfied in my life and talking to that, I may never have found the industry that would completely change my life. My first foray into network marketing was with a company that offered deregulated electricity and natural gas services, and while network marketing wasn't even on my radar, the more I learned about the industry, the more I saw my opportunity to make a clean break from corporate America. After one year working it very part-time and experiencing the power of residual income, I decided to go full-time into network marketing, guns blazing!

Within eight years, I had achieved the highest rank in the energy company, was a Top 50 earner, and found myself traveling for the company as a speaker, coach, and trainer. However, the constant travel began to take a toll on me and my family, and I knew I still wanted to be part of something in healthcare where I could truly change lives while working from home. When I was presented with an opportunity to join a new health and wellness movement with a truly unique platform, I jumped at the chance to be a part of it. This platform was the first of its kind, bringing both pharmaceuticals and nutraceuticals into consideration in an online assessment powered by science and designed to give individuals not only the vitamins they need, but to also block what they don't need—to ultimately personalize and customize health and wellness based on someone's unique genetics and epigenetics. It's been very rewarding, and I love coaching people on how to be the best version of themselves, not just physically or financially through our company, but also emotionally, spiritually, and relationally.

A Personal Growth Plan with a Compensation Plan Attached

Almost everyone in network marketing would tell you that they joined the industry for the money. However, I didn't start for personal financial gain. I was already making a lot of money as a pharmaceutical rep, or at least, what I thought was a lot of money back then.

I joined my first network marketing company to earn money for my church's building campaign. I wanted to save the world, and I knew I could save the world by first helping my church. I was willing to push myself and make that leap more for my church than I was for myself. But I had no idea of the impact that network marketing would have on my life and legacy.

In the eight years I was with my first network marketing company, I truly failed my way to the top. I grew as a person and a leader and learned I could impact others through my journey and with my story.

Whatever you're thinking, whatever you think you've done or haven't done, that was me and network marketing. I had pity parties, I pouted, I quit, and I came back. My struggle in my journey from employee to entrepreneur was rough, and I finally got to a point where I could no longer blame the compensation plan, the products, or my upline. I had to take a good, hard look in the mirror. It was ME. Eventually, you have to realize that *you*, and only *you,* are responsible for your results. The only way we can reach the next level in any area of our life is to grow, which means we need to be open to learning from others. As global leadership expert John C. Maxwell teaches in his "law of the lid," your level of success will never exceed your level of personal development.

The folks that are at the top of almost any industry I have found to be the most humble, coachable, teachable, and generous people on the planet. They've learned that you have to be open to grow, and you have to keep pushing. Every entrepreneur needs the mindset to be the best version of themselves they can be to live out God's purpose for their life.

"It's not what you know, it's who you know." When you are in symbiotic relationships with other entrepreneurs, you can't help but be successful. Your network becomes your net worth. As Zig Ziglar said, "If you help enough people get what they want, you'll get everything that you want." When you serve, it seems to come back to you tenfold, sometimes out of places you least expect.

Bikini Bodybuilding Champion

We had just launched our health and wellness network marketing company, and I had become the number one income earner. It was a busy, hectic time, and I was going through challenges as part of transitioning away from my old company. Because of the stress, travel, and dinners, I ironically, was unhealthy and had gained 25 pounds.

The summer my daughter was 18, she was preparing to go off to the University of Alabama. She wasn't going to be continuing in soccer and was planning to participate in sorority rush. She was concerned about getting out of shape over the summer. One day, she walked in the kitchen and said, "Mom, I think I want to do a bikini contest."

When she said this, I instantly pictured a shot girl in a bar at happy hour—so, no. But actually, she was following a friend from high school on Instagram who was in training for NPC Bikini Bodybuilding. She showed me her picture and said, "I know this girl and the guy who's training her. Can I do it?"

So, I took her down to the gym to meet the trainer. He told my daughter, "It's going to take 16 weeks to get you in shape for a competition. It would really help if you had an accountability partner."

She looked me up and down disapprovingly and said, "Well, you're the number one income earner in a health and wellness company. It wouldn't hurt you to do it."

I went into bodybuilding with two agendas. One was to spend more time with my daughter. The second was that this might help my business. Perhaps I could recruit people at the gym or sell some products. I had no idea that I would find myself four months later standing on a stage, placing top five in NPC Masters Bikini.

I'm competitive, so I decided to go back into training and came back the following year, at age 49, and won first place at NPC Battle On The Bay, then went off to compete at the national level. It was eye-opening, and I certainly didn't expect all the blessings that came back to me. More than getting in shape or getting healthy, I was blessed by the people that I accidentally inspired along the way.

People still want to talk about it. They still ask me about my workouts, what I ate, and about how much confidence it took to go out on that stage. I tell everybody it was a mental battle the entire 16 weeks. You think it's about the food and the workouts. That was tough, but it's really about the mental discipline and the commitment to stay focused. I learned that anytime I've ever said, "Oh, I could *never* do that," that maybe I really *could* do that.

I truly think God was trying to teach me a lesson through this whole experience. I was not meant to just talk the talk. I needed to learn to walk the walk. For years, I had told people, you're limitless, you can do anything. But when my trainer said I should compete, I thought he was being ridiculous. After all, who would want to see a 48-year-old on stage in a sparkly bikini?

Everybody says my transformation must have been hard. It was hard, but the hardest part was posting my "before" picture. I wasn't sure I wanted to post a photo that would allow everybody to see me 25 pounds overweight with an abdomen scarred from three C-Sections and a recent robotic hysterectomy. It wasn't the greatest picture of me, but I'm very glad I chose to share it. Now I show those pictures proudly because I've seen how being authentic in sharing my transformation story has helped others.

A Health and Wellness Movement

In addition to building a health and wellness company, I just launched my own website, Grow With JMo, to further utilize my John C. Maxwell training certification via one-on-one coaching, and am expanding my public speaking and leadership training. I've also created the Killin' It Collective, a social media-based podcast, to help entrepreneurs share both their successes as well as their challenges with other entrepreneurs. This platform has also helped me fulfill what I believe is my purpose in life: to connect great people with great people and connect great people with their own unique, God-given greatness.

As an entrepreneur, I've personally struggled with "captivity through activity." My norm in the beginning was to be constantly stressed out and operating at an emotional deficit. Long ago, one of my mentors said to me "the higher you climb, the stronger the wind blows." The best way to handle it all is to first ground yourself mentally, spiritually, and physically every day. I tell the people I coach to start each day with gratitude, affirmations and meditation—to get out, get fresh air, exercise every day, and invest in personal development. For my Christian friends, I encourage spending time in the Word and going back to what God says about who you are and whose you are, to take every thought captive and focus on what is pure, right, lovely, and noble. If you take that time every day, you will remain in a peaceful and positive mental state and remain open to learning and growing.

I love my company and the life-changing health and wellness movement we have created. We are six years in, and we are changing people's lives, helping them do life better physically, financially, emotionally, spiritually, and relationally, every single day. What I love most, however, is the health and wellness movement I've created within my own life and, as a result, in the lives of others. As John C. Maxwell says, "Success is when I add value to myself. Significance is when I add value to others." That is when you transcend just "making a living" to leaving an enduring legacy.

Connect with Jennifer Moran, her coaching, and an opportunity with IDLife on

Facebook: Jennifer Maret Moran and Jennifer Moran Official

www.growwithjmo.com | growwithjmo@gmail.com

BILLY BROWN
Taking the Lessons from a (Failed) Golf Career to Finance

Billy Brown is a three-time Oklahoma Golf Association amateur champion and a seven-time club champion in Nashville. Billy talks about the lessons from golf and mentors that helped him become a successful commercial lender, real estate syndicator, and mentor.

Early Influence of Entrepreneurship and Sports

My parents owned Brown Tire, a regional tire distribution company. They grew up with nothing and built their business from the ground up. They had it all...then lost it all in 1998.

Although they succeeded for a time, the word "*rich*" was almost a slur in our house. I developed a strained attitude towards money and wealth that I later worked to overcome.

My parents were involved with Oklahoma State University (OSU) wrestling program. I spent a lot of time with the champion wrestlers. But I was not built to be a wrestler.

I was also not a natural at golf, but I loved the competition. I applied the work ethic from the wrestlers to my game. Eventually, I found myself on the team at OSU. A few of my teammates became NCAA champions and eventually earned their PGA Tour cards. But not me.

Lessons From Golf

All my life, I wanted to be a professional golfer. I burned every bridge to pursue that dream. I tried at least three different times to get on tour. I blew through my $40,000 in savings in 18 months. Financial stress off the golf course led to poor performance on the course, and my career was short-lived.

It's incredibly difficult to make it in professional golf. I grew up with wrestlers as my mentors and had the privilege of living on-site at the Olympic Training Center when I worked at USA Wrestling. I saw their training regiments, and I applied their vicious warrior mentality to golf, but still failed.

Since leaving golf, I assumed if I applied that same mindset in business, I would win. I've since learned the law of reciprocity. Give first, and it will be returned in multiples.

A Leap of Faith and a Fall from Grace

In 2003, I ran away from home and moved to Nashville. I had to borrow money from my grandma for gas. I spent five years bouncing between jobs and unemployment.

By 2008, I got fired from my job at a gym. I decided I would use this misfortune to make another run at professional golf.

I got a job at Banana Republic unpacking their shipments at 4 AM three times a week for $8 an hour. I was still broke. Church members stuck cash in my mailbox so I could afford gas, food, and mortgage. I borrowed my friend's '86 Chevy Suburban because I couldn't afford a car.

Golf was going well. But I knew I needed a sponsor to give myself enough time to make a serious run. I met Mike Hardwick, founder of Churchill Mortgage. Mike was kind enough to buy me lunch and listen to my (bad) business plan—yet he still said yes!

In the fall of 2008, all hell broke loose in the financial markets. Mike called to let me know he had to back out. I was devastated. This was long before I knew how to raise money. The only other gentleman with money that I knew said the dreaded words when I came to him: "I would have said yes three months earlier."

Everyone was holding on for dear life then. My only blessing was I was already broke, so when the recession hit, I didn't have far to fall.

After exhausting all my resources, I had to pull the plug on my lifelong dream. I had no money. I was broken and ashamed. An ex-girlfriend's mom sent me $500. I still have the letter today. When that money ran out, I had to suck up my pride and send **the email** to Mike. I asked, "Can you help me? I'm broke and need a job. I'll clean toilets. I don't care." Mike's response was quick and uplifting. He would hire me.

I balled for 15 minutes, mourning the death of my dream. It was the first of a few times I was truly BROKEN.

But, it was time to go to work. Mike taught me to be a loan officer at Churchill Mortgage, Dave Ramsey's preferred mortgage provider. I learned the ropes as fast as I could. He assured me of two things 1) with the new regulations, everyone was starting from zero, and 2) there wasn't a mistake I could make that couldn't be undone.

Because of the uncertainty of The Dodd-Frank Wall Street Reform and Consumer Protection Act, commissioned loan officers did not know day to day if the loans they originated would close or how their compensation would be affected. Three years of this took its toll.

Another Failure

I got up from the desk, ran down the hall, opened the door out on the fourth-floor veranda as fast as I could, and jumped off the roof.

At least, this is what I wanted to do.

I stopped short, sat on the edge, and screamed inside. I began to cry.

I'm not sure what made me not jump. In my heart, I felt I deserved to die. My inner voice said failure should be fatal. I should be able to succeed, but wasn't even producing the minimum.

Why did I stop short? Maybe I didn't want to disappoint my mentor, the owner of the company, who took a chance on me two years earlier. Maybe it was the mess I would create for my family having to, yet again, clean up after my mess of a life.

It began with an email from underwriting. Yet another loan was going to be declined. I was crushed.

Why couldn't I succeed when I was given this opportunity? Just a few years earlier I was flat broke and broken. Now I'm given this chance only to fail?

That moment on the roof was a wake-up call. I sought professional counseling to help cope with the stress, but it didn't fix the root issue. I hadn't discovered my genius...yet.

I knew the mortgage industry was not my career calling, but I loved finance. What I didn't know was the OTHER types of financing tools available. That curiosity led me to the real estate investing community where I fell in love with tax-advantaged passive income partnered with lending tools specific to investors!

I didn't know where to start, so my wife and I took a mentor to dinner. The first step was quite simple. We needed to get in *more* debt by buying a duplex. We rented out our first house and the second side of the duplex. We went from having a mortgage payment to getting paid to live!

Lessons

Looking back, what I thought was a failure was really preparation. It was one of the roughest times to get into the mortgage business, but it ignited my love of finance.

I learned systems, processes, marketing, lending policy, and how to solve complex problems with creativity. I learned how my brain really worked and embraced it. I realized I was only able to help a certain number of people through what I had been doing, and I started to think that there had to be a more creative way. I just didn't know what that was until a few years later.

Business and Family

When my parents created their business, that business owned them. I swore I would never let a business own me. It just seemed awful. The family was provided for, but everything else declined. My wife and I believe time is our most precious treasure, not money. I can always make more money. I cannot make more time.

With that in mind, when I launched Investors Capital Group in 2019, we made the decision to limit the number of clients we would work with so that we could provide higher quality service. The "extra" time allows us to find more investments, invest in time with the family, enjoy life, and travel. Although we enjoy our work, it is not the center of our lives. We don't work just to work. We work to invest in ourselves, our daughter, and real estate. That investment paid off in 2019 when we syndicated an 81-unit apartment and partnered on a large office investment.

When I do work, I work to serve. It is about more than the transaction for me. My greatest professional joy is to coaching "step up" investors from the perspective of a commercial lender. When most people see "lender" they see "transaction." I want them to see a relationship.

Focus on Your Strengths

Failure was my greatest teacher. I also learned to focus on what I am good at. The more I develop my gifts, the more I am able to bless others. When I followed advice to work on my weaknesses, I was miserable.

The advice I now give is to stop trying to be perfect. Be you. God has it under control. Make the best decision you can and enjoy the ride. God made you for a reason. It wasn't an accident, it was on purpose. Believe that and live out your gifts boldly.

When you do need help, ask. NOT asking for help is selfish. It takes away from others' ability to use their gifts to bless you.

Finally, the biggest lesson I learned from golf was to be prepared and pull the trigger. Trust the preparation and release the results.

Billy Brown is founder of Investors Capital Group, a concierge commercial loan brokerage company that maximizes clients' ROI through strategic loan partnerships. With his experience, he can proudly say he is a "lender that can MAKE you money."

BillyBrown.me | Facebook.com/BillyBrownLending

Founder of The Golf Sanctuary. MyGolfSanctuary.com

ANDRE PARADIS

How Dancing Led Me to Helping Men and Women in Relationships

Andre Paradis is CEO and founder of Project Equinox, entrepreneur, speaker, and author. His passion is alleviating the misunderstanding and pain between men and women in all relationship orientations by teaching the concept of gender intelligence and energy polarity. Andre is also host of the podcast How the Culture Gets It Wrong.

Lonely in a Family of Seven

I am from a French-Canadian Catholic family and was born number four out of five kids. My parents were radically religious, to the point where most everything else seemed to be neglected. I remember at age five feeling that I was born to the wrong family. It felt like somebody had made a terrible mistake. There was a palatable disconnect between me and the other six members of my family that was profound and disturbing. I'll even say, terrifying as a child. I became obsessed with figuring out why I felt like I didn't fit in and how I could feel abandoned, lonely and invisible in a family of seven.

I was a kid that couldn't really fit in and connect to anybody well, so I became an avid observer of everyone and everything around me, especially people's behavior.

My first grade teacher gave me the attention I needed. In my eyes, she was giving me the love my mother didn't and wouldn't. I became the teacher's pet and soon her favorite. She would come over to me at recess, rub my head, and say things to the other teachers like, "Isn't he sweet? Look at his sweet face." I loved the compliments, the attention and actually being visible to someone. I couldn't believe that somebody liked me, especially a woman like her (she was beautiful), so I quickly became THAT guy. I couldn't fit in anywhere well, but the ladies liked me. That was HUGE.

A Natural Dancer

I went to a private high school that offered a lot of opportunities to students. At the beginning of the school year, a girl came up to me and said, "I want to do ballroom dancing for PE, but you have to sign up as a couple. Would you want to be my partner?" I loved to swim, but ballroom dancing for PE would mean I wouldn't have to change clothes or get wet in the Canadian winter. Plus, she was super cute, and I would have the opportunity to hold her in my arms. Yes!

I had never danced a day in my life. I knew nothing about it. But, somehow, everything the teacher showed us I could instantly copy. I became the king of the class. This was the first time in my life I felt I was really good at something. It was a "built in" unexplainable and unexpected gift. It was a incredible boost to my confidence.

Dancing connected my soul to my body. I had been sad for a long time, and this made my heart smile. There is something about moving your body in time to music. When the two vibrations come together in sync, the feeling is euphoric. I realized I was going to do this for a living.

Celebrity Dance Career

At age 19, I moved 3000 miles away to Vancouver BC on the West Coast to get away from my family. The transition was tough. I had no connections, no skills, no resources, no training, no family and zero money. I didn't speak English, only French. But I could dance.

Ballroom was popular on the East coast, but not so much in the west. There were no ballroom studios, so I ended up in a jazz dance studio. That was a whole different kind of dancing, much more demanding physically but the challenge excited me. After only three months of training, I earned a scholarship. Unbelievable! Then another, and another. I never paid for any of my professional classical and jazz training ever! I ended up constantly surrounded by mentors and teachers who believed in me and wanted me to succeed.

Within a couple of years, I was invited on my first tour. I was in Los Angeles for vacation, at a dance party for professional dancers. I didn't know anyone, but it was a crowd I was trying to join. I was dancing with my girlfriend when I noticed this older man looking at me. He was with a bunch of young guys, and his continuous gaze started to creep me out. When he came up to me, I was prepared to blow him off. But then, he told me he was looking for somebody to replace a dancer in his show and I was just what he was looking for.

That was the beginning of my career and my very own Hollywood story.

I was on the road for a year and a half making good money doing what I loved. It wasn't exactly what I had imagined for myself, but being an exotic dancer had huge advantages for my self-esteem. I received such attention and admiration from crowds of women night after night. I could have never imagine that.

But, life on the road is not glamorous. Touring is fun for a while, but the schedule is very demanding. Five cities a week, and really no way to keep up your dance training. You start to lose your finesse as a dancer, your strength and your timing start slipping.

I returned to Los Angeles to get settled and find an agent. I started booking work, and that led to me dancing with Michael Jackson, Prince, Paula Abdul, Julio Iglesias, and countless others. I had the ultimate career, traveled the world and it was absolutely a dream come true.

Understanding Women

My observation of the human condition that started as a child never stopped. After my dancing career, I made a living through different businesses. At a business development conference, a couple I met on a break invited me to attend a workshop in Los Angeles. I loved workshops! So I agreed before I even knew what I was getting into.

The workshop was called "Understanding Women". This was in 2006. At that time, I thought I knew women pretty well. But by the end of the workshop, I realized I knew absolutely nothing. That workshop changed my life! I ended up taking the company's entire curriculum to learn absolutely everything I could.

I became a workshop leader for a short time before moving on because of the politics of the company. That's when I realized this field was much wider than the curriculum I had already completed.

I began study with other masters like Dr. John Gray and his research on the differences between men and women on a chemical and physiological level, Shaunti Feldhahn who teaches love and respect (from the Bible's perspective), Esther Perel a therapist in New York City teaching the dynamics of sensuality and sexuality within relationships, how people love, why people cheat, and why relationships fail. Allison Armstrong taught on the level of anthropology and instincts that are a million years old that still run many of our behaviors, actions, and reactions in life. Then finally, I studied three and a half years with Dr. Pat Allen who brought all these elements together along with the masculine and feminine energy dynamic studies and the power of the quantum energy of words.

After nine years of in depth learning in that world, I began to integrate all of those teachings, along with my life long observations. This led to my own and unique relationship dynamics cocktail. It is both easy to learn and works quite fantastically. It is my passion and mission to share what I have learned and support those who look to overcome the many challenges that come from attaining and maintaining an intimate love relationship to create long term connection and happiness.

The Difference Between Men and Women

In the past few decades, we have pushed this idea of equality between men and women in our culture. The thinking is that if we're equal, everything is going to be better. We did this by empowering women and softening men. Of course, that seemed to makes sense. And doing that worked to make money, build businesses, and careers. But in the matter of love relationships, this is the absolute kiss of death. Because we are, in fact, extremely different! Complete opposites is an even more accurate way to put it.

Good news is that our differences make us beautifully complimentary. Ballroom dancers are not equal. Partners are two different, opposite parts that become a whole. That's the magic of a healthy love relationship.

Our natural dynamics were set eons ago in the time of hunting and gathering. It was a way to assure our survival.

We think we're better than that today because we're more intelligent, educated and civilized. Sure, we have knowledge and we're smart, but our bodies are still surprisingly driven by millions of years of survival training.

Women naturally are more spiritual driven and have a sense of God that most men have to meditate to reach. Women live through their hearts and naturally help men become more heart-centered, gentle, sensitive, aware, and connected. The divine feminine help men out of their heads and bring them into their hearts.

This is good for men, however, men don't live in their hearts like women do. Men spend most of their time up in their heads, to plot, to plan, push, produce, build, provide, protect and conquer. Again, that's how we had to be, and still have to be, for all of us to survive.

Modern life is more difficult for women, especially women in the workforce. It's very demanding and exhausting to compete with men, and there's a huge price to pay for that eventually. Fortunately, the negative effects don't have to be permanent. When a woman brings a man into her life, he will typically want to help and ease her load. When he steps up and becomes HER rock, she can relax, let go and flow back easily into being more open, present, and feminine which eases her anxiety, stress and makes her feel better. When she feels better, she naturally becomes more loving, nurturing, connected and radiant towards most everyone.

Clearing Obstacles to an Ideal Relationship

My message stands out in the crowd, and most of my clients come to me through referral, or after reading my blog or listening to my podcast usually because nothing seems to work out in their intimate relationships. On our first coaching call, within the first 20 minutes, I know what direction a client needs to go and how to address their issues. Once we agree on where they want to go, we clean up obstacles and set about getting there through practices in either one on one coaching, group coaching, and/or workshops. I have found this works for both couples and for single people who want to be in a healthy long-term loving romantic relationship.

My customers become raving fans. The ultimate gift for me is watching a client go from thinking this is never going to happen for them, to actually getting everything they want in an intimate relationship. Last year I officiated the weddings of four couples who were my clients. I can't describe to you what an honor that is.

We all want love. Get clear on which energy you bring and learn to dance rather than step on each others' toes. Find Andre Paradis's coaching around gender intelligence for relationships (regardless of orientation): www.projectequinox.net. andrecoaching1@gmail.com.

Instagram: Relation Dynamics. How the Culture Gets It Wrong podcast available on request.

LISA HAISHA
Actress Turned Philanthropic Soul Blazer

Lisa Haisha is an experienced life coach and founder of The SoulBlazing™ Institute and the non-profit foundation Whispers from Children's Hearts. Lisa teaches women, men, and couples how to "show up" in their lives with her fearless expression as a globally sought-after life counselor, life coach, and mentor.

I Always Wanted to Be an Actress

I moved to Hollywood when I was 22 years old. I'd wanted to be a star since I was ten when my maternal grandmother shared with me and my four sisters how an intuitive told her that our mom (a Southern belle) would marry a foreigner (which she did), that she'd have five kids, and that one of them would be a star and very rich. I claimed it on the spot, and that moment never left me. I just didn't know how that would work. Having an Iraqi father who was very strict, we weren't even allowed to move out of the house until we were married.

My parents ended up divorcing when I was 19 years old, which now gave us more flexibility, but I chose to live with my father, which included his rules. It was tough not being able to go out but one night a week, but doable because of my bigger goal of being an actress in Hollywood. I channeled all my energy into studying the biographies of the great actresses of the day and the past as well as saving money. I was obsessed with the sacrifices the top actresses made to create their dreams.

Meeting Madonna and Travel

One day, a friend told me Madonna was coming to our school, San Diego State University, to perform her first live concert, The Virgin Tour. I was ecstatic. Madonna was my hero. Her father was very strict and Italian, but she'd broken through and expressed herself in a way that was groundbreaking at the time. She was self-actualized while I was still stuck in my cocoon, dying to burst free and fly.

I went to the concert, and afterward, my friend and I found out where the band was staying and decided to go to their hotel. We sat waiting at the bar, and an hour later, the band showed up, but Madonna was not with them. They headed for the elevator. We quickly approached them and told them how much we'd enjoyed the concert, and they invited us up to their room. Score.

We had a great time being in this rare situation. We felt like groupies... really living life. It was a big deal for two small-town girls with no real-life experience. At around 10 p.m., the party was starting to get a bit wild with more groupies and friends packing the suite. The alcohol started flowing. I was having a good time chatting with Madonna's keyboard player, so we exchanged phone numbers before I left to meet my curfew.

Over the next three months, we kept in touch with late-night, two hours calls. He invited me to concerts all over the country, but my father reminded me that I wasn't allowed to spend the night away from home, even though I was 20 years old. Finally, I decided to rebel and meet them in New York for the five-day tour finale. I felt it was my destiny and I couldn't pass it up. I started saving money and then decided (since I may not be able to leave my house again) to add a two-week European vacation to the trip.

When the time came to leave, I left a note for my father explaining that I had to go, and quickly left while he was at work. When I arrived in JFK airport, my "boyfriend" picked me up, and we went straight to a gathering where I got to meet Madonna. It was the moment I had been waiting for. She was rude at first, outright ignoring me, while flirting with my boyfriend and others, but after a few days, she warmed up.

I was confused by her behavior. We had such similar conservative upbringings, but she was so liberated! So when I got my chance to have a conversation with her, one of my first questions was, "How did you self-actualize into Madonna from being one of seven children in a patriarchal family?" We spoke for about 15 minutes, and here's a paraphrase of what she said:

> It's hard when as a child you didn't have the freedom to think the way you want or to experience life freely, but the advice I would give you is to travel. And you have to travel alone, so you can make all the decisions yourself, be brave and meet people, and explore ideas and activities with no judgment from your family or friends. We're so brainwashed from birth and indoctrinated into our parents' viewpoint on life. You have to dig deep and learn who you are—what your soul came here to express.

I took her advice seriously, and that's what I did. I went straight to Europe for an exploration of my new ideas. I went with my best friend, but we were very independent on the trip and did our own thing. Since then, I've been to over 80 countries, and in 50 or so, I traveled alone. Some of my adventures include: meditating in an ashram in Nepal and hiking the Himalayas (part of them), studying with the Sufis in Cappadocia, taking San Pedro in Peru with Shamans, studying with aborigines in Australia, modeling in Tokyo, and going on an adventure to Iraq to meet Saddam Hussein. I immersed myself fully into these experiences that were presented to me, just like Madonna advised me to do.

I was told to trust my intuition and expect miracles because they are everywhere. I was told that everything has already happened and we just need to claim it. I took that to heart. I felt it meant if you want something, ask for it because if it's a strong desire, it is fate. But be careful what you wish for.

Moving to LA to Become an Actress

After I returned from my whirlwind vacation, I moved to LA to become an actress, fueled by a memory of my grandma's prediction that I would be a star. I ended up meeting an agent on the train ride up from San Diego. I felt that it was meant to be. She got me work right away. I was booking small jobs and then bigger ones, earning good money. However, I was an ingenue, and everyone wanted me to do nudity or a love scene. I had several #MeToo moments. I was way too conservative for that and had to quit. Not being able to take great roles because of the R ratings and the casting people or producers wanting favors on the side was depressing.

When I realized acting wasn't for me, I met with the owner of my favorite 24/7 restaurant and the hottest new hangout in Hollywood, Gorky's Café and Russian Brewery, and suggested we start an open mic night called Hollywood Underground. He got on board. They already had the first microbrewery and bands playing each night. The open mic would be from 1:00 a.m. to 4:00 a.m., Thursday through Saturday, when business was slow. Almost immediately, we welcomed stars like Chaka Khan, The Brat Pack, and Iggy Pop, since the restaurant was already a hot spot for celebrities. Watching these stars create material each week to perform and test inspired me to write. So I wrote my first screenplay with the help of a book called How to Write a Movie in *Twenty-One Days* by Viki King.

Getting My First Movie Made

As funds were getting low, I got invited to go to Japan for a three-month modeling gig. I took it and pitched the idea of investing in a Hollywood movie to everyone I met. I ended up raising a million dollars. That led to me producing, writing, directing, and acting in a small part my independent feature film called *Psycho Sushi*. It wasn't the best film ever made, but the experience was invaluable.

After making the movie, I realized that we do all have a destiny to a certain extent, but achieving our desires is about whether you take the torch and follow through with it, whether you're able to see the miracles presented to you, and whether your mind is free from chatter enough to hear the whispers of your higher Self guiding you toward your dream. You have to be brave and believe in yourself. You don't have to know how you'll get there, but you do need to follow the breadcrumbs.

Discovering My Iraqi Heritage

When the film project was finished, I had a lot of questions about my Iraqi heritage, which I felt had held me back my whole life, especially in decision making, people-pleasing, and relationships.

My childhood was still affecting my life, as it does for most people. I felt I was still rebelling or conforming, and nothing was from my soul. So, I read self-help books and attended workshops, but it seemed like going to Iraq and learning about my father's culture would be most beneficial—so that's what I did.

The year was 1998. I booked a ticket to Jordan because, at the time, there were no flights into Iraq because of the Gulf War "no-fly zones." I made my connection in New York. At the airport, I met a woman who was also going to Iraq. She was an emigration attorney from Michigan a few years younger than me, and we connected right away. We both were looking for an adventure and to be inspired. We knew we were heading into danger, and it didn't really matter to us what happened. I asked why she was going, and she said, "I want to die but can't commit suicide because it'll hurt my family."

And I said, "I want to get kidnapped so I can escape and write a tell-all book about the experience." We both laughed.

She wasn't really suicidal, and neither was I. Though we were both somewhat successful and high-functioning, we were both broken in other ways, feeling depleted and dead inside. We wanted to see action, to put ourselves in a situation that would wake us up. At heart, we were both funny, alive, and adventurous people, not so much depressed as wanting to feel alive again. We could even laugh at our horrible states of mind, and yet it was serious enough to cause us to set out for Iraq alone—until we found each other.

We landed safely in Amman, Jordan, and learned that on the bus ride from Jordan to Iraq there were five stops where people were often robbed or kidnapped. We looked at each other and thought, "Perfect. We'll make sure we're the ones that get kidnapped." Whenever we stopped, everyone was quiet, but we made an extra effort to start a conversation with the Generals checking our bags for paraphernalia or anything not allowed. We would say things like, "Oh, let me find my passport and visa. It must be in my Gucci wallet." We were trying to let them know we had money, and we'd be great candidates to kidnap. But they couldn't be nicer—all five stops. We made it safe and sound to the El Rasheed Hotel, where all the journalists and media stayed because it was in the Green Zone in the center of Baghdad. Now we just had to figure out how to meet Saddam, ask him questions about the mentality of Middle Easterners, and meet his sons.

My dad and my new friend were both born in Tel Keppe, an Assyrian town in northern Iraq (the same town where Saddam was born). When we visited, all they had was caves connected to each other where people lived, a school, an ice cream truck, a liquor store, a church, and an orphanage.

We went into the orphanage and started talking to the kids. They asked us, *Why does the world hate us? Why doesn't anyone love us? Why do they let us hurt like this?* I fell in love with these kids. I saw myself in them. I had felt the same way. I wanted to give them a voice and memorialize their words.

Then, I visited more orphanages in Jordan and Israel and talked to the children there too.

Whispers from Children's Hearts

Over the next five years, I went to 15 countries to visit orphanages and asked the children the same three questions: *Is God fair? If you had one wish, what would it be? Who in the world would you want to meet and why?* That ended up becoming a book, *Whispers from Children's Hearts*. That book launched my speaking career. I spoke in schools and gatherings across the globe, sharing the words of the unheard children.

I continued traveling the world and aiding SOS orphanages, who have places in 135 countries. Soon, other people became interested in getting involved. That turned into a non-profit. I didn't charge money, but rather, everyone who joined had to bring a suitcase of supplies and help. We'd visit orphanages or knock on poor people's homes near the orphanages to ask them what they needed. If they needed a new roof, we'd hire a local roofer, so every penny spent went to the community and the kids.

Adopting and Raising My Daughter

After doing that work for years, I decided to adopt a daughter. It was a magical experience and helped me heal in more ways than I could ever have expected. I got to put my energy into giving to someone else and focus less on me. She was so full of joy and love and made me laugh so much, and still does!

However, I couldn't travel as much now that I had a child, so I transitioned to using my reputation to highlight other people who were doing amazing work on a grassroots level locally in the US. I put on an annual Legacy Gala with over 300 guests, raised 20k for their non-profit, and gave them a lot of publicity with over 30 media outlets present.

When I did travel, I brought my daughter to do social work, helping build and repair schools and playing with the kids in various orphanages. Watching my daughter make friends with kids in different countries has been incredible. I want to pass the torch to her so she can continue to live her life with an open heart, be aware of the diversity in the world, and not be threatened by other cultures.

This part of my personal journey has helped me let go of my "shoulds" and my desire for achievement and material things. Now it's all about what I can give back. Once you make that switch, your whole life changes.

The SoulBlazing Process

Today, I teach clients a process I call SoulBlazing. We talk about the seven Impostors who live on the stage of your brain, wreaking havoc in your life, and about your Authentic Soul, who lives on that very same stage. We have to train the Imposters and put a leash on them. Our Authentic Souls know who we are and our mission on this Earth. Once you can understand how your personality is here to assist your soul's journey, magic happens. Once you discover this, you get grounded. Then, through meditation, you can stay focused.

Awareness is an essential ingredient in a fulfilled life. If you would spend 10-15 minutes in the morning planning your day... If you would set your intentions, create space for a two-minute meditation and create and say your affirmations, stretch, look in the mirror, and tell yourself that you love you, or whatever it takes so you feel you're showing up for you... then the rest of the day will run itself. All this could be a twenty minute morning that would change your life forever.

I delve into this on my show, *SoulBlazing with Lisa Haisha*, on Amazon Prime Video. I interviewed thought leaders, trailblazers, and *Guinness Book of World Records* holders to get their story of how they made it, the choices they had to make, and the obstacles they had to overcome. It's about the baby steps they took, how they showed up for themselves, and how other people showed up for them. If you have one person who believes in you, that's really all you need.

Your obstacles are all in your head. Your success is determined by what you believe you can do and whether you step into opportunities. Success is about not having fear of the unknown, not having fear of people, not feeling that you're less than. It doesn't matter where you are in life, it's who you are. If you don't show up for yourself or give yourself love, you can never be there for others, and others cannot fully be there for you.

People say I'm lucky, that life just works out for me. I am not lucky. My life is very conscious. I show up for myself, and when I do, my choices are different.

To learn more about having Lisa speak for your organization or about her SoulBlazing method go to Lisahaisha.com | IG: @LisaHaisha

JIM RICHARDSON
The Impact of Attitude for a Man on a Mission to Address the Housing Crisis for Autistic Adults

Jim Richardson is the co-founder of Stonebridge Equity Group and the nonprofit Neuro Diverse Living (NDL) focused on solving the housing crisis for adults with autism by developing smart-home enabled neurodiverse personal care homes.

Parents, Role Models

My mom and dad were the greatest people, and like parents are for most kids, my first true role models. When Nancy and I talk about what makes us a great couple, we think about our parents and their influence that made us better people... likely the same things that made my mom and dad really wonderful people.

My mom and dad were forever in love and never more than a foot apart. They always held hands: sitting on the couch watching TV, walking down the street. My dad always treated my mother with the greatest respect, and I believe that I grew up in the shadow of a true gentleman. He was confident but mild mannered, soft spoken, and a career blue collar guy. It wasn't what he said, it was what he did. Even though he's no longer here, he's the voice I hear when I'm faced with a tough situation. I am my father's son and am eternally grateful for his wisdom and love.

When Bad Things Happen, Your Attitude Is Really the Only Thing You Can Control

---

"The longer I live, the more I realize the impact of attitude on my life. The remarkable thing is we have a choice every day regarding the attitude we will embrace for that day. We cannot change our past. We cannot change the inevitable. I am convinced that life is 10% what happens to me and 90% of how I react to it. And so it is with you... we are in charge of our attitudes."
– Charles R. Swindoll

I had a very serious car accident when I was in my early twenties and a seatbelt literally saved my life.

It was a cold winter night, and a gentleman fell asleep behind the wheel of his car. When we collided, my car spun out of control and rolled side-over-side down an embankment. When I came to, the police had broken the passenger window and were pulling me up through it. From there, I had four back and neck fusions with plates and screws holding my spine together. I may have broken my back, but never my spirit or resolve.

I think it was God's will that I survived, but I never let pain alter my attitude. I think my positivity goes back to my upbringing. I was raised always being good spirited and good natured. I had numerous surgeries and was out of commission for months on end, but I just kept pushing through. I had been given the opportunity to go on disability, but at age 26, I didn't want that for me or my family. I had children. I had responsibilities.

In another twist of fate, I was once again faced with adversity. In 2001, I was diagnosed with a brain tumor at the top of my cervical spine and, within four days of the diagnosis, was readmitted for more major surgery. Then, in 2014, without warning, a metal plate from the first operation in my neck broke, so I had yet more surgery to remove the original plates and install new hardware. Nancy was wonderful in helping me get through another one of life's hurdles. Life is too short to surround yourself with negative thoughts or people. I have so many things I still want to accomplish, and that would only slow me down.

When something bad happens, you really have two choices: you accept adversity and move on, or you let it consume you and take you down a never-ending spiral of self-pity and despair. I've got powerful positive messages of inspiration posted everywhere in our house. I have always looked at my attitude as the one thing that no one can take away from me. I am totally in charge of and responsible for how I react and believe that how we react to adversity determines our path.

Service Above Self

Two years ago, Nancy and I got involved in our community's Rotary, an amazing organization. I love that it's a group of like-minded people, mostly entrepreneurs, some professionals, who come together with the sole purpose of giving back to our local community. Recently, I was voted to be on the board of the Central Bucks Rotary and asked to lead the Fundraising Committee. Service above self is the motto of the Rotary. I think that is a great way to live, always putting somebody else and their needs before your own. It keeps me centered and humbled.

Autism and the Housing Crisis

I believe Nancy and I found each other during a time of our lives when we needed each other more than we could have ever known. We were put on this earth to take care of those with autism and other intellectual developmental disabilities, which was the inspiration and genesis for our nonprofit, Neuro Diverse Living.

Nancy and I are the products of a second marriage. We have been married for 21 years. Her son, now my stepson, Michael was two and a half at the time we met and fell in love. Michael is now 26, and in raising a son with autism, you appreciate the challenges a family with an autistic child goes through. I have witnessed this challenge firsthand.

One of the things we've always talked about is what will happen to Michael when we're no longer here, and we have learned this is a problem on a level we could never have imagined. We are not alone in our thinking and know there is a huge gap in the market. The CDC just reported on May 15, 2020 that there are over 5.4 million adults in the United States with ASD. The Pennsylvania 2014 Autism Census projects that there will be over 73,000 adults in Pennsylvania alone receiving services by 2030. The Autism Housing Network estimates that 87% of autistic adults live with their parents, but only 22% want to live there. There's no doubt that the 2020 Census will see those numbers rise even further.

Despite investment of billions of dollars in research, early diagnosis, interventions, and education, autistic adults graduate high school "onto the couch." Most are unemployed or underemployed, socially isolated, and have been largely supported by their aging parent caregivers. Without access to alternative and sustainable housing options, autistic adults are at risk of homelessness and likely to be "placed in the next empty bed" of a group home or adult foster care far away from their hometown.

Desiree Kameka, Director of the Autism Housing Network, stated,

> We know from the contacts made through our website that there is a large percentage of autistic adults already experiencing homelessness. Due to social and communication impairments, many can't get past an in-person job interview and thus they can't afford housing. They experience crisis when

their parents pass away as they are left without support with the upkeep of everyday life. They often fall victim to mate-crime or predatory/abusive relationships.

Soon, two or three out of every 100 adults in any community could be affected by ASD. What will happen to them when their family is no longer there? Why should their expectations of living as independently as possible be any different than their neurotypical peers?

We've done well in our careers and our businesses, and we can take care of Michael's needs for the rest of his life. We came to realize that if we can take care of our son, why couldn't we help 10 more, 20 more, or even 50 other families dealing with these very issues?

Years ago, individuals like Michael were going into institutions or nursing homes, bouncing from family member to family member, or worse, becoming homeless. There are currently very few suitable places for Michael to go where he can thrive and become a successful member of the local community. If we did nothing to plan for his future not only as a healthy adult, but also for any circumstance where he might get sick and for when he ages, where would he stay when he needs assisted living and medical care?

The housing crisis for adults with autism isn't coming, it's here.

We are on an ambitious journey to build lifelong, safe, and sustainable smart-home enabled housing for adults with autism and other intellectual developmental disabilities. The response from families we've talked to about this has been overwhelming. We believe it's something we can do to benefit dozens of families with similar needs to ours while leaving a legacy behind for my family by developing a repeatable model that others can leverage and take to their hometown.

I have just turned 65 and want to spend the rest of my productive years making Neuro Diverse Living a reality. This is the time: I've got the right attitude, mindset, energy, and desire.

Lessons Learned

We are truly capable of anything we put our minds to and are willing to work hard for. I believe most people want more out of life but are unwilling to take responsibility for their lot in life. Instead, they blame everyone and everything but themselves. Take personal responsibility for every facet of your life and never let anyone's small-minded comments or criticisms stand in the way of your goals.

1. Time is the ONLY commodity that is not renewable.

2. Pain is temporary. Quitting lasts forever.

3. If I am the smartest person in the room, I'm in the wrong room.

4. Associate with people who have accomplished what you want to do. Never stop learning.

5. If you want something you've never had, you have to do things you've never done.

"We are not the highest version of ourselves we can imagine; we are the lowest version we can accept."

– Sam Ovens

A tax-deductible contribution to 501(c)3 charity Neuro Diverse Living will enable Jim and Nancy Richardson to provide viable housing and employment opportunities for adults with autism.

Visit https://neurodiverseliving.org/ways-to-contribute/ or contact Jim at https://ndl2020.org/contact-jim to make an impact.

TROY HOFFMAN
The Fire That Becomes a Passion

Founder of three-time Inc 500 honoree Simpluris, Troy Hoffman builds impactful companies and people. He speaks globally on leadership and entrepreneurship, holds degrees in performance management, psychology, and multinational financial management, and has built seven-figure companies and legacy-leaving organizations.

A Family of Go Getters

I grew up one of the luckiest kids in the world because of the influence of my family.

My grandmother went to college back in the forties when women didn't go to college. Her dad had an affair with her mother and then just left them, so she had to earn everything herself. In her lifetime she interviewed two different sitting presidents in their hotel rooms and built a huge clothing company for women's fashion right after World War II and had shops up and down the East Coast. She had a mermaid brand before mermaids were popular.

My dad never made much money but had a passion for learning. He was super sick as a kid and then met a chiropractor who helped change his health. For his entire life, he had no immune system and so was constantly sick. When my brother and I were ten and six, my parents sat us down and said the doctors gave him a year to live. Even so, he kept working to change his health. He was able to keep himself alive another 30 years. During that time, he attended chiropractic and neurology seminars and went from being an electrical contractor with his own company to a chiropractor. He opened a health clinic and in the process started learning from Tony Robbins. That's how I got to meet Mark Victor Hansen as a kid. I would later be his chauffeur for the day when Mark was in town speaking at an event.

I grew up in an environment where it seemed very normal to start something, to build a company. Being exposed to that set the stage for my future.

I got into Amway when I was 17 and devoured the books, tapes, and personal development functions. It changes who you are and the way you think. You start to see the possibilities where others can't, and as a result, you take action and accomplish things other people never would. I discovered what could happen if I studied the attitudes, behaviors, and success secrets of giants. It will change the way you show up in every area of life.

Find a Way to Serve

I once tried to sneak into a seminar because I didn't have money for the $189 ticket. Back then, I was making $6.75 an hour as a lifeguard and was working on some other businesses. But I got caught. Instead of tucking my tail and going home, I asked what I could do to help with the seminar. They asked if I had a car. I had just bought a brand new Toyota Camry, so they asked me to pick up the speakers from the airport for the event. It was my great pleasure to do so! This opened a new idea for me, the idea of serving. I picked the speakers up and drove 30 minutes from Orlando Airport to their hotel, carried their bags, and asked them if they needed anything. This allowed me to talk to incredible people one on one and learn from them in a way they would not have shared on stage. And I would repeat this again and again.

A Remote Culture

Today, I run a three-time Inc 500 nominated class action settlement company, Simpluris. We also deal with corporate remediation and data breach and do a lot of backend legal processes for law firms. We have a massive software platform we built for the legal administration industry

13 years ago that we are now making available more widely. We are presenting the opportunity to very large government agencies, attorney general offices, and Fortune 500 companies to serve their administrative needs.

When we started Simpluris, I was living in California and my partner Zach was living in Georgia. From day one, we had to build remotely. We were bi-coastal with remote offices around the nation.

At the onset of stay at home orders with COVID-19, we were lucky to already have well-established remote systems and culture in place. We didn't miss a beat. The challenge for us was that work started dropping. So, we started converting everyone available to sales and marketing.

We needed an online marketing group because a lot of the cases we were seeing, such as bankruptcies or class action lawsuits, required a notice through Facebook and Instagram in addition to banner ads to reach as many people as possible.

We didn't have the expertise, so we needed to attract top talent. However, we didn't have enough work to sustain them. The creative solution was to start a supplement company. We mastered online marketing. We also started a coaching and consulting business to learn how to build online businesses, sell online, and market online.

Launching Balancegenics

Because supplements is a fluctuating business, we had to get creative. We started with one product, made it successful, added the second product, made it successful, then added a third product and made it successful. We've been able to go from zero revenue to $150,000 a month in a year and a half. On top of that, it's self-sustaining with a cross-company team that we shift as needed. We have a huge team of online experts that are fantastic at marketing and we continue to roll out new products.

The long-term vision is to expand into a complete service. Balancegenics has a software team that is elite. The customer is able to order Q&A testing and receive recommendations. We also pulled in Glenn Depke who ran Dr. Mercola's clinic for him and other experts to consult on product line design. The architecture of the product line is designed so that the different product colors align with your test results. Whether you are looking to improve sleep, detoxification, or hormones balances, we are able to help.

Develop the Positive and Clear the Negative

To reach my current level of success, I had to learn who I am, what I can do well, and what I cannot do well. I had to learn how to release the fears, doubts, anger, and emotional baggage that we put on ourselves as entrepreneurs and release what I call entrepreneur PTSD. We get hit with all these problems over and over. It never ends. But we can choose how we cope with those challenges emotionally. By developing emotional strength, challenges no longer bring us down, they fuel your passion and ability to execute.

I need to change my thoughts and way of viewing the world constantly, so I journal. Critically, I also go back through what comes up for me when I journal. I love Byron Katie's teaching because of the way it retrains and reframes your mind. When we get triggered by something, there is a gift within this. I look for that gift by asking myself: *Why am I being triggered? How is my reaction a reflection of me? How do I release this negative emotion?* I practice this regularly. I also work with Dr. Doug who clears emotional triggers in the body and one of the original founders of neurolinguistic programming on a weekly basis for a couple of hours. I constantly am addressing my internal emotions and dialogue and clearing triggers and traumas that come up.

I consume veggie drinks consistently every day. I've been doing it for decades, as much as I possibly can. I'm obsessed. Lately, I've also focused on making sure I stay hydrated and get enough sleep. I do supplementation consistently every single day and I'm constantly getting rid of the negative.

Once or twice a day, I try to book "napitation." For 10 minutes, I do meditative box breathing, and then I take the 20-minute nap. As a result, I have multiple sections throughout the day when I'm on fire and able to crush it.

On Sunday or Monday morning, I take time to go through my calendar for the week. I book everything I think can think of in each area of my life. This includes time for walks, snacks, journaling, my veggie drinks, and taking showers. I make sure that for all seven days I'm booked as much as possible. Then I check the next month to see what is coming up. Finally, I review the previous seven days so I know what I have been committing myself to. If I don't take these steps to plan my time, my day becomes a constant barrage of stuff that knocks me off course.

At the same time, the more successful you are, the more requirements there are of you. At age 44, I'm realizing I can't do everything. It's great to have chill time and not have to book EVERY day full. Once in a while, it's okay to break the routine. I have been decommiting more and having fun in the process.

Sustainability Is Personal Faith

I'm getting clear on what I need to have to sustain. Sustaining in business is a challenge. Building something for one to three years and growing a company that goes from zero and then grows fast is great. But a lot of those companies also disappear, and a lot of people give up. They are able to go three to five years and get massive results, but going decades is a challenge.

For every challenge there's an opportunity and for every opportunity there's a challenge. Accept that you're going to rise and thrive. Keep getting out of bed and keep going by tackling it again.

Find Troy Hoffman, founder of Simpluris, on Instagram at @HoffmanTroy and on Facebook as Troy I. Hoffman. For questions about speaking at one of Troy's events or questions regarding his company, text him at (850) 322-8261. Visit balancegenics.com for healthy personalized supplements.

GREG JUNGE
Doubling My Business Income Through New Learned Habits

Greg Junge went from failed starts at new success habits to rituals that doubled his income for three years. After years of the rat race in Phoenix, Greg became a real estate investor in 2012, a full-time Realtor in 2015, and a Homes for Heroes® specialist in 2019.

Creating Good Habits

I really struggled with creating good habits. I thought about what I was giving up rather than the results I was about to receive.

I read Dean Grazioso's book *Millionaire Success Habits* in 2018 while in Costa Rica celebrating my birthday and my one-year wedding anniversary, but I didn't take any action to create new habits. Why? I wasn't ready.

I then read *The Miracle Morning* by Hal Elrod six months later and tried to force myself to wake up early, work out, etc., but it only lasted for two weeks before I reverted back to my old habits. Why? I wasn't ready!

I re-read *The Miracle Morning* about a year later because I needed the motivation again, not the information. Something clicked this time, and I was ready!

Sleep Divorce

My wife and I had never heard of a "sleep divorce" until friends of ours told us that they sleep in separate bedrooms because they both snore. I immediately thought YES! I value a good night's sleep, so I drew up the sleep divorce papers and served them to my wife. She got the king size bed, but I negotiated a brand-new mattress for myself, so we both came away winners.

Since then, we both sleep much better, and it forced me to create a whole new routine. The room I was exiled to didn't have a TV, which was one of my first concerns. How was I going to fall asleep without it? I have always slept with the TV on, starting in grade school.

Consciously designing a new bedtime routine, I stopped watching TV and started listening to podcasts relating to mindset, habits, and real estate while falling asleep. This change alone has helped me sleep better. I soon realized that creating one good habit can move the needle pretty far, but creating multiple habits that compound on one another can be life-changing.

Tweaking and Maximizing Habits

I'm always tweaking my habits to make them stronger and more effective. After I read *The Miracle Morning* for the second time, I started out with waking up early every day and riding my spin bike in my home office while watching TV. I'd put on an old show that I didn't have to pay attention to like *Seinfeld* or *King of Queens*. One day I thought, how can I take this habit to the next level? Instead of watching TV while working out, I started listening to podcasts. And, why not listen to a motivational or habit-forming podcast? It now feels amazing starting my day with these two habits.

When I think I have developed a great habit, I ask myself, how can I make this more beneficial? I try to be consciously aware of my habits to maximize my time and productivity.

Creating one habit feels good, but tweaking it to maximize your experience feels great. Next level thinking is when you have one habit, improve upon it, then commit to the process. Before you know it, you have four or five really strong habits that you've developed, and the power of your brain allows you to complete them automatically without thinking.

Make your initial goal ridiculously easy so you know you can accomplish it, then add to it.

At first, my goal was to wake up every morning at 6:30 a.m. and workout. Once that became automatic, I added reading and writing to my morning routine. I then added 15 minutes of stretching, and so on. Before I knew it, I had a lot of habits on autopilot, and it set my day up for success.

My Morning Routine Exploded My Business Growth

Initiating a "sleep divorce" and creating this new morning routine has helped my business income double for the past three years. I am much more productive and much healthier because of these habits. These two changes have given me more energy, more time, and have allowed me to focus on what matters: creating more great habits. The results of those habits trickle down to allow my business to grow faster than I could imagine.

Early Career

I bought my first home in Phoenix in 2010, and then repeated that process a couple years later. All of a sudden, I had a rental property and my life as an investor began.

During this time, I was working in a cubicle as a W2 employee. I was talking to my buddy, and he asked, "Why don't you become a Realtor?" I loved real estate, and I had no desire to be in a cubicle for 30 years. I started as an investor in 2012, then became a Realtor in 2015, and now really enjoy balancing both.

My biggest takeaway when I transitioned from a W-2 employee to full-time Realtor was the importance of having support. When I first met my wife, Mandy, I transitioned through a few jobs before working in real estate. She encouraged me and understood my passion for real estate and investing. I'm so grateful for her continued support.

Homes for Heroes®

As a Realtor, I'm affiliated with a national program called Homes for Heroes®. Founded in response to 9/11, the program allows me to give back by donating a good portion of my commission directly to heroes like firefighters, law enforcement, military, health care workers, and teachers. These are people in our community who I have tremendous respect for and are major contributors to society. They have tough, demanding jobs that most people, including me, either don't want to do or aren't able to do. The least I can do is help them save a substantial amount of money when buying or selling a home. It has been great fun to volunteer and give back to people that otherwise I would never really have a way to thank. Thank you, heroes!

Advantages of Real Estate

I'm a little bit of a tax nerd. There's a lot of complexity to it, and I'm not a CPA, so I can't give advice, but I do think a lot of people overlook the tax advantages of real estate. It's not really sexy or fun talking about how much money you're going to save on your taxes, but to an investor, it's a huge advantage.

Real estate is a private investment, which I like better than public investments (stocks). I feel there are more ways to make money in real estate than stocks, but that's my philosophy, and there's no right or wrong answer, just personal preference.

Simple but powerful, in real estate the tenant is paying down your mortgage. That's huge. Who wouldn't sign up for that over and over again?

Being a Realtor

There are some tips and tricks that I like to give to my clients, especially first-time home buyers. I try to be really clear with my communication, explaining the three or four major steps, which step we're on, and what they can expect next. I'm really upfront with timeframes and what I expect of them and what they should expect of me. Every client is different, which makes it fun!

I like relating to people and building relationships. I'm not that salesperson that goes, "What do I have to do to get you in the house today?" I don't like those kinds of salespeople, so I don't project that onto my clients. At first, it was slow going getting clients, but eventually business came, and it's either sink or swim. At that point, I found I was swimming, and I really enjoyed it. It wasn't just about making commissions; it was doing something I really had a passion for: helping people.

Build great relationships and great success must follow.

Reputation is everything in real estate! As a Realtor, you don't want to be known as a commission-hungry agent or somebody who is unethical. It all comes down to relationships, and doing what's best for the client.

Greg Junge holds an international rental portfolio and gives back through the Homes for Heroes® program. He's married to his beautiful wife Mandy and is supported by great friends and family. Learn more about Greg and Homes for Heroes® at PhoenixAZHeroes.com and SevenFigureCapital.com for real estate investing.

TODD STOTTLEMYRE
Lessons From My Dad, Mentors, and Baseball

Todd Stottlemyre is a former 15-year professional Major League Baseball player and winner of three World Series championships as well as a successful entrepreneur, speaker, and bestselling author.

Growing Up in the Shadows of Greatness

I grew up in baseball royalty. My dad was Mel Stottlemyre, who played and coached with the New York Yankees and was part of some of their great teams. He was surrounded by many future Hall of Fame players and coaches.

I'm so grateful that my brothers and I got to go to work with my father every day during his pitching career with the Yankees. We got to go to the stadium, put our Yankee uniforms on, be in clubhouses, dugouts, and outfield, and roam the fields during batting practice. Monument Park was like our monkey bars.

Inheriting my father's environment, associations, and teammates like Whitey Ford, Yogi Berra, Mickey Mantle, Thurman Munson, and Bobby Mercer, and further, the way they went about the game, how they acted when they won, and more importantly, the way they acted when they lost, was a very special opportunity I treasure to this day.

My father meant so much to our family and was a true legend, not just in the sport, but also as a father and man. He was ten times the father privately than he was as a public persona. I'm forever grateful for him.

Dad constantly told us, "You need to be you. Don't worry about who I am and what I've done. You be you." I have now transferred that message to my kids. My father allowed us to spread our wings and dream. He was always very helpful while we were dancing in his shadow because that was a big shadow, and it came with a lot of baggage.

Almost Leaving the Game

I got really vulnerable in 1989, my second year in the big leagues, and almost walked away. But the dream was always bigger than the setback. I was sent back down to the minor leagues the second time consecutively, and I was frustrated. I was like anyone else at 23-years-old being told they're not producing, not performing, and not good enough to stay in the major leagues. I had given my life to this. I had put in all the hours and made all the sacrifices, but I was still being told I wasn't good enough. At that point, my buddies from high school had moved on, gone to college, and started careers, and the career I chose was telling me I wasn't enough.

I remember driving back to the minor leagues from Toronto to Syracuse by myself in silence, no radio. I had all my belongings with me, and many times I pulled over, asking myself what I was doing. Even if I got back to the major leagues, was I ever going to be good enough to stay, or was I just wasting my time? I called my father, and he listened. He was a pitching coach for the New York Mets, and he said, "Listen, I would love for you to be a starting pitcher here in New York with me, but not the way you're pitching today."

I thought, "Wow, Dad! Maybe, is Mom around?" I was feeling sorry for myself, and my father just wasn't putting up with it.

He said, "Man, you have so much more!" He had belief in me when I had lost my belief.

I remember pulling into MacArthur Stadium around six in the morning. The sun was coming up, and no one was there. I was the only one in the parking lot, had been up all night, and was at my wit's end. I started dozing off, then came to and thought, "You know, I'm just going to go all in. I'm going to be the first one at the stadium and the last one to leave. I'm going to do everything I can to get better every single day. If I fail, I'll be okay, even if I fail in front of the whole world. They can say what they want, and at least I'll know that I went all in on my dream and did what I believed was right. I can call it a lesson and move on. If I succeed, I get to succeed in front of all those people telling me I'm not like my father, and I'm not good enough!" And, I went all in.

If I Would Have Quit

That was the only time during my amateur, professional, and minor league baseball career where I had self-doubt. I almost walked away. I didn't have the vision that I would get called back to the big leagues, play for 15 years, or play on three World Championship teams and get paid tens of millions of dollars. I didn't know I was going to play for a Hall of Fame manager or that a lot of my teammates were going to go to the Hall of Fame.

I couldn't see any of that because I was ready to quit. Where I was is where most people quit, and not just in sports, but in life, from a marriage, job, or situation. It's where they decide they're just not good enough. It's a wall you run into that you either get over or around, or the wall becomes your ceiling forever.

If I had walked away, I wouldn't have come to believe that everything is possible. I wouldn't believe that I can create my own destiny. My mindset today is, if I'm not good enough, I have to grow into something else to achieve my desires. I need to grow to fit the dream.

My Greatest Loss in Life Was My Greatest Win

My little brother was 11 and on his third bout with leukemia when they said his only chance for survival was a bone marrow transplant. In 1981, our whole family got tested to see if any of us was a match. I was the closest match.

I remember all the needles they used to pull the marrow from my hips, then how they put it through an IV and into my brother. A couple of weeks later, he was bouncing around the hospital and doing great. They were even talking about allowing him to go home with a follow-up plan. Two days later, he went into a coma that he never came out of. Because his body rejected my marrow, I felt like the killer.

My brother had served others who had the disease every chance he had. He didn't have one ounce of quit, and he fought to the end. He didn't just teach me how to live, he taught me how to die. When you're in touch with your mortality, you remember tomorrow and today are gifts.

I carried guilt and sadness for a long time. It became a problem because the feelings that didn't heal showed up in every aspect of my life. The darkness I was holding inside would come out when I was performing and when I was competing. When that hate and guilt came out, I would turn it into an animal.

The Toronto Blue Jays had just won back to back World Championships. I was a kid of 28-years-old, and a two-time World Champion. On paper, I had everything. But when I looked in the mirror, I couldn't stand the person looking back at me because he had something to do with killing my little brother. I knew that if I didn't heal, this was going to control my life.

The Day My Healing Started

Harvey Dorfman, author of *The Mental Game of Baseball,* was a big deal in my life. He was a well-known sports psychologist and the go-to guy for major league players. In 1993, Harvey taught me about the thoughts we have, how powerful they are, and how your brain and heart are connected. We spent 12 hours together that first day. My healing started when he asked if we could go back to 1981.

He asked me, "Would you do it all over again?" I told him I would have. Then he said, "Let it go, champ. If you would lay down all over again, then it's time you let it go. If you would have said no, then my answer to you would have been then fix it today and start changing the way you live your life. Start glorifying your little brother instead of crucifying you and everyone around you because of that situation." In 1993, I started journaling and studying the way I thought.

I don't think I would have ultimately turned the corner of my career if I had not done this work. I had been spiraling into black-out anger and going back to apologize for what I had done. When I didn't have control of something or when something wasn't going my way, watch out. Harvey had me do a seven-day challenge of journaling every emotion. My intense anger became my trigger. When I started to get to that point, I had to write what I was feeling. Then we went through what I had written together.

Retiring From Baseball

After retiring from baseball, I decided to take a year off. My family had never been on a summer vacation, and I wanted to go somewhere with no pressure. We traveled many places. At a certain point, you have to go home. In the middle of my first year off, my wife started wondering what I was going to do next. My neighbor was a director at Merrill Lynch. He invited me to his office one day in 2003, and I walked out with a job. I decided I would give it a shot and learn new things.

I knew that teams win, and I always accomplished a lot as an individual because I was a part of a team. So I built a team to talk to major and minor league players and agents and raise capital and an asset management team. And we did extraordinarily well.

In my fifth year, I woke up, looked at my wife, and said, "This will be my last day." I couldn't see myself working in an office the rest of my life. I went to the director that day and quit, but stayed 30 more days and met with every client to help the team retain every one.

Not long after, I got inspired and co-founded a hedge fund. I raised capital and ran the fund for eight months. I participated in and built a network marketing group and loved it because I was building a team and helping others dream. I was also involved in a lot of businesses from Wall Street firms to network marketing and owned a lot of companies. I was going from industry to industry, looking for my next Major League Baseball and couldn't find it.

The Call That Led to the Book

My mother called and told me I needed to get to Sammamish outside of Seattle—now. My father wasn't well. I went straight to the cancer hospital. He was running a fever of over 105 and wasn't sure who I was. My dad, my coach, my mentor, and my best friend didn't know who I was.

Three days later, his fever came down. The doctors didn't know what was going on, but my father led our family out of the hospital, refusing a wheelchair to walk out with a cane.

He said he wanted to take a drive through the mountains. As we drove through Snoqualmie, he said, "Todd, someday I might buy a cabin up here." That night I couldn't sleep. All I could think about was how was it possible he could see himself owning a cabin in the mountains when we just wanted him to get through the day. I realized at that moment, he was giving no power to his current circumstances. He wasn't playing a victim. Instead, he continued to be optimistic, fight the fight, live with zest for life, and see the good.

The next morning, I said, "Dad, I'm going to write a book."

For the first 50 years of my life, I used every example and lesson I came across for my benefit to become the best version of me. But I had never allowed it to pass through me to someone else. That night, I decided that I was going to dedicate the rest of my life to other people and see if I could help someone else become more so they can live their dream. I wanted the book to be relatable and about something I've lived through, overcame, and learned from. That's how I developed the nine steps. Every step was a lesson and a trampoline to the next level of my life.

Opinions of Others

When speaking to audiences, I often ask how many have ever let the opinions of someone close to them affect what they do. It still blows my mind to see how many people raise their hand. People get so emotional about other people's opinions out of fear. Sometimes we hold ourselves back more for fear of others' opinions than for fear of failing. Failing is not really the fear. The idea of failing in front of a friend who gave a different opinion is a much bigger emotional fear to overcome. That's why other people's opinions can crush.

I had to overcome the opinions of other people in the sport of baseball and in business. Every time I took on a new venture, I had to remind myself that if I did not overcome that fear, I would not get there, and I hate losing more than I enjoy winning.

My Father's Passing

I was at my father's side when he died. He went to heaven with not one regret. My father did everything in his life he wanted to do. He visited every place he ever wanted to visit. He lived out his dreams. At the same moment, I had this feeling come over me, the opposite of the hate, sadness, and guilt that entered my body with my little brother. For my father, I felt sadness and gratitude.

I decided I was going to test drive the word gratefulness, study it, intentionally be in it, and see what happens. Since then, that word has shown up everywhere because of my mind growth and personal development from people like Jim Rohn and Kyle Wilson.

The night my father passed, I took my journal out in the guest bedroom of his home. I titled the page "Lessons," and started writing everything that I could think of, every situation I could capture, every lesson he taught me, every moment we had. I wrote until I had to stop. About a week later, I wrote a blog about my father and how he truly lived a legendary life and left a legacy. I captured part of that legacy in my journal because I was grateful.

Todd Stottlemyre is a former professional major league baseball player, winner of three World Series championships, author, and speaker. More information about his book Relentless Success, *his online program, and contact information can be found at toddofficial.com.*

TODD SULZINGER
Intentional Steps Towards Financial Freedom

Todd Sulzinger is a former Silicon Valley finance executive turned real estate investor, syndicator, and mobile home park consultant. He founded Blue Elm Investments to help people harness the power of group investing. His focus: creating quality, affordable mobile home park housing options.

A Traditional Role Model

I was born and raised in California, the middle son in a family where my dad went off to work each day and my mom stayed home and managed our household.

My grandparents and great-grandparents were business owners who worked long hours and faced financial uncertainty as pharmacists and restaurant and motel operators. Watching their parents struggle led my parents to seek a more stable and secure middle-class life. Not long out of high school, my dad got a job with the defense contractor Lockheed. With just a high school diploma (he'd later go on to earn an AA degree), hard work, and a bit of luck, he created the life he dreamed of. Forty-two years later, he retired from Lockheed at age 62 with a pension and financial security.

My role model was exactly like that of nearly every kid in my neighborhood. Get a good job with a stable company, work hard, retire young, enjoy the good life. It seemed like a pretty good option to me.

Never let where you've come from determine where you want to go.

Chasing Corporate Success

After graduating from San José State University with a degree in finance, I landed a job as an early employee at a technology startup in Silicon Valley. The company was growing fast, and there were opportunities for me to grow with it. After just a couple of years, the CEO asked me to move to England to help lead finance operations for the company's European subsidiaries. It seemed crazy at the time, as I had little experience to prepare me for the job, but I quickly discovered the value of being thrown into the deep end and having to figure out how to swim. I spent two years traveling around Europe and honing my finance skills. More importantly, I learned how to navigate unfamiliar cultures and how to build credibility with people who had more business and life experience than I had, and I gained confidence that I could add value even as I was learning.

My experience in Europe taught me an important lesson: We are often more capable than we give ourselves credit for, and we have an amazing ability to succeed—and even thrive—when we are presented with big challenges.

Believe in yourself and act "as if" you are already the person you want to become.

When I returned from England, I realized I needed a new challenge. So I did what people in Silicon Valley often do—I set my sights on a company on the way toward an IPO. I soon landed at another startup and experienced the excitement of taking a company public. But soon after the IPO, the company was acquired by a larger firm, and my job was eliminated in a "synergistic cost-cutting measure." Two failed "can't miss" startups later, I felt the personal toll that long hours, travel, and commuting were taking. I began to wonder if there was a path to financial security for myself and my family that didn't involve chasing a pension or an IPO.

My "Millionaire Next Door"

After moving back to the US from England, I became friends with my neighbor Paul, an unassuming, older gentleman who drove an old truck. He was soft-spoken and walked slowly, slightly hunched over. As we got to know each other, he would say things like, "I have a rental down the street I have to check on," and "There's a strip mall I own across town," and "Oh, this commercial building I own downtown needs attention", and finally, "If you ever consider moving, I'd like to buy your house."

Over time, I realized this quiet, down-to-earth guy—my "middle-class" neighbor—owned millions of dollars of real estate. He was the millionaire next door I wanted to be.

Listen and learn from those you want to emulate.

Paul helped me see that there might be another way to achieve financial security.

Finding My Own Path

I decided to learn all I could about investing in real estate. I immersed myself in books and started listening to my first mentors, Robert Helms and Russell Gray, on their *The Real Estate Guys Radio Show*. More importantly, I also started attending their monthly networking events and met a tribe of people who were gaining financial freedom through real estate. These connections showed me the immense power of networking. Spending time with people who were more experienced than I was exposed me to wisdom and insights I couldn't learn from books, and unlocked access to resources I wouldn't have found on my own.

"You are the average of the five people you spend the most time with."

– Jim Rohn

After several years of research and education, I took my first uncertain step into real estate investing. With introductions from Robert and Russ, I met property providers and managers I trusted and purchased several rental properties in Texas. While it was daunting to invest in properties located over 1,500 miles from where I lived, my property managers made it easy for me by taking care of the day-to-day details and providing wise counsel when decisions needed to be made.

My rental properties began to generate income, and I decided to branch out. Through my network, I met a team of people involved in real estate syndications—an investment approach where groups of investors pool their money to buy larger real estate assets than they could afford individually. Before I put together my own investment projects, I invested in several other syndications to see the process from an investor perspective.

As I gained experience and confidence, I began to wonder if I could use real estate to generate more than passive income. Could I actually use real estate to leave my career in corporate finance?

Once again, I dove in to learn what I could and turned to my network for ideas.

Tapping Into My Entrepreneurial Roots

Andrew Carnegie once said that 90% of all millionaires became so through owning real estate. Today, it remains one of the primary ways people build generational wealth. However, while people understand the benefits of investing in real estate, they're often scared away by concerns about managing tenants and not knowing how and where to invest.

I began to realize I might be able to use what I'd learned to help others invest and secure their financial future. I'd spent most of my corporate career developing financial models for multimillion-dollar companies and helping communicate complex financial information in simple, straightforward ways. I knew I could use these skills to analyze real estate details and help people understand the ins and outs of investing. And so, I began to dig deeper into the idea of organizing real estate syndications.

Syndications happen with all kinds of real estate investments, but as I learned more, I became interested in one specific kind of asset. Mobile home parks are a little-known, profitable niche in the world of real estate, and I was intrigued by the key factors that make mobile home park investing so desirable: the growing need for affordable housing, almost no new park construction, shrinking supply due to redevelopment, and the ability to purchase family-run parks and quickly add value by investing in infrastructure and improving management practices. I loved the idea that I could turn neglected mobile home parks into safe, clean, affordable places for families to live while providing investors a safe place to invest their money.

I committed to leaving my corporate job, reduced my hours at the medical device startup I was working for, and developed my business plan for a mobile home park syndication business. I formed a relationship with a nationwide mobile home park consulting company with many years of expertise managing and turning around struggling parks to increase their profitability. This partnership took years off my learning curve and enhance my credibility with investors.

With a draft business plan and this partnership in place, Blue Elm Investments was born!

"Alone we can do so little; together we can do so much."

– Helen Keller

One year after founding my company, I closed on my first mobile home park syndication and left my corporate job. Six months later, my investor group and I purchased another mobile home park, and I expanded my business to provide consulting services to people who want to buy and turn around their own mobile home parks. I'm excited to be building my own business and thrilled to be able to share what I've learned with others and to help them take steps toward their own financial freedom.

In retrospect, I should have taken action sooner, which is a common refrain I've heard from successful entrepreneurs and investors. When you're ready to achieve your dreams, create your plan, and take action to move forward.

My Success Habits

William S. Burroughs said, "When you stop growing you start dying." I strongly believe that happiness and success stem from a desire to continually become a better version of yourself. Two habits have been particularly impactful for me.

My first personal development mentor was Darren Hardy, who I discovered when he was the publisher of *SUCCESS* magazine. Darren's inspirational messages began to permeate my thinking and gave me confidence and motivation to push forward towards my dreams. I start each day by watching his *DarrenDaily* video. These short videos never fail to get me going with a success mindset and a powerful boost of positive thoughts.

I've long believed in the power of journaling but struggled to figure out the "right" way to do it. What to write? How much to write? How much time to spend? I followed a recommendation from entrepreneur and author Tim Ferriss and started using a beautiful little book called *The Five-*

Minute Journal. The journal asks you to contemplate three questions in the morning and two in the evening about gratitude, affirmation, and a positive mindset. It has simplified journaling for me and immediately began to change how I experienced my days. Powerful things happen when you intentionally fuel your mind with gratitude and possibility, and answering these questions consistently every day has compounded to make a big impact over time.

I've recommended both *DarrenDaily* and *The Five-Minute Journal* to countless people, and I hope you'll find value in them too.

One last piece of advice: As you strive to achieve your goals, believe that your success is inevitable. When in doubt, just take the next small step, and you'll be that much closer to reaching your dreams. Good luck!

Connect with Todd Sulzinger, founder of Blue Elm Investments, to diversify your portfolio with passive real estate investing opportunities in mobile home parks at www.blueelminvestments.com or todd@blueelminvestments.com. Find DarrenDaily at www.darrenhardy.com/darrendaily and The Five-Minute Journal at www.intelligentchange.com

MAHEALANI TREPINSKI
From Nightmare to Natural Healer

Mahealani Trepinski is an intuitive natural healer and integrative nutrition health and life enrichment coach. She uses Christian NLP in her speaking and coaching and specializes in craniosacral, energy, and medical massage. Her passion is to educate and help bring the body, mind, and soul to homeostasis.

Natural Healer Helps Your Mind & Body Return to Homeostasis

Natural healers believe in the ability to heal your body without medications. As a natural healer, I'm not against Western medicine. I believe you can heal yourself the way God planned by using food, herbs, natural ways, and the power of the mind. If you bring the mind, body, and soul together, you can treat your whole body as one and bring it back to homeostasis.

Homeostasis is your body's state at equilibrium. When you are in homeostasis, you have a stable internal environment as we have when we are born.

We can get our bodies into homeostasis by first getting our minds back to the way they should be. By eliminating negative thinking, you raise your thought patterns. In the body, if you have negative issues stuck in the muscle or tissue, they can be removed by craniosacral massage or neuro release. Then we assess what you are feeding your body. We need to remove all the processed foods and chemicals you have been ingesting and breathing so we can bring everything back to the way God intended.

You Are Not What They Call You

When I was young, I frequently reversed numbers and words. Teachers were not trained back then, and they said negative things to me. My brain just wasn't connecting. I grew up thinking I was not going to be good enough at anything. Worthlessness is still something that tries to haunt me today.

I was transferred to public school and got pushed through. When I was a senior, things started clicking. I met Coach Jeff Davis, my second mentor. He was a lifesaver, and we are still good friends today. Coach Davis influenced me to become an athletic trainer. I became one of his prize students. It made me feel amazing and as though I could achieve anything.

I never finished college because it would have required many remedial courses. While I was there, educators began to acknowledge dyslexia as a real issue. I learned that certain colors could help. I found rose helps my brain not to flip the words on the page. I use glasses with pink lenses. I don't think you can ever 100% overcome dyslexia, but I've learned ways to deal with it.

A Nightmare

I am the baby of three with two older brothers. I was unplanned and was born three and a half months early and was not expected to live through the night. I believe I am here for a purpose.

My dad was in the military for 31 years and retired as a Command Master Chief. He was very strict at home. There was abuse, and it was a very negative environment. It made me who I am today.

I left my abusive home and married someone worse than my father ever was. My ex-husband was verbally, physically, and sexually abusive to me, but he didn't show that until I said, "I do." Everything started on our wedding night. None of God's creatures deserves such abuse.

I was still young when I got pregnant. He had an affair and left me for someone else who was married and also just had a child. So, I became a single parent.

I decided I could not continue school to be an athletic trainer coach and be a proper parent. The work schedule of a trainer was too demanding. I truly believe to be a good parent, you need to be there for your child, especially if you are the only parent. I did multiple things to make ends meet, including moving in and out of my parents' house. That was difficult because my dad hadn't changed for the better yet, and I didn't want my son to grow up in that type of environment.

Seeing Daylight

I ran to my church for support. They helped me out tremendously, financially and with counseling.

In 1999, I tried corporate life and did not like it. So, I decided to work for a chiropractor. It was an old school chiropractor, and they didn't have the liberties chiropractors have now. If I knew that back then, maybe I would have become a chiropractor, but instead, God led me to go to massage school.

I had no idea why I would do that. I thought massage was fluff, and I wanted to help heal people. I listened to Him anyway, put myself through school, and learned that massage has so many natural healing properties.

Since, I have been able to work on Dallas Cowboys, Olympians, and the Dallas who's who as well as teach at a massage school and in continuing education. It turned into an unbelievably awesome practice.

Benefit of Multiple Perspectives

When my dad started getting sick with cancer, I thought there had to be a way to cure this. So, I went to school for integrative nutrition and food for medicinal values.

In 2012, I graduated as an integrated nutritionist. I learned if your work, personal life, God, or family are off, every part of you will be off, including what you eat. That's why my nutritionist training included life coaching. The disciplines go hand in hand. I eventually got married again to an amazing person. When I met him, I had been going to counseling and doing NLP. That's when I started using the NLP to help rewire my subconscious mind.

I prayed for guidance. I got clear while working with Kyle Wilson and his Inner Circle. I met Mike Davis who taught *renewing of the mind*, which is NLP backed with scripture. Through him, I received my master practitioner certificate.

I have enjoyed learning many different skills which serve my practice. I can look at my client's issues from a nutritional, craniosacral, NLP, or spiritual point of view and ultimately see the big picture.

Getaways & Retreats

I need a place to retreat where I can get grounded. That's why I like living in nature. I like to meditate, pray, and sing. I also like to go to retreats to learn new things and enrich life.

Getaways are a way I can continue to help people. I have retreats that incorporate everything I practice. My goal is that when you leave the retreat, you will know what you want in life, how to achieve your goals, who you are on the inside, and your purpose.

We all face challenges and setbacks. There are times I slip up and backslide. I strongly recommend having a coach who can help in these situations. I have benefitted from having multiple coaches, especially coaches who specialized in different areas of my life.

I'm a very intuitive person, and I can read people, so I've got to resonate with my coach. It's important to sit down and talk with a prospective coach to see if they are going to be a good fit with you. I tend to procrastinate on the things I know I should be doing to grow, so I need a coach who is going to stay on me. Having a personal coach has also been a tremendous help to keep me centered and on point with my life.

I work to keep my vibration/energy high. When my energy is high, I can resonate with other people and bring them to that level.

Gratitude helps me keep my energy levels high. I spend time every day writing what I am grateful for. It may be as easy as "I am thankful for my cup of coffee," or it can be big like "I am grateful and thankful that my father had a peaceful exchange into heaven."

When I work with a group of people, it is important to manage my energy level and stay grounded. Before I go into that situation, I ground myself. It's like putting a bubble around yourself that only certain things can penetrate. I think about it like Wonder Woman bands. When anything negative approaches, I deflect it with my bands. If there is too much coming at me, then I will take a break to recenter.

Visualization

I keep a journal, and rather than just focus on my present state, I also write where I want to be. I do visualizations because what you think about and what you see, you will bring about. I do a vision board every year and put forth the steps to achieve the items on there. I put the board in a place that my subconscious will see it, and by the end of the year, I accomplish 90% of what's on the board.

Action is key. You can't just put it out there. You have to put forth effort. In the Bible, it says ask and you shall receive, after doing as He asks, Matthew 7: 7-8.

Just keep pressing forward. Don't give up when it gets hard. You might take two steps back for every three steps forward, but you are still making progress.

Mahealani Trepinski is an integrative nutrition trained health and NLP life coach and CranioSacral LMT in the Dallas-Fort Worth area offering a variety of natural body healing services to help you achieve your higher and better self. mahealani@healingmasters.us / healingmasters.us / @HealingMastersLLC

PANCHAM GUPTA
How I Multiplied My Engineer's Salary Into Passive Income and Time Freedom

Pancham Gupta was an engineer in the financial technology industry for 14 years and now is a full-time multifamily syndicator with $43M of assets under management. Through his podcast, The Gold Collar Investor, *Pancham is passionate about teaching personal finance to high-paid professionals who lack investment experience outside Wall Street.*

First Generation Indian Immigrant
I grew up in India in a middle-class, small business family and came to the US in 2003 to get my master's degree. As a kid, I was fortunate to have access to food, clean water, and a good education. My parents made sure that I went to a good school and had access to a good education. I was a very shy kid.

India is unlike the US, where kids get to pursue their passions. Growing up, we were brainwashed into choosing between being either a doctor or an engineer. If you had managerial aspirations, you could choose to go for an MBA. It did not matter what you wanted; if you did not choose one of these professions, you would be considered a failure. The peer pressure from the adults, and the kids as well, was huge. In general, people made their decisions based on what their peers wanted or what looked good. It was not based on what they wanted to do or what would be prudent for their situation. I am not trying to demean this culture or look down upon it. It's just the way it was back then.

A Gold Collar Worker
I was very good with math and science, so naturally, I chose to become an engineer. As a kid, computers fascinated me. So, I decided to become a computer science engineer. Four years later, after graduating with my bachelor's in computer engineering, I came to Carnegie Mellon in Pittsburgh to pursue my master's.

At the time, I thought I would get some work experience in the US after graduation and then move back to India to start something of my own. I really wanted to be an entrepreneur growing up. I had the entrepreneurial genes of my dad.

Right after graduating from CMU, I started working for a big financial technology company in New York City as a computer programmer. I started making a six-figure salary, and every year that salary grew. If you have followed the growth curve of pay for good programmers in the last 10 years, you know the increase is staggering. Computer programmers are the new bankers of the 90s, and rightfully so. I believe technology is going to change the world.

I truly became a gold collar worker, an employee who was making a six-figure salary and had money to invest but had no knowledge in investing outside of some Wall Street paper products.

Delayed Plans
Hard work and persistence always wins over intelligence.

I was undecided if I was going to stay in the US or go back. In 2009, my wife and I almost sold all of our stuff to move back to India, but we found out that we were expecting a baby. That delayed the plans for another year, and leaving the US became harder and harder.

Years went by while the desire to start something on my own still burned inside of me. I founded two startups with partners and allowed my partners to take the lead. I could not quit my job as I was still on a work visa. One of the startups was for the US market, and the other one was for the Indian market. One failed as we couldn't get the VC funding, and the other failed because my partner and I couldn't spend enough time. I lost quite a bit of money, but I learned a lot.

A Real Estate Addiction

By 2012, I decided to invest in US real estate. Subconsciously, I knew that I would not be moving back to India. I was always interested in real estate and grew up seeing my dad investing in it. I started educating myself about the market around me. I started going to open houses every weekend for for single-family homes. Going to open houses turned into an addiction. I was spending all my time just going to open houses and talking to brokers with my wife. It became part of our lives, so much so that my three-year-old son learned a bunch of terms about houses.

First Purchases

If you stay at it long enough, it will come together. I bought my first rental house in 2012 with a partner while I was still living in a rental apartment. Three months later, I bought another one also in the suburbs of NYC. They were not cheap. However, the mechanics of passive income while building wealth were getting vetted out in my head. I did not realize back then, but this was the opening of a new world of investing for me.

A few years later, I ended up buying small properties in five different states. I dabbled with Airbnb as well for a year and managed to do a flip with a partner. I realized that I enjoy real estate so much that I wanted to make this my full-time thing. And, I wanted to scale up.

Education Binging and Scaling to Multifamily

Buying single-family houses did not seem like the way to go. What I was doing worked well, but it would be years before I could replace my income. I did not see myself working in a cubicle all my life for someone, and on top of that, I liked real estate so much more.

Focus is the key in this world full of distractions.

I started educating myself with books, podcasts, and blogs. Instead of open houses, books and podcasts became my friends. I used my three-hour commute to educate myself. At my kids' soccer games and birthday parties, I listened to podcasts. There was a period when I did not watch TV for a very long time and we got the cable disconnected. That lasted up until the soccer World Cup, but we turned it back off afterward.

I decided I wanted to scale up by buying apartment buildings. After all these years of learning the investing game, I knew that whatever I try to do, someone else has done it before. I was not inventing an iPhone. I was following a path that has been followed by many others before me. I could learn from their mistakes.

Mentors Compress Time Frames

I thought of hiring a mentor, however, being an A student all my life and an engineer on top of that, I had too much confidence that I could figure this out myself. I would make many mistakes along the way, but I would learn from them. So, I tried to do it myself. I failed. I tried again. I failed again, and this repeated a few more times.

Then one day, I had an epiphany. It's all about compressing the time frames. I mean you can learn all these things by yourself, but it will take years. If you want to learn something quickly, learn from someone who has done it before. It's not about how smart you are. It's about how quickly you can acknowledge what you do not know and find the right help to bridge that knowledge gap. With that realization, I decided to seek help. I hired a coach to help me with my journey of buying apartment buildings using syndications. My partner and I ended up buying $8M dollars worth of apartment buildings in eight months.

Along the way, I have also educated myself about other asset classes outside of the apartment buildings and started investing in those passively. There are so many opportunities out there for people who have the money to invest while working high-paying jobs. They can use their investments to build passive streams of income so they DO NOT have to rely on a 401k, i.e. Wall Street, for retirement. In the process, I also realized that this information is not easily available and it takes a lot of time and motivation to learn it.

Quitting My Job

I decided that I would quit my job and start educating people about investing outside of Wall Street. I put together investment opportunities that help people create income streams and achieve diversification.

It's 80% psychology and 20% the actual mechanics in anything that you do.

The decision to quit was not easy. I liked my job. I was going against the wishes of my wife and my parents. Even so, I made it my mission to help high-paid professionals learn about their opportunities and become financially educated. I could not do that while I was working full-time. Podcasting seemed like the best medium for me to start this journey, so I began my show *The Gold Collar Investor*. I hope I can bring value to my listeners and have an impact on their lives. This was just the beginning, and since then, opportunities to share what I have learned continue to multiply.

If I Can, You Can Too

If a first-generation Indian immigrant with no financial background or knowledge, a three-hour commute every day, a demanding fin-tech job in NYC, and a family with two kids can learn to invest and build passive streams of income, you can too. Hard work, focus, and persistence is the key. I absolutely love the Henry Ford quote: "Whether you think you can, or you think you can't—you're right."

Pancham Gupta offers a free e-book on his top six reasons to diversify outside of Wall Street. Download it at www.TheGoldCollarInvestor.com/download.

Subscribe to his podcast at www.TheGoldCollarInvestor.com/subscribe or email at p@TheGoldCollarInvestor.com

MICHAEL BLANK
The Focus System of Three Things

Michael Blank is founder and CEO of Nighthawk Equity, a $75 million multifamily investment company, and a leading multifamily authority. His education company has produced his bestselling book, Financial Freedom Through Real Estate Investing, *his top-rated podcast, live events, and coaching programs.*

Failure Is Earned

I didn't figure out I was an entrepreneur until I was in my mid-thirties. I was taught to go to school, get good grades, and get a good job. When I realized I wanted to go out on my own, I started reading the biographies of famous, successful people. I noticed a pattern. Everyone, without exception, had failure, sometimes repeated and most often almost catastrophic failures. I considered myself a pretty successful person, and I had never had a failure of any sort. I thought that obviously something was wrong with everyone else and I was the normal one.

When I finally became an entrepreneur full time, it was unsettling to realize that I controlled nothing. When I was employed, I felt like I controlled my destiny. If I worked hard and maybe played a little office politics, I knew I was going to get promotions. As an entrepreneur, I found I controlled very little. I couldn't control whether people walked into my restaurants. I couldn't control how much money people would invest with me. I certainly couldn't control the market. Failure was almost inevitable.

While failure is not pleasant, my early failures shaped me into the person I am. I'm much more resilient today. I am much calmer in stressful situations. I've now been through failures several times in several ways, and I think that if someone has not failed in a big way, they are not truly an entrepreneur. I don't welcome failure, but there's always a lesson in it that will propel me to a higher level.

First Failure

My first real exposure to entrepreneurship was in the restaurant business. At that time, I had a bunch of money from my involvement in a very successful IPO of a software startup in the late '90s. I had gone from being an employee dependent on a paycheck to having more cash than I knew what to do with.

Then I read *Rich Dad Poor Dad* by Robert Kiyosaki and realized the money I had in the bank or the size of my salary was inconsequential to my true wealth compared to passive income derived from my assets. As an employee with savings, I was making interest dividends at best, which did not give me financial freedom to live my best life. My solution was to purchase a cash flow business—a restaurant franchise, then another, and another.

The recession came, and I lost my IPO millions in a restaurant debacle. I share the full story in *Resilience: Turning Your Setback into a Comeback*. I lost all my cash, lost another $200,000 in lines of credit, and maxed out all my credit cards.

Development of Passive Income

I was lost, but I believed I couldn't have quit a safe, cushy job to go on an adventure only to crawl back to a safe, cushy job. That could not be my lesson. I couldn't see how that's what God would want for me. I updated my resume and was close to getting a job, but after a lot of reflection, I realized that real estate might be my way forward.

I had taken an apartment boot camp, and I had flipped a few houses and actually made money. Real estate made more sense. It was less risky. So, like so many people do, I started investing in single family houses. Everyone was flipping, so I did too, but it was like another job. If I was not buying, fixing, and selling houses, I was not making money. I realized I had created my own rat race. That's when the light bulb went on. I needed to hold real estate.

I would need a portfolio of more than 50 houses to reach my passive income goal, and that just wasn't reasonable for me. That's when I got into an apartment building deal. It was very scary. But, when I started receiving mailbox money, I was all in. Getting involved in multifamily investing was the best, fastest, most reliable way to become financially free.

Biggest Investing Mistakes

Real estate generates cash flow, has unbelievable tax advantages, and is less risky. What's the catch here? The only catch is you have to have an open mind and educate yourself.

A Deal Maker Live event is a magical environment we created all about multifamily investing. The overall goal is helping attendees do their first deal. If they can do that, the second and third basically follow automatically.

The biggest mistake I see people make is not getting into real estate investing at all. Typically this is because of their fear of the unknown. Getting out of your comfort zone is always nerve-wracking, but even with the failures I have gone through, I have found every moment of this journey worth it.

My battle cry is, let's help other people become financially free so it empowers them to live a life of significance.

Focus Is Required for Balance

Successful entrepreneurs I have studied realized that the classic sense of balance doesn't exist. Balance means that you're spreading yourself evenly among different categories. If I were to spread myself thin across all categories, I wouldn't be doing a good job in any one.

Focus is critical. Be fundamentally intentional with everything you do. This requires a large degree of self-awareness. Be very intentional about how you use your time. If I'm going to work, I'm going to work. If I'm going to play, I'm going to play. Don't do anything with 50% intensity.

Intentionality requires systems and a plan. Once a quarter, I take myself on a retreat for eight hours. I don't think about how I did in the past. Instead, I set goals for the next time period, usually 90 days. Then I set similar goals for smaller time frames: this month, this week, and today. Gary Keller's *The One Thing* is really useful in this because it helps you identify your most important goals.

In my world, the *one* thing is a little too minimalistic. So, I always work in threes. What are the three things that will move the needle in every timeframe? The three things I want to get done today should contribute to the three things I want to get done this week. That should contribute to the three things I want to get done this month. That should contribute to the three things I want to get done this quarter. And that should contribute to the three things I want to get done this year.

Systems of Success

The other critical system is scheduling a time for these things. Tuesday mornings and Thursday mornings, so one full day per week, I set aside as my strategic time. I do not take phone calls or set meetings. This is when I do deep work, the three things I identified that will keep the ball moving. I get my entire week done in that time period. The rest of the week, I am firefighting, on phone calls, checking emails, on Slack, and doing so many other things. As entrepreneurs, we're constantly firefighting, which becomes a problem if you never actually get to the important things.

I chose mornings because I'm more of a morning person. After around 1:30pm, I'm great on email, but it's not deep, productive time.

The Three Things to All Areas of Your Life

You can also apply the system of three things to all areas of your life. I apply it to my family, spiritual, health, etc. Secondly, you have to look at each of your goals on a regular basis and ask yourself, "How am I doing on these goals? Should I change the goals? Should I step it up a little bit?" Don't be surprised if you need to adjust. This is actually beneficial.

I love this system because when you think about doing something meaningful, anything from losing weight or doing your first deal, there's potentially infinite steps to achieve this goal. It can overwhelm you to the point you don't even get started. So, I like thinking in terms of three. If you're embarking on a journey, it is easy enough to identify the next three things you should be doing. They could be simply making a call, reading a book, and taking that meeting. Write them down and do them. Don't put any thought into the rest of the journey. Just execute. When you check those off your weekly list, it's very satisfying. Then, come up with the next three things.

All of a sudden, three months later, you look up, thinking, "Holy cow! Look at all the stuff I've done." Sometimes it's good to have the big picture, but the big picture can also be overwhelming. Get in the habit of doing the next three things.

Crash Test Dummy of Financial Freedom

I consider myself to be the crash test dummy of financial freedom. In hindsight, I see that starting with flipping single family homes was unnecessary. You don't have to start with single family homes and then graduate to multifamily investing. It's a misperception that multifamily is much more difficult or more complicated. That's what we teach our students. Multifamily real estate, for an active or passive investor, is the fastest, most replicable business in the world to generate passive income and, of course, long-term wealth.

I am proud to be the leading authority on apartment building investing in the United States and passionate about helping others become financially free by investing in apartment building deals with a special focus on raising money. I have helped students purchase over 2000 units valued at over $55M through my training programs and plan to continue doing so.

To learn more about Michael Blank's online and live education and coaching, visit TheMichaelBlank.com for free resources. Listen to The Apartment Building Investing Podcast, *a top 100 investing podcast on iTunes, watch on YouTube, and read* Financial Freedom With Real Estate Investing.

JOHN ASSARAF
Are You Interested or Are You Committed?

John Assaraf is a two-time New York Times *bestselling author and mindset/performance expert. As an entrepreneur, John has built five multimillion-dollar companies and has been featured in eight movies, including* Quest for Success *with Richard Branson and the Dalai Lama and blockbuster hit* The Secret. *Today, John is the founder and CEO of MyNeuroGym.com, a company dedicated to using the most advanced technologies and evidence-based brain training methods to help individuals unleash their fullest potential and maximize their results.*

Early Years Growing Up in Montreal

I was born in Tel Aviv and lived there until I was five. In 1966, my parents were tired of raising their children in war-torn Israel and moved my brother, sister, and I to Montreal, Canada, a logical choice because my parents spoke French. My father was born in Morocco.

From ages 12 to 16, I was involved in a small street gang doing breaking and entering, selling drugs, and fighting against rival gangs in the neighborhood for power. I was getting into a lot of trouble in school, the law, my parents, teachers, and other families.

At the time, I played a lot of sports, and I got a job at the local community center. They gave me access to the exclusive men's health club. Every night after work, I would shower and go into the men's sauna. That's where I would hear these extremely affluent individuals talk about success and money, what was happening in the economy, their families, and travel. These were lifestyles I had only seen on TV. It shocked me. Just like me, they were immigrants. A lot of them didn't go to college. Many left high school because they had to work. Something sparked in me. I wanted to have a life like theirs. Maybe one day, I could feel great about myself.

A Troubled Teen Meets His First Mentor

I was 18 years old, and my brother was 27 living in Toronto, Canada. I was getting into trouble, and my parents and I knew I was one wrong decision away from jail. I'd already been in detention centers. So, 350 miles away from where I lived in Montreal, my brother arranged a lunch meeting with a man named Alan Brown and told me to take the train. I didn't have a car.

We met this man for lunch, and he started asking me questions about my life, deep questions nobody had ever asked me. Why was I doing the things I was doing? Why did I want to get out of school? Why did I think I was only worth 65 cents an hour? Then he gave me this 1982 goal setting guide.

It asked: What age do you want to retire? What? I still aspired to get a job! I put down 45. How much net worth do you want to have? I had to ask what that was, then I put $3 million, but it could've been $3 billion. What kind of house do you want to live in? What kind of car do you want to drive? How much money do you want to give to charity? What kind of lifestyle do you want? What kind of clothes do you want to wear?

Are You Interested or Are You Committed?

I gave Mr. Brown the papers, and he said, "Good, now you're dreaming. I have another question. Your answer will show us whether you will achieve this or whether you won't. Are you interested in achieving these goals... or are you committed?"

"What's the difference?" I asked.

He said, "Son, if you're interested, you'll do what's easy and convenient. If you're interested, you'll come up with stories and excuses for why you can't. You'll not do what it takes, and you won't develop the discipline, habits, mindset, or skill set required to achieve those goals. All those goals are achievable. I have achieved each of those immensely. If you find that rather than interested, you are committed, you will let go of your stories, excuses, beliefs, habits, and all of the reasons you are saying to yourself you can't."

I remember getting chills. "Well, Mr. Brown, I'm committed." And I had no idea what that meant.

He replied, "Great. In that case, I'll be your mentor." He shook my hand. "The first thing I want you to do is to move from Montreal to Toronto."

I launched into, "I don't have any money. I don't have a car. I don't have a job. What do you mean move to Toronto?"

Mr. Brown said, "See how fast you're going back to your excuses? Are you interested? Or are you committed?"

Then he asked me to enroll in real estate school. I HATED school. I didn't do well in school. I flunked out of math. I flunked out of English. I was voted most likely to fail in life by my basketball squadron. Mr. Brown pointed out that this was my story.

You Must Decide

It was $500 to sign up for real estate school back then. He told me, "First, you make the decision. Then you figure out how to do it. Then, you become the person capable of doing it." Three weeks later, I moved to Toronto, moved in with my brother, and enrolled in real estate school. I passed the real estate test without cheating, and then I went to work in one of Mr. Brown's offices.

Alan Brown really had nothing to gain. His mentorship was out of total pay it forward compassion, love, and desire to help another human being.

That was the beginning of shifting my mindset. I began to become aware of the story I was creating of my life. Many of my beliefs about myself were disempowering me, but I hadn't understood that.

Taking Time Between Building Five Multimillion-Dollar Companies

I've taken three years off twice in my life.

The first was in 1997. I bought and became the sub-franchisor for RE/MAX in Indiana, and I built that company as the CEO for over 10 years. I wasn't the smartest kid on the team, but I learned what the people that preceded me did, implemented what worked, and tweaked what needed improvement. I then hired somebody to run it for me. I took three years off to enjoy my second son when he was born.

I took another two and a half years off, and in 1997, I was part of the senior team that took bamboo.com (an internet company that did virtual tours of homes, cars, hotels, and even the Mars Rover 360) public on the NASDAQ. We built that company to two and a half billion dollar value on the stock exchange.

I started another business with a dear friend that did extremely well. Then it failed miserably after some business partnership challenges. I made some mistakes. I didn't adjust to the circumstances. We closed it. I was in the depths of despair over the loss of millions of dollars of my money and investor's money, 72 employees, and my good reputation.

How to Turn Any Failure Into Fuel for Future Success

I was drinking way too much alcohol. I haven't had alcohol in 10 years now as a result of how much I was drinking during this challenging time. I could drink from 6:00 p.m. until 11:00 p.m. and then go back to work at 6:00 a.m., which really was not healthy.

After that, I was able to go deep within and create transparent, radical honesty with myself. I was able to inspect what I did and didn't do well, what I hid from, what I was embarrassed of, and what I was ashamed of. I dug deep with the help of some really good mentors and a psychologist. I took all of the lessons and dove headfirst into the field I am in today: the neuroscience and neuropsychology of beliefs, self-image, and fears.

When I came back out, my failure gave me an appreciation of the difficulties of startups and what entrepreneurs face. There are positives to failure that make us a better person. How do I turn my failure, limiting beliefs, and low self-image into my fuel for future success? I learned the skills to reframe things so that they empower versus disempower me. There are psychological techniques to do that.

When you understand how the brain works, you can use it to lift you up instead of put you down. That's the power of the human condition. We can take any condition and flip it so that it's constructive instead of destructive. Then these conditions become the building blocks of our success instead of the reasons we continue to fail.

I built a mega-successful company out of my pain and my successes. It's been magical. Now, I'm the healthiest I've been in my adult life at 58 years old.

How to Respond Instead of React

Fundamentally, I have a brain. It's an organism. I'm not my brain. The question is, how does my brain work? First of all, we are biologically, neurologically wired for survival and the avoidance of pain above all else.

If there is a painful experience that has led us to believe something will be painful, emotionally or physically, then our brain's millions of years old, programmed reaction will move us away from that as a protective mechanism.

When a trigger inspires an automatic reaction, there's a place between the stimuli. In that space is our ability to respond instead of automatically react. Without training, we're going to react based on the highest level of our skill. With training, we can learn to be aware of disempowering emotions and respond instead.

The Power of Your Mind and Thoughts

Let's say I failed and lost money. My family had to move homes because we went bankrupt. I made such a stupid decision, and people laughed at me. How do you shift and use that as your fuel for success?

You could say to yourself, "Because of that, I'm not good enough, not smart enough, not worthy."

Or instead, you could say, "I'm going to rise and use the pain and suffering that my family and I have experienced as my fuel to succeed. Because of that, I'm smarter, more worthy, more knowledgeable, more skilled. What can I do now to build upon that?"

When we shift the frame in our mind, we also shift our neurochemistry. In fear, we activate stress hormones: norepinephrine, cortisol, and adrenaline. We go into fight, flight, freeze, or faint (the four F's). This occurs in the Frankenstein part of the brain, the self-critical part that tells you why you can't or shouldn't.

But the second we ask ourselves, "How do I turn this into my fuel for success?" we activate the left prefrontal cortex, the genius part of our brain that can figure out how to achieve the goal. I prefer to activate what I call Einstein instead of Frankenstein by asking, how can I, why must I, what will I do? Now I have activated dopamine, serotonin, and, if I shared with other people, oxytocin. These neurochemicals start the motivational process, activate the motor cortex, and cause us to take action instead of falling back into the reasons we can't.

Our choices and awareness directly affect our neurochemistry.

Thoughts on *The Secret*

In the movie *The Secret*, I shared a story. I had goals, strategies, timelines, and vision boards that I looked at every day. I would visualize and emotionalize each so I could actualize what I wanted—the old Napoleon Hill stuff. Crazy enough, I ended up living in an amazing home that I'd cut out of a magazine. HOW DID THIS HAPPEN? When I cut out the picture, I didn't know where the house was, let alone how much it was.

In 2000, after we took bamboo.com public and I retired for a few years, I hired quantum physicists, quantum mechanics, anybody that I thought might shed some light on how this was possible.

I started to envelop myself in the neuroscience and neurochemistry and learned about the law of resonance. Let's throw away the airy-fairy, metaphysical understanding of the law of attraction that most people are talking about, the "think, believe, and you'll achieve." That's bull. It's "think, believe, feel, and TAKE ACTION until you achieve."

When you get your head, gut, and heart in alignment with the right strategies and tactics, then your brain, this electromagnetic switching station, tunes into your desired results. You can deliberately tune your brain to the frequency of the physical, emotional, mental, financial, spiritual, and relationship goals that you have. That is the law of attraction as I know it, the law of harmony and resonance.

How to Marry the Inner Game and the Outer Game

There's no human being that doesn't feel like maybe they're not good enough. Anybody who tells you they don't is lying, or they're not playing a big enough game. In my book Innercise, I remove that veil of ignorance. I want people to realize: There's nothing wrong with them. It's totally okay to feel insecure when you're going after a goal that you don't know how to achieve. This is caused by neurochemicals. Neurochemicals cause me to either take action or not. What if I could understand the process better? What if I then become skilled at that process so that I could get it right?

I learned many years ago, amateurs' practice until they get it right, and pros practice until they can't get it wrong. My company NeuroGym supports people in that practice. When you marry the inner game with the outer game, that's when you can start to achieve predictable transformations and results.

Achieving Your Vision

Do we know how to get in shape and stay in shape? Make more money? Build a business? Write a book? Be in a great relationship? YES! For anything that anybody wants to achieve, we have all of the how you need for a lifetime. Your problem is not how.

Ask yourself, "Am I prepared to do the work?" I want Olympic level results, which means I must match my thoughts, emotions, behaviors, and habits to my vision and goals.

The question is, what's holding you back? Whatever it is, limiting beliefs, low self-worth, fears, we know how to fix that. The key is: Are you willing to do the work necessary to eliminate the obstacles, so you achieve the dream? If you're not willing to do the work, stop complaining and stop having these big goals and dreams.

To get John's bestselling book Innercise, go to www.ignitemybrain.com

Learn more about John's company, NeuroGym, at www.myneurogym.com

Follow John Assaraf on all social media channels.

Facebook: https://www.Facebook.com/JohnAssarafPage

Instagram: https://www.instagram.com/johnassaraf/

Twitter: https://twitter.com/johnassaraf

YouTube: https://www.youtube.com/user/JohnAssaraf

RICH DANBY
Mentors Helped Get Me Where I Needed to Be

Rich Danby is an entrepreneur, real estate investor of over 20 years, a private money lender, and former president of the Ottawa Real Estate Investors Organization (OREIO). He has a television background as a producer/director and is a very talented speaker.

My Three Brads

There were three prominent people in my life, and their names were all Brad. The first is my brother Brad who is two years older than me. Growing up, he looked out for me, loved me, and helped me navigate a challenging childhood. He was and still is my hero.

The second Brad is my best friend. We met at school, coincidentally the same day I moved out of my parents' house at age 16. We were inseparable. After high school, he moved to Ottawa to go to university. I came to visit and loved the city. Five months later, I decided to move to Ottawa, and I've been here ever since. We still hang out regularly.

The third Brad was a complete stranger. I had a very difficult relationship with my parents, especially my dad. Brad knew my friend's parents through his church and found out my story. At my friend's house one day, Brad said, "If you're ever facing the streets, my wife passed away a few years ago and my kids moved out, so I have an extra room if you need it."

A month later, I moved in. Brad was a Phys Ed teacher. He quickly realized I had very few clothes. He went to his closet and started offering me shirts, including his 1989 Detroit Pistons NBA Championship t-shirt. By the time he offered me a third shirt, I thought I had better stop saying yes, because I was afraid there was going to be a catch. I was always waiting to find out what the catch was, but it never came.

That first night we went out to eat. Brad told me there were no rules, other than getting home at a decent hour and staying in school. He told me as long as I was doing the right things, he wouldn't need to step in. My first thought was, "No rules? He's making a big mistake trusting me. I'm going to screw this up." Thankfully, that never happened. Brad's trust in me opened up the door to helping me grow, achieve, and believe in myself.

He taught me how to drive and helped me get my driver's license. He was a great mentor who led by example, and that changed everything for me. He showed me unconditional love and gave me the confidence to step into my potential. We all have the ability to be that person for someone else. The impact that a complete stranger had on my life turned everything around.

Becoming a Dad

Growing up, I remember feeling sorry for myself, wishing I could have the relationship with my dad that some of my friends had with their fathers. My dad made my childhood painful in many ways.

Today, I realize all that pain served a purpose and I'm grateful for it. Those experiences taught me to appreciate my children and love them in a way I wasn't loved as a kid. I now have the relationship I always wanted; the only difference is I'm the dad. When I talk to my kids, I make sure that I talk with them, not at them, that they know they matter, and that I care about them. Being a father is a privilege. I am very blessed to have four children to love and be loved by.

Ambition Came Early

I always felt like I had to prove myself and prove to my father that I was good enough. One of the earliest jobs I had was selling flowers door to door at age 16. That was my first job, after I moved out. I would walk up to the door, knock, and say, "Hi, my name is Rich. I'm from the Student Employment Program. Would you like to buy some flowers and support us? We also give to underprivileged children."

It was $3 for two flowers. Every time they pulled out a $5 bill, I would say, "For just one more dollar, you can get two more, if you like?" That job made me realize I was awesome at sales. The owner and other employees couldn't figure out how I had sold so many flowers so quickly. They would send me out with 50 in a big bucket, and I'd be done in an hour and asking for more. By the end of the day, I often put over $100 cash in my pocket. I became pretty good at making money at an early age.

As I got older, my ambition started to grow. I got a job selling cars at a car dealership. I remember my brother writing me a letter saying, "Congratulations, I'm so proud of you. You've got the world by the balls." And I remember thinking, *I do. I made it. I have a career.* I was 19 years old and so proud of how far I had come. I was completely content having a car, an apartment to live in, and being able to cover all my basic needs.

That was true until I had kids. Once I became a father, I decided how I was living wasn't good enough. That's when I kicked it into high gear and entered television broadcasting.

You're On Air

I had been selling cars, bartending, and DJing, but broadcasting seemed exciting. It sounded perfect for me. For two years I worked for a news station. That was a lot of fun because I got to see everything in Ottawa. I went everywhere. I lived by the second hand on my watch, constantly moving to get as much news as possible on the air. I was being queued up to become the next sports anchor for the news station, and at the time, that was my big dream! I was working towards that goal when I was offered a job as a producer/director at another TV station. The job paid $10,000 more, and I now had a young family to support, so I decided to let my dream go and went behind the scenes.

At that time in my life, my dreams were for sale. If I could go back in time, I wouldn't have given up so easily on the dream. I had an awesome 15-year career surrounded by incredible people so I don't regret any of it, but the lesson I learned is to follow your dreams, not the money.

Real Estate Luck, then Mastery!

In my early 20s, a family member offered to loan us a down payment to buy our first home. A year later, we were randomly approached and asked if we would consider selling. We did a quick renovation and sold the property, making a $66,000 profit. That was a big wake up call. I saw the power of real estate firsthand, and I've been investing ever since.

I took the profits from that property, reinvested them into a three-unit building, renovated, refinanced, and within a few years had three properties. It was a great start to what would eventually become my new career.

Shortly after we got married, my wife Christina became pregnant with our son. At the time, a lot of my TV friends were getting laid off as the world started to shift from TV to the internet. I knew my days at my current job were numbered.

I needed to do something. The only thing I knew that had really worked for us was real estate, but our success was more luck than it was strategy. I decided it was time to turn to Google and start searching "how to invest in real estate," which led me to a local real estate club. A few months later, I attended my first meeting, and that one decision altered the course of my life forever. That was my first big step on a path that eventually led to mastery!

Coach, Speaker, Expert

I never intended to be a coach. I really enjoyed being a professional speaker traveling across Canada, inspiring people, and teaching them how to create wealth through real estate. As a result, people started asking if I would coach them. I wasn't planning to build a coaching business, but gradually, as I got call after call, I started raising the price in an effort to discourage people from hiring me because I was busy doing real estate deals. In the end, I really love helping people, and my private coaching practice continues to grow.

I love talking to seasoned investors, but the group I love talking to most are people who are being introduced to real estate investing concepts for the first time. So many people think investing is out of reach for them because they're not smart enough, or don't have the time, or money. They don't realize those are not real obstacles. The real obstacle is the real estate of your mind. As a coach, at the beginning, that's the primary thing we focus on.

As I became increasingly known as a real estate expert, I attracted a lot of investors who wanted to participate in my deals. I had more money than deals, so unfortunately, many potential investors would be forced to go off and find another way to invest. I decided to find a way I could still help those people, so I became a licensed mortgage agent, specializing in private lending. I'm essentially a connector between people who have money and people who want money. As a private lender, investors can secure their loans against first or second mortgages, and often there are opportunities to participate in the equity. I use my experience and expertise to help analyze deals and protect investors from making bad decisions.

There's massive opportunity everywhere. You just have to recognize they're opportunities.

Morning Routine

I love 5:00 a.m. because nobody else wants to wake up that early. It's quiet, peaceful, and very productive. I try to maintain the same activities in the same order until, eventually, they become a habit. Exercise, journaling, and Bible study. Exercising often leads to creative ideas. Journaling allows me to log thoughts, aspirations, and practice daily gratitude. It's also great for releasing myself of any guilt, shame, or negative thoughts. It could just be something as simple as not waking up when I planned or overeating unhealthy food.

It takes time to develop good habits, so you have to experiment until you discover what routines work best for you. It's like we're downloading new software. We just have to be consistent until the new software becomes our new normal.

People often give up because they screwed up. It's not about being perfect, it's about progress. Success is a dial, not a switch. It takes time. There will be disruptions to our routines. Trying to be perfect every day is not realistic. I've learned not to measure my success in days, but instead to measure in weeks, months, and years. Journaling allows me to look back and see how far I've come. I am blessed and grateful.

Reach out to Rich Danby, a real estate investor, private money lender, and professional speaker.

www.richottawainvestments.com, www.richdanby.com, www. mastersofrealestate.com

FB: https://www.facebook.com/rich.danby.5/

Twitter: https://twitter.com/richottawa

rich@richdanby.com

JESSICA WATERS
It's Not About Your Stuff

Jessica Waters is a master-level professional organizer, guiding clients through the murky waters of their internal and external chaos and disorder, vanquishing it for good. Ever the adventurer, she is a passionate volunteer disaster relief worker with the American Red Cross.

Inside Out

My dad, a Harvard-educated and irresistibly charming man always had a desk littered with scraps of paper, used tissues, unfinished snacks, and pens that no longer worked. Piles of paper covered the surface and books and file boxes obscured the floor, making it almost impossible to navigate the room. He could never find anything he needed, a personality quirk which contributed to the stress and agitation in our family growing up.

My father's inattention to the world around him infected his closest relationships—by the time I graduated from high school, he had married and divorced three times, we had moved 11 times, and I lived with the ever-present sense of being lost and alone, even with two "adults" in the house.

In stark contrast to my dad's retreat into unconscious distraction, my stepmother ruled our family in a way that squeezed the heart and soul from wherever we lived. Growing up in an environment suffused with tension and conflict affected decisions and relationships in all areas of my life for years to come.

As a teenager, I was not allowed to close my bedroom door. Personal space and privacy were not an option, and feeling heard, seen, and respected was not part of the family culture. With no outlet for individual expression, the atmosphere was stifling, heartbreaking, and lonely. As kids, we were simultaneously neglected and micro-managed, and it never felt emotionally safe to explore who we were or what we wanted out of life.

There's No Place Like Home

I spent many years trying to outrun the heartbreak and trauma of my childhood. Although I was determined to live differently, my young adult life was spent distracting myself from the pain as best I could, moving... seeking... always yearning for the elusive place called home. While I was busy careening through life, I could never have imagined how later on, by working intimately with people grappling with their clutter, I would open my heart to compassion for myself and my family. I had observed early on from my dad's behavior how one's surroundings can be a window into the internal mindscape, and without realizing it at the time, I was on the path to putting this insight into practice as a professional organizer.

Relocating frequently had taught me to get good at examining why I was holding onto things and then letting them go if they no longer suited my goals. I love passing on this hard-won ability to those confronting their own inner turmoil. Often as we work together, people begin to look years younger as they work through buried memories, feelings, heartache, regret, remorse, and guilt in their piles of stuff. It has been both humbling and gratifying to stand witness for others on their journey to enlightenment.

Magic Fairy Dust and How It All Began

In my 20s, I embarked on a cross-country adventure, staying with friends along the way. At some point during each visit, I would open a cabinet or closet door and ask if I could organize that space. Later in life, those same friends would thank me for how much more functional their house felt after I sprinkled my magic fairy dust, and over a decade later, when I heard about a woman who called herself a "professional organizer" on Oprah, I knew I had found my life's work: helping people learn how to let go of the things in their surroundings that hold them back, so they can come to a place of forgiveness for themselves and others. I was born for this.

Giving Yourself the Space to Make Room

Working side by side for over twenty years with those impacted by disarray, I have witnessed how confronting your clutter with compassion can be an effective way to uncover who you are and what you want. Decluttering is not a rational process, it's primarily an emotional one, and once you allow that, forgiveness and empathy can prevail, affecting a deep and lasting change.

Because letting go is intensely personal, anyone who is helping you must be able to be present without being invasive. That way, you feel supported, not judged or pressured, and have the space to examine what arises in safety. People often tell me that decluttering with someone close can feel too confrontational, as the loved one may be more focused on the outcome rather than the journey and too impatient to step back and allow you your process.

Streamlining your possessions and organizing your life must be in line with the way both you and the others in your home interact with your space. If you rigidly impose a protocol that you read in a book or saw on YouTube, chances are you and your family won't keep it up. Whichever way you choose, it must include taking everyone's needs into consideration, which means: expect to compromise. Letting go of control is a critical part of the process to healing.

Disrupt the Status Quo

The current trend towards "extreme decluttering" is on the rise—touching every single item in your space and deciding if you love it transforms your life in unimaginable ways—although the process is not without its challenges and disruption. One way to counteract inertia and backsliding and have an easier time getting through the intensely emotional moments is by focusing on making decisions about what you want to keep rather than what you want to get rid of and welcoming the upheaval as the start of a new chapter!

It's Not About Your Stuff

Clutter is never about stuff, it's about the backlog of feelings, beliefs, strategies, and (of course) possessions that hold you back, paradoxically keeping you from having what you want. It can manifest in many forms: financial challenges, time clutter (procrastination or over-commitment), a chaotic physical environment, or even relationship clutter (loyalty to energy vampires and guilt-mongers stealing a part of you every time you connect).

Things you don't love take up precious real estate both physically and emotionally, silently radiating guilt and shame. Simply put: Clutter is anything that drains rather than energizes you. Use that as your gold standard whenever you are called to let go.

Once you release the emotional clutter you have projected in an item, detaching from the item itself is easy! As an example, a well-known speaker in Los Angeles had a shelf full of high-ticket conference CD sets that she had received from fellow presenters over the years. When we approached the shelf, she instinctively gasped, "I feel so overwhelmed!" As she held each box and asked herself: "Does this give me energy or does it take energy away?", in a matter of minutes, she was able to whittle down the collection to only what was valuable to her and never looked back.

Embrace the Chaos

A phone coaching client told me that after he wrote letters of forgiveness to his ex-wife and (deceased) father, he was able to achieve his goal of completely decluttering and decorating a spare room into a home office in a couple of days.

Another solopreneur told of allowing herself to let go and wail out her grief and how that catharsis cleared the way for an office organizing blitz she had been avoiding for years. It feels like magic, but gently facing our demons is the most important work we can do as human beings.

Be Open to the Wild Unknown

Because moving, downsizing, changing relationship status, or clearing out the belongings of a deceased loved one are huge and often painful life transitions, they also provide an incredible opportunity to wade into the emotional abyss and completely redesign the trajectory of your life.

You never know how being intentional can change your life. Working with a successful marketing entrepreneur who yearned to find a partner in love, I suggested she clear a space in her closet and leave a nightstand empty for "him." Sure enough, after many years of doing life solo, within a couple of months she reconnected with a high school sweetheart and they are still happily married, over 15 years later!

Getting organized isn't about redistributing your possessions so they fit better; it's about coming to terms with any emotional or circumstantial issues you have projected on your stuff. Until you stop rearranging your junk, stop buying the latest tidying-up book or nifty new organizing container, and start decluttering your thought process, the change you say you want simply cannot happen. Embrace the chaos! Accept that discomfort and vulnerability are an integral part of that process and you may uncover courage you didn't know you had.

Jessica Waters offers a transformative 2-3 week intensive decluttering service at your home or online, as well as webinars and declutter coaching via video chat.

Reach her at: www.facebook.com/inperfectorder

508-237-7994 | Jessica@inperfectorder.com

LOUIS MELO

The Power of a Work Ethic, Passing on Years of Experience to Others

Louis Melo is the founder and CEO of Atlantis Properties, which specializes in property management services for single-family homes, townhomes, duplexes, apartments, and small commercial properties in Santa Clara, Santa Cruz, San Mateo, and Monterey counties in California. He is also a real estate broker, investor, and syndicator.

The Power of a Work Ethic

In 1974, our family immigrated to the United States from the Azores Islands, Portugal. We settled in the San Jose area in California, where my grandparents, aunts, and uncles lived. I've lived here most of my life. My parents worked very hard, and they offered us the opportunity to live the American dream. I am very thankful for the sacrifice they made for the entire family. At age seven, I arrived in America with no clue about the opportunities our great country had to offer. Well, the road trip started, and I was on the way to find out what hard work, honesty, integrity, and persistence could achieve.

During my senior year in high school, I worked part-time in a real estate office. I loved everything about real estate at an early age. In my early 20s, I worked in property management and in hotels. Working in real estate at that age sparked my interest in property management. I interacted with the property owners and tenants and was able to see the entire cycle of managing properties.

I got my real estate license when I was 19 years old and sold for a few years. I also bought my first property at 19 with the help of my parents financing it. From there on out, I loved real estate even more. And throughout the years, I found myself coming back to property management. I consider it a rewarding and challenging business.

Exploring Horizontal Career Opportunities

At age 23, I decided to pack my bags and move to Hawaii. I got my Hawaii real estate license, worked for a real estate developer in their commercial management division, and learned all about commercial real estate. Hawaii was a much slower pace than the Bay Area, but I learned to adapt quickly. I am grateful for the experience of living there and the friendships I developed, some of which I still have today.

I came back to California at the age of 25 to work in finance at the corporate headquarters of an established staffing organization. Shortly thereafter, I moved to customer service at a high-tech company.

At this point in life, I knew I did not want to work for anyone else. While working my full-time job, I started my property management company Atlantis Properties on the side, part-time, operating out of my condo. I worked on building my business anytime I could pick up properties, meet with clients, or show properties. I used to do the accounting late-night at my kitchen table.

After a few years, I went full-time, and the company took off. I focused on networking with local property management groups, investment clubs, and building relationships, and the company grew quickly. It's now 20 years later, and the company is doing very well.

Understanding the Property Management Business

In the property management world, you've got to be very organized, stay focused, and be tough but professional. There are a lot of things to keep track of in our business, and there's a lot of oversight by government agencies that impact our business.

In property management, you have to be compassionate but at the same time be crystal clear that you are running a business. You cannot get emotionally involved, and you cannot let any conflicts that come up get to you personally, otherwise, you'll never be able to sleep at night. It's important to remain focused and resolve problems quickly.

Over the years, I've had my challenges, but I've learned a lot and have put procedures in place that help protect my business and clients. We rely on systems. Some we've created ourselves, and of course, there are guidelines we must follow from the various agencies that have oversight in our industry. We use many standardized forms provided by real estate associations. It's so important to be educated and stay current on the laws and keep our clients informed of the latest legislation that impacts their real estate portfolio.

When you buy a rental property, you will have a long-term relationship with your property manager versus the short relationship you have with the real estate agent who sells you the property. Choosing the right property manager can make or break you in regard to the successful management of those properties.

We have grown even more quickly than I expected. We don't really do any advertising now, and we work almost entirely on referrals. Every day, I would say, we get at least one referral or more, most of which are from an existing client or a real estate associate. It doesn't happen overnight, but it's pretty exciting that it is this way now.

With my team, I like to hire based primarily on personality and work ethic. I can teach a team member everything they need to know about the company and the industry. My first priority is to make sure that they're going to blend in and work well with my team.

Real Estate Investing and Syndication

I am now investing in California, Florida, and Tennessee and am looking at other states where it makes sense. I also own in and am looking to invest in other properties in Portugal. I think it's always a good time to buy because you can always find something worth buying. If the cash flow numbers work, then why not buy it? I buy properties for myself, especially for the long-term. Many of my clients own properties in Silicon Valley, and many have owned them for many years. I see the wealth they have built in real estate. I believe real estate is the best long-term investment there is for cash flow, appreciation, and tax benefits.

Passing on My Years of Experience

I want to share all my years of experience in property management and put them into a book, and share some of the crazy stories and difficult situations that I've gone through in the business. There are honestly more than I can tell, but hopefully, it will help others when they build their own companies in this industry. I hope I can pass on the motivation and work ethic to others who want to start their own business.

In business, you have to work hard and smart because success does not come without challenges and obstacles. You've got to just stay focused and disciplined and never give up. It will work out, and before you know it, you'll look back and won't even realize what you've done over time.

Being around like-minded people as well as going to events and organizations like The Real Estate Guys keeps me motivated and focused. Every day, I wake up excited about real estate and what challenges lie ahead.

The main thing is to stay focused. I lost focus in my 20s and got sidetracked and probably could have built my company much faster. But I did still learn a lot from the experiences. There have been many challenges, and sometimes you get too focused on it rather than saying, "Hey, this will all be over with, things will get better." As you go through the years in the business, those things that seem to be a challenge are no longer a challenge, and you find yourself saying, "why did I worry about that?"

People ask me all the time if I'm going to retire and go live in my house in Portugal. The word "retire" does not mean the same thing to me as others. I enjoy what I do, and it's not really work for me. I could do this 24 hours a day and still be excited. I think that's a necessary part of the focus. If you do what you love, the success will come.

Louis Melo is the founder and CEO of Atlantis Properties. He is also a real estate broker, an investor, and a syndicator with 20+ years experience. Contact Louis directly at (408) 515-3746.

Email: louis@atlantisproperties.net

DR. KARL JAWHARI
Physical Health, Wealth, Success!

Dr. Karl Jawhari is the founder of Core Integrative Health and a chiropractic doctor for celebrities, athletes, and high profile individuals. A seasoned entrepreneur, Karl has coached over 450 other doctors on how to run an efficient office and is a successful real estate investor.

Watching and Learning

I learned my work ethic from my dad. He drove a truck throughout Venezuela selling shoes and would be gone for three or four days at a time, sometimes weeks. When I asked him how his trip went, he would always say, "It's great. This is what we have to do to be able to live." Having three very driven older brothers further impacted my understanding of work. Seeing this taught me that you have to go out and work.

At the age of 10, my parents took me back to their home country, Lebanon. I attended an American school where I learned the basics of the English language. As I grew, so did the country's civil war. My father felt it would be safer for me to leave Lebanon and go to the US at the age of 17.

It was a shocking move. I didn't know what to expect. I will say, knowing nothing will be handed to you makes you tougher. In the US, I decided to continue straight into college. I got my bachelor's degree at the University of South Florida and continued my doctorate in chiropractic at Life University in Marietta, GA.

From Pain to Purpose

At one point, I thought I was going to become a dentist. But fate had a different path for me. I was a martial arts instructor through college until I injured myself during a tournament. The pain in my back wasn't going away. I tried the usual measures of pain pills and steroid shots, but neither worked.

Next, I went to a chiropractor, and he helped me tremendously. My pain was gone, and I fell in love with the profession. I decided I was going to be a chiropractor. My wife and I call it *from pain to purpose*. That was my new purpose. I knew that was how I wanted to help people.

A New Focus

Once I finished chiropractic school, I opened my first practice in Denton, Texas. I was told once you open the doors, people will come. But no one showed up. Then something happened that completely changed my mind.

In June of 2004, sitting at my desk, I realized there was not enough money in the bank account to cover rent. Anger and fear just came over me with tears flowing, I questioned my emotions. I realized I was angry at myself because I wasn't spending enough time with my son and wife. I was angry because I realized I was taught to become a very good doctor, but not a good business person. I wore only one hat, the technician hat. I decided to read books to find some answers, so I looked outside my industry to those who were doing the best in business.

A New Outlook, 80/20

I wanted to know how the big companies were growing and how they became successful. I returned to my books by Tony Robbins, Jim Rohn, and Brian Tracy. There was a common denominator between the definition of self-development these men held. It really hit home for me when Tony Robbins stated that 80% of success is mental and 20% is biomechanics.

This meant I did not have to know everything or understand everything before I did it. I just needed the right mindset. So I did a deep dive into mindset. With a new set of eyes, I realized I went to school to become a good technician. My challenge was to teach my mind how to think for the rest of my life to take me to the next level.

Being *in the business* and working *on the business* are two different things. Anyone can build a business, but if it's dependent on you showing up to work, then it's not a business. That's a high paying job.

Like Grant Cardone says, "How do you create attention? That's marketing." I started studying the top marketers from Joe Polish to Dan Kennedy. Some people call it "sales." Instead, they should think about it as communication. How do we properly communicate with someone about our services, goals, and purposes? I had to learn how to do that. You need to be able to communicate with people to sell your services and sell yourself. Selling has had a bad rep but when you look at it from the perspective that if I don't sell the patient on why he needs the service, he might end up not doing anything or doing the wrong thing at which point you have robbed him from living at his full potential physically and mentally.

I'm in This Profession for a Reason

Decades later, people have often asked me how I stay motivated, and the answer is I have connected to my *why*. When I first started this journey, my whys were my kids, my family, and spending more time with them. I accomplished that. Then I had to think about my patients.

These people have gone from doctor to doctor, and no one has been able to help them. Some of them have had corrective surgery, and they're still in pain. I needed to step up and be a hero to all of my patients.

I altered my thinking to become that hero. I vowed to treat my patients as if they were my own family members. I made this my personal mantra, and to this day, it is a mantra we follow in the office. My why today is to expand into other parts of the world to help and protect more people.

Global Mission

I looked outside my industry to see how other people grew their empires. Essentially, it's about reaching the masses and being able to serve them. I've had the pleasure of taking care of Grant Cardone for multiple years. Being around him and being a student of his philosophy has helped me mentally get to that next level and thing BIG.

Five years ago, I decided what we were doing was not enough. People were coming to us for chiropractic, but if they needed a steroid shot as well, they had to find another doctor. I didn't necessarily agree with traditional medicine like the steroid shot, but I could advocate for a natural alternative. We had to be more comprehensive and hire the medical staff to support that. People love it. We see patients in-house and take care of all needs in one place by using different technologies like regenerative therapy, spinal decompression, laser therapy, and natural nerve treatments with FDA-approved machinery.

Fundamentals to Success

My dad drilled into my head: Don't lie, don't steal, treat people the way you want to be treated, and learn how to properly communicate. My secret sauce is persuasion through ethical communication, which has helped me scale my business to where we are. So, naturally, to work in our organization, you are required to train and drill in communication every day. You should have full confidence in your product or service and therefore have no need to pressure any client into a sale. That will set you apart!

I always want to surround myself with high thinkers. I don't want to be the smartest guy in the room. I want to learn from other people. Plugging into Grant Cardone and studying his methods of sales and communication has been tremendously helpful for me. I've also joined other groups like Joe Polish's 25K group and Kyle Wilson's Inner Circle Mastermind and have met some interesting people and celebrities. It's really important to be surrounded by people that you can look up to.

One of the first lessons I learned was from Jim Rohn and Tony Robbins: write your goals. I write my goals every single day, no matter how I feel. I might skip one morning if I'm traveling, but it's a must. This keeps me focused on what I'm trying to achieve. Grant Cardone has taught me, if you write them twice a day, you amplify them. And if you're having issues, you can write them three times a day. I have a few goals that, realistically, are not reachable, or might take me a lifetime to get. And then I have other goals that are more immediate. When you rewrite your goals, you refocus on what's important to you. You're taking control of your mind.

If people are willing to pay the price, get educated, and learn from others that have already succeeded, new opportunities in business, family, and financial success, will open up.

Dr. Karl Jawhari invites anyone interested in his practice to come and visit. He also invites health questions and offers free advice

(972) 239-7444 | Drjawhari@aol.com

JOSH AND EMILY HOUSER
The Power of Partnerships

Founders of Houser Capital Group Josh and Emily Houser have acquired over 2,700 apartment units in the last three years. Josh has been investing in real estate since 2002, in finance since 1999, and is now a residential mortgage broker. Emily has invested since 2014 and is an avid entrepreneur.

Better Together

"Life is an echo. What you send out comes back. What you sow you reap. What you give you get."

– Zig Ziglar

Everything we do has a ripple effect on those around us. Whether by choice or by chance, we participate in partnerships every day.

If you're married, you're in partnership with your spouse.

If you're employed, you're in partnership with your coworkers.

If you're self-employed, you're in partnership with your customers.

We partner with others because we can accomplish more together. This is one of the greatest lessons we have learned in recent years.

Ten years ago, a powerful partnership seemed like a dream. We both had suffered the pain of failed relationships, yet we still desired the chance to succeed. When we met, our connection was immediate. We were an answer to each other's prayers. While those prayers were born out of pain, it's amazing to see how God used our experiences to create a partnership that could enrich and encourage others.

There are limits to what we can do alone, but surrounding ourselves with the right people allows us to grow and accomplish more than we can on our own.

We experienced this again in 2017 as we started expanding our real estate business. Wanting to pivot from small multifamily deals into larger multifamily projects, we recognized our limits. We realized that to scale our business, we needed to scale ourselves. But we didn't know how. We took action and sought to find someone doing exactly what we hoped to do, and thankfully found our mentors Mark and Tamiel Kenney of Think Multifamily. Joining their group changed the trajectory of our business.

Under their mentorship, we learned the importance of relationships in business. Investing is a team sport. Our relationships with mentors, partners, and investors became key to our growth. The incredible thing about getting around individuals who inspire, teach, and motivate you is that it naturally creates an authentic desire to reciprocate and give back. We began looking for ways to add value to the team with our skills and abilities and shifted the focus from ourselves to others. When you work as a team, you can scale and grow much faster and share in the benefits together.

Andrew Carnegie once said, "Teamwork is the fuel that allows common people to attain uncommon results." Over the last three years, thanks to the partnerships we've formed, our portfolio has grown exponentially. We could not have accomplished this on our own. It has been a humbling journey to say the least! Most important are the families we serve, the communities we impact, and the lifelong friendships we've created. We are blessed to count our partners among our closest friends and consider many of them family. In setting out to grow our own business, we found true fulfillment in helping others succeed and grow with us.

Master Your Mindset

We have discovered the true value of becoming lifelong students, striving to improve our skills and mindset. We made the decision together to go all in, investing our time, financial resources, and energy. This commitment has included traveling to events, joining mentorship and mastermind groups, educating ourselves through podcasts and books, as well as getting involved in our local real estate community. At times, we are in awe of the caliber of people we are surrounded by. The key is showing up! We've never once regretted going to an event. There is always something to be learned and new connections to create. There is unlimited value in finding a mastermind group that inspires and helps you achieve your goals faster.

To further our mindset growth, we joined Dr. Shannon Irvine's Epic Success Academy. She teaches about how the human brain, while complex, is also simple. The brain does not know the difference between reality and what you tell it. We all have beliefs that are created from past experiences. While our subconscious brain serves to protect us, the limiting beliefs can become automated and hold us back throughout our lives.

EMILY: I realized the extent to which my subconscious beliefs have played a role in my personal and business journey. When we first started traveling to multifamily events, I felt rather intimidated and out of place. For years, I have disliked being in the spotlight, standing in front of a crowd, or having all eyes on me. Overall, I am a very social individual, but for some reason, certain situations have a way of making me feel uncomfortable. This does not serve me well. I have come to realize that stories created from my past experiences were blocking my ability to be my authentic self and fulfill my purpose and mission in life. My deepest desire is to make a difference in this world, help others, glorify God, and live to my fullest potential. I'm still working through these challenges, but had I not taken the first step out of my comfort zone, no progress would be made. It is amazing to see how my comfort zone has grown over time, adding up to significant growth. Is the fear still there at times? Absolutely. But I have seen huge progress and know it's something I can and will overcome! Over time and with work, it will get easier.

JOSH: When we made the switch from small to large deals, I wrestled with limiting doubts: *I don't have enough experience...What if we can't find the right partners.... What if we fail?* These doubts were based on fears of the unknown. My protective brain craved safety and familiarity. As I worked to identify and address these fears, I intentionally pushed myself out of my comfort zone. I refused to stay in the "safe zone" and play less than full out. I couldn't wait for things to be perfect. If I did, I would never take action. I had to take the risk. A job done is better than a job not started! As I pushed through my fears, I grew. While growth can be painful at times, I believe conquering fear allows you to pursue your unique, God-given purpose.

"There are no limits to what you can accomplish, except the limits that you place on your own thinking."

– Brian Tracy

Pay attention to what you allow yourself to think. Your thoughts create emotions, which create beliefs, which lead to decisions and actions, which become habits. Since habits are what ultimately lead to success, your future is being created by your thoughts!

Be Who You Are Becoming

If you allow yourself to step outside of your comfort zone, amazing things can happen. Investing in yourself will ultimately help you invest in others and have a positive impact on the partnerships in your life. There will be bumps along the way, failures, and disappointments. But don't let failure define you; rather, let it refine you! When you fail, fail forward. We become stronger by learning from past failures. Be intentional and relational. We strengthen and build relationships by investing in them daily.

Looking back, it is humbling to see our transformation. Together, we have been on a journey of self-development, mindset shifts, and strengthening relationships. With hard work and daily habits, our business continues to grow, and we are able to do what we are passionate about while helping others enjoy the benefits of investing. Having an impact on communities makes this business even more rewarding and fulfilling.

The way you show up now will have a huge impact on how people remember you. What you do today will be a reflection of where you'll be three months, six months, or five years from now. Step out in faith and take action, even if you don't feel ready. There is a plan, a purpose, and a mission for your life that only you can fulfill. Step into the person you were always meant to be. One day you will thank yourself for pushing through challenges and never giving up.

Josh and Emily Houser are real estate investors, entrepreneurs, and founders of Houser Capital Group. Learn more about multifamily investing, creating passive cash flow, and financial freedom at housercapitalgroup.com.

Email: josh@housercapitalgroup.com and emily@housercapitalgroup.com

RON WHITE
2x US Memory Champion, Creator of the Afghanistan Memory Wall

Two-time US Memory Champion Ron White is a speaker, author, and trainer. He has been featured on Stan Lee's Superhumans, *National Geographic's* Brain Games, *CBS'* The Morning Show, *and more. Ron is the creator of the Afghanistan Memory Wall, his tribute to fallen soldiers in Afghanistan, where he served in the US Navy.*

Paper Boy of the Year

My first job was a paper route at age 14. While the typical kid would sign up one household for the paper per day, I signed up 8 to 10. It was the first time I felt good at something. If you got eight sign-ups in three months, you won a season pass to Six Flags. In a weekend, I was getting me, my parents, and my sister a season pass. I was *Mid-Cities Daily News'* carrier of the year. It was a fun time, and it taught me lessons that carry me to this day.

At 18, I worked as a telemarketer for a chimney cleaning service. It was brutal. One day, the man who picked up interrupted my script to say, "Ron, we don't want our chimney cleaned. We're trying to sell our house."

Then I said the words that changed my life: "Sir, don't hang up the phone. If you're trying to sell your house, you're going to need a clean chimney." I was only 18, but I knew how to overcome objections.

Laughing, he asked me, "Do you want a job?" He offered to pay me more than I was making, which was a pretty safe bet! I took the offer.

Determination Launches Speaking Career

It was July of 1991. And I was beyond eager to start my new position. At the time, there was a popular infomercial on TV for Kevin Trudeau's Mega Memory. It seemed like magic to me. Now, I had the chance to work with them.

When I started telemarketing for them, I observed their speakers going out to give presentations and sell, and I knew that's what I wanted to do. The company wasn't interested. I was 18, and they didn't have a speaker under 28. Most of them were closer to 40, and all were established in business.

So, I joined Toastmasters and invited my sales manager to go with me. I wanted him to see me speak. Once he did, he said, "Ron, you need to get a tent and do revivals. You can speak!"

I said, "I don't know if I want to do revivals, but maybe...memory training?"

That's when a speaker, who was bringing in a remarkable $30,000 a month, quit the company. There were two choices—cancel all his speeches or get a new speaker. They had no speakers in training, but they had me. Even if I didn't make any money, they wouldn't come out any worse than if they had canceled.

The first year, I was terrible, the worst in the company, by far, according to the numbers. With the generous coaching from the president of the company, it took me a year to achieve the company average. Now, 28 years later, I do much greater than that. I just had to take that time to learn.

Memory Expert, But No Special Ability

People always want to know when I realized I had special memory ability. The truth is, I don't have a special ability. I learned a system which anybody can learn. People will say, "I remember the face, but I don't remember the name." That's because they look at the face but never see the name.

The mind remembers what it sees, so you have to visualize what you want to remember, whether it's a deck of cards, phone number, poem, quote, or speech. The first step is to turn what you want to remember into a picture. The next step is to place that picture somewhere. This step is a technique called the mind palace, which has been around for 2500 years. Put simply, in the mind palace technique, you use your house to memorize things.

The majority of people can say with confidence that they can memorize three words. The magic of the memory palace is that you can use this system to memorize three items, one hundred items, or 7,000 items once you understand how it's done. The trick is to apply the technique to what interests you—a speech, your classmates' names, or knowledge that is going to help you in your job.

Naval Service, US Memory Champion, and World Record

When September 11th happened, I joined the Military as a Navy Reservist at 28 years old.

I served in the United States Navy from 2002-2010. In 2007, I was deployed to Afghanistan. I was an Intelligence Specialist. IS1, Petty Officer 1st class.

I did 51 convoys, but I saw no combat action. There is nothing extraordinary about my service or deployment. It was just a regular deployment like many others. But countless men and women were in extraordinary circumstances. Combat veterans and too many others paid the ultimate sacrifice.

When I got back, I decided I wanted to compete in the US Memory Championships. I hired a coach, United States Navy SEAL TC Cummings. He taught me a lot about mindset and discipline. He had me memorizing cards underwater. He had me memorizing cards in noisy bars. He had me changing my diet, getting up early, and training like a Navy SEAL would train for war so that I would be a well-trained brain athlete for the memory tournament.

I won back to back years, becoming a two-time USA Memory Champion, and set the record for the fastest to memorize a deck of cards in the United States. That record held until 2011.

The Afghanistan Wall

After winning, I wanted to do something more special with my memory, something I was passionate about. As a Veteran of Afghanistan, I decided to create a tribute for everyone who died there, so they would not be forgotten.

2,400+ US Military died in the War in Afghanistan. As a Veteran and an American, this deeply affects me. I've memorized the rank, first name, and last name of each of the fallen. 2,400 names is over 7,000 words, and I memorized each of them using the mind palace. I travel the USA rewriting each name entirely from memory on an expansive traveling wall to honor their memory and service.

When I was memorizing that wall for a year, I lived in solitude. I took a book filled with each soldier's name with me everywhere I went. When I was sick, I was memorizing. When I was tired, I was memorizing.

I'm humbled by all who have come to witness this across the country and at major events like NFL games, NASCAR races, MLB games, Independence Day at the National Mall in Washington

DC, and on Veteran's Day. I have countless stories of how The Afghanistan Memory Wall has made an impact on friends and family of fallen soldiers that shake me to my core.

Every time I set up the wall, I brief my helpers beforehand, because I know what is coming. "I don't know when it will happen today, but it will. Someone is going to walk by this wall and ask what it is. In an instant, their eyes are going to fill with tears, and they will be barely able to contain themselves. Then they will give us a name and ask us if it's on the wall. I will take them to that name, and they will stand in silence with tears running down their face."

When I began the process, I didn't know any of them personally. Now I feel like I know all of them. Not just their names, I feel like I know them. Honoring and giving respect to others has given me purpose and a mission which I would not trade.

My Day Job

Since 1992, I've been a full-time speaker and trainer on the topic of memory. Companies and organizations have me come and speak at their conventions and to their teams.

I make memory entertaining. It is something I love doing. I also have multiple courses on memory, including Black Belt Memory.

I love what I do because it impacts others, adults and children alike! I do not have a special memory, and anyone can learn to do what I have done, whether it's setting the world record for the fastest to memorize a deck of cards, winning and defending the US Memory Championship, or memorizing the names of 2,400 fallen soldiers. That is what I love to teach.

The 2X US Memory Champion and professional speaker Ron White can be found at www.blackbeltmemory.com, YouTube, Facebook, and Instagram.

Email: ron@ronwhitetraining.com | Podcast: www.americasmemory.com

MICHAEL BECKER

How I Went From Bank Teller to Over $700 Million in Assets

Michael Becker is principal at SPI Advisory, LLC overseeing property and asset management, accounting and taxation, renovations, and investor relationships. They have purchased over 10,000 apartment units and own over 700 million in assets. Michael is also co-host of The Old Capital Real Estate Investing Podcast.

I Was Paid to Learn How Money Works

I came from a modest background. My father fixed appliances for a living and my mother was a school secretary. We certainly didn't want for any necessity, but we didn't have many luxuries. My dad had a strong work ethic and instilled that in me.

I was an okay student through high school and ended up at the University of North Texas, where I had a nice, eight-year college career and earned a bachelor's degree. Ultimately, school led me to start my career in banking.

I had retail jobs and mowed lawns in high school and didn't enjoy it, but I always worked and saved money. I would spend a little and save some more. I wanted to learn how to make money into more money. That was what intrigued me about banking. I figured if I could learn how the banks work, I could learn to make more money for myself. I don't have the highest mathematical acumen, but luckily the math you need to do what we do today is very learnable. I really wanted to learn, and I wanted to have more than I had growing up.

I Watched My Clients Get Rich

I was earning a big salary and nice performance bonuses. But then, I noticed my clients were getting rich! I made it a point to interact with my most successful clients. I realized they weren't necessarily smarter than me, but they were taking action while I was content being an employee.

I felt like a working stiff, stuck paying high taxes. In contrast, my clients were making all this monthly cash flow and not paying any tax because they understood the tax law and how it favors real estate investors and business owners. I looked at the daily of my boss and my boss's boss and knew that wasn't the future I wanted. I was in my early 30s. A couple other things happened in my personal life, and I finally decided it was my time to take action.

Jumping Into Real Estate Full-Time

I started buying little single-family homes. I was building my confidence. I bought 16 rental properties, one at a time. In 2013, I bought a large apartment complex with another investor. That same year, I met my business partner. I was about 35 when we bought our first deal. We did four deals together while we kept our day jobs before we decided we were sick of making other people rich. I figured if I failed, I still had enough life left. I could go back and be a banker again. If I didn't take my shot, I would not shake my depression, and I would regret it. It was time to take a chance and work for ourselves. I left the bank in 2014.

Today, we have purchased over 10,000 apartment units. We sold several of those, so we currently own about 700 plus million in real estate and multifamily in Dallas-Fort Worth and Austin. I can't believe how much we've done in a relatively short period of time.

Start Small for Exponential Growth

Once you decide to take action, do everything you can to get an education. Build your integrity and your ability to show you know what you are doing. People have to know, like, trust, and have confidence in you to invest in you.

Your first deal will be the hardest. Going from zero to one is really hard. Going from one to two is exponentially easier. Even if you start small, you can scale really quickly. Start small and make small mistakes first with small dollars. It's not a linear business, it's an exponential business. As you achieve bigger deals, your confidence will grow as well.

Communication and Incremental Improvement

Communication is key with everybody, especially when there are multiple counterparties in a transaction. If it's a negotiation, learn what the other parties want. A good outcome is a deal where they get what they want, and I get what I want. And it's not always monetary. Just understanding that when I get into a new situation gives me confidence. Confidence is earned by going through challenging situations. Today, stressful situations don't bother me as much as they did a few years ago because I've lived through firestorms and got the job done.

After every deal, we do a post mortem. We write down the bad and add to the ever-growing list of stuff to never do again, and we write down the good and add to our ever-growing list of things to look for. Fortunately, now that we've done so many deals, what we add to the bad list is pretty minor. But, at the beginning, these lists held many big learning moments. We've only gotten to where we are through incremental improvements. I think being a good leader is knowing that just because you do something one way doesn't necessarily make it the right way. The only way we will continue to improve is by reflecting and making adjustments.

Saying No

The bigger we get, the more opportunities come our way. It gets to a point where you have to balance what you say yes to and what you have to pass on. The biggest cost in life is opportunity cost. Anything you do is at the expense of something else. We all want to help people, and at the same time, we can't take on every project. If we're busy doing a bunch of small deals, we're not able to take on the big deals. Saying no has gotten easier over time as I've gotten more practice.

I wish I'd had more foresight when I started the business. I didn't know how big we were going to get, so at the beginning, I was giving out my personal contact details including my cell phone number. You get to a point where that's not sustainable. Too many people were contacting me, and listening to their proposals and saying no time and time again was really eating up my time. Now I do not give out my phone number, and I have a firewall up so other people can handle smaller decisions. I try to preserve my mental capacity for the bigger decisions and use my personal resources in the highest and best use of my time, which is finding deals and finding money. That's how you make money in this business: you find capital, and you find deals. Everything else is noise.

People Are Your Business

I don't think of myself as a natural salesperson or marketer. Here's what I find effective. If you understand and believe in the benefits of the product or service that you're selling, you can communicate those to your counterparty for their specific situation. I've also found that although going up on stage isn't really my element, I am much more comfortable and effective speaking from a platform and allowing prospects to approach me, than I am going out and speaking to strangers one on one.

I'm the co-host of *The Old Capital Real Estate Investing Podcast* with Paul Peebles, a very successful commercial mortgage broker that focuses on multifamily lending and support. It's really heavy-hitting, no fluff, and about apartment investing. We provide tactical, actionable content. We get about 50,000 downloads a month, which is surprising given it is such a niche subject matter.

We have people all over the world. Once a year, we have an annual The Old Capital conference to get together. This year we had about 700 people at the House of Blues in Dallas. Lou Holtz was a keynote speaker. Previous years we've had Roger Staubach and Robert O'Neill, the gentleman who shot and killed Osama bin Laden. We do a couple events throughout the year as well. We can do a lot of what we do remotely, but there's huge value in seeing the people who you've been working with face to face.

Freedom Lifestyle

As we've grown bigger, and as I've gotten older and started thinking about the legacy, I feel it's my job to not mess up what we have built.

Many of my best friends are people I know through the business. In September, I had the opportunity to travel with 12 colleagues to Germany for Oktoberfest for six days, completely sponsored by one of our banks. That was pretty awesome and a great cultural thing that I've always wanted to do. We all do business together, and we go back a long time, to my banking days. We got to reflect back on when none of us had money. For us to build our independent businesses to get to where we are now and share that trip is pretty cool.

My job is flexible. I always have something going on, but I don't need to be in the office to do the vast majority of it. Every year, I challenge myself to come up with money to take the family on a trip to Hawaii for two weeks in the summer. I'm trying to go to Europe every year now. We went to Ireland and then Italy for the last two years. I love that I am not tied to a desk, and this work enables me to design a lifestyle that allows my family and me to experience the world.

Listen to The Old Capital Real Estate Investing Podcast *on iTunes, Stitcher, YouTube, or wherever you get your podcasts, and contact Michael Becker about speaking on www.oldcapitalpodcast.com and www.SPIadvisory.com.*

SHELDON HOROWITZ
Second Changes, Setting Goals, and Mentoring Others

Sheldon Horowitz is a Zig Ziglar Legacy certified trainer and a lifelong student of personal development with a goal of positively impacting millions of people in his lifetime. Sheldon is also VP of business development, overseeing a team of 150 people for a $60 million company, Coast to Coast Computer Products.

Growing Up

I was raised Jewish in Southern California, and I lived a pretty traditional two parent household life. I had my bar mitzvah at age 13 and was very actively involved in my temple and volunteering up until the age 18. I was taught that a traditional education was the way to have success in life. I finished high school, then I went to a couple of different schools, a four year university then a two year community college. I think I finished two classes total out of four semesters. I just didn't want to go.

Eventually I was done with school, and I wanted to make money. My first job was at a bowling alley. That was something I was super passionate about and very competitive with. I wanted to be there all the time and even ditch college to practice. I was there for a couple years and moved into coaching and running all the junior programs. I loved working with younger people.

My Big Wrong Turn

From there, I worked an office job for a couple of years, answering phones and taking orders for a gift basket company. In hindsight it was all meant to be, and it was definitely a learning and growing process, but, unfortunately, I chose to help myself to company funds for a few months. When I finally got caught, I was told my services were no longer needed.

While I was working there I had been homeless, or actually living in my car for the better part of a month, and then my car broke down. Then I was couch surfing, staying at a few friends' places until I was let go. From there, I met with some friends down in Long Beach, California, and basically spent about six months living there. I think I worked a total of two days over six months.

I was really resourceful though. I always made sure I had food to eat and clothes to wear. And, I used to smoke a lot of weed, so I always made sure I was well taken care of on that front. I did that for about six months, while I was driving a rental car that I wasn't paying for. So, stolen. One morning at two o'clock, close to eight police cars pulled me over, guns drawn, the whole thing. I pretty much blacked out the rest of that experience.

I got to spend my 23rd birthday in jail. I was there for five or six days, and they let me out. Thankfully, the car had been returned in good condition.

When I got out, I had $40 to my name. I took a couple of buses to my mom's house. She let me stay there. I'm sure they heard through the grapevine I had gotten in some trouble. I hung around the house for about two weeks watching scary movies and smoking a bunch until my dad came by and said, "I know you're looking for a job." Technically, I wasn't really looking, but I figured that was my clue that I probably should be.

I was fortunate to be given the opportunity at an entry level sales position at Coast to Coast, the same place I am now. We are known as a second chance company. We give people opportunities that normally wouldn't get them based on the way society looks at people if they have a record. They gave me a chance starting at the very bottom.

I earned a little above minimum wage, which was more money than I'd ever made before. I saw pretty quickly there was potential. I was around people who were making a good living for themselves and living a good lifestyle. I thought, "They're no better than me. They don't want this any more than I do. I'm going to do it." That first year, I really struggled. I worked hard and I put my mind to it, but I was horrible at the job. Again, I was fortunate that I worked with my dad. We were able to do enough business together for me to stay on board and learn.

Goals Unlocked My Future

Then, the founder of our company introduced me to goal setting. Unless it was for sports, I'd never had goals. Really, I didn't know what having goals meant. He spent about an hour with a group of us, taught us how to write goals, how to do affirmations, and about our subconscious mind and our reticular activating system.

Within months, I started to see the positive benefits of goal setting, and my life started to change. I was starting to take care of some basic financial needs, and some records of the past were starting to improve. So, I thought, if this works, why not go for it?

I got an email from our manager about a seminar for the late, great Jim Rohn. A ticket cost more than I had to my name, $600 or $700, plus a flight to Texas, plus room and board. My dad was gracious enough to front me the money, and the company also reimbursed me 50%. They invested in my personal growth, and paid my dad back over the next three months. At the seminar, I was on fire every day. I felt like Jim was talking to me. It was life-changing.

He had us write down 50 goals. That was really tough. I've since walked countless people through the same exercise over the years. I've found that the first 10 or maybe even the first half tend to flow pretty easily. Those are immediate need, urgent pain points, and that's as far as most people are able to see. However, the most valuable goals come out in the second half. At the time, I had no idea I was affecting anybody, let alone myself, but one of the goals I wrote down was to positively affect millions of people over my life.

I still have that list of goals. I couldn't even get to 50, but looking back, there's a good chunk that I've accomplished. Some of them aren't really meaningful to me anymore and other ones I'm still working on. That was almost 13 years ago. It's amazing the power you can have over your life. I highly recommend to anybody to take a day or a weekend to fully check out of your current emotion and habits, go to a fresh place, to look at yourself and your goals from scratch.

Experience Yields Wisdom

One of my big goals is to help people not live through the same mistakes I made. We all have to make our mistakes, but they don't need to be as extreme as mine were. What really drove me into some bad habits was not believing that I had much of a future. If you can see it for yourself, there is a future for you.

When I graduated in the late 90s, I expected to make $40k a year in an entry-level position. Maybe I could work my way up over time to $60k a year. This was right when real estate was really getting more expensive in Southern California, and I saw that if I didn't spend a single penny of what I earned, it would still take five years for me to save a 20% downpayment for a home. After I paid my bills and paid off any college loans I took out, it was going to be a freaking long time before I had that 20% for a down payment. And I thought by the time that happens the values would have increased anyway, so it was never going to happen.

As a result of this thinking, I fell into a bit of an addiction to get rich quick gambling. Just put it all in and go for the big hit. That behaviour led me to make some pretty bad decisions.

For years, I tried to hide that part of my personality and be the very calm, collected, consistent person that I felt was the opposite of how I had been before. And then I had a revolutionary shift in my thinking. I realized that if I learned to harness my biggest weakness, it would ultimately be my biggest strength. If I loved taking risks, I'd much rather play in high stakes that are win-win—really great learning experiences, helping other people, making investments in the company, and so forth. I've learned to love that aspect of myself. Not everybody has the guts I do. I am truly excited to be in a place in life, around the kind of people, and in a system where I can go 100% with my God-given uniqueness in alignment with the principles of personal growth and helping other people. I'm happy where I am.

Teaching Yourself to Grow

It's not a road without roadblocks. We all face those. I've found that I need to assess myself regularly to make sure I am staying on the path towards my goals. The mentorship I've had at our company has been a huge gift. I committed myself to personal growth and put myself through automobile university, listening to thousands and thousands of hours of material to put myself in a position where I'm able to share and help other people. I've always liked coaching, helping other people, and being of service. Then I realized that can be in alignment with success and a good life. As Jim Rohn says, service to many leads to greatness.

Daily, I say affirmations. I was taught that an affirmation is reprogramming your subconscious mind. You're training your reticular activating system to notice things that are necessary for you to have what you want to achieve. Our brain is designed to match our internal picture of reality with the external picture of reality we perceive. All our brain wants is for those two pictures to match. If they match, we are comfortable, not necessarily happy, but comfortable. If you see yourself in a destitute, poor, horrible situation in your mind, and that's what you see outside, you're not happy, but you're comfortable. Comfortable is not where growth happens. Growth happens when you expect something greater than what you see. When you expect less than what you see, the concept of self-sabotage comes in. So, I do daily affirmations to reprogram my picture constantly. That is a nonnegotiable habit.

I've learned when challenging situations happen, I don't have control of what goes on in my own head. Over time, I've learned different techniques you can use to consciously cut down on the amount of time you're down. Where you might have been knocked down and stayed down for years, you can turn those years to months, those months to weeks, weeks to days, and eventually almost instantly go from getting knocked down to gratitude. You can very quickly take responsibility for the situation and where you are, even if it's not your doing, and be thankful for the opportunity for growth.

When I have a challenge. I can consciously choose to shift. If I'm honest with myself and I take a self-assessment regularly and ask myself those more difficult questions, I can bring myself back into a positive state. From there, everything's easy.

For information on joining Sheldon Horowitz and his team at Coast to Coast Computer Products, email sheldon@coastcoast.com. To reach Sheldon about speaking or mentorship, or if he can be of service in any fashion, find Sheldon Horowitz on Facebook.

BJ JOHNSON
From No Shot to Olympic Basketball

BJ Johnson teaches sports professionals how to create a financial safety net through real estate while benefiting communities. BJ is a Villanova University alum with three Olympic gold medals in basketball as assistant director at USA Basketball and director of college scouting and player evaluation for the NBA's Brooklyn Nets.

My Early Love of Basketball

I grew up in North Carolina, the fifth of six children. I was two years old and my mom was pregnant when my father passed away. This put our family in a tailspin. Growing up without a father was a major challenge.

In Love with the Game

I wasn't very talented in basketball, but at around 13 years old, I just fell in love with the game. My goal was to earn a college scholarship and make it to the NBA. Everybody laughed at me. But, I believed it was possible. I didn't have access to all the resources that some of my friends had. I didn't have guys I looked up to that could teach me the game.

While others went to basketball camps and joined summer leagues, I taught myself by watching videos and reading books.

There were a lot of players more talented than I was. I was often picked on because of my awkwardness. Being told I had no future in basketball was embarrassing, however, I couldn't help but work hard because I loved playing so much.

There might be players more talented, but I knew nobody was ever going to work harder than I would.

I wanted to live a life of no regrets. If I was going to do something, I would go for it with all my heart.

Real Determination

In the 11th grade, my skills started catching up with my desires, but injuries kept me from getting a college scholarship offer. I went to Villanova University and was determined to make the team as a walk-on.

I worked out relentlessly, never going out on the weekends, closing the gym every Friday and Saturday night with my 77-year-old Jewish friend who worked as an attendant.

And, I was cut the first try out.

After getting over the disappointment and embarrassment, I kept working relentlessly until the following year's tryouts my sophomore year. They ended up canceling those tryouts, but I told myself that I would keep trying. If I got cut every year, then I would at least know it wasn't meant to be.

A Dream Come True

I chose to be a manager for the women's team and continue to work on my game with them. My junior year, after a women's practice, I was running stairs to prepare for the next men's tryouts when the men's team began practicing.

The coach called me downstairs. I expected to be kicked out, but instead, he invited me to be on the team!

This was huge! I played two years under Steve Lappas. Then, I played for Jay Wright, who gave me the scholarship I had always desired and the opportunity to play. It was a dream come true.

Limbo Becomes an Opportunity

After graduation, I was going to play in China. I got into law school but deferred so I could go overseas first. That opportunity fell through at the last minute. It seemed my basketball career may be over.

I was stuck in limbo with my opportunity to play and my opportunity to continue school closed. That's when my old youth pastor reached out to see if I wanted to come to Colorado Springs to help them with their ministry. I moved out to live with him and his family and started a job at Lockheed Martin doing software engineering.

A few years later, I was unsure of where I wanted my life to go next. Serendipitously, I found out that the USA basketball team was also based in Colorado Springs. I was ecstatic at the idea of pursuing my highest passion again. I reached out to Sean Ford, a fellow Villanova alum and national team director. When a position opened up in the team's management, Ford offered me an opportunity to apply.

USA Olympic Basketball Team

I was selected in 2005, the same year that Jerry Colangelo and Mike Krzyzewski took over. Life couldn't have been better.

In 2009, I was asked to help establish the inaugural Junior National Teams for the U16-U17 competitions. Our teams won every competition from 2009-2016 going 52-0, and we were selecting large numbers of players that would go on to be drafted into the NBA. At this time, I moved over to the men's national team and was the chaplain for the World Championships and Olympic Games 2010-2016.

I had tremendous success at USA Basketball, including three Olympics and countless gold medals. I'm very fortunate to have been a part of that group including Kobe Bryant, LeBron James, all those guys who I learned a lot from as role models behind the scenes. When you share a journey to success like we did, there's a special bond that connects you.

Brooklyn Nets

At the height of my success, I was looking for another challenge. I met Sean Marks, current general manager with the Brooklyn Nets. Even though this was my opportunity to finally be in the NBA, when he offered me my current position, I took a hard look because the team was in dire condition. In the end, I believed in him and his vision, and it was time to transition.

I had traveled quite a bit internationally, developing a global view of the game and relationships with younger players getting ready to enter the NBA who I knew would benefit the team. I was hired as coordinator of player evaluation in 2016 and quickly elevated to director the following year. I currently coordinate our amateur scouts and consultants for a team that has gone from the worst in the NBA to being on the verge of completing one of the fastest rebuilds in league history.

Building a Family

After extensive medical testing, it was determined that my wife Pauline was not able to have children. This was a devastating blow to her and our family.

After healing, we decided that adoption would be our path. Going through the adoption process and the training offered by our adoption agency prepared us to have a child and strengthened our marriage. Everyone's adoption story is different. After putting our profile up, we were selected fairly quickly by a prospective family in February 2016.

After the first several weeks, communication dropped between the agency and the birth mom. We thought she had changed her mind, and we were ready to be placed back into the pool.

However, a few months later, the birth mom decided to proceed with adoption, and the agency reached out to see if we were interested. We prayed about the decision and also decided to move forward. Our baby boy was born 11 days later on July 15, 2016.

I was in Houston preparing to head to Chile, and my wife was in North Carolina. We got on the first available flights, met in Kansas City and headed to Topeka, KS to meet our newborn. He was named on the hour drive to the hospital: Emory for what the birth mother desired and Marcellus to honor my wife's late brother. I was able to hold him for an hour before heading to meet the team in Chile while my wife stayed behind to care for him.

In Kansas, a mom has 12 hours to change her mind about an adoption. This is significant, as Emory's birth mom did want Emory back, but not until the next day.

The birth father was unresponsive and would not relinquish his rights. A little over two days after Emory's birth, he contested the adoption. Because the birth father chose to fight for custody, my wife had to remain in Topeka, KS for five weeks, alone, as a first-time mom while I was in Chile until a court order was issued. The birth father kept the case alive, but wouldn't show up for court appearances. The final court case was set for Dec 8, 2016, and he was a no show again.

We were granted custody that day. It was a tough journey to walk through, but every bit was worth it.

Now, we have started the process of finding our second child. There are so many children that are in a situation where they need homes. Most of them end up in the foster system, and some find permanent families through adoption. I now enjoy helping to provide other families with the resources to get through this process because our son has brought so much joy and had such a profound impact on our lives.

In the Game, There Are No Guarantees

Throughout my career, I have seen that scouts and general managers in this industry have very volatile positions. Even with great skills and experience, our jobs are not guaranteed, and you never know what's going to happen next season.

Like many investors, reading *Rich Dad Poor Dad* in 2004 had a profound impact on me. My wife got us going on our real estate journey. Just after we got married, we moved out of Colorado Springs in 2009 and kept her house to rent out. We saw that we could earn money and that there were major tax benefits. This could be our safety net beneath the unpredictable sports industry. Colorado was a great market for us, and now we are diving into the North Carolina market where we continue to grow.

As I've gained experience, I've developed a passion for helping guys like me. When this is your sole income and you can lose it in a heartbeat, new opportunities become critical.

I enjoy the successes my wife and I have had with small multifamily and single family deals. I enjoy taking something that was in bad shape and making it a good place to live. We desire to take this model into targeted areas of North Carolina and bring profit through community transformation.

Lessons

Throughout my life, perseverance, discipline, and determination have been my tools to achieve my great successes.

Growing up, I watched my mom persevere and figure things out every single day. Through her efforts, my siblings and I were able to get through college and we are all pretty successful professionally. The foundation of my life is based upon what she has done to show me what truth, perseverance, discipline, and determination are all about.

I've learned to view my setbacks and struggles as assets not liabilities. Every disappointment is a necessary stepping stone on the journey to success.

Contact BJ Johnson, founder of Metamorph Investments, LLC with over a decade of real estate experience rehabilitating, stabilizing, and creating great value for investors and communities at

metamorphinvest.com | bj@metamorphinvest.com

KEVIN EASTMAN
Leading in the NBA, in Business, and in Life

Kevin Eastman, now a professional speaker and author, spent 13 years in the NBA as an assistant coach with the World Champion Boston Celtics and as an assistant coach and vice president of basketball operations for the Los Angeles Clippers. He spent 22 years as a college coach, including 11 as a head coach. Kevin was inducted into the hall of fame at his high school, university, and his home state of New Jersey. His book, Why The Best Are The Best, *is a bestseller and is used by many sports and corporate teams around the country.*

Losing My Mom, Finding Basketball

My mother died tragically when I was six years old, so my dad worked long hours to provide for my brothers and me. He did his best to balance running his company and providing for three kids...not easy for anyone. Consequently, I had to figure out many things about life and growing up on my own. Sadly, I have no memories of my mom, and just wish I could have had more time with her. I wish I remembered the lessons she taught me, but I'm sure they are part of who I have become. Fortunately for all of us, my dad was a tremendous role model.

I don't know why I fell in love with basketball, but I am so glad I did, as it has been a huge part of my life. I was a shy kid, and basketball provided something I could do on my own. You don't need anybody else in order to get better—just a boy, a ball, and a dream. I was that boy, and I had the ball; the dream was to play basketball for as long as I could.

I went from having fun shooting hoops in the driveway to becoming passionate, then all-in committed to basketball. That commitment earned me a college scholarship and a short professional career following college. When my playing days were over, I had to figure out what was next. Coaching became my new passion, and that, with the same commitment I had to playing the game, has allowed me to experience coaching the game at the highest level.

What Creates Greatness

I had the good fortune to coach in the NBA for 13 years and to win a World Championship with the Boston Celtics in 2008. I was alongside the best of the best, all the while keeping notes of what I learned from the players, coaches, and others in the organization. I wanted to figure out what made "The Best" the best, and I set out to do so through observation, listening, reading, discussing, and learning from others.

One of my key mantras is this: Success lies in simplicity; confusion lives in sophistication. When writing my book, I wanted to simplify the lessons and concepts as much as possible so the reader could immediately take action and apply the lessons to their lives.

Another philosophy I have lived by is that success leaves footprints, and it is our job to find them, to follow them, and to fit them. Not all footprints lead to success, so be careful where the footprints you follow are taking you.

Being a Great Leader

I have been around several great leaders during the course of my life, and each one has left a significant impression on me. Among other shared traits, I believe they are all thoughtful and caring people. I have seen that being an effective leader does not have to include getting angry and demeaning others.

One of the most important things we can do as coaches and leaders is to provide positivity and hope. We must understand, people want to be appreciated, recognized, and valued, so we must do our part to make sure that is part of our leadership philosophy as well.

I was fortunate in that my dad was a great leader. Like other great leaders—and parents— he led by example, helping us make our way by showing us that he lived his values every single day.

Leadership Velcro

How do you get your followers to stick to you so that they're following only you? I call that leadership Velcro. After studying some of the best coaches, CEOs, and VPs, many of whom are close friends of mine, I have found a few common qualities among these successful leaders that create loyalty from their followers and separate them from the pack.

Humility. Great leaders find a way to be "in charge" and lead effectively while still being humble.

Vulnerability. The leader doesn't have to have all the answers, but someone in the organization should have those answers. Great leaders are open to ideas and suggestions brought by others.

When I first took over as vice president with the Clippers, there was a culture of "no." New ideas brought by anyone were met with negativity and were routinely rejected. After years of this treatment, some had understandably stopped giving their best to the organization. So I wondered how I could let the staff know that our new culture would be different.

In our first meeting, I said, "I know it's been a tough time these last few years. Some of you have told me exactly this. But I need to tell you one of the staples of our culture. We are going to live this every single day, and it's going to be great. We now have a culture of *know*." I could see all the air go out of the room as they heard the last word. I said, "Under Doc Rivers' leadership, we spell that word differently. The old regime spelled it N-O. We will spell it K-N-O-W. We want to *know* what's in your head. When you have an idea, you have to let us *know*. I'm here to tell you, as the vice president, I do not have all the answers. But I've seen you guys work. I know what you're capable of. The answers are in this room. Don't be afraid to let me know a good idea."

Likability. Many say, "They've got to trust and respect me, who cares if they like me." In my mind, there must be some level of like. Fortunately, likeability is easy. Be friendly. Know names and use them; people love to hear their own name, especially from a leader.

Empathy. As leaders, we walk in two pairs of shoes every day. The first pair are the ones from our closet. Man, do they feel comfortable. They fit. But there's another pair of shoes. Those are the shoes in your employees' closets. You may wear an 11. They wear an eight. Those size eights are uncomfortable, but you must learn to walk in those shoes too. We need that empathy more than ever today.

Values. People follow people who have strong values and who live those values every day. Values aren't just those things you have on the wall or on your website. A true core value is something you're willing to be fired over.

What are your core values? When people know them and see you live them each day, that's when leadership Velcro happens. That's when those you lead want to meet the challenges you put before them. They want to stick with you, to follow you wherever you lead them.

How to Work With People

We always hear that we need to know what makes people "tick." I believe we must care about what makes them *talk*, because if we can get them to talk, we have an opportunity to find out what makes them tick. We also must care about what makes them listen, because if we can get them to listen, we have a chance to influence the way they tick.

It all comes back to relationships. Who cares if we have a Hall of Fame player on our team if he won't listen to us and won't do what we've asked him to do in order to win the game that night? You have to develop relationships to become successful in any arena.

I use an acronym, REAL leadership:

R Relationships. You can't lead people properly unless you have a strong enough relationship with someone such that you're comfortable talking about what matters to them.

E Example. Simply put, be who you want them to be.

A Attitude. We need a positive attitude so we can provide hope for the people we lead. Sometimes it's not what you *know* but what you *bring* that day.

L Listening. This is critical to leadership. Do you listen to respond or do you listen to understand?

To become real leaders, we want to cover the four attributes in REAL. Sure, we have to have a vision and processes, but to me, that acronym defines true leadership.

Leaving A Legacy

I have a list of what leaving a legacy means to me—my "Elite Eight." A legacy is created for the future so that when we leave, our beliefs and lessons remain for others to learn from them.

It's all about doing the next right thing for someone else. A legacy is others-driven, not me-driven. I don't want to leave a legacy so my name stays around. I want to leave a legacy because I want my lessons to possibly help someone 20 years after I'm gone. A legacy is built one conversation, one touch, one word, one person at a time. A legacy challenges me to have a different mindset each and every day.

To me, a legacy is about listening. A legacy is about sharing. A legacy is about depth...staying a little longer in conversations with people. It's about impacting and inspiring. A legacy is about others first. It's not about having success, but about what I do with that success. Most legacies are built on sharing and caring, not how high you went up the ladder.

The power of a legacy has nothing to do with numbers but has everything to do with lessons and touches. It's the people we touch and the lessons we leave for others. Even by simply living a principled life, you can leave a legacy for someone who you may never know but who sees how you lived and tries to follow your example.

Legacy starts with the person in front of you. No one else. I have spoken to crowds of thousands and to leadership teams of 12. The people in front of you are the most important people in your legacy at that moment. You're sharing to help them get to where *they* want to go, not to help you get where *you* want to go. You leave a legacy by doing your part in your piece of the world.

Kevin Eastman is a professional speaker and author, and an NBA World Champion coach. His bestselling book, Why the Best Are the Best: 25 Powerful Words That Impact, Inspire, and Define Champions *can be found at www.kevineastman.net. To inquire about speaking engagements, email wendy@kevineastman.net. Follow Kevin on Twitter @kevineastman.*

STEVE LLOYD
Living My Best Life

Steve Lloyd is the founder of Stone Bay Holdings LLC and is an expert at raising capital with over $150 million in real estate and over $175 million in private capital raised. Steve lives in Siesta Key, Florida, where he owns multiple vacation rentals and spends his free time mentoring entrepreneurs and investors with a passion for helping others live their best lives.

Early Entrepreneurial Passion

My passion for entrepreneurship started young like most entrepreneurs. At eight years old, I was responsible for delivering 142 newspapers every day. At 10 years old, I was working in a local pizza shop, which I was running by the time I was 16. I eventually bought the shop when I was 20. I had this passion that was fueled by every success and obstacle I encountered. Everything that came into my path, I leveraged into something that could serve me.

If you're not passionate about your business, you're chasing the wrong dream. What makes your eyes pop wide open every morning? It's all about waking up every morning excited for the day you've been given. Owning a pizza shop my entire life wasn't the dream I was chasing as a kid, but living life on my own terms and having the potential for exponential growth was, and every step I've taken in life has been a step in that direction.

The Power of Leverage

Entrepreneurs have to understand and be able to harness the power of leverage in their businesses. While I was still a pizza shop owner, Dave Van Horn took me to a real estate meeting. As I was taking everything in, I remember thinking, "If we could just raise a hundred thousand dollars and pay an 8% return, then we could lend that hundred thousand dollars to somebody else and charge them 16%. We'd create an 8% arbitrage." This is what we call leverage.

I could scale this up as well. What if instead of one hundred thousand, I raised a million dollars. For every million I raised, I could make $80,000. The lightbulb went off. "Heck, if I could raise a hundred million dollars, I'm going to create some serious wealth in my life."

Learning how to leverage goes beyond leveraging money. You also need to leverage people and their skills. I'm an expert at raising private capital. As an entrepreneur, you learn early on to stick with what you're amazing at. I have 12 strategic partners who excel at finding distressed assets for us to buy. So, I leverage my partners' skills, and we all focus on what we're great at. No one is wasting time doing things they don't love or don't excel at.

Morning Gratitude and Reflection Daily

Every single morning, before I do anything else, I take 10 to 15 minutes to just be grateful for everything I have. Sometimes, it seems like life isn't going well, or there can be a crisis in your business, but when you start creating a list, you realize how quickly you can come up with 40 or 50 things you can be grateful for in the moment. Start with the simple things in life, like you're breathing, you're healthy, it's sunny out, and so on.

You have to be grateful for what you have because there's so many people that don't have what we have. We usually concentrate all of our energy on the few things that are holding us back in life, so that we forget about the abundance of good we have right now. When we realize this and really fill ourselves with gratitude, it fuels us for the day ahead and puts us in the right mindset.

Spend Time Visualizing Your Ideal Future

Sit down every morning and think about yourself driving a yacht, making a big real estate deal, walking into a nice hotel, whatever the future may look like for you. But visualize yourself in that future, actually doing the things you aspire to. Don't just think about the beach house you hope to own one day, think about you and your family in the house, cooking breakfast, drinking coffee on the porch, living in the house, looking out the window at the beautiful view.

You see these images in your mind every morning, and it gets into your subconscious. It's like a short movie that I play every day. You're spending 10 or 15 minutes every day already living that life. When you get into this habit, your goals come way sooner, like it did for me, because you already feel like you're living it. Imagine exactly who you want to be and what you want to be doing.

Another way I keep my goals at the front of my mind is what I call *the toothbrush effect*. Write your goals on a 3 by 5 index card and keep them on your bathroom sink next to your toothbrush. Twice a day, read through your goals while you're brushing your teeth in the morning and at night. A lot of entrepreneurs have big goals for themselves and their businesses, but they get lost because they're not thinking about them every day and visualizing. Keep your goals front and center, and watch how quickly they become reality.

Get Yourself a Strong-Willed, Hard-Core Accountability Partner

It's amazing how much entrepreneurs and leaders have people pull us back and tell us we can't. I just show them I can. As an entrepreneur, you fight for independence, freedom, and living life on your terms. But it's a long, hard road. It takes six to seven years to create success in your company. I see so many business owners and entrepreneurs who get two years into their business and decide that it just can't be done, quit, and move on to something else. You have to realize that you're starting over. Constantly starting over is going to dramatically set you back.

A big part of this is finding an accountability partner you can trust, that will keep you on track, and even call you out when needed. About 10 years ago, I was two million dollars in debt, and for a bit, I was going in circles trying to find a way out. I was able to keep pushing through everything because of my amazing accountability and business partner Kerry Faix who supported me and was loyal through the storms. Kerry kept saying, "Take one bite out of the elephant every day." And that's what I did. One bite every day, until all the debt was paid off and my businesses were thriving.

When everyone is trying to hold you back, find the few that believe in you, want to support you in your journey, and are going to keep pushing you to always be better. You always want to practice fair exchange in your relationships though. Make sure you are giving back as much as you are receiving. One person can't be doing all the work, and this goes for all relationships, in business and family. You maintain healthy relationships with the people who matter in your life by keeping fair exchange in mind when interacting with others.

Pivot When Necessary

A lot of people won't change until something traumatic happens and they're forced to change. You have to get ahead of this. Always be willing to admit when something isn't going well or something needs to change. Create a plan and take immediate action when necessary.

A massive mistake entrepreneurs make is they put all of their money back into their business. You need to have different investments outside the company you own all working for you and have money in your savings. You need multiple buckets of investments. They can be simple investments. Start with $500. It's about getting started.

Living My Best Life

I recently moved from Pennsylvania down to sunny Siesta Key in Florida. It has been a huge transformation. I have owned vacation rentals here for years, 50 yards away from the #1 beach in the country. I realized that I love the lifestyle. Now I am so focused on my health and am healthier than I have been in a long time. I go bike riding and paddle boarding every day, and I've already lost 57 pounds. I go out on my wave runners every day and ride next to dolphins in the Gulf of Mexico and overall am creating a magical life here.

I have people coming to visit me from all over the country, and I'm helping them live their best lives too. I've helped a group of people lose close to 1100 pounds in just a couple months and helped them start pursuing their biggest dreams. I've always dreamed of living on an island, and now that dream has come to fruition as I've created wealth. I'm getting ready to buy my first yacht, and I'm so excited to keep living my best life and helping others do the same.

I feel blessed and honored to be an entrepreneur, and I feel like it's my duty to give back to up-and-coming entrepreneurs and help them avoid some of the mistakes I've made. Have an open mind to do whatever you want to do, and don't let anyone hold you back. Make today the best day ever because you will never get it back.

For advice on building your business or living your best life, contact Steve Lloyd by visiting his website at www.SteveLloydMBL.com or find him on Instagram @SteveLloydMBL and YouTube at www.youtube.com/SteveLloydMBL.

REBEKAH LOVELESS
Anthropology, Pushing Boundaries, and Personal Growth

Rebekah Loveless is an archaeologist and founder of Loveless Linton, Inc. which offers archaeological compliance services to local, state, and federal agencies as well as private developers. Through commitment to ethical practices and a solutions first approach, Loveless Linton, Inc. has changed archaeology.

Bones

I am really not a fan of dirt, so it's kind of funny that I'm an archaeologist. It all started as a child. I guess anthropology and archaeology are just something I was meant to do. My first memories of being fascinated with the human skeleton were made at The Museum of Man, an anthropology museum in San Diego. It was by far my favorite museum. Every Tuesday was free museum day, and my mom took my sister and me to our local city park where all the museums are located. My poor sister always had to endure the hours we spent in that museum. There were displays of human bones, I was absolutely fascinated.

Anthropology is a very broad discipline. You can focus in archaeology, physical anthropology, cultural anthropology, linguistics, or primates. My pivot point was a physical anthropology class where I learned I could study the human skeleton professionally—human osteology. Today, I have two degrees in anthropology and operate an archaeology firm that partners with developers to legally and ethically handle the discovery of archaeological resources and human ancestral remains.

Moral Dilemma

After I graduated, I fell into my first job. My partner had a Native American archaeology monitoring company at the time, and they brought me in to do preliminary bone identification at the site before formal identification by a medical examiner. In archaeology, there are categories just like there are in life: making tools, cooking, building houses, and burials. On this particular excavation site in San Diego, they were finding a lot of bone. I worked with them for a while before I followed a promising opportunity to another established company.

At this archaeological company, things were a bit different. In archaeology today, unfortunately, there is a relationship dynamic between archaeologists, Native Americans, and developers that is not ideal. Often, developers think that the archaeologist and the Natives are there to slow things down, which is generally not the case. The problem lies in the structure of the discipline and the lack of cross-discipline training. Archaeologists are specially trained to identify cultural and historical artifacts, but are not trained in legal mitigation, permitting, or basic business practices. Native American communities are primarily interested in the preservation and respectful treatment of their cultural material. All too often, archaeologists are tasked with being the liaison between the developers and the Native American communities and simply don't have the business sense to involve interested Native American communities until it is time to level the site. That's when we run into trouble; lack of communication and preparation leads to short cuts, cover ups, and conflicts in the field.

When working with human remains, "we speak for those no longer able to speak for themselves," and advocate for the respectful repatriation of their physical remains to family and descendants. Psalms has a similar quote: "Speak up for those who cannot speak for themselves; ensure justice for those being crushed. Yes, speak up for the poor and helpless, and see that they get justice," (Proverbs 31:8-9 NLT). Identifying an individual allows that person to be returned home, provides resolution and answers for the family, and allows that person to be buried according to their cultural customs.

When we were working on a particular site, there were a lot of human remains coming up. These bones had been there a long time, but they were the ancestral remains of people who are still alive today.

I was responsible for identification of remains. A large number of bones that we found on site were positively identified as human. When this happens, legally and ethically, the game changes. Work slows, a new plan of excavation practices is created and goes into place, "most likely descendants" are identified, and more. It is a legally defined and a professional practice. The problem is, this slows down the project, requires more work by the archaeological firm, and costs the builders additional money if it had not been budgeted for. So, the company I was with at the time glossed over the discovery of the remains.

They generally acted as though these discoveries were unimportant in comparison to the timeline of the project. State and Federal laws differ slightly when it comes to environmental practices and laws, and there were some things that I felt violated our legal obligations and were questionable.

This presented an ethical dilemma for me. So, I spoke up. And because I was not in line with the company, they terminated me.

Of course, it was frustrating at the time, but this was a launch point for greater opportunity. I've never had a mentor to fall back on. I had to learn that the only person I can count on is me, so I better be someone I can count on to do the right thing, be a good person, help where I can, plus be accountable and dependable.

Do what's right, not only for you at the time, but what's right by you and right by your heart.

Ethical Archaeology

After I was let go, I took some time to finish my masters degree and get the credentials I needed to become a principal investigator so I could operate solo and start my own company.

With my life partner Brandon, I created a company that links Native American and archaeological agendas to provide better services to developers as well as more professional and respectful archaeological practices. We chose to focus on solutions, not roadblocks, and to give the Native American community impacted by the development a seat at the table in the discussion of every project component. This is the most efficient way to legally repair the relationship Native people have with their traditional landscape.

A big part of my work is fighting for the dignified, responsible, and legally compliant methodology for identifying human remains within an archaeological context. Every piece of bone is equally as important to a complete skeleton and should be treated as such. This is in accordance with indigenous culture and local, California, and Federal laws. Identification of human remains for the purpose of repatriation is my passion.

Identifying an individual allows that person to be returned home, provides resolution and answers for the family, and allows that person to be buried according to their cultural customs. The identification of bone as human or potentially human allows the individual whom the fragments belong to be treated as human and allows descendants of that person, or their living cultural group, to be allowed access to the remains and the cultural items that may have been associated with the burial. They can rightfully claim their people and their space. Many Native American people have been shoved into a small corner of undesirable land and erased from US history, and we especially see this in San Diego history.

Our vision is for archaeologists and Native Americans within each region to come together on a single platform to not only treat the resources appropriately, but also support developers in fulfilling their timelines.

As a result, we have changed the archaeological practices in our county. Now, people more often follow the legal protocol and call the correct people to identify remains and "most likely descendants" have a say in the treatment of the remains. In general, agency and archaeological professionals are more educated on and follow the laws in place, and policy and protocols on the treatment of human remains is more standard within the profession in our county. With our ethical treatment of remains, we are cutting-edge and have moved an industry!

Establishing Professional Standards in a "Cowboy" Culture

Brandon and I are very excited to have recently written a chapter in a textbook titled *Ethical Approaches to Human Remains: A Global Challenge in Bioarchaeology and Forensic Anthropology* next to some big names in our field addressing areas for growth we see in archaeology.

Since archaeologists in the US are still a bit of a rogue "cowboy" culture with few professional standards, it is up to the individual company or archaeologist to know and abide by legal protocol and cultural recommendations. And at the end of the day, if they don't do things properly, there are often no repercussions.

So, Brandon and I sought a solution. In addition to educating the forensic community regarding their responsibilities for archaeological bone identification, we would address a potentially larger industry-wide issue in the US of underqualified osteologists. In the US today, anyone with a semester of human anatomy, regardless of whether they've ever seen archaeological human remains, can claim to be a bone expert. And unfortunately, we are seeing this happen.

California law says medical examiners or coroners are legal experts that can identify human remains exclusively. However, most of these folks are focused on recent forensic cases and don't realize their obligation to archaeological remains. This creates this void that underqualified osteologists are too ready to fill. Forensic professionals assume that archaeologists have a system and trained experts, but we do not.

So, Brandon and I presented at the Annual American Academy of Forensic Sciences to educate the community and ask for their help. Eventually, we would like an Academy-endorsed list of qualifications for someone to call themselves an osteologist. That hasn't happened, yet.

There has been a big paradigm shift from "all archaeology is for the enhancement and satisfaction of the white man's knowledge and curiosity." There was, and unfortunately in some cases still is, very much a finders keepers mentality. Many in the new generation of archaeologists understand that everything we do, everything we excavate or disturb, negatively affects a living person, population, or culture, and we have a duty to be respectful stewards of their well-being by properly handling material culture. We are not entitled to another person's possessions, story, trauma, or culture.

To make our view understood, we had to contradict the "good ol boy" mentality of "archaeology belongs to science first." I was extremely nervous because people who employ that mindset are able to make or break anything within the American forensic and academic communities. But with Brandon by my side, I had to speak up. I was his access to the platform. Brandon is Native American, and when it comes down to it, we were telling his story. I couldn't hide behind fear.

Brandon and I also started a non-profit to provide resources in areas that are incorporated in archaeology and cultural resources but that are not really part of the development process. We continue to expand, and we are developing expert-level consulting where clients may ask questions to a principal investigator on call and have access to Native American input, regional expertise, and legal expertise. The vision is a one-stop shop for all compliance questions and solutions.

Pushing Boundaries and Personal Growth

Be comfortable with being uncomfortable. I've learned to enjoy being uncomfortable because that's where change happens. Without that uncertainty, everything stays stagnant. I've got to experience things that may make me uncomfortable to grow. I experienced that when I was pushed into starting my own business. Being uncomfortable keeps me moving.

Rebekah Loveless is an archaeologist and the founder of Loveless Linton Inc. More information on Loveless Linton Inc.'s services can be found at www.loveless-linton.com. Email: rebekah@loveless-linton.com.

DUSTIN MILES
Lessons From a Real Estate Investor, Balancing Life with Real Estate

Dustin Miles is a seasoned real estate investor, syndicator, and entrepreneur. As CEO of Cowtown Capital Group, he has purchased approximately $90 million in assets. His passion project, The School of Income, educates new investors about the possibilities and strategies of building passive income.

Childhood Entrepreneur

I've always had a knack for starting businesses. By age eight, I had a thriving candy business at Westcreek Elementary in southwest Fort Worth.

My bus driver even dubbed me the "candy man." The school actually threatened to kick me out if I didn't stop selling candy, but in my opinion, that was only because I was cutting into their profits. I also mowed lawns, sold baseball cards, and always looked for ways to make money. Although money has its place, the real attraction for me is the competitive part of the entrepreneurial game.

Once I got to college, I had an internet business. This was pretty early on in the development of the internet. At that time, Pokémon was hot. I didn't know anything about it, but I knew I could make money. I sold Pokémon cards through websites like Yahoo Auctions and eBay. My college apartment was half-filled with Pokémon cards. Looking at my room and shaking their heads, my friends had a great time asking me if I needed to have a heart-to-heart.

Transition to Real Estate

The Pokémon gig, although profitable, was short-lived. The bubble lasted about 18 months.

After college, I moved to College Station to work as an engineer. I wanted to be in fuel cell research and development, and the company I worked for was one of the few with fuel cell opportunities. After College Station, I lived in San Francisco for a year before heading back home to Fort Worth where I then transitioned to carbon nanotube research.

While still in College Station, I noticed a few work colleagues had rental property. In San Francisco, I started attending various real estate seminars that resulted in people running to the back of the room for a "deal." I read *Rich Dad Poor Dad*. It was a great book. However, one of my main influences was *Your Money or Your Life* by Vicki Robin. What a title! I didn't agree with all of the premises behind it, but it really inspired me in terms of creating passive income and achieving financial independence. Between these books and seminars, I was hooked! And my journey to financial independence began.

I started finance blogging in 2007 when blogging was big. The exercise didn't fare too well, but I met many interesting people, some who are pretty big today.

While blogging, I found a few local real estate groups in the Dallas-Fort Worth area and hired mentors until I found one that stuck. I started flipping houses and had a few rental properties. I continued to attend real estate investing Meetup groups and met people that owned 50, 100, 500, and even 10,000 doors. I was hooked! I found someone willing to teach me about investing in apartments. I tend to dip my toes in the water rather than jumping in, so I started my apartment investing passively with a friend. I wanted to see how it was done. After watching, investing, and closing on my first apartment deal passively, that was all I needed to start syndicating my own deals!

223

I stopped blogging, stopped flipping houses, and began the process of selling my single family rental portfolio while still working full-time as an engineer. In 2013, I moved to multifamily investing. I have done ten multifamily syndications to date valued at $90 million and raised over $20 million dollars in equity for the acquisitions. I still remember my first syndication. It was 109 units in Haltom City, TX. We acquired the asset for a little over $4 million and raised $1.65 million for the purchase. I was nervous for that deal. I remember waking up in the middle of the night to check the rental comparables and constantly reviewing the numbers to make sure the deal made sense!

In 2018, I went from full-time engineer to part-time, just two days a week. I was cautious (probably overly cautious) about leaving my job. I never wanted to be in the position where I HAD to go buy apartment deals. That would be a complete disservice to my investors and myself.

Teaching and Learning From Others

I find success investing in a diverse set of asset classes, and I want to share my experience and mentor new investors. I created The School of Income to educate people about the value of investing, passive income, tax benefits, that there are multiple ways to put your money to work for you, and that there are alternatives to the stock market. Ten years ago, I didn't know regular people like me could invest in large scale apartments. I thought that was reserved for large corporations or families with generational wealth.

The School of Income is the resource I wish I had when I was getting started. It is a labor of love. This education platform is what I was trying to build in 2007 when I started blogging, but I didn't have the insight, knowledge, or connections at the time. We are creating a community of givers, and we want The School of Income to be the ultimate resource for passive investing in the world.

Lessons I've Learned

Last year was pretty hectic for me. I had about $40 million in transactions going on along with my part-time engineering job and finalizing a divorce. It was probably the most challenging time of my life.

Self-care was critical for me, so I worked out 5-6 days a week to keep my head clear and my body in shape. I am extremely grateful for all of my amazing friends and family that supported me. I'm also extremely grateful that the divorce was finalized amicably and that we are able to focus on co-parenting our son. I'm proud we co-hosted our son's birthday party just a short two months after the divorce had been finalized.

I realize a lot of people struggle in their marriages and relationships. I encourage anyone who is facing these issues to talk openly with a professional counselor. If it can't be a professional counselor, speak to a trusted friend. I was embarrassed, so I didn't tell anyone about what was happening in my life, and it was tough being alone. I didn't tell most of my friends and family members what was going on until it was decided we were moving forward with the divorce. Even if you are in a very healthy relationship, I would encourage you to see a marriage counselor and a counselor for yourself as well. As we treat our bodies with medical checkups, it makes sense to have a checkup mentally to make sure everything is okay and no issues are creeping in. We are all human, and it's easy to get busy and not realize there are issues that must be addressed.

Marriage counseling and seeing a therapist were amazing for me. I was most enlightened by *The 5 Love Languages* by Gary Chapman. I had built up many walls, and it took an event like this to bring the walls down. As a man, I know there can be a stigma around going to a professional. I was very tempted not to share this in a public setting. I am sharing this because I hope it helps someone. Divorce is a taboo topic. The lack of discussion is potentially part of why half of all marriages in the US lead to divorce. Whether counseling helps your marriage survive or not, once you bring the walls down, you are able to develop those deep human relationships and connections I think we are all looking for.

The process leading up to my divorce made me a better person. As a result of this work, my self-awareness and empathy shot through the roof. After the divorce, my goal is to be the best ex-husband I can be. It didn't really matter who was right or wrong. If my ex-wife is in a good spot in life, she is going to be a good mom to our son, and he is going to be in the best position to lead a happy and healthy life while making a positive contribution to society.

Always a Student

I enjoy teaching others, but I'm also a student (and always will be). When I want to learn about another asset class, I start by seeking out an expert in that space. I let them invest my money and learn along the way. This way, I can learn and make money with minimal risk to my capital. It is much easier to learn when you immerse yourself in a topic. There is only so much you can learn from a book or class. To master something, you have to do it. With new endeavors, I tend to enter gradually, so I can test the water before I just jump in the deep end. I have to determine whether it's a good fit for me.

In all my endeavors, from swimming laps to multifamily investing, I have set goals and hired a coach to help me. Why reinvent the wheel? It is much easier to partner with or hire someone who has already achieved what I want to achieve. I can save time and heartache by shortening the learning curve. I'm all about finding the expert who will help me achieve my goal in the most effective and efficient manner.

One of my habits is finding the best people in an area I am interested in and making friends with them. I want to hang with the best, because as Jim Rohn said: "You're the average of the five people you spend the most time with."

The Importance of Giving Back

I'm a capitalist, and I like making money, but you can't take money with you. Rockefeller and many others since have provided an excellent example of giving back. I've done well, and I really want to make an impact on the world. One year for my birthday, I started a Facebook fundraiser to raise money for a local Fort Worth charity, Cancer Care Services. My mom had cancer about twenty years ago and survived, so the cause is personal to me. I wanted to serve on their board, but I wanted to give value to them first. I told my Facebook followers I would match each dollar donated. We raised a little over five thousand dollars. In addition, Hayden Harrington and I hosted a charity event for Cancer Care Services raising another seven thousand dollars through our multifamily meetup, Momentum Multifamily.

Later that year, to my excitement, Cancer Care Services asked me to join the board. It's been a pleasure, and I've met some incredible people. As I continue to grow, teaching others, caring for my family, and sharing the wealth I accumulate will always be my priority.

If you would like to and connect with Dustin Miles about investing, please go to www.schoolofincome.com or www.dustinmiles.com. You can also connect via email at Dustin@schoolofincome.com.

TIM COLE
Bringing Honor and Healing to Veterans

Colonel Tim Cole is a retired 31-year Marine leader, author, speaker, and enthusiastic advocate for military Veterans and their families. His passion is helping families and friends understand their Veterans' service and honor their military heritage.

Blue-Collar Kid

I'm a blue-collar kid who grew up in the shadows of industrial steel mills of Northwest Indiana. My grandparents were sharecroppers in the Missouri Bootheel, laboring in exchange for living on the owner's land. After Dad served during the Korean War, he married Mom, and they moved North where he found work in the steel mill. They escaped a life of poverty and became successful in the eyes of their family.

Growing up in an uncertain family environment created by alcoholism meant life as a kid was chaotic and confusing. These formative childhood years came with embarrassment, shame, and guilt, impacting self-confidence and self-esteem.

School sports helped pull me out of that home environment. I was not a great athlete, but chose to show up, suit up, and get in the game. That was my attitude—get in there and do the very best I could. Sure enough, I began to have success in athletics. Even though I was a C-level player, I made the freshmen basketball team and played four years of football. Although I was not a big guy, I was strong, quick, and played with aggression. Our team was not expected to do well my senior year, but we went to the state playoffs.

My friend's father, Mr. Wilson, became a mentor to me. He was confident I could play college football. My parents didn't have high school diplomas, so they felt a high school diploma was a great achievement. Mr. Wilson showed me how to write letters to college coaches and then drove me to visit colleges. With his help, I'm the first in my family to earn a college degree.

The Front Office

After graduating with a business degree, I moved to Kansas City, where I found a job at a small family-owned metal fabricating plant. I had grown up pouring concrete, moving brick and mortar, patching roads, and dumping garbage, so I understood how to do blue-collar labor. I didn't know what my business degree could do for me, so I went for what I knew, working in the plant as a machine operator. A few weeks into my new job, the owner came over to me and asked, "Do I understand you have a business degree from Graceland College? I want to give you a job in my front office." It turned out he was also a Graceland graduate.

That year I learned how a business operates. The owner was a one-man show. I was fortunate to witness and learn everything from purchasing materials and equipment to hiring and firing from right outside his office.

The Realization

Later, I was hired by a Fortune 500 company. Things around me began to change. People were getting married, buying homes, and having families. When I witnessed a coworker die from a heart attack at the office, something inside me clicked. I needed to get away from the corporate world for a while and challenge myself.

So, I went to the Recruiters that afternoon and enlisted in the Marine Corps at age 24.

I was looking for a challenge, something that would test me. Nothing would test me like becoming a Marine. I knew I could always go back to an office job.

A Patriot

My patriotism is not blind. It comes from an understanding of the opportunity that is available in our country, and that I have experienced. My two grandfathers were sharecroppers, and my dad an eighth-grade educated steelworker. There is no fault in earning a living and taking care of your family in these ways. Still, I am so truly grateful that I had other opportunities to permit me to do what I am doing today. This country gave me the opportunity to be who I have become.

In America, it doesn't matter who you are, you can get an education if that's what you want. And education isn't the only answer. There's a bit of entrepreneur in me, and I have many entrepreneurs in my circle. I am convinced more than ever; this nation is the place where with personal responsibility and deliberate effort, nearly anything can be achieved. There is tremendous opportunity to advance yourself and your family's standard of living.

In my 31 years of military service and in my private, corporate world, I've traveled all over the world. And yes, I've seen some desperate places that do not have the advantages we have in the USA, places that remind us that people at the poverty level in the USA are amazingly among the top 10% wealthiest people in the world.

Our history, far from perfect, yet an amazing heritage of opportunity fuels my patriotism. I've learned what happened in World War II. Nations of the free world were so close to a different outcome—students of history do not have to imagine how the world would be. I feel humbled and grateful for our greatest generation. And it wasn't just those who were fighting the war. Our entire nation came together. It was Rosie the Riveter, victory gardens, and coupons to buy rationed items like sugar and tires. I love honoring Veterans who have served because they actually protect our hard-won liberties and freedoms.

To Honor and Bring Healing to Veterans

After a full career on active military duty, service members are honored with a formal retirement party. Commanders often attend. An award is presented to the retiree, and the medals they earned are honorably displayed in an awards case. Their family is present and they are given flowers and gifts. On active duty, I saw and conducted a number of these retirement ceremonies. It's a memorable and edifying event. Corporate retirement events are rare these days, and may have a cake, and are generally much less formal.

I once asked my dad where his military awards were. He noted he received one award and didn't know where it was.

I knew I could write off and find out about my dad's awards. I did that, and I was intrigued by what I found. I wanted to honor my father's military service, so I assembled a medals display made with dad's medals. His was the first medal awards display I created.

Because of my military service, I knew exactly what the medals were and what it took to earn them. I gave the award display to dad at Christmas in front of our family, who did not understand what these awards meant. As I explained each of the medals' service requirement and recognition, I witnessed my dad get choked up. Nobody had ever talked about him and his military service in a way that was so honoring. It helped our family understand what he had accomplished.

After Dad got misty-eyed, I asked him why. He said, "The military helped change my life. It pulled me out of backwoods Missouri. I began to have confidence that I could do things others could do."

Having witnessed that, I began doing the same research and honoring for a number of other family members and friends. People often asked me to do it for their dad or grandpa. This began in the early 1990s, and now I have held a couple hundred of these ceremonies to honor men and women who have served our country.

The Process to Honor

First, I research. I go into the archives, both the National Archives and the family's records. I read everything I find. For this part, I am a genealogist.

Next, I am a military jargon translator. I do research, and I interpret it. In my 31 years with the military, I've been enlisted, an officer, and I've worked with all of the branches of service. I know rank structure and military awards. I can put in context what it takes to earn each award and what it means to have earned them. For example, when I find out what World War II infantry division a person served in, I know exactly where they went in World War II based on my references and resources. The story of the Veteran begins to come together in context with the time in which they served and what the world was like at that time.

Once I uncover and understand the Veteran's military story and awards, I put it all together in a display case and ceremony that will honor them. Many times, the family has never been given any of this information. Veterans of the World War II generation are renowned for not talking about the war. The Korean Veterans did not really come home to a celebration. And the Vietnam Veterans had to literally hide their military service from fellow Americans.

People who have served in the military have not traditionally had their stories told. I have seen just how truly healing it is to have somebody else tell their story, especially someone who knows context and perspective. Although the best events are the ones where the Veteran is still with us, one of the most memorable ceremonies I created was for a World War II Veteran that had passed away. The family did not know his story and came to learn he was a genuine hero.

It is my mission to help families learn about their patriarch or matriarch in a new way and to honor them as Veterans. When I tell their stories, they receive honor, and honor is healing. Subsequent generations gain a legacy and family heritage of military service in which they too can take pride. Who should you honor for their military service?

To learn more about how to honor the Veterans in your life, reach out to 31-Year Marine Colonel, speaker, and Veteran advocate Tim Cole at www.coloneltimcole.com, Email: tim@coloneltimcole.com, Facebook: www.facebook.com/tim.cole.940, LinkedIn: www.linkedin.com/in/james-tim-cole-382b8914

RICK GRAY
How Anyone from Athletes to Real Estate Agents Can Build Success Through Systems and Processes

Rick Gray is an Executive Coach and the cofounder of Gem State Modern, a real estate brokerage team in Meridian, Idaho. He is also the founder of Rick Gray International and is a speaker, trainer, outdoor enthusiast, American Ninja Warrior, race car driver, father, and lover of life!

Taking the Leap of Faith

I grew up listening to Jim Rohn. My dad used to get the Nightingale Conant audio series Insights, so I grew up listening to Earl Nightingale, Zig Ziglar, and Jim Rohn—who was my favorite. There's something about Jim that resonated with me. I memorized all of his material and loved the stories he told to bring his points to life.

On the back of one of Jim's programs, I saw that his business was based in Irving, Texas, so I wrote a letter to Jim inquiring about working for him. About a month later, Kyle Wilson, founder of Jim Rohn International, invited me to fly to Dallas and meet with the team. I jumped at the chance, bought a plane ticket, and when I came back home, I told my wife that I was putting my real estate license and thriving business on hold to work with Jim Rohn International.

I was 26 years old, and although I was making money in real estate and had 36 listings at the time, I'd rarely been out of the Northwest. I knew there was more to life, and I craved experience. It was time for me to experience more of the world.

Working at Jim Rohn International, we would travel to different cities across the US to talk to sales companies, do a 30 to 40-minute presentation, and then promote attending an event with Jim Rohn. On my second day, one of my coworkers got sick and could not do their presentation for a mortgage company in downtown Dallas, Texas. Everybody thought we should cancel, but instead, I said I'd do the talk. I didn't even know the talk yet, but I was so eager to impress everyone that I knew I had to learn it quickly. I spent that whole evening and night doing the talk over and over again in the warehouse where all of the boxes of Jim Rohn books and cassette series were stored. I slept for one hour that night on the couch in Kyle's office.

I was scared and nervous to do the presentation the next morning, but I had total confidence in the material. I knew when the seminar was going to be and the cost because that was on the brochure. I also knew that if I forgot the talk, I knew Jim Rohn. I could teach them about Jim and I'd had his material ingrained in me for years. I showed up almost an hour early and sat in my car rehearsing the presentation in the parking lot. There were 10 people at the talk, and I had six sales! This was the start to an amazing four years of traveling the country and doing hundreds of presentations.

Systems Create Success

In 2000, after the seminar business started to wane and be replaced by online programs, my wife and I moved back home to Bend briefly before going back to West Linn, Oregon. We got back into real estate together as partners, and I was also doing sales training for companies in Portland.

Our son was born in 2006, and our daughter was born in 2008, which had a big effect on our business. Real estate in 2006 was great, but I remember very well, in May 2007, the phone stopped ringing. The real estate market shut down, and it stayed shut down for almost three years. The great recession had just begun, and I was blindsided.

I had thought I was skilled in real estate because my wife and I were making good money as a team. After 2007, I realized our success was the result of a good circle of influence. A lot of people knew who I was, but I didn't have any systems. Until then, I had been good at GETTING business, but I didn't really know how to BUILD a business. If business didn't just come to me, I was stuck. That was a really hard lesson.

2007 and 2008 were the most difficult financial years of my life. But, looking back, they were necessary as they forced me to learn the power of systems and how to actually build a business. Now, in my coaching and training, I ask people, Do you want to get business, or do you want to build a business? There's a big difference. I was getting business for years, but I didn't really figure out how to build a business until I had to. When you hit rock bottom, you are forced to figure out how to move ahead in a different way. It's painful at the time, and I wish we didn't have to go through it, but in the end, I am much smarter and better because of it.

Why Process Trumps Outcomes
When my son Alex was five years old, we lived right across the street from a golf course in Meridian, Idaho so one day I took him to the driving range. I wouldn't consider myself a great golfer, but I enjoy playing. Golf is a notoriously difficult skill sport, so I didn't expect much from my son that day, but to my surprise, at five years old, he was hitting the ball really well immediately.

I thought, "Wow, he's a natural. Maybe I should get him a coach." We had a great junior golf program with Jonathan Gibbs of the PGA as the head instructor. My son's first lesson was one hour with Johnathan as the private coach. During that hour, Johnathan taught him three things: the approach (where the ball should actually be in relation to your stance), the rhythm of the swing, and his body position on the follow-through.

A great wisdom I've learned over the years is to be a process-based thinker rather than an outcome-based thinker. But, during this lesson, I was still an outcome-based thinker, and Alex wasn't hitting the ball very well. So, after watching him be inconsistent for about 45 minutes, I finally asked Johnathan the question, "At what point do we care where the ball goes? Because he's not hitting it very well."

Jonathan set me straight with this point, "Rick, I don't care where the ball goes. We're laying a foundation for his swing right now." That may sound obvious to you, but I was 42 years old, had played golf most of my adult life, and had never once thought about that. I was always reacting and adjusting to results. If I sliced it, I would change my stance and my grip. If I hooked it, I opened the clubface a little and tried to sweep my swing more. And because I always adjust to results, I have never developed a consistent golf game.

Today, my son crushes me at golf at 14 years old. Why? Because he went several years without caring about results. He mastered a process, and now the results are there.

I relate that to business, especially real estate, when I coach agents and brokers. How many agents in business are constantly chasing the next deal, the next client, the next commission, but never stop and build a business? Never master a system that is duplicatable and scalable? Agents who are always adjusting to results never have consistency. Agents who put systems in place that are scalable and repeatable have leverage and thriving businesses. This lesson had a major impact on me, and I see it show up so often in business that I speak on the topic regularly.

I do a lot of talks on habits, and one of the bigger points I make is that habits are more important than goals. Goals are great for setting direction, but systems and processes are what get you there. There's so much emphasis in our society, especially in the personal development industry, on setting goals. I'm a really big believer that habits and daily behaviors outweigh goals. Habits, if kept up long enough, have the power to change your identity. THEN it's easy to do the right thing because that's just who you are.

Living Your Intent

You don't get what you want in life, you get what you intend. You get to choose your habits, then your habits choose your future. I've been coaching for over 10 years, and I have been a licensed real estate agent and broker for 26 years now. I get joy and satisfaction out of helping other people build and grow a thriving business. In my coaching business, it's not uncommon for my clients to double or triple their business in one year as a result of a shift in mindset, developing consistent systems, and being focused on the right things.

Outdoor Adventure Lifestyle and American Ninja Warrior

My wife and I love the outdoors. We were very intentional about moving to Meridian, Idaho because this is paradise to us. I love to snow ski, water ski, ride dirt bikes, rock climb, and fly fish, and all of that is within an hour of our house. My wife and I really wanted to raise our kids with this lifestyle, so we decided to expand the real estate team from Portland to the Boise area.

For my lifestyle and schedule, it works best for me to work out early in the morning. My focus is on agility training, ninja obstacles, and rock climbing, not necessarily pushing weights. I compete in the Ultimate Ninja Athletes Association and love Ninja Warrior because it's so different from traditional workouts. Overcoming obstacles takes a lot of upper body, core, and grip strength. It's anaerobic fitness—short bursts of high-intensity effort—which is how I've trained for years. I placed 19th at the Ninja World Championships in 2018.

People might think that I am very scheduled and consistent, yet in reality, I might (on a whim) load up my dirt bike, drive an hour into the mountains, and ride all day. I love spontaneity, but there are certain things that I realize I must be disciplined in to get the results I am looking for. In my personal life, eating well is one of those things. In real estate, it's lead generation. I have also developed valuable reading and journaling habits. You can pick and choose areas to be really focused and disciplined in and let the rest of your day unfold naturally. You only need enough discipline to establish a habit. Many successful people look very disciplined from the outside, but the reality might be that they have just developed the correct habits, so it looks effortless. Making the crucial activities for your life and your work a habit is the easiest way to ensure your eventual success.

I have committed to use my abilities and talents to help other people show up as their best selves. As Jim Rohn would say, "Use your gifts, and they will make room for you." Take some time to discover your gifts and then build habits around them. This is the best gift you can give yourself and the rest of us.

Find more on Rick Gray, Executive Coach, speaker, founder of Rick Gray International and cofounder of Gem State Modern real estate at www.rickgray.com, email: Rick@RickGray.com

Instagram: therealrickgray YouTube: Rick Gray International

Facebook: https://www.facebook.com/rick.gray.754 and Rick Gray International

ADAM LEVY

Alcohol Professor and Founder of International Beverage Competitions

Adam Levy is co-founder of the Internet Security Company NetTects and founder of the International Beverages Competitions Group, which runs beer, wine, and spirits competitions around the world. He is also known as the Alcohol Professor, a prosumer website and online magazine covering all things beer, wine, and spirits.

Early Years

I was born at Mount Sinai Hospital in Manhattan and have lived within the same 25-mile radius my whole life. Growing up, I always had jobs: raking, snow shoveling, waiting tables, etc. I worked my way through college at Rutgers University, and that took me on a longer route than the normal four years to graduate. I am, to this day, a loyal Rutgers sports fan. GO RU!

While I was still attending Rutgers, I started a job with AT&T, but after several years, it was time to leave my comfort zone, and I began working with pre-IPO technology companies. I enjoyed the success of the dotcom era, but I also lost a good friend who sat next to me for two years in my executive MBA program on 9/11. That loss, along with the impact of 9/11, sent me into a tailspin. I felt if there was ever a time to start my own company, it was then. On top of that, the economy and the technology industry were sputtering after 9/11. So, when my best friend, the best man at my wedding, proposed that we start a music equipment company together, it seemed like perfect timing.

What Is Success Without Passion?

All of a sudden, I was manufacturing, importing, and distributing guitars and bass gear around the world as well as doing artist relations for top musicians playing in Bon Jovi, Destiny's Child, Prince, LeAnn Rimes and other bands. I had no real passion for the music equipment industry, and I started it just so I could start a company. Five years into it, my best friend was gone, as I had bought him out early on, and I lost all my money.

I was so focused on trying to keep the company afloat, I could not see anything else. As an entrepreneur, especially with your first, your whole identity and sense of value is wrapped around the success of your business. My wife said to me, "It's either the business or it's your family." I had to make the hard decision. I had to shut it down.

I realized that even if I had turned it around, I was never going to make enough money for all the effort I was putting into the company. I was working in an industry that I had no passion for, and I did not enjoy it. Looking back, it was doomed for failure from the start.

While running my music equipment company, I did not properly monitor my burn rate and cash flow. Now in my ventures, I am vigilant about my cash flow. I have freelancers and agencies who work for us on monthly and annual retainers. Their work may spike between February to June and the rest of the year will be dead, but they're still getting paid the same monthly amount. Why? Because I know the importance of understanding my burn rate and fixed costs.

Traveling the World and Drinking Good Stuff

I have always been passionate about drinking good stuff as a craft beer freak first, then a whiskey freak. I was reading an article in *Malt Advocate* magazine about how their results differ from other well-known spirits competitions. The startling statement was that, on average,

85% of those who submitted to these competitions won a medal like it was third-grade soccer. I knew I needed to start a respected competition for the trade and the consumer.

I had recently read the book *Blue Ocean Strategy* and knew I needed to start my competition with my philosophy of judging the liquid by its category and price. Consumers buy based upon price. Why not judge based upon price? I started the New York International Spirits Competition with this philosophy in 2010, followed by the wine competition and beer competition. In 2014, I expanded globally into Melbourne and Berlin, and then, in 2018, launched the Asia competition based in Hong Kong. Liquor is my passion. I like drinking good stuff, eating well, and traveling well.

After closing down my music equipment company, I returned to the tech industry to a company that I had originally invested in years earlier that could use my help. In 2013, I co-founded NetTects, an internet security company based in New York with a former coworker and good friend. Our clients range from large financial funds to media companies, hospital groups, regional banks, and manufacturing. We have experienced network engineers who work for us, and our business comes by word of mouth from clients and the manufacturers we work with.

The Long Game, Reputation First

In the tech world and the liquor world, credibility is huge. Unlike the music industry, I knew the tech industry when I started NetTechs with my partner. I had been in the industry for over 12 years and had existing relationships with customers as well as manufacturers. Our clients know we are their part-time CTO as well as their advocate when dealing with manufacturers when solving their technical issues. All our new business comes from word of mouth from our customers and the manufacturers we work with.

I have a saying, *There's greed and there's greedy*. I have greed (I'll make money), but I'm not greedy. Our mentality in our tech business is thinking long-term, and I have the same mentality with my relationships in the liquor industry. The trade knows we are not a medal factory when compared to other competitions where on average 85% of those who submit win a medal. I have been able to launch global competitions and have had introductions made on my behalf based on my reputation and the strong relationships I have built in the liquor industry. My website Alcohol Professor is also well-respected for our content because we do not pull punches even to the point that we have exposed things that went against my core values.

Relationships, Trust, and Principles

When someone is in my circle of trust, that's important to me. We have walked away and fired tech customers when we could not trust them to do the right thing. We are very fortunate that we enjoy working with the great majority of our clients and manufacturers.

I operate my personal and business relationships by my Dad Rule. If I'm sitting with my dad at lunch, and someone who I have done business with approaches our table, yelling at me, upset with me—maybe they didn't get a gold medal, maybe they thought a tech deal went bad, whatever it is—I'm clean and clear if I can turn to my dad and honestly tell him, I did the right thing, and that person is wrong.

Reciprocity and Expertise

I've been with Entrepreneur's Organization for many years. EO has also been a great source of business mentorship and allows me to be around other highly successful, principled people. I have met many great people on their domestic and international trips as well as when I visit different cities. Every year, I go to Melbourne and have dinner with the former chapter president and a few others who have become friends. Immediately, we deep dive and really just share. If I have a question or even need a couple of staff people for a competition I am hosting, he'll call the local chapter on my behalf. They support me, and I've given back to them.

You have to have the mentality that you're willing to give back.

Another time, I met a distiller from South Africa who is in EO who was having an issue with a US importer. I provided a backup plan for her, just in case. Now, if I ask anything of her chapter, she'll ask on my behalf, within reason, of course. She will make the effort because I made the effort. I just wanted to help another member of EO.

The Industrious Farmer

When it comes to business, I'm a seven days a week guy. My second wind and most effective time is nine o'clock at night to midnight because I'm not getting distracted with inbound calls and emails. Technology has allowed me to be connected, whether I am home or traveling around the world. Some of my tech clients get a laugh when they know I am working on their quote while I am sitting in my Airbnb in Hong Kong and respond quicker than a competitor. When I am home, I go to bed to Asia, wake up to Europe, all while dealing with New York during the normal day. It is hard for me mentally and physically to be untethered.

A good entrepreneur is a farmer who knows they have to constantly make improvements to make their farm more productive. I always feel there's a fence to fix, a wall to paint, or a seed to plant to prepare for the next harvest.

Like most of us, I have more ideas than time. I tell my staff that it is their job to annoy me to do my job and stay focused. As soon as you can afford it, outsource whatever you dread to do. Otherwise, you will push it off, and in the end, it will hurt your business.

On Retirement

I have worked hard to be this lucky to enjoy this life. I plan to leave technology 7-9 years from now. I will always continue to build and grow the liquor competitions worldwide, and I have a few a other competition projects I am working on for the future. The liquor business is my creative outlet that allows me to follow my passions as well as generate income. If you are fortunate enough to find a way to generate income while following your passions, then pursue until you are no longer able to.

Learn more about drinking and tech professional and New York native Adam Levy and the Alcohol Professor at www.alcoholprofessor.com and on Facebook at International Beverage Competitions.

SHERRY PATTERSON
Change Your Mind, Change Your Life

CEO, investment Realtor, event planner, speaker, and mentor Sherry Patterson has built businesses in seven industries. She provides free education, elite training, masterminds, and a mentorship program for investors and Realtors. She believes her success comes from helping others achieve their goals.

I May Appear Blessed

Change. What a scary word.

We all develop our habits, personalities, fears, attitude, and insecurities at a very young age. Most of these are a result of our home life, parents, and experiences. Pretty much all of us have had challenges in our lives. How we chose to handle those challenges determined how they affected us.

A friend who I have known since childhood once said to me, "We haven't all lived a blessed life like you."

At the time, it made me angry. I thought, *You have no idea what I have been through.* I wanted to blurt out, "Oh yeah, did you grow up with an abusive, alcoholic stepfather? Were you made fun of all through school? Did you live in a house where the anger and hate were palpable in the air? Did your boyfriend kill himself on his 21st birthday?" I could have gone on with the challenges I have faced. But I chose to not respond. In the following days, I thought about this more and realized that instead of it making me angry, it made me proud. Apparently, I have changed my life enough and handled my challenges in such a way that to others, I appear to have a blessed life.

This did not come without a lot of work. So many use their experiences as a crutch, the reason they cannot do something. Instead of poor me, YOU must be the change. YOU must want success bad enough to go get it, no matter the challenges!

How I Saw Myself

As a teen, I was so insecure. I was skinny with a potbelly. (Where do 25 feet of intestines go? OUT!) So, kids at school called me an Ethiopian. I wanted to wear tight jeans like everyone else, even though on my skinny legs, I am sure it looked ridiculous. I would wear thick sweatpants under my jeans and then put safety pins all down the inside of the jeans to make them tighter. I also stuffed my bra. I am sure this was obvious to everyone. In PE, we had to change in the locker room. Every day I would go in the back behind a curtain just hoping no one would see me or what I did.

At 15, I joined a gym and started lifting weights. At 18, I became a personal trainer and was determined to change the way I looked. Instead, I should have been trying to change how I saw myself.

I have now worked out and lived a healthy lifestyle for 35 years. Unlike I was as a child, I am not a naturally thin adult.

Insecurities and Fears

I had a mean, alcoholic stepfather that was mentally and sometimes physically abusive. My mother worked and stayed upset most of the time. She endured my stepfather's abuse for 21 years until he passed. There is not enough space here to go into the rest of my family issues.

I was never involved in anything, never played any kind of sport, drank way more than I should have, and got in more trouble than necessary. I think I was just looking for love and attention somewhere. I needed a feeling of belonging. I had no idea at that age that I had everything I needed for happiness and self-worth within myself.

At age 20, I dated a boy I had gone to high school with. We broke up not too long before his 21st birthday. On his birthday, he committed suicide. This broke me. I too wanted to die. At that point, I had a decision to make. I could use these experiences as my "poor me" excuse for the rest of my life or I could choose to change. I looked at my life and identified where I was, what my crutches were, and who the toxic people were. I decided who I wanted to be and where I wanted to go, then I set goals and made a plan to get there. As I did this, I realized that it wasn't me that was broken.

To Overcome the Challenges in My Life

I first sought out counseling. Then I started listening to and reading self-help books. I distanced myself from the toxic people. I took classes in behavior modification—so many I ended up with a double major with my business entrepreneurship degree. Later, I received a master's degree in metaphysics.

The changes in my life didn't happen overnight. It is still a daily decision to choose happiness. Everything we do is a choice. If you get nothing else from this, I want you to understand that you choose every single second of your life. Many things come to us by chance, but how you chose to act on them determines the outcome.

We get so comfortable in our lives and with our habits that it is difficult and scary to even think about change. But without change, we cannot grow. For those of us who dream big and want to continue to be better every day, we need to look at our lives daily and adjust. I don't feel like we should be searching for our "purpose." We should focus on what makes us happy. If we take steps to live and choose a positive, grateful life, doors will open, and success will follow.

Experienced CEO and Entrepreneur

On my journey to self-improvement, I was fortunate to get a job in early 1994 with The People's Network as an event planner. This is where I met Kyle Wilson.

I had no idea of the opportunity I had been given. I planned the events and traveled to three cities a week with Jim Rohn, Brian Tracy, Les Brown, and others. I got to listen to them repeatedly, had all their materials, and learned so much from these mentors. This launched my career as an event planner that I have continued for 25 years and led to my success in owning nine other businesses.

Realtor, Real Estate Investor, and Educator

For the last few years, I have immersed myself in investment real estate as an investor and Realtor. I train and mentor both Realtors and investors on how to build an investment real estate business. I have three events monthly with free training for a wide range of experience from beginners to syndicators. I also have elite training, a mastermind group, and one on one mentoring. I enjoy helping others grow their wealth.

Your Choices Make Your Success

All the success I have has come with a lot of hard work and a lot of mistakes. I have learned that each thought we have, word we say, and action we take is a choice. Once you decide who you want to be, you must take massive action to change your thoughts and habits to create your happiness, no matter how uncomfortable it is. Here are a few things I do to keep me focused on the right choices and to manifest my goals.

I wake and say, "Good morning, (–day). It is going to be a GREAT day!" then think about all the things I am grateful for. I meditate, including my affirmation to set my intention for the day. I get up and work out. Then, in the shower, I visualize light streaming through my body to the center of the Earth to ground me. As that light grows roots and grows up around me, I grow into a money tree. I do this to attract money.

When I get in the office, the first thing I do is look at my vision board and say my affirmation. Next, I watch *DarrenDaily* then write my Morning Mindset in my *High Performance Planner* by Brendon Buchard. I then check my goals in *Living Your Best Year Ever* by Darren Hardy and make my things to do list in order of priority. At the end of the day, I write in my evening journal.

I take the last hour of the day to read or listen to something educational before bed. Once in bed, I close my day with gratitude and set my intention for what I want my brain to work on while I sleep.

I have, in fact, had a blessed life. If not for the people and experiences in my life, I would not have been challenged and may not have felt so compelled to fight so hard for my success. I also feel like my journey has helped me be a better parent. I could write a whole book on my wonderful husband of 24 years and my extraordinary children. Although this only touched on the challenges in my life, they have been minor compared to most. I am not better than anyone else. I made a choice to change my life and work to be better every day, to help others be their best, and that is something that I believe anyone can do.

Are you ready to make a change? Do you want to grow your wealth? Set goals you have no idea how to achieve and conquer them with Sherry!

Sherry@aspirerealtyteam.com | 817-822-2640
WWW.REI-TRAINING.COM
WWW.ASPIREREALTYTEAM.COM
www.facebook.com/groups/REITRAINING/
Instagram: @aspiredbysherry

HOWARD WHITE

Principle Based Marketing, Connecting, and Mentoring

Howard White is the founder of Business Growth Dynamics, a training and consulting firm, and founder of Top Choice Products, a collegiate apparel merchandising company. He's also a John Maxwell Coach and a board member of 100 Black Men of America who has worked with two Fortune 500 companies.

Hometown Work Ethic

I learned a strong work ethic growing up on a small farm in Prentiss, Mississippi. It's a small town, but there are more great people from small towns than there are from the big cities.

I grew up with 100% entrepreneur tendencies. I didn't have a garden. I had a field with rows of cucumbers 100 yards long. We'd pick them, put them in sacks, and take them to a store to sell. We'd keep the profits after we paid my father back for the seeds and fertilizer. I didn't realize it at the time, but he was teaching us that all business has a cost.

He was a building subcontractor for most of my life. We would help him, wiring houses and plumbing. Eventually, my brother and I were finishing houses while he was elsewhere with his crew. It taught me my work ethic and instilled in me the idea of multiplication, doing more than one thing at a time to drive revenue and make income.

The Power of Mentorship

I went into engineering. In a small town, I was top percentile in math, but when I got to school, I realized I didn't know much. My fourth year, my mother said to me, "Son, you're not enjoying college." This took me back. I thought I was loving college. I had just won student government president, I was on the state board, and I had finished the last semester with a 3.5. She said, "No, you're not enjoying engineering." She was right. She advised me to become a teacher. That was going to add another year or two to school. She was so convinced this was my calling she offered to pay for the extra time.

As I got ready to graduate, I met MacArthur Sholas through my position as student government president. This relationship made me realize the power of mentoring, a critical habit for success. He had the insight that I would not enjoy being a traditional engineer, and suggested, "Why don't you go into sales as a sales engineer?" I'd never heard of that. Most people hadn't, but his firm looked for engineers to sell technical products because engineers take calls from engineers. So I started selling the materials used to make circuit boards.

Your purpose will keep hitting you until you answer that calling.

My last semester in college, I had seven hours to fulfill. So, I volunteered at a mentoring organization called Big Buddy, which I still work with now, coaching an elementary flag football team for a season. It was a blast. When I got ready to graduate, one of my college professors presented an opportunity: teaching in Jamaica. I would have loved to, but I turned it down. I had a job in hand and was headed off to corporate America. But, that purpose, and I truly believe my purpose is helping others win and realize dreams and dollars by teaching and training, would come back to me, and would keep hitting me until I finally answered that call.

Fortune 500 Salesman of the Year Quits at the Top

I worked for two Fortune 500 companies. When I was first hired on at the second company, it was the week of the national sales award conference. As I was watching people receive their rewards, I said to myself, "Okay, just wait. I'm gonna be on stage soon." Two years later, I was salesman of the year. But I was miserable. This was no fun. So I decided to leave the company while I was at the top. If something felt wrong while I was at the summit, how was I going to feel when I came to an inevitable valley?

I left corporate America without a game plan. I don't recommend that, but I knew I couldn't stay there and milk it, being unhappy and not doing my best. Then I would be doing a disservice to the company and the people who trusted me. I guess the principles that I learned back in Prentiss, Mississippi kind of took over. I can say, even only being at the company a short time, being faithful and honest paid off. The national manager actually called and said, "Okay, Howard, we're gonna do some things for you that we normally won't do, just because of how you handled this." And he continued to pay me, knowing that I was doing other things. Some people call this karma, but it's just core principles. I like to say principles are few, processes are many.

Power of Pivot

I ran into an awesome opportunity back at school to get into merchandising, selling collegiate apparel. We have a physical store by Southern University in Baton Rouge. Most people know the other university, LSU, and there are hundreds of LSU stores in the city. There are two stores focused on Southern University.

There were many challenges to overcome, and the key was I had the desire to solve my situation. I was all in. My wife and I were newly married and had just had a baby without health insurance. I was figuring out how to support a newborn and pay off the hospital bills, including a C-section. I'm glad to say, we made it work. Our son is doing great and now in college.

Business is a constant pivot. If you play basketball, you have a pivot foot. Once you take up your dribble, your pivot foot is planted, looking for the next opportunity. You remain ready and willing to pass the ball and move to the next opportunity. That's what I've been able to do. We soon expanded into commercial vending, and we've been able to work with brands such as Essence, Blue Cross Blue Shield, IMG, and the National Trucking Companies. We've developed great relationships, and we do some really exciting things. There are always challenges, but each challenge allows us to come up with good solutions.

Training-Consulting Business

Over 10 years ago, Capital One did a series for small business owners, and I joined the team to do their marketing training. One day, a trainer for another segment canceled. They needed someone. The material was far out of my realm, but I looked at the content and thought I could teach it. Principles are few, processes are many. If I understand the principles, I can teach it. I got great reviews, and I started thinking, I like this. Why am I not doing more of this? That was right around the time John Maxwell started his coaching and training company. If I was going to learn from someone, why not learn from one of the best? I joined John Maxwell's team.

Two years later, John Maxwell was expanding overseas, and we went to Guatemala to introduce our event attendees to the round tabling process. It's a great format and process we teach for teams. 150 trainers went in on a Monday morning to learn the methodology and how to work with the volunteer translators. By Saturday morning, our 150 trainers had trained in three-hour blocks of small groups of 30 to 70, almost 19,000 people.

Then they went on to run 30 weeks of roundtables that trained, in the first year, over 200,000. That is the power of a seed. That was one of my top five life experiences.

Since then, we continue to focus on small business training. We do a lot of soft skill training: problem-solving, creative thinking, and effective communication. Actually, rather than soft skills, I call these essential skills. Today, a lot of people in the workplace struggle with those three skills. You may have the technical skills to get you the job, but lacking these soft skills will keep you in a cubicle. If you really develop your essential skills, you get promoted up and out because you're able to connect with people and solve problems for your clients.

Next Level Essential Skills

I had a big vision. The successful are always moving to another level, always doing new things. And each level requires a new set of skills. As one trainer, how many people can I reach? Just me training by myself? Not a lot. How much can you make? Well, you can make a good living, but not much more. So I created a train the trainer module: Next Level. It's six modules we train and license to a group for them to continue to learn and pass on to others. We have Next Level Prep (high school), Next Level Collegiate, and Next Level Corporate.

Last year, I was meeting with the director of the mentorship organization Big Buddy. She said they wanted soft skills training for students to prepare them for work and future success. They could bring in speakers, but honestly you never know exactly what you're going to get.

I shared my Next Level vision with her. I envisioned 20,000 students each month interacting with this in five years. She hired us to develop and implement our program. We would train the college students so they could train the high school students. We trained 10-12 college students over a seven-week period and then supervised their training of 300 plus high school students on those soft skills.

We learned from that, and we're doing it again with them this summer and expanding to other sites for second stage beta testing so we can really fine tune it. Then we begin to go out to the masses. Ideally, we will get this into the school districts. Most of the modules are 10 to 20 minutes, 30 at the most, so they can be used throughout the year to supplement existing curricula.

Principles in Vision

Vision. Have a clear vision for yourself and a clear vision for your business. Then, be able to communicate that to all stakeholders, your potential clients and your team members. If it's a true vision, it's going to require a team. With Next Level, there's no way I can train 15,000 high school and college-age students every month. The vision is the overall guiding piece that allows me to move that many people. As we move forward, that vision will grow and change. Remember, vision is always about your future, not your past. And your vision must be a dynamic, vivid vision. Check out the book *Vivid Vision*. Make it so vivid it becomes tangible.

Business Success Is Like a Good Gumbo

1. Know where you are. As a business owner, you must fully understand where you are in your business and personal life. This begins with understanding the numbers. A few of the KPIs (Key Performance Indicators) you must know are sales, marketing, administration, and leadership numbers. Check out my first book, *TOP Secrets to a TOP Performing Business*.

2. Mine your relationships. Depending on what you're trying to do for your business, ask yourself, what do I need to do to either grow to the next level or maintain? Set those numbers, and then determine how many conversations, I call them Business Growth Conversations (BGCs), you need to have each day to make that happen.

3. Prioritize sales training. As a business owner, if you have not been formally trained in sales, get some sales training. Trying to sell without formal sales training is like taking an ax out of the box and trying to chop a tree before you sharpen it. You'll get there eventually, but you're going to take a whole lot more strokes than you need to.

How did I get here? I've asked a lot of questions and made a lot of mistakes. But more importantly, I'm willing to listen to other people's ideas.

Success is just like a gumbo. Good gumbo is made from a whole lot of different stuff, and everyone has a different recipe. It's hard to say what exactly goes into a great gumbo, but you sure know it when you taste it. Each great gumbo is going to be different, and that's okay. It's the same in business. There's no one way to solve your problem.

To connect with Howard White about specialty products, consulting, or coaching, visit yournextlevels.com, topchoicepromo.com, or call 225-442-8911. To set a meeting guaranteeing at least 15,000 new dollars in ideas if you're an established business owner, visit the online calendar at 15kmeeting.com.

TOM ZIGLAR
Growing Up Ziglar

Tom Ziglar is a speaker, trainer, and the CEO of Ziglar.com, as well as the author of Choose to Win: Transform Your Life One Simple Choice at a Time. *He is the son of the legendary Zig Ziglar.*

Having Zig Ziglar as a Dad

I didn't really feel the pressure of growing up with a famous dad. I'm just not wired that way. It was such an incredible experience having Zig Ziglar as a father. My sister Julie, on the other hand, felt so much pressure that she wouldn't even bring her problems to mom and dad. They thought her life was perfect, but she was dealing with the same stuff everyone else deals with. Even in our house, everybody was unique.

Dad traveled a lot, and while we were in school, he was gone up to three nights a week 40 weeks a year. But when he was home, he would change his schedule so he could take me to school and play golf with me. For me, that was normal.

Dad was intentional, and when he was with us, there wasn't the distraction. He was different than most people. He wasn't afraid to say no to people, which took a lot of burden off his shoulders and allowed him to make us a priority. This is a really powerful leadership concept.

Joining the Family Business

When I came into the Ziglar company, I had to work my way up. I was 30 when I became the president and CEO. And it wasn't until 10 years ago that I started speaking and training. I'd never wanted to. Why would I go out there to speak when we had the best in the world? Some of that was personality, some of it was fear.

I finally got talked into it and liked it, but it wasn't fun while I was getting ready for it. It was nerve-wracking, and my stomach would do somersaults. I did it a few more times and then finally had to have a "sit down with myself in the corner" talk and say, "What's my worry? What am I anxious about?" I realized I had burdened myself with the idea that people wanted me to be Zig Ziglar on stage.

I had to step out of myself and ask, "Do people really want you to be like Zig Ziglar on stage?" The answer was no. They want me to have the same principles and values but to be the best version of myself. When I am not myself, it comes across as fake, a mask. That put the pressure in the right place, in developing myself and understanding what people needed.

I realized it wasn't about me or the opportunity I had to speak. It was about every person in the room.

I engaged Paul, my Shakespearian-trained speaker trainer who coaches Fortune 100 CEOs in Europe and voice coaches movie stars. I flew to Dublin, Ireland and spent two days with him. I needed somebody who knew of Zig Ziglar but wasn't in the fan club. Sometimes you run across people who are such a fan that they won't tell you what you need to hear. I needed somebody to shoot straight. Working with Paul, I realized that while I could be myself, I could not ever wing one of my speeches. The top in any profession never wings it. They have diligent intentionality about perfecting their skill.

What You Feed Your Mind Determines Your Appetite

One of my favorite quotes from my dad is, "You can change what you are and where you are by changing what goes into your mind." About 10 years ago, I was 60 to 65 pounds heavier than I am now. I got sick and tired of being sick and tired and was praying for purity—not that I was off doing any of this impure stuff, but I was just sluggish and feeling icky. A voice in my head said, "Why don't you eat pure?"

I made the decision to eat food the way God made it: no chemicals, no preservatives, and organic whenever possible. Six months later, I'd lost 50 pounds without ever being hungry. So I came up with this quote: "What you feed your mind determines your appetite."

My favorite quote is, "You are what you are and where you are because of what's gone into your mind." For six months after I decided to eat pure, I read everything I could get my hands on about what the body needs nutritionally. And I started craving that stuff.

"What you feed your mind determines your appetite" is literal, but it's also figurative. It's really simple, who do you want to become? What do you have a burning desire and a passion for? Feed your mind that.

Lessons Learned From My Dad

The number one lesson I learned from my dad was, control your input. Be intentional about your input. There's no action that happens without someone first thinking about it. When we intentionally choose the right input, what we read, what we listen to, and who we associate with, that changes our thinking. Our thinking changes our beliefs. Our beliefs also change our thinking. It's a loop. In turn, your thinking changes the actions you take, and the actions you take affect your results. Your input determines your outlook, your outlook determines your output, and your output determines your outcome. Input, outlook, output, outcome. It all starts with what we choose to put into our mind.

I was in Nashville having dinner with Dan Miller, a great friend who wrote *48 Days to the Work You Love*, and his 25-year-old grandson Caleb Miller. My book *Choose to Win* is about habits. The fastest way to success is to replace a bad habit with a good habit. Caleb said, "How do you know if you have a bad habit?" It's astonishing how awesome a question that is, because most people may feel it's obvious what's a bad habit. Not necessarily.

I said, "If your goal is to get lung cancer, then smoking is a great habit. Here's the problem, most people don't have clearly defined goals or a purpose, something they want to achieve in their life. To test if you have a good or a bad habit, ask if what you are doing is taking you closer to or further from your goal."

The second lesson dad taught me was about input. Instead of making decisions for me, he would ask me, "What do you want to become? Is that going to work? Do you still want to do that?" He was doing Ninja Jedi mind tricks on me and ultimately teaching me how to get a clear direction of where I wanted to go.

My Perfect Start Routine

Every morning, I follow a routine I call The Perfect Start. The first two to three hours of the day, I have quiet time. I'm reading and getting my priorities done. I try to learn something new every day that I can share with someone else for their benefit.

Somebody once asked me at an event, "What was the one thing that made Zig Ziglar who he was?" He spent two hours a day, minimum, reading, listening, researching, learning something that he could internalize, simplify, and then share with someone else for their benefit. That last piece is the key—for their benefit. I encourage people who want to be like Zig to, for five minutes every day, be real and intentional, read or listen to something, internalize, simplify, then share it with someone else for their benefit. If you do that for a year, it will totally change your life.

I share The Perfect Start in my book *Choose to Win*, but basically, I have four or five sections to it. I get alone in my office with no distraction and do a process called Two Chairs, one chair for me and one for God, and we have a five-minute conversation. I ask God questions, and then I listen for four and a half minutes.

God, do you know what's going on?

God, are you big enough to handle it?

God, what's the plan?

It's hard being quiet, meditating, and just listening. Then I read or study some Bible devotional. Then I get into whatever the major thing is.

Two or three times a year, I'll do a gratitude practice I call 66 Days of Gratitude. For 66 days in a row, I write down three things I'm grateful for. Day one, I start with three things I'm grateful for. On day two, I read the previous day. Then I add three new things to the list. By the end of the 66 days, I have almost 200 things I'm grateful for. There's a reason for 66 days. Habits take anywhere 21 days or longer to create, but 66 days is the average.

Most people are naturally focused on identifying things that can hurt us, so most people are bent a little negative. I think it's just the way we're wired. We don't want to get hurt. In the old days, it was the saber-toothed tiger. These days we don't want to be taken advantage of. When you start looking for new things to be grateful for, you actually train your mind to start thinking that way. And that's a powerful way to think.

The other habit I really like is what I call The Mental Model. Brain science backs this up. If I have an important business meeting, a meeting with somebody on my team, a speech, a training, or a podcast, I write it down on my calendar. Then that morning, I spend one minute in my mind envisioning the answers to a few questions: Who's the audience? What's their biggest need? What are the drivers of the people there? What are they worried about? What would be a win for them?

I start playing in my mind how the event might go. If I'm going to sell something, then I think as a salesperson. What are the objections they might have? What are they going to hear from the competition? Who are the influencers in the group who might have a say in this decision?

What I'm really doing is creating slots in my mind capacity for when we actually have the conversation. It can either go exactly the direction I want, or it could veer a little bit, but it doesn't matter. Either way, I'm prepared in advance for what could happen. That makes me more productive and makes a much better outcome in general. Allowing the subconscious to work on the situation before you get there prepares you.

What Inspires Me

I got a six-minute video from a lady whose brother had been really struggling. He made a lot of bad life choices. He tried to commit suicide, and then he got COVID. She said she had given him tough love.

Finally, in the hospital with COVID, he realized he had to make a change, so she said she would help him. He arrived home, and when a Ziglar book showed up, he asked if he could read it. He read it three times in a week with all the notes.

Stories like that inspire me. I am grateful for every single time I am able to share a life-changing message and then see the ripples it creates.

Tom Ziglar is the CEO of Ziglar.com and the author of Choose to Win: Transform Your Life One Simple Choice at a Time. *Order his book at www.ziglar.com. To book speaking engagements, email tom@ziglar.com.*

CLAIR HOOVER
Dream Big, Work Hard, Bless Others

Clair Hoover is a 20-year investor and entrepreneur in self-storage, mobile home parks, car washes, housing, and laundromats. He is the president and CEO of Freedom Storage Management, is a sought-after speaker, serves on the Pennsylvania Self Storage Association board of directors, and is active in men's ministry.

The Starting Block

I was born in the beautiful farming community of Lancaster, Pennsylvania. My early life was spent living and working on our family farm. It was not always an easy life. Finances were never in abundance, but my parents always found ways to find joy in lean times and make the most of what little we had.

My dad had a tremendous work ethic. Living on a dairy farm, that meant working seven days a week, 365 days a year. Kids growing up on farms often experience adult responsibilities early in life. The challenges my dad offered me through tasks on the farm built character and problem-solving skills at a very young age. I learned what it meant to be a man working by my father's side and those values have served me well throughout my adult life.

My father encouraged me to choose a different path than he did. Although I showed little motivation and promise through my teenage years, I was frequently told I had great potential. The reality was, I had no real dreams and thus no reason to push myself to achieve.

Wake Up Call

Statements starting with "I will never" are much more powerful than "I will" statements. "I will never" statements forced me to dream big. An "I will never" is usually born out a painful experience. After graduating from high school, I decided to take a little time off from pursuing my education. I knew that if I was going to go to college, I had to treat that with a different level of commitment than I did my high school experience.

I spent a few months working for a local construction company. I remember it was so cold that every hour, they would give us a five-minute break to thaw out our toes and fingers. There were moments my feet were so cold I thought it may be wiser to pour the hot coffee down my boots than to drink it. Somewhere during those cold days on job sites, I made an "I will never commitment." The commitment was "No matter how hard college might be, if I am warm, I will never quit." I chose an accounting degree.

They say Intermediate Accounting separates the men from the boys, and many accounting students choose that hurdle as their exit ramp. I clearly remember staring at that intermediate accounting textbook, hating every minute. Something in the back of my head said, "But you're warm." That got me through. Having a "Why" became very important in my life.

Prior to college, I did not see a clear reason to excel at anything. The effort I could visualize promised very little, if any, benefit. In college, I finally found a reason to apply myself. Good grades meant financial grants and academic accolades with the promise of better-paying career options. I finally found a reason to work hard, and to my surprise, I was a good student. I was able to graduate with honors in less than three years.

Dream Big

Early in my career, I began meeting extraordinary people who were doing amazing things with their lives. As I got to experience some other countries and cultures, I began to increasingly value the opportunities I had available to me having been born in the United States.

Growing up, I assumed there were limits on how far I could go because of who I was and where I started. The truth is there are no limits. You can pursue any and every dream you have in this amazing country.

I soon realized that if I continued putting an average effort into planning and living my life, I was going to get average results. However, if I chose to put in extraordinary effort, I could achieve extraordinary results. I developed a passion for seeing how far I could go if I put everything I had into every endeavor, every day. Remember, success is measured not by where you are in life, but by the distance you traveled from your starting point.

Work Hard

Two of my favorite quotes about working hard are "The elevator to success is out of order, but the stairs are always open," and "The man on top of the mountain did not fall there." I was fortunate to develop relationships with some amazing leaders who helped me understand the value of setting goals and the joy of achieving them through hard work. Successful people are often characterized as being lucky. When confronted with that view, I love to explain that I have found that "the harder I work, the luckier I get."

The great philosopher Socrates said, "The unexamined life is not worth living." I love learning from the life choices that other great leaders have made. Every ten years, I take time to intentionally seek out men who are 10 or 20 years older than I am and ask them to speak into my life from their experience. What can you see about the next ten years of my life that I cannot? What should be important? The year of my 50th birthday, I asked: Now that I have some margin in my life, should I slow down or keep the pedal to the floor?

I secretly wanted the majority of them to recommend slowing down. But, 9 out of 10 said keep the accelerator to the floor because someday your health or other life events will force you to slow down. Another guy said, "Go as fast as you can, for as long as you can, to bless as many people as you can."

As much as I enjoy working hard, a balanced life requires strategic planning for times of personal care and revitalization. My daily strategy is to incorporate three pillars into each day. Health, wealth, and relationships. In the morning, I start by focusing on both physical and spiritual health. In the middle of the day, I focus on business and wealth building. And the evening is spent with others developing and nurturing relationships.

Bless Others

One of my mentors told me that I would do well as I built businesses for my personal benefit, but when I found the joy of building them to bless others, I would find real success. That spoke to me. My *why* became wanting to create some margin in my life, specifically in my time and finances. Now, when God puts somebody in front of me who needs help, I have the capacity to do something about it. My goal is to be a blessing to family, friends, and organizations dear to my heart.

I have watched people sacrifice the best years of their life to reach the top of a ladder that did not bring them happiness. Every successful person I know understands how to climb a ladder. The best of the best know it's even more important to focus on what is waiting for you at the top of the wall that you have chosen to climb.

247

If you have been fortunate enough to make it to the top floor in your endeavors, your next greatest responsibility is to send the elevator back down. I am passionate about encouraging others to live the best lives they can live as the best version of themselves, because I have been blessed. I realized that "success" is winning, but "significance" is helping others win. As you live this out, you will find that you cannot shine a light on another's path without lighting your own. Blessing others has always led to more joy in my life.

Life is surprisingly short and incredibly precious. Now that I have tasted what it means to dream big, work hard, and bless others, I want that for everyone. You get one shot to enjoy this thing called life. Why not make the most of it?

Life is not a journey to the grave with the intention of arriving safely in a pretty and preserved body, but rather to skid in broadside, thoroughly used up, totally worn out, and loudly proclaiming, "Wow, what a ride."

– Eric Blehm

Dream big, Work hard, Bless others.

 *To reach Clair Hoover about investment, entrepreneurship, or ministry, email him at clairhoover@comcast.net. Learn more about Freedom Storage Management at freedomstoragemanagement.com. For details on ministry and the National Coalition of Ministries to Men, visit NCMM.org.*

DR. NICHOLAS J. SCALZO
How I Came Out of My Shell to Deliver Corporate Training at Its Best

Dr. Nicholas J. Scalzo is the principal architect of OnTrack Training, adjunct professor at multiple respected East coast colleges, author of Radical Organizational Change and Organizational Memory *(2009), and co-author of #1 Amazon Bestseller* Resilience: Turning your Setback into a Comeback *(2018).*

Unexpected First Job Leads to Lifetime Career

I grew up in Laurelton, Queens, New York, which was a wonderful little town. I had a great childhood with many friends, some of whom I am still in contact with and see a few times a year. I went to St. John's University on Long Island with the goal of becoming a math teacher. In my senior year, I began working part-time at JP Morgan on Wall Street, going to classes in the day and commuting to New York City for the evening shift.

When I graduated, JP Morgan offered me a full-time position. Within six months, they promoted me to supervisor in the bonds/ADR department. Two years later, I had to overcome some obstacles when I wanted to advance but was instead selected to become a member of a newly created training department. This would prove to be an excellent opportunity that would change the trajectory of my life. I was basically an introvert, and my new role forced me to develop the skills and confidence to speak to audiences and facilitate seminars for various levels of leaders. I was fortunate to have the support of my senior management and work with professionals who provided opportunities, feedback, and encouragement which enabled me to develop into an expert training professional able to speak in front of large audiences at all levels with skill and confidence. This is where I developed my passion for organization development and training. I am forever grateful to all my managers and colleagues at JP Morgan.

The Student Becomes the Teacher

I started teaching at colleges in the mid-80s. While I was at JP Morgan, I started pursuing a master's degree while also traveling the world for work teaching seminars. When it was time to graduate, I became aware that I was one elective short. The electives to choose from were all focused on leadership, communication skills, and management—all courses which I taught for JP Morgan in England, France, Nigeria, the Philippines, and the USA.

Concurrently, I was also working on a performance evaluation system at JP Morgan and wrote my master's thesis on performance evaluation. There had to be another option, so I met with the dean, and we agreed that I would conduct a performance evaluation seminar for NYIT. That's how I fulfilled the requirements for my master's degree. Subsequently, the dean asked if I would become an adjunct professor in the School of Management.

Benefits of Needs-Based Training

Shortly after, I established a consulting and training company, as a side business, to work with select client firms or individuals who want to excel in leadership practices, developing high-performing work teams, interpersonal skills, etc. If an organization has someone who is a diamond in the rough, I'll work with those individuals. Sometimes I use assessment tools to identify the skills that need development and create a coaching program tailored to their specific needs.

I learned early on in my training career that you could develop the best training program available, but if that's not what people need, there is no added value or benefit, and it will flounder. The service I provide is knowledge and skills with a focus on practical application for the individuals or the team which they can use on the job. Theory is nice, but you've got to apply it. So, I look for individuals or senior management teams that are ready and able to make a commitment to act when the training is over.

September 11th

September 11th was pivotal for me. I was a year into my doctoral studies. When the towers were hit, I was at work when, all of a sudden, I saw papers floating past the office window. That only happens when there is a ticker tape parade. Surprised, I said to a colleague, "There's no ticker tape parade today, is there?" We went to the window and saw the tower in flames.

I worked in HR at the time, so I immediately went back to HR to help implement our disaster recovery plan. While in the meeting, on the 49th floor, the second plane flew past our window and we watched it go into the second tower. You could feel the concussion and the heat from the impact.

Heading home that evening, there was an eerie silence, and everything was covered in a blanket of gray snow. There was a UPS truck abandoned in the middle of Water St. On the rear window of a car, someone wrote, "Welcome to Hell." The subways weren't running, so I walked the four miles from Wall Street to Penn Station where I took the Long Island Railroad home.

From the Ashes

As what happened settled in, especially the huge loss of life from the attack was devastating. One company, Cantor Fitzgerald, who our company interacted with on a regular basis, lost over 700 people.

During the next week, I drove to George Washington University in Virginia for my onsite class sessions. One class focused on organizational memory, and it hit me like a brick. What happened to the knowledge and skills of those people that Cantor Fitzgerald lost? Would the company ever be able to recover?

I decided to focus my dissertation research on radical change and organizational memory because of the devastation that Cantor Fitzgerald and other organizations suffered with the tragic loss of their valuable people. This led to my successful dissertation, the presentation, and winning of the Best Paper Award at the Conference on Corporate Communication in Wroxton, England (2005), and my first book, *Radical Organizational Change and Organizational Memory*.

The Importance of Respites

I think it's important to recharge your batteries. When I pursue interests unrelated to work, it takes my mind in a different direction. If I'm working on my classic car, running a marathon, working on a home project, playing my drums, traveling with family, or playing with Lionel trains, my mind takes a vacation. I find these activities to be a respite from day to day stresses, and it prepares me to take a new perspective on problems or challenges.

As I think back to my childhood, I realize how my father influenced my approach to solving problems. You see, my father started out as a welder for the Coast Guard and ended up running the base at St. George Staten Island. Occasionally, he'd bring me to work. I learned how to weld, burn, and heliarc weld. I spent time in the paint shop, carpentry shop, metal fabrication, and on the ships. I learned many skills, including how to analyze the issue or problem, visualize the solution, design the approaches to overcoming challenges and solving through hard work. I find a lot of comfort in that and working on those kinds of things still today.

Wisdom and Advice

I find when you get caught up in something and frustrated because it's not going the way you want, you've got to stop and step back. Remember when we were kids, we used to hear, "Stop, look, and listen." We need to take a breather and walk away for a while. When our emotions rise, the brain shuts down. When you're getting really frustrated, you've got to stop and think it through. I tell my children many times when they are frustrated to stop what they are doing and approach the problem as a puzzle—I still do that.

Also, as the saying goes, "attitude is everything." Having a positive attitude toward challenges and problems allows one to approach things with a constructive orientation.

Things are going to be great at times and other times they're going to be tough. The journey of life always presents hills and valleys and level ground. Just move along and don't sweat the small stuff. We must develop and continuously fine tune our skills in being resilient.

Lastly, we must have a constant thirst for learning. Continuous learning is extremely important if we want to navigate and adapt to what the world presents to us. We only need to look at the advances in technology to know that we must continue to learn and grow. I am now 70 years young, and I still learn every day. These days I am learning more about how to use social media as a tool to share my knowledge, skills, abilities, and experiences. You need to be willing to put the effort in to learn. At times it may be tough, but we must do it to move to the next level and be a better version of ourselves than we were yesterday. We have a choice to grow and move forward or stop and become stagnant. I prefer to move ahead.

Continuous learning, stepping back, and resilience are especially critical today as we deal with COVID-19, the lockdown of the economy, and recent societal events that have multiplied the intensity of uncertainty and emotions we are experiencing.

Connect with author, professor, coach, and HR/OD consultant Dr. Nicholas Scalzo for coaching for individuals and groups. He specializes in leader development, conflict management, team development, and organizational change initiatives.

njscalzo@ontrack-training.com | 516-241-3801

APRIL CROSSLEY
Single Mom to Investor, Lendor, and Mentor

April Crossley is a no-bull investor who helps people grow wealth with real estate. A teenage mom, April graduated college, began a healthcare career, started a real estate business, and grew that business to retire at the age 35. She currently flips houses, owns rentals, and is a private lender.

Sixteen, Pregnant, and on Welfare

If someone would have told me when I was 16 and pregnant that I would retire at age 35, having millions of dollars of other people's money to invest in my company and money of my own to loan to others... I would have told them they were talking to the wrong person.

Instead, at age 16, I had people telling me I would be on welfare for the rest of my life and that my life was over. And then, I had one person in my ear believing in me like no other, telling me to go to college and make a good life for myself and my son. That one person was my mom. So I did. Every morning I woke up extra early, drove my son to daycare, and drove to high school. I then did the same thing with college.

During this time, I didn't live the normal life of a 16-21 year old. I lost most of my friends, slept an average of 4-5 hours a night, and gave up most social things to put my head down and accomplish my goal of graduating.

At age 21, I graduated college and started my career as a respiratory therapist. I thought I would work in healthcare until I was 65 years old and then retire. I was taught to go to college, get a good job, and work hard to save for retirement. I had no ability to think any bigger. I wasn't surrounded by anyone that knew differently. After working a few years, I signed up to start school for my master's degree. After all, the only way to get more money was a higher degree. Right? Wrong.

Thinking Bigger

When I met my now husband, he was a bigger thinker than I was. One day, I picked up a book he was reading. It was all about buying real estate, growing wealth, and how everyday people retire from their jobs early in life by doing this. I remember reading partway through and telling my husband, "This book has to be a lie." I couldn't believe that it was possible to not have a job or that owning houses could help you get income and retire early. My husband had two rental properties at the time and started explaining to me how it works.

I was instantly fascinated and started asking tons of questions. I was driving my husband insane with questions. I needed to learn more. So, we took some classes on investing in real estate. After learning more, I decided to drop out of my master's program to pursue learning about real estate in my spare time.

The First Deal

I talked to anyone and everyone, asking them about their experiences in real estate. I wasn't scared that I didn't know what I was doing. At the time, I was working in a hospital with patients on life support machines. If I could learn how to run someone's life support machine, I could learn anything. What scared me was that I had no money. How do you buy real estate with NO money?! Despite this fear lingering in my mind, I figured I would just keep going and learning and see what happened.

I started looking for houses. I eventually found one and took it to my husband to tell him I wanted to buy it. With my student loan debt, rent, and providing for my son, I was paycheck to paycheck. My husband knew someone in real estate that was flipping houses. So he took him the deal. The gentleman offered to do the deal with us and split the profit. He would bring the money, we had to put in the sweat equity. So we did.

Becoming a Deal Finding Master

At the end of the project, I found out that the money to pay for the project didn't come from the guy we partnered with. It came from another guy who just loaned out his money to people to do real estate deals, a private lender, a guy who had money but did not have time to find or work on real estate deals. He just wanted to loan his money to real estate investors for a good return. At this moment, a lightbulb went off for me. I realized I didn't need money to do real estate investing.

I decided I would become really good at finding deals and just take them to people with money to fund them so they could make a return without having to find the deals and doing all the work. I became a deal finding master.

The private lender that did the loan on our first deal asked us if he could continue lending money to us for more deals. So I made it my job to find more deals. But, I still was not thinking big enough.

Funding Retirement at Age 35

I knew I had enough money from him to do three deals a year. Three deals a year would retire me from my full-time job. After 13 years of working in healthcare full time, I retired. I was making enough flipping houses that I didn't have to continue working for someone else, and I wanted to run and grow my real estate company full time.

My retirement at age 35 brought with it everything that being 16 and pregnant did. My coworkers told me I would come crawling back in six months. My friends told me I was crazy. When I told my mom who was VERY successful in healthcare, I thought she was going to pass out. BUT, while she wanted me to be cautious, she was very proud and supportive. To this day, she is my biggest fan.

After retiring, I had time to read more books, learn more, and spend more time around other people in real estate investing. I read a book about using other people's money to buy real estate, and it finally dawned on me that if I could find more people that had money to invest, I could do more deals and grow my business faster. I set out to meet more people that had money to invest in real estate.

A Very Embarrassing Meeting

While seeking out more private lenders, I had one of the most embarrassing meetings of my real estate career.

I met a gentleman for coffee to discuss his interest in investing. He was a more experienced investor than I was. He started asking me questions about what I was invested in other than real estate. I proudly told him I had a Roth IRA and some old 401k plans from prior hospitals I worked at. He asked me what they were invested in, what returns I was getting, and what fees I was paying.

I couldn't answer his questions. I could feel myself sinking into my chair. This meeting was not going like I thought it would.

He finally asked me, "April, if you know about real estate and you are successful at it, why are you investing in things you don't understand? April, you need to look into investing in real estate with your Roth IRA and 401k. Look into a self-directed IRA." I wrote this down and politely, quickly tried to end our meeting. I was nearly blushing because of my ignorance. Why would this man invest with me as a private lender?

As embarrassed as I was, I went home and looked up "self-directed IRA." Turns out, this embarrassing meeting was the push I needed to become a private money lender using my IRA and old 401k. I never imagined I could be the one providing money for other people's real estate deals. Once again, I could not think big enough and did not know enough until I got around the right people. The most embarrassing meeting of my real estate career gave me the biggest leap.

Growing Wealth for Good

When I was a teenage mom, no one talked to me about the importance of growing wealth and financial freedom. Today, I feel it is a disservice to everyone if you are not growing wealth. Being able to pay off my debt with real estate has allowed me to help others who are less fortunate. It has allowed me to empower other women to stand on their own two feet financially. I have helped countless people retire early from their jobs and become more financially stable in retirement with real estate. The best part is that all of this will have a ripple effect! All because one girl in debt learned how to become financially free! All of these people will teach more people. I can't think of anything more fulfilling that will have a greater impact on so many lives.

LESSONS:

1. **You can do anything if you want it bad enough.**

2. **Get around people who think bigger. (I will never go without a coach or being in a mastermind ever again.)**

3. **Become fascinated and ask lots of questions.**

4. **Don't let fear paralyze you—continue with the pieces you have and team up with others that have the pieces you don't have.**

5. **Add value to people who know more than you. Put in sweat equity, and do work for them in exchange for learning.**

For some free, no bull, real estate education, go to April's YouTube Channel: April Crossley. Follow her for inspiration on Instagram: April_Crossley and learn more about her at www.lazygirlrei.com. For more information on April's investment groups contact her: crossleyproperties@gmail.com

CHRIS WIDENER

Humility, Kindness, and Service, Lessons I Learned From an NBA All-Star

Chris Widener is widely considered one of the top speakers in the world today. He is a member of the Motivational Speakers Hall of Fame and was named by Inc. *Magazine as one of the top 100 leadership speakers in the world. He is the author of 22 books and has sold millions of copies in 14 languages and he has worked with legends including Jim Rohn, Zig Ziglar, and John Maxwell.*

It was 1977, and I was 11 years old. While most kids my age were just trying to get through sixth grade, I had just gotten my dream job: ballboy for the Seattle Supersonics! I had been a fan of the Sonics growing up because my dad was one of the first season ticket holders. He had four courtside seats right on the floor. I mean, when you sat in the chairs, your feet were on the court! He got those tickets in 1967 for $2 a seat. As you know, courtside seats at an NBA game now go for as much as $15,000 a seat, depending upon the team. I was a huge fan and had always loved watching not only my team, the Sonics, but also all of the great old-time NBA superstars like Wilt Chamberlain, Jerry West, Willis Reed, and so many others.

I had always wanted to be a ballboy, and after my father passed away, my mother stayed in contact with a friend of my dad's who was friends with the owner of the Seattle Supersonics at the time, Sam Schulman. When I got old enough, she reached out, and since they needed a ball boy, they hired me. I couldn't believe my good luck! I was thrilled, even though the Sonics were not very good at that time.

Two months after I started the job, I fell off a roof one afternoon while goofing around with some friends and broke both of my arms. I had no idea how this was going to affect my ability to do my job, and I only hoped that they would let me keep my job. I would soon find out at the next home game.

When I showed up for the next Sonics game, I went into the training room where my boss, trainer Frank Furtado, was taping the ankles of Dennis Johnson. Frank was a short, stocky, curmudgeon of a man who in a previous life had been the wrestling coach for Seattle Pacific University. I was terrified of him!

Dennis, or DJ, as he was known, was not a star or a household name but was just breaking out as a player. Even though the Sonics were terrible when I first started working with them, they changed coaches 22 games into the season and hired Lenny Wilkens who would take the team to the seventh game of the NBA championship that year before losing to the Washington Bullets. They would then go to the championship series again the next year, where they would beat those same Bullets in five games. DJ would win the NBA Finals MVP that second year and go on to be one of the best defensive players in NBA history with a Hall of Fame career spent mostly with the Boston Celtics.

Seeing my two broken arms in casts, both Frank and DJ looked at me and chuckled. I was funny looking with two casts up to my biceps. I asked Frank if I could keep my job. He said, "If you can do your job, you can keep your job."

Unfortunately, there wasn't much chance I was going to be able to do my job because the first thing I had to do every game when I got there was to make two five-gallon jugs of Gatorade and haul them 200 yards to courtside. First, I had to get the jugs, then I had to fill them with water, then I had to rip open the Gatorade packets and stir them with a giant stirrer. Then the real problem: they weighed a lot! There was no way I was going to be able to get them from the locker room all the way out to the court in any sort of reasonable time, and there were no carts to use at the time.

I went into the room to make the Gatorade and barely got it done. While I was making it, DJ came in and told me to drag the jugs outside the locker room (so Frank could see me doing my job) and wait for him to go do his shoot around and warm-ups. So I did. It was all I could do to drag those jugs twenty feet outside the doors of the locker room, let alone 200 yards to the court. It took me a couple of minutes just to drag them from the back showering area out through the front doors and into the hallway that led to the tunnel.

After waiting for a few minutes outside of the locker room, out walked DJ. He handed me a basketball and said, "Carry this." Then he picked up both jugs and carried them to the court for me... for the next *six weeks* while my arms healed. I cannot even imagine an NBA player doing that for someone today. But this was a different era, and DJ was an incredibly great guy, and this was the beginning of a great relationship. I stayed in touch with him long after I was gone from the Sonics and he was a superstar for the Boston Celtics.

His act of kindness enabled me to keep that job, a job I would have for seven years, and which was one of the highlights of my life. At the age of 13, after the second year of working for the Seattle Supersonics, we won the NBA championship, and I was in a ticker-tape parade with 500,000 people through downtown Seattle. That was an extraordinary experience I still look back on today.

What made what DJ did for me even more amazing was that the first 100 yards was through underground tunnels, but then the doors opened up to a concourse that the players had to walk through, past all the fans, to get to the court. Every game for six weeks, DJ humbled himself and let the fans see him carrying the jugs of Gatorade so a little kid could keep his dream job. I thought it was really great at the time, obviously, but as a grown man now, I recognize what a humble gesture it was for DJ to do that for me. There was no stopping for autographs or pictures for the fans. He was just helping a little kid get his job done.

This to me shows the spirit of true humanity, one I've tried to embody myself through the years. Love. Humility. Kindness. Service. Regardless of age, race, class, or anything else. DJ was just one human helping another human along the path of life.

DJ passed away in 2007 from a heart attack while coaching. He left a profound impact on my life and how we should treat one another.

Here are a few of those lessons I've tried to live on my journey to success.

Humility. No matter how big you get or how successful you become, it is important to be humble. This doesn't mean that you don't know how good you are or that you don't have faith in your strengths. It means that you don't consider yourself better than other people. It means that you are always willing to help and encourage and view people as your equal. It means that you're even willing to be perceived as less than you actually are in order to be successful. One of my first mentors was the CEO of Mars Candies. He taught me to always answer my own phone. That seems like a small and insignificant lesson, but even when he was the CEO of one of the largest and most well known companies in the world, he answered his own phone. After my speaking career took off and I was experiencing at least a small level of fame and fortune, I still answered my own phone. And the interesting thing is that people were always shocked that I answered my own phone. Still to this day, I answer my own phone. It may just be a small example, but I've always kept it as something that keeps me grounded.

Kindness. All throughout the day, we are given many opportunities to decide how we're going to treat the people we come in contact with. I do believe that it is our choice. I have always tried to choose kindness. At the end of my life, I want to be able to look back on and know that in my journey to success, I didn't treat people poorly. The world is filled with people who've achieved so-called success, which for many really just means building a well known business or making a lot of money, who left a wake of people in their past. It doesn't have to be that way.

I know quite a few very successful men and women who are also kind. They treat people with love, respect, and decency. That's my choice as well. I may not always be perfect at it, but it is always my intention. I try to find a chance in every situation to be kind.

Service. I consider true greatness to be servanthood. Most people consider greatness to be dominating other people and winning at all costs. I believe in something different. Zig Ziglar used to say it best when he would say that you can have anything you want in life if you would just help enough other people get what they want out of life. I think that that's very sound advice, and it has been true in my life as well. I try to find ways to serve my wife, my children, my friends, and the people I come in contact with each and every day. The Bible says that we should consider other people's interests more important than our own. That's what service is. It doesn't mean that you don't take care of yourself, but that you always take care of other people, exceeding even how you take care of yourself.

My lessons for success? Humility, kindness, and service. I'm still thankful to this day that I learned those lessons as an 11-year-old boy from one of the best NBA players of all time, Dennis Johnson.

To access Chris Widener's books and trainings or to contact him about speaking, go to ChrisWidener.com.

ZACH HAPTONSTALL
Laser-Focused Competitor Mindset of a High Success Individual

Zach Haptonstall owns and manages more than $48 million of apartments in Arizona. He's also the president and co-owner of a large Phoenix hospice organization. He played college football and was also a live news broadcaster, bringing a competitive spirit to multifamily investing. And he's just 28 years old!

Work Hard and You Will Get There

Growing up, we weren't dirt poor, but my family had filed for bankruptcy twice by the time I went to high school. I never had an abundance mindset or understood you can create your own wealth. However, my parents encouraged me to do well in school. They told me if I did excellent there, I could get a degree and do better than they had.

I wanted to dominate everything I did. In high school, I was in honors classes and got good grades. I went on to play Division II football at a small school in Colorado. I strived to play in the NFL, but I kept getting injured, and it started not to be fun anymore. Still, being an athlete taught me mental toughness and discipline.

After football, I wanted to be a sports reporter, so I got a bachelor's degree in broadcast journalism at the Cronkite Journalism School at Arizona State. My athlete's mentality came with me, and if I wasn't going to succeed in football, I was going to succeed in every class. I graduated with a 4.0 GPA, summa cum laude.

Live News Anchor and Sports Reporter

I was a live news anchor and a sports reporter on Arizona PBS, and I hosted a show on Fox Sports Network Arizona.

It was great being on TV at first, but I quickly realized that journalists don't make a lot of money and work crazy hours in a very political and stressful environment. I had paid for school myself by working 40 hours a week while I was a full-time student, and everything I made I used to pay for school, but I still had a lot of student debt. It wouldn't be possible for me to pay down the debt without sacrificing the freedom to live the abundant lifestyle I had been working towards. I decided I didn't want to pursue journalism further. I was passionate about sports, but not that job. I was there for a total of five or six months.

While I was in journalism school, I worked 40 hours a week for a medical equipment company delivering oxygen machines, wheelchairs, and all other sorts of medical equipment nights and weekends.

As I was leaving journalism, my former boss told me about working in healthcare marketing. I would go around Phoenix to hospitals, doctor's offices, and assisted living facilities to offer home-health and hospice services to patients and their families.

I never wanted to be in healthcare, but my goal was to make money and be the best of the best at whatever I was doing.

Laser-Focused Achievement

I started in home-health and hospice marketing at the end of 2013 as an entry-level marketer. Over a four-year span, I became the top hospice marketer in the Phoenix market, the director of marketing, and then a co-owner in the company. During that time, I also earned my MBA, going to school nights and weekends while putting in 50 to 60 hours of work a week.

It sounds weird, but hospice care is an extremely competitive, lucrative, and cut-throat private business. There are more than 100 different hospice companies here in Phoenix, the largest market in the nation for hospice care. A hospice company is only as good as its marketers. If you can't sign up patients, the company dies.

By the time I was 23, I was making more money than both of my parents combined. I paid off my student loans and my car and paid for my MBA in cash.

But I was burnt out. It wasn't my passion. I wanted to gain back control of my time.

Moving the Needle

December 2017, I met a guy at a family Christmas party who owned a bunch of mobile home parks. He recommended I read *Rich Dad Poor Dad*. I was planning to quit my job, and it was like it was meant to be.

I read the book, and my mindset totally shifted. When I moved back to Arizona to live with my parents and attend ASU at age 18, I was reading Dave Ramsey and all about killing my debt and being financially conservative to achieve my goals. I came to believe that Dave Ramsey has a good philosophy to get out of debt or for a beginner investor, but it's not good to truly build wealth. Now I wanted to learn about equity, passive income, and owning businesses.

I had $260,000 in my bank account. I had no plan, but I decided to resign, live off my savings for at least 12 months, and look for ways to create passive income through real estate.

I didn't know anything about real estate. I had only bought a single-family home that I lived in. I cut all my personal expenses. I canceled Netflix and Spotify. I spaced out my haircuts—anything I could do to save money. I learned, consuming as many books and podcasts as I possibly could.

Every day I woke up and tried to move the needle.

Originally, I was looking at investing in mobile home parks because they're a good cash flow vehicle to create passive income. I found and called over 90 mobile home park owners in the Phoenix metro area. Maybe six answered. One was interested in selling. I made him an offer, but someone outbid me.

Before I knew it, four months went by. I felt I wasn't accomplishing anything. It was very discouraging. When I had my hospice job, I woke up each day knowing what I had to do. Now, I was completely unsure of what I needed to do to achieve my goals.

My fiancé Grace and I had started dating the year before. At this point we were living together. She was extremely supportive and believed in my dream.

On Your Own

Six months went by, and I lost all my confidence. Was this the right thing? People thought I was crazy.

I cold-called a bunch of property managers, brokers, lenders, and attorneys and built a team. But, I still didn't have partners. And I didn't have a high net worth or high liquidity to sign on real estate loans. So, I joined a mentorship program focused on multifamily investing in Dallas for $30,000. I already learned all about the numbers. But this would be the network I needed.

The group worked in a particular way. You would go out and find a deal, then if the coaches approved the underwriting, you could raise money from other people in the group, assuming you'd built relationships with them and were SEC compliant.

Three months went by, and the group had not approved any deal I presented, saying they were each too aggressive. That's when I met another member, Robert Szewczyk. He also lived in Scottsdale and was a high net worth, high liquidity guy. He had been trying to get into the multifamily market as well. We liked and trusted each other, so we decided to partner.

It had now been 10 months since I left my job. I was making no money and very aware that by this time of year I could have made $150,000. Robert and I found a 36-unit, $3.4 million deal. I analyzed it, and the numbers worked. Based on our track record, the group wasn't going to approve this deal, so we decided to put in an offer on our own.

The offer was accepted! We got the deal under contract, and Robert and I each deposited $25,000 of non-refundable earnest money.

Because we had not followed the group's rules, we were on our own. We need to raise $1.4 million to close the deal. It was a high-stress time. In multifamily syndication, people will say there's a ton of money sitting on the sidelines just waiting to find a deal. But that's not true. If you don't have a track record, they don't invest. It's very difficult to get started.

All In, Life Savings on the Line
You've got to do whatever it takes to make it work.

I started the year living off my savings with $260,000. I dropped $30,000 on a mentorship program. Probably idiotically, I was also renovating my house at the time, leaving me with a little more than $160,000.

I put the remaining $160,000 in the deal. It was everything I had left after grinding away in the hospice industry for four years. But I believed in the deal.

We found a few other investors and closed on the property in February of 2019, just four months after we put it under contract.

Doubling Down
In the midst of our first ever raise, I was looking ahead. We put that first deal under contract October 2018, and we would finish our raise February 2019. Mid-raise in December 2018, I set a goal to have 1000 units by the end of 2019.

The problem was I was out of liquidity. I had gone all in on the first deal.

In December 2018, I decided to sell my house, the first house I bought, to get the $100,000 of equity out of it.

The move paid off: in April 2019, two months after the first multifamily deal, we found a portfolio of two properties with a combined 135 units, totaling $13 million! The week after I sold my house, I wired $100,000 as a nonrefundable deposit. I was all in again! Currently, after two years, we are blessed to own $48,000,000 of apartment assets in Phoenix.

Promoting a Relentless Warrior Mindset
The summer of 2018, before I joined that mentorship group, I was really down and putting a lot of unhealthy pressure on myself. I was getting very negative.

Around that time, I read *The Miracle Morning for Millionaires* by Hal Elrod. I immediately put new habits into practice. Before, I was staying up late until 12-1:00 a.m. I assumed I was a night person. Regardless, I was not getting the job done, and I wanted to be more productive.

So, I started going to bed at 10:00, then 9:00, then 8:30. Before I knew it, I was waking up before 5:00 AM.

Beginning in 2018, at least five or six days a week, I wake up early, drink a bunch of water, wash my face, have turkey bacon and eggs (which I make ahead each week), then go into my office to pray and meditate. I'm Christian, and my faith in Jesus Christ got me through the hard times. It doesn't matter what your religion is, but time in silent meditation or prayer with deep breathing does so much to relax the mind and relieve pressure.

After prayer, I journal about everything I'm grateful for. Then I work out, even if it's only five minutes. When I have more time, I put on an audiobook and go to the gym.

When I skip out on this routine, especially sleep and exercise, I feel anxiety. With anxiety you are more prone to give in to fear. When you feel at peace, you're more ready to attack challenges. You have to have a relentless warrior, champion mindset.

Giving Back in Phoenix

In the Phoenix market, I saw there was a lack of community for investors. Grace and I decided to start a multifamily meetup with the intention of providing valuable content because a lot of what we know is hard to access.

After our first several successful events, we started calling our group Phoenix Multifamily Association. All I do is invite speakers, show up, and speak. Grace organizes absolutely all of the logistics. Usually, we have a panel of real estate professionals including experienced investors, brokers, and property managers. The purpose is to provide content and quality networking to help people get in the game.

Each Day Matters

My story now sounds cool, but at the time, it wasn't. I was in a dark place, miserable and lost. I tell people, to get into multifamily, you don't need to do what I did. I was in a unique position. I didn't just quit my job, I gave myself a launchpad of healthy savings and a year to figure it all out. I also was able to live inexpensively and Grace and I didn't have children to support at the time.

What you do every day builds up. In *Mastery*, Robert Greene says that even when it seems like things aren't going, if you're pushing, the wheels are turning, and things are moving forward. Just be disciplined, be consistent, and keep pushing, because you will break through. That has matched my experience. We've got big goals and we'll continue to do just that.

Connect with Zach Haptonstall, President and Founder of ZH Multifamily in Phoenix about Apartment Investing or the Phoenix Multifamily Association:

zhmultifamily.com | (602) 859-5458 | zach@ZHMultifamily.com

TAKARA SIGHTS

Entrepreneurship to Apprenticeship + How to Work from Home

Takara Sights is a skilled editor, writing coach, and bestselling author. She is passionate about hearing, creating, and sharing great stories as well as sustainable living, design, and nature, especially animals.

Exceptional Education

My mom worked hard to become a surgeon. My dad was able to work from home for the majority of my childhood, and he taught me his practical skills, frugality, and creativity. I was able to go to all private, college-prep schools. Eventually, my parents would become investors and share some of what they learned with me.

I was accepted to the University of San Francisco and enrolled as an architecture major. I enjoyed each of my challenging classes, but I was staying up all night, multiple nights a week for homework projects. While I was getting praise and good grades from my professors, the criticism was difficult to take, and I didn't feel I was enjoying the work enough to make it my calling.

I thought long and hard about other possibilities. A university career counselor suggested I look at each major's required classes and choose the one with the most requirements I was interested in. I chose environmental studies and started a position as an RA (student resident advisor) in the residence halls my sophomore year. The RA job and the community I joined became a big part of my identity, and the experience remains a highlight of my life. Combined with my classes around sustainability in environmental studies, college became a fulfilling study of building happy, healthy communities.

Creating Your Opportunities

I was developing countless skills, but I was not deeply thinking about what I would do for a career. Unlike architecture, environmental studies did not lead to a career track. While I expected opportunity, I had no concrete plans. So, when I graduated, I felt launched into space. I moved in with my mom two hours outside San Francisco.

I always had an interest in animals, and I started volunteering with adoptable dogs and cats at the San Francisco SPCA, exotics including zebras, tamarins, macaws, and pythons at Oakland Zoo, and sick and injured native wildlife like songbirds, opossums, hawks, and owls at Lindsay Wildlife Hospital in Walnut Creek. Each opportunity was incredible. At the same time, I followed the environmental studies path through a part-time paid internship helping San Francisco public schools meet the city's sustainability goal of zero waste by 2020.

Volunteering and a part-time internship were not going to pay my eventual bills, and I didn't want to live in mom's house forever, so I was looking for a way to make real money, preferably passive income like my parents had earned through real estate investing. My mom forwarded me an email from Robert Kiyosaki about private label products fulfilled by Amazon, and I started a company selling eco-friendly home products.

Shifting Purpose

Surprise surprise, building a business is difficult. I chose my product well, and over the first Christmas, I sold out, received lots of five-star reviews, and made a profit. Then things went downhill. I felt pressured by my supplier to place increasingly large orders and borrowed money from my mom to do so. Summer was slow, and customers complained of problems with the product's non-replaceable batteries, which had gone bad sitting in Amazon's warehouse. The supplier said the batteries had to be soldered in to be imported from China into the US.

I was at a loss. If bad reviews kept coming, I might not be able to sell on Amazon at all. While I wanted to expand my line and searched for a second product, I wasn't convinced going into more debt with unsolved problems was wise.

As a new member of Kyle Wilson's Inner Circle Mastermind, I turned to the group for help. They provided lots of wisdom, but I struggled to implement.

I met Kyle on The Real Estate Guys Investor Summit at Sea with my mom. He heard that I was an entrepreneur and interested in writing (I also had dreams of becoming the next JK Rowling), so he invited me to author a chapter in *Passionistas*, which he was publishing.

I enjoyed writing my chapter, and Kyle was looking for someone to help edit the book. I had seen in the Inner Circle what Kyle could do in marketing and selling. I thought working with him would be a rare opportunity to learn from him and would allow me to turn my business around and possibly teach me how to sell lots of my future books.

Proving the Work

I had education and natural talent strengthened by a lifetime of avid reading, but little editing experience, so Kyle agreed to work with me on a trial basis. He gave me small tasks and feedback once I completed each. We grew together over time. Kyle has been incredibly generous with his wisdom and mentorship, and I have gained invaluable knowledge and experience through being associated with him.

In some ways, I think of our partnership as an apprenticeship. He allows me to peek behind the curtain of his decision-making process on each project we work on. Unlike an apprentice, I believe that rather than Kyle grooming me to do what he does, he is mentoring me to leverage my unique skills and passions to help others and accomplish my personal goals. It's possible I could eventually learn through solo entrepreneurship what I have learned (and will learn) from Kyle, but I doubt it, and certainly, not at this speed.

By the third book Kyle and I created and published, I closed my Amazon business. I think about starting again sometimes, but I also now know how difficult it is. Many programs promise you can "make your millions" in a couple hours a day. For me, it would take years of dedication to get to the level I want, and to stay the course, I would need commitment to a greater purpose beyond making money. I was missing that in my business the first time.

Today, Kyle and I have curated and published nine Amazon bestselling books, including this one, and are beginning the 10th. Through Kyle's Inner Circle and with each book, I have associated with and gotten to know personally incredible, accomplished, principled people who have become friends and mentors. I have benefitted from my ability to work from home, in LA the last three years, and to earn my living from anywhere in the world.

How to Work Well from Home

I have been working from home six going on seven years since I graduated from college. I went from being an RA working and living with my best friends to working alone for the majority of each day. At first, working from home, especially as an introvert, was THE DREAM. After a few years, I found it increasingly challenging but have developed key strategies to maintain my morale and productivity. As the world has rapidly shifted into more people working from home, and likely continuing to work remotely in the future, I would like to share small pieces of wisdom I have gained.

Structure and organization are your friends. I am a neat and organized person, but especially with scheduling, I have to push myself into preparation and planning ahead. To convince myself to do this, I adopt the frame of mind that I am helping a future Takara, who I care very much about and who is probably going to be struggling.

I wake up feeling like a bewildered time traveler unsure of who I am, when I am, and what I am supposed to be doing. To combat this, I plan my schedule for the week on Sunday nights and my schedule for each day at the end of the workday prior. I use a blank notebook to hold all my schedules, notes, and to-do lists in one place. Each two-page spread holds one day, with my schedule and tasks on the right and notes on the left. I also lay out my clothes the night before and make an effort to get dressed to a level that I would welcome other people seeing me, even though, on most days none of my clients or co-workers will see me. It helps me feel energized and a part of the thrum of life. I also meal prep or plan my menu in advance whenever possible. This greatly streamlines the day and reduces binging.

I also have set work hours which I make public with my friends and family. Interruptions and distractions still will come, so I prefer to start early and, ideally, be done before my housemates come home. For light days, I have backup projects pre-planned to help me maintain momentum and combat energy lulls during work hours.

Pre-empt monotony and isolation. Maintain a list of places where you can work for variety and in case you need to relocate due to disruption. I recommend the majority of your options are quiet places, especially if you make phone calls for your work. With safe places to go limited now, these locations will likely be within your house or outside, perhaps on a blanket in a park during off hours. If it's an option for you, use your phone's hotspot in places without wifi. Now that Zoom calls are frequent in my schedule, I also keep a list of places with acceptable noise pollution and backdrops for video calls.

Invest in quality audio equipment. Great music can have a significant positive impact in your day and I have found speaker quality has a notable effect on my experience. I don't look to spend a lot, but I do look for what sounds good to me. Although Apple's Airpods are not the best sounding headphones, I do love them for their hands-free and noise-canceling features. Also, you want to be able to hear everyone you communicate with remotely clearly and for them to hear you clearly. It may be strange, but when I am on the phone, I have found it helpful to look at smiling pictures of the person I am speaking with. It helps me concentrate on the speaker and feel connected. If you can find a compatible coworking buddy, nurture the relationship and spend structured coworking time together.

Create a supportive physical environment. Do your best to create a comfortable workspace with a work surface of appropriate size and height with a chair and monitor height that reduces back and neck strain. If you are short and your feet do not rest on the floor when you sit in your desk chair when it's adjusted to your desk, as mine do not, you may benefit from a footrest. The hours you spend in this chair add up and take a toll on your body, so do what you can to eliminate stress points and remember to stretch. Look away from your screens often to avoid eye strain. The recommendation is to gaze 20 feet away for at least 20 seconds every 20 minutes. I find I work faster with a mouse than with a trackpad. I keep fidget toys on my desk for antsy moments during tight deadlines when I cannot get up and stretch but need an outlet. I recommend classics like a Slinky, Play-Doh (which also has the benefit of being quiet), or a set of play magnets.

I also have found it beneficial when I feel my work environment is beautiful and I want to be there. Framed posters, plants, and different textures: fabrics, metal, glass, and wood are my go-tos. I also recommend putting up pictures of your friends and loved ones if you are often alone. Even seeing a photo of a loved one can trigger the brain to feel connected. Reducing clutter also has a beneficial effect on how your space looks and improves efficiency. With fewer things, it's easier to put everything in a suitable place, and everything you have takes less time to find.

Create zones between your work and living, even if that means simply storing your notebook, laptop, and pens in a backpack when you are not working. I have gone from having an office, to having a secretary desk in the living room, to working at the kitchen table and using a backpack for storage. It all works as long as you have a system.

To connect with Takara Sights, and to receive a free copy of Passionistas: Tips, Tales and Tweetables From Women Pursuing Their Dreams, *email tsights@gmail.com with Success Habits Book in the subject. You may also find her on Facebook and Instagram.*

ELI KING

Barefoot Amish Farm Boy to Real Estate Millionaire

Eli King is a full-time real estate investor and owner of We Buy Houses Lancaster LLC specializing in flipping houses and purchasing long-term investment properties since 2010.

Eli is a values-based family man passionately serving others and providing opportunities as he once received.

Down…. But Not Out

Shocked, I hung up the phone. It was a Saturday evening in March 2009, and I couldn't believe my boss had just laid me off work, effective immediately, due to the economic recession. I was newly married, only 21, and I depended on the income to feed my family and pay rent. What would I do now?

I wasn't sure, but in my heart, I decided if that's all the better employers could do for me, I wouldn't give them another chance. Resolutely, I faced west….and chose the entrepreneurial road.

Bringing in the Hay

I grew up in Perry County, Pennsylvania on a 120 acre dairy farm. Our family was part of the local Amish community. Some of the best memories I have are our family working together on the farm. We were always working hard. We needed to get up early to milk the cows, and everybody's help was needed. We learned a lot about teamwork in those early days.

Sometimes you've got to get the hay in before it rains. Times like those you learn how to constructively deal with pressure. And then, when you beat the rain, you have a great sense of accomplishment, and the blisters from stacking thousands of heavy bales become a badge of honor. We know we pulled together and gave it our all.

Today, thinking back to those days is like an energy reservoir. I know that if I rally my team and we give 110%, we'll pull through any difficult situation. Even if we don't get it in before the rain, we know we gave it everything we had, and we'll get up tomorrow looking for the next victory.

Making Lemonade…with Lemons!

I always thought I would be a dairy farmer. That was what I knew. I loved being on the farm. But life doesn't always work the way you think it will.

When Rebecca and I married, I moved to Lancaster County. I was 21 years old and didn't have much money. Farm ground in Lancaster is expensive, and start-up costs for farming are high, so we held off. I got a construction job, and we settled into our cute rental home.

Within months, I got laid off from my job and was forced into self-employment. By 2010, I was flipping houses and quickly got to be really good at it! Gradually, we let the idea of a farm go and transitioned into where God had led us.

Five years after we married, we had the opportunity to buy a beautiful property close to Rebecca's parents, where we've lived ever since. That sealed the deal on the farm. We would just not be farmers.

Making Hay While the Sun Shines

When I was young, I latched onto any money-making idea I could get my hands on. I would scrape snow and salt the neighbors' drives, catch nightcrawlers after dark and sell them to fishermen, raise bunnies to sell for pets, and much more.

At 18, I started working for a roofer. Soon, I was doing additional roofing projects on the side evenings and weekends. I just had a passion to get into business and produce income.

After losing my job in 2009, I was faced with bleak choices. Either get another job, maybe only part-time, that would barely pay the bills. Or, start my own roofing business in the worst economy in recent history, in an area new to me, where I had no industry contacts, no customer base, and barely knew which way was east or west.

Two roads diverged in a wood, and I—
I took the one less traveled by,
And that has made all the difference.

– Robert Frost

I started selling and installing roof replacements, knocking door to door evenings and Saturdays. I was scared, but in my heart, I was selling my dream of providing well. That motivation kept me going through these tough times. I'm very grateful to my father-in-law for providing odd jobs to fill in the gaps. Even still, many days I had no work, and I'd sit at home reading books. Two books I read had a huge impact, *Rich Dad Poor Dad* and *The Slight Edge*. They taught me what I do today can have a dramatic effect on our future.

In 2010, I "happened" to meet a real estate mentor. He helped me start flipping houses. The real estate market was very weak, and there was work everywhere. All you had to do was look at houses with a Realtor, place a few offers, and you'd have properties. With our work ethic and the motivation I had to prove myself, I got pretty aggressive flipping houses. We kept renovation budgets and timeframes where they needed to be and started turning big profits. Our team started having a lot of fun, and in ten years we've sold 181 properties. I love flipping houses!

Still Making Hay, Rain or Shine

I started flipping houses because it was quick money. I could put needed cash in my pocket immediately. Still, having read *Rich Dad Poor Dad*, I knew the power of long-term investing. I knew I needed to build our business into something bigger than myself to sustain me through any season. Flipping is the active part of the business, but whether I'm flipping houses or visiting family in Indiana, our long-term rentals are paying themselves down and increasing in value. I have special appreciation for that because when I was a farm boy, very little got done unless you did it.

It's been interesting to watch our rental portfolio of 80+ properties grow from single family homes to include apartments, midsize townhouse complexes, a commercial property, and several self-storage facilities. What could the future, Lord willing, look like? Read *The Slight Edge* to find out!

If You Believe in Yourself, You Will Invest in Yourself

You need to be willing to invest in your growth. I'm blessed that my mom always instilled in me this belief. She wouldn't let us sit too long in self pity or tolerate too much whining, but rather would shift our focus to somebody that had it worse or how we could improve the situation.

She had me read *Gifted Hands* by Ben Carson, M.D. After reading that book, I realized I have a lot to be thankful for. Even though I felt I had to work harder than other children my age, even though our family was always short on money, and whatever else I was whining about, we honestly had a whole lot to be thankful for. Mom would remind us it's just a period, and really wasn't as bad as it felt at the moment. Remembering that advice still helps to this day.

Mom taught us you're not going to change anything by whining. You need to take action. You have to believe in your abilities enough to have the confidence to take action to change your situation.

When I got laid off from my job, I could have said, "Life sucks," and went and found another job that paid less or only offered part-time work. But I knew that wasn't going to get me where I wanted. So, I put my small life savings on the line to pursue my dream of being able to financially provide for my family.

Exponential Give Back

Along the way, we've become acquainted with Christian Aid Ministries in Berlin, Ohio (330) 893-2428 and their SALT microfinance solutions for third world countries. How it works is each local person in the group saves money and contributes. Once they've raised their goal, the local leader decides who gets the first loan. The recipient then goes out, starts their business, and pays the loan back. The money then goes to the next entrepreneur. The average loan is $160 US dollars.

Since I was a little boy learning how to run the farm, I've understood the major difference a little seed money can have. What's really exciting is this isn't just once and done. When we make a contribution, that money keeps rotating to the next hungry entrepreneur determined to break the cycle of poverty. When he pays his loan back, it goes to the next guy. It's a very powerful concept and we enjoy being a part of it.

Five Success Habits to Live By

- **Be Friendly. Value Relationships.** Be intentional about pursuing, developing, and maintaining valuable relationships with valuable people.

- **Be Optimistic.** It's much easier to spot opportunity if you believe it's there.

- **Be Resilient.** The tough times will come for beginning entrepreneurs. Bounce back.

- **Be Grateful.** A spirit of appreciation, humility, and generosity is appreciated by all, and will convey you are a leader that cares.

- **If You Believe in Yourself, You Will Invest in Yourself.**

Be intentional about investing in your growth. It's seed for future opportunity.

Eli and Rebecca King and son Michael live in Strasburg, PA, in the local Amish community. Hobbies include hiking, running, and beekeeping. To learn how you can invest well in a growing real estate company, contact Eli: (717) 598-2661, webuyhouses@pcfreemail.com, or P.O. Box 22, Strasburg, PA 17579.

MARK VICTOR HANSEN
Lessons From the World's #1 Bestselling Author

Mark Victor Hansen is the co-creator of the world's bestselling book series, Chicken Soup for the Soul, *with almost 500 million books sold. He is also a prolific writer with 397 books authored and co-authored and a serial entrepreneur now involved in sustainable energy and co-chairman of Metamorphosis Energy, LLC. Mark has appeared on* Oprah, The Today Show, *and* CNN. *He is known as a philanthropist and humanitarian, working tirelessly for The Horatio Alger Association, Habitat for Humanity, The American Red Cross, March of Dimes, and Childhelp USA, among other organizations.*

My Dad Was a Danish Baker

My dad came to America from Denmark with only an 8th grade education. He came to a country he had never been to, where he didn't speak the language and didn't know anyone, but it was that or stay in the dangerous climate produced by WWII and die. The United States is truly the land of opportunity and the home of the brave.

My dad was young, and he learned modest English and to read. He started a little bakery and did okay but never had a lot of money. My dad desperately wanted his boys to take over the bakery. When I started selling greeting cards at the age of nine to earn the money for the bike of my dreams, he saw that I had business acumen. He believed in free enterprise, and would say, "The more enterprising you are, the freer you are." He decided the bakery would be my legacy. But if you've ever had to knead bread by hand for an hour, you know it feels like your forearms will fall off. I knew that wasn't the life I wanted for myself.

Meeting Buckminster Fuller

While I was at Southern Illinois University, Dr. R. Buckminster Fuller, as Chairman Emeritus of the Design Department, spoke to 5,000 students at our weekly convocation series. He was 71 and I was 21. Bucky, as he was affectionately called, had 15 doctorates at Harvard and lots of inventions: geodesic domes, dymaxion cars, all kinds of really cool, world-transforming innovations. He came out saying, "We're going to talk about cosmology, cosmogony, epistemology, synergetics, cartography, and more. We're going to figure out how to make the world work for 100% of humanity." I wanted to help humanity, so after I heard him speak, I went to his office and begged to work with him. I got to travel and work as a research assistant and then co-worker with Buckminster Fuller for seven years.

He was always writing. Bucky said: "Everyone of us is born a genius and gets de-geniused. Every one of us is a human guinea pig. We're supposed to test ourselves, see what the limit of our peak performance is. People tell us we aren't good enough to succeed at our peak levels, and eventually, we believe them."

He taught me that once you plug into a higher level, you get in tune with the infinite. The spiritual world runs all that is mental, which runs the physical, which ultimately facilitates our personal results. In short, this means imagination is one of the keys to unlocking your infinite potential.

I imagined I could sell a billion books. I haven't sold a billion books yet, but I'm over halfway there.

Bucky was a futurist and mythologist. In his book *Utopia or Oblivion*, he said we can choose utopia or dystopia. Either things are going to be a magnificent paradise or we can wreck them.

SUCCESS HABITS OF SUPER ACHIEVERS

Both options always and only coexist because the law of polarity always exists. The point is, if enough of us embrace positive thinking and right actions, we have the power to do wonders.

If you think, "I can't do it. I'm not strong enough. I'm not enough," you won't be. But, if you start saying, "I really have a wonderful mind and powerful resources," you are setting yourself up for unlimited achievement, success, and opportunities galore.

Like my friend Bob Proctor says, "You don't have a good mind or a bad mind. You have a mind that's either trained or untrained. You must decide to discipline your mind." Perhaps you want to have a great memory. Decide to have a great memory, then tell yourself, "I've got a great memory." Then, one day, you start doing the work to create a great memory.

I believe all of us can do this. Everyone's got a genius talent, skills and abilities, but it's different for each of us and requires enormous self-discipline to action. Everyone has a destiny. It's your job to discover what that is and then go fulfill it. My wife and I co-authored the book *ASK! The Bridge From Your Dreams To Your Destiny* to help each and every person discover and realize their individual destiny.

Chicken Soup for the Soul

Jack Canfield and I met serendipitously while hearing each other speak at the Mandela Conference in San Diego, California in 1989. We immediately befriended each other. I got Jack to think bigger, write bold goals, and really start telling heart-touching and soul-penetrating stories. Over the next three years, if we were off speaking somewhere, Jack and I met to write the first *Chicken Soup for the Soul* together. Simultaneously, we were also getting rejected by every agent and publisher we talked to—144 rejections to be precise. Even our agent literally fired us, saying "no one wants this book," which cost him many, many millions in lost commissions.

When we were finally agent-free, we found a small independent owner/publisher in Florida, Health Communications, Inc., that agreed to take our book, if we would agree to buy 20,000 copies at $6 each. We were desperate and said yes.

Chicken soup was what Mom or Grandma gave each of us when we were sick. Jack and I thought the soul of America was sick, in pain and trouble. We would soon discover that the soul of the world was also ailing and in profound pain.

We decided to test our stories and created seven mandatory discernments to help us find stories that people wanted and would read, reread, and share widely.

The stories in *Chicken Soup for the Soul* had to connect with the heart and soul of our readers. Not only that, they had to inspire instantaneous behavioral change. We wanted people to read each story and think, "Whoops, I'm going to change my perception." We wanted these stories to have a cause, a heart-touching, soul penetrating-energy to them. We wanted readers to feel each story in their stomachs or have a, hopefully, happy tear come to their eye.

Eventually, the first *Chicken Soup for the Soul* book was published on June 28, 1993.

Every time Jack and I appeared on stage sharing our stories, we enjoyed a table rush of sales that was beyond compare. Our book became the gift book phenomena of all time, according to our cover story on *Time Magazine*. People were buying books. And more importantly, they recommended and shared books within their spheres of influence.

On a daily basis, I was doing two to three radio interviews, many times from a payphone at an airport between planes. It was exhilarating, exciting, and occasionally exhausting.

We had set BIG goals! And the results eclipsed even our lofty goals! As of today, we have sold over 500 million *Chicken Soup* books worldwide.

I love those stories because I think life is a story—it's either a compellingly interesting, irresistibly good story, or it's boring. You and I are made in the image and likeness of God. In Ephesians 2:10, it says *"We are God's masterpiece."*

As God's carefully sculpted masterpieces, all of us have got to chip out our imperfections, and self-sabotaging behaviors. Stories subtly help each of us to do that. Reading other people's stories either builds you up or helps you to realize your weaknesses and mistakes and gives you the chance to overcome them.

Turning Trash to Cash

With Buckminster Fuller's influence, I wrote down seven initiatives I would take on in my life. One of those initiatives is to take the world's pollutants and turn them into resources. Today, I am part of a company that does what I call "turning trash into cash." After 20 years and $300 million in development, we are able to recycle every atom available in a recyclable source with no waste created. We get metal back to metal, glass to glass, fuel to fuel, almost 100%, which is really cool, and more importantly, desperately needed, so we can have abundance for all.

On average, 60% of all garbage is water. When we compress our source material and distill it, we vaporize that water, generating atmospheric water—what that gives us is clean pure water and cleaner air. The best part is, with our processes, we can do plastics. There is a huge amount of plastic pollution in the ocean, which I believe we're going to have to clean up in this decade. That alone is a $50 trillion business, and we've got the resources to do it.

Meeting My Wife

When I was single after my divorce, I wrote down 267 things I wanted in my ideal woman and published it in *Chicken Soup for the Soul The 20ᵗʰ Anniversary Edition,* about love. I thought nobody would ever meet all those values, virtues, characteristics, and qualities, but I figured as long as I was going forward, this was what I wanted.

At an event, I saw a vision of loveliness in one of my many seminars. I asked someone if she was married, and they told me they believed she was divorced. Later, in the VIP room, I saw her on the other side of the room and watched a woman spill a glass of red wine on her white pants.

So, I went over and said, "I know where the club soda is." She agreed to go with me, and fortunately, we were able to rescue her pants. A bit later, it was nearly 10 o'clock, and I asked if she had eaten dinner. She said she had not. And I said, "Me either, but I can't stay here. There's a thousand people that want two minutes of my time, and that'll vaporize us. I want to be with you." She agreed to join me for dinner, and we had a great time, equally impressed with each other.

And that started our relationship.

Crystal and I are a formidable couple. We're two hearts, but we have got one soul. We wrote our new book, *ASK! The Bridge From Your Dreams To Your Destiny* together. She wrote the parable that starts *ASK!,* and the publisher said, "This is the most compelling parable ever. I've never read a parable three times in a row." She can make stories so magnificent, so believable, and so understandable. We believe we will and have had invitations to make it into a big screen movie.

Key Success Habits

You create your habits, and your habits create you. We must, especially as we mature, objectively look at our habits and determine which habits are working for us and which are not. Many people don't pay attention to the bare essentials.

My wife taught me great sleep habits. It's got to be totally dark. We listen to certain music. She's a master clinical hypnotherapist, amongst other things. We've got an extraordinary bed and perfect pillows. The environment is important, but it's also critical you go to bed happy. We pray out loud with each other before bed to sleep, and it works. Pray for yourself, your family, your businesses, and your city, county, country, and the world. As a result, we have an exalted love experience.

Next is nutrition. I take 78 herbs and vitamins a day. Each morning I wake up, wash off, and have fresh fruit and nuts, which are great for the brain. In addition to taking all the right vitamins, you need omegas. You've got to have really superior nutrition if you're going to live long and prosper. Genesis 6:3 says we shall live 120 years. My goal is 127 years with options for renewal.

You also have to exercise. If I'm in town, three days a week I do muscles because you've got to stay solid. It's a discipline that can be hard to do because there are so many interruptions, however, exercise is a minimum daily mandate, like brushing and flossing my teeth. Dentists say, "Just floss the teeth you want to keep." I say, I have one body temple in this lifetime and it is mine to sculpt, improve, and keep superbly healthy and happy daily.

And of course, your mind has got to be programmed to be positive rather than negative. You've got to be an addict of great, inspiring books, audios, podcasts, and, most importantly, people.

If you have the right habits, you'll be healthy, and you'll feel good. How you feel counts. You want to feel like a million bucks every day of your life. If you're going to reach your destiny, you've got to get there with joy and fulfillment, and why not make everything a memorable experience?

To order Mark Victor Hansen and Crystal Dwyer Hansen's new book, ASK! The Bridge From Your Goals to Your Destiny *go to Amazon.com. For speaking events and more information, go to www.markvictorhansen.com.*

BEN NELSON
Real Estate Entrepreneur, Syndicator, and Realtor: Destination Specialist

Ben Nelson is a real estate entrepreneur, principal of Steadfast Investment Group, Realtor, and family man in Portland. He's an investor with a mission and passion for helping others learn the business, make strategic investments, and get from their current scenario to where they want to be.

A Starting Point

I started out about as small as you can. My first investment was a $2000 mobile home that I remodeled and resold. Even though it was a relatively small investment, it was extremely nerve-racking. It was a new world to me, and there was a lot to learn. I've grown from there into additional remodels, small development, and syndication.

On that first purchase, my client needed a different solution. Putting their home on the market was not what she wanted. She had a lot of emotional baggage with the house and just needed to be done. The best solution for her was something quick and easy. It was about recognizing what she needed and providing a solution that worked for her, not about me getting a deal.

Analysis, The Double-Edged Sword

I'm very analytical, almost to a fault. It's a double-edged sword. I often feel I have to learn all the details before I can take action. It's something I have to keep in check. However, my analytical side also helps me make careful and calculated decisions so I can do my very best for my clients, partners, and investors. Part of the hesitation comes down to a fear of making a wrong decision. But if you don't take action, you'll never make right decisions either—you just stay stuck. In this business, you have to get involved and learn as you go. Much of your knowledge you will gain through experience.

Being Passionate & Personal

I love what I do. As a real estate broker and investor, I get the opportunity to offer solutions that are outside the box. I approach every client's situation from a personal level and present solutions based on their needs and goals. Everyone has the situation they're in and their idea of where they want to ultimately end up. My goal is always to help them get to that destination in the way that most appropriately addresses their needs. For many sellers, putting their home on the market is a great option, but others may have a unique need. In fact, many of my personal acquisitions started out as sales appointments and through conversations with the seller we uncovered a better solution. Every one of those situations, *they* chose the route they felt was best for them, not me. This ability to look from a consultative role and not just be transactional is often missing from this business.

Choose Carefully

When you're first starting out, you're just trying to get clients. As I built my business, I've honed in on my ideal client. There have been a couple times when I have not said "no" to a client and it's come back to bite me. Sometimes they're negative or draining people. I don't want to be around that kind of energy. Sometimes it's just we don't quite click. Either way, if you have a gut feel that it isn't the right fit, it's okay to pass or to refer them to someone who can better help.

Being Around the Right People

Influence is so important. There are a lot of people out there with a ton of knowledge and experience, and many of them are willing to share it with those that want to learn. Those are the kind of people I want to be around. I have an abundance mindset and love teaching as well. I share my experiences, successes, and failures with others to help them avoid those pitfalls and have quicker success. When you surround yourself with amazing people on a regular basis, it's going to expand your world of knowledge and raise your bar of possibility.

Working with people you trust and who you're aligned with philosophically also opens up opportunities to collaborate. It's a competitive industry, but if you have the right mindset, there are abundant opportunities to work in joint ventures or help each other. It's easy to want to keep an opportunity to yourself, but I've learned that it's a lot better to share part of multiple big pies than to have all of a smaller one. Sometimes not being willing to collaborate means you don't get a deal at all, and part of something is definitely more than all of nothing! I don't view others in the same field as competition. We can do more together than we can alone.

Overcoming Obstacles

As an investor, you make the best decision you can with the information and experience you have at the time. Often, it's the right decision, and sometimes it's not. We bought a commercial building a few years back that was outside the scope of what we had done before. Ultimately, we made a poor decision on the purchase and were not positioned properly for what needed to happen after the purchase. We paid too much for the building and ended up having to sell for a significant loss. We needed to know our product better and make slower decisions. This had been an emotional decision and an easy transaction. We didn't have outside vetting from a third party like an appraiser or a lender. Sometimes when things are too easy, it's easier to make a poor decision. Challenges and hurdles can actually be beneficial, as they make you stop, think, and work through the process. The result definitely stung, but we learned a lot and built a couple of great new relationships through that experience.

When things don't go as planned, you need to step back and ask yourself what the lessons are so you don't make that mistake again. The first part of that process is admitting you made the mistake and not placing blame somewhere else. Own it, learn from it, and be better in the future. There are always pieces within a failure that you can benefit from if you take the time to figure out where things went wrong and what you could have done differently. You should never waste a failure by moving on without gaining the lessons.

Success Habits

My morning routine sets the tone for my day. I make sure I'm up before the rest of the family to have quiet time alone. I do some pushups and stretching just to get my body moving, then read my Bible, spend time in prayer, and do some reading. I also spend a little time working on something that's going to increase my knowledge and challenge me in new areas. My mornings are about getting my mindset in the right place and planning my day.

There's so much to learn, and things are constantly changing. If I don't continue to stay up on what's new in the industry and what's going on in the market, I'll fall behind very quickly. Every day I'm listening to podcasts and reading whatever I can to increase my knowledge base. This is for myself, but it's also for my clients who rely on me to be at the top of my game.

Practice What You Preach

One of the most frustrating things to me is seeing agents that don't own investment real estate selling real estate as a great investment opportunity. Knowing logically is not the same as knowing from experience. It comes across as completely disingenuous if you're pitching that someone should buy a product as an investment that you don't invest in yourself. If you really believe it, you should own it too.

You also can't truly know all the benefits of investing in real estate unless you've experienced them for yourself. You're not going to be able to speak the language of an investor, show them the benefits, and most importantly, help them make *strategic* investment decisions. Real estate is everywhere. The key is to make sure you're buying the *right* real estate to reach your investment goals.

Why Real Estate

I believe real estate is the best investment you can make, and there are many reasons why. There are tons of tax advantages—the government incentivizes us to buy and provide quality housing. You can tap into the power of leverage by using other people's money, which multiplies your returns and lets you buy more property. Typically, someone else is paying you for the use of the property, which means they're essentially buying the asset for you. You can influence the value and equity by improving the property or how it's managed. Generally speaking, and if you choose well, you also benefit from appreciation of the market over time. All of these things and more, blended together, means a much greater total return than most people realize at first glance.

Take Action

There are too many benefits to owning and investing in real estate to not find a way to get involved for yourself. If you've thought about getting involved in real estate or want to take it to the next level, let's work together to get you from where you are to where you want to be. Don't sit in the stands. Get in the game.

"You can't make money on real estate you don't own."

– The Real Estate Guys

To get in touch with Ben about starting or growing your real estate investment business, and for a free initial investment consultation, send an email to consult@BenJacobNelson.com or connect on his website or via social media.

www.BenJacobNelson.com | Facebook.com/BenJacobNelson

ALFREDO BALA
Traveling the World Loving and Leading Others

Alfredo Bala is the CEO of Mannatech, a global direct sales company doing over $150 million annually. Alfredo has over 40 years in the direct sales industry and has built businesses and impacted lives in 59 countries around the world.

Global Opportunity of a Lifetime

I began my working career in a factory in Providence, Rhode Island earning $1.65 an hour in 1980. My first acquaintance with the direct selling industry truly changed my life.

Direct selling, network marketing, multi-level marketing, or any name you give to the industry really is personal development with a compensation plan attached to it. It is the opportunity to create a life on your own terms, which is exactly what the industry has afforded me over the last 40 years.

I feel very unique and blessed because I've had the phenomenal opportunity to work eye to eye and belly to belly with people in 59 different countries. I realize how different, yet how much the same we all are. In every country, from China to Chile, from South Africa to Sweden, human beings want the same things. We want freedom and flexibility, to be happy, to take care of our families, and to have the opportunity to do something exceptional. The industry has given me each of those things plus the opportunity to share those immeasurable gifts across the world and see post-communism Poland in 1992, the wall fall in Germany, and South Africa just after apartheid as Mandela was coming onto the scene.

I have seen all of that, and it all came from one phone call when somebody asked, "What are you doing Tuesday night?"

That Tuesday night when I walked into that meeting, I discovered the concept of residual income and the opportunity to be in business for myself for less than a hundred dollars. I walked out of that meeting with the dream. For the next 10 years, every night when I would talk to someone about my business, I said, "One day I'll be traveling the world visiting my businesses."

In 1991, I started traveling the world. I traveled to 108 countries, physically working in 59 countries. As a result, I am a rich man because I have lived many lives in one lifetime.

Providing Real Value

Success in business comes down to delivering value. During an interview, I was asked about my feelings on money. I said, "Money is the score keeper of how much value you have provided to a number of people. The more people you have provided value to and the more problems you help solve for other people, the more money you will eventually earn."

Money is almost the cherry on top of the satisfaction you have in being able to provide and deliver value to fellow human beings. Marketing is about showing your customer that the price of the product is a fair trade for the value you are delivering. The companies and people that are going to succeed and stay around for a long time are those that provide the most value to the most people.

I'm a huge promotor of network marketing because at the end of the day, whether you succeed or not, you will always carry something from the industry with you that is going to be of value to you. The serendipity of network marketing is that if you get engaged, regardless of your level of success, we're going to leave you better than we found you.

Hundreds of people in my lifetime have come back to me, some were around me for 30 years, some for 30 days, and said something I said or did was the catalyst for them to go on to be successful in real estate, in insurance, as a father, or as a son. Really, all that is incorporated into the added value of the industry.

It irks me when I hear people make generalizations about the industry and totally miss this critical part. When they only focus on results—did they recruit a person, build a team, create volume, or get big commission checks—they completely miss the investment in the person. The results of investment in a person are going to be priceless because their success is on a totally different level. You must consider the whole person and what they've become holistically, not just what they did.

The Lifetime Impact of Mentorship

I remember the first personal development tape I ever listened to. After that first meeting, they gave me a tape called *Rubber Bands*. It was about the potential of the human being for being stretched. A rubber band has no value and no purpose unless it is stretched. And you can draw parallels between a rubber band and a person. The speaker Charles Paul Conn doesn't even know I exist or how much of an impact he had in my life. Before I started this work, I had never heard of positive versus negative thinking, the power of a dream, and the power of verbalization and visualization. Each of these concepts, which had such an impact on my trajectory, came from people who have no idea they ever impacted me.

Seven years later, Charles Paul Conn did a speech called "Promises to Keep." That speech is why I decided to do this work for the rest of my life. One event, one speech at midnight in Virginia Beach, totally grounded me. I'm here today because I heard that one speech from that one person. Investing in other people is an amazing legacy we leave behind and an amazing tool that we have through our industry. We have the opportunity to make them think and think differently than they have in the past based under the influence of friends, family, teachers, and other mentors.

Leadership is being willing to do more than you are asking others to do, setting the right example, and putting others first. People choose you to be a leader because you have provided value for them. Leading others is a privilege they give to you. I see my role as a leader as being a servant to the people I lead more than I see leadership as people doing things for me. I earn the right to lead every day by demonstrating that I care for others, their wellbeing, their legacy, and everything else they care for.

Bill Britt, one of the biggest names of greatest impact in network marketing, epitomizes the concept that in every adversity lies seeds of greater opportunity. I was fortunate enough to help him grow his empire from three to 60 countries and work with him on and off the stage. I watched the man work with some of the top leaders in the industry. You can't put a price to that education. There's not a day in my life when I don't think about how Bill Britt would have handled a situation. I channel him on a regular basis and want to honor his memory. I want what I learned from Bill Britt to be known to as many people as possible around the world.

Keys to Long-Term Legacy Business Growth

Mannatech is a publicly traded, 25-year-old Texas-based company. We are in 25 countries and in two hot markets: wellness and the work from home industry. The phenomenon of the gig economy provides folks the ultimate opportunity where you can not only earn as you learn, but also build a financial legacy by representing products that are very needed today.

We have spent 25 years and millions of dollars in clinical studies developing impressive technologies for the immune system. The focus is ensuring safety, quality, and efficacy at every turn, in addition to ultimate value.

For me, it starts with an obsession for the customer. I consider every one of our distributors to be our customers because they are the frontline users of our products. If there's one thing that is not negotiable with me, it's not taking care of our people and customers in the highest standard possible. It's really about creating a culture from top to bottom that is endeavoring every single day to make that experience for our customer better and being able to measure it so that we can improve it.

In this space, safety is number one. We want our products to have the highest-quality, because our products are something people are taking in, and a dependable degree of efficacy. As a publicly traded company, we must be transparent. That transparency creates a trust. Without trust there is no transaction. Not only must we be trustworthy for our consuming public, but we must also build trust with our associates who depend on us for their lifestyle and multigenerational financial legacy.

Everything we do will keep us in business for the long-term. Being patient, not cutting corners, and operating at the highest level of ethics will preserve the life of this company. And the life of this company impacts the lives of families in 25 countries.

I'm very proud to have represented and worked with Mannatech for the last 13 years. I believe we are one of the companies that will be iconic in this space because of our commitment to delivering the very best value we can to a world that needs what we have. Health is your first wealth.

Continuous Growth and Positive Intention

I believe that I have to manage the input if I want to ensure the output. So, I start every morning listening to a little round speaker in my shower. Personal development has been part of my life for 40 years, and it's made all of the difference.

I believe in the concept of *kaizen*, the Japanese concept of continuous improvement, and hold myself to that in all areas of my life. It's to be constantly curious about things and about being in this continuous learning mode of self-directed education. I am willing to do the things that others are not willing to do so that I can enjoy the things that others won't be able to. And that means being able to on a personal level to make the right sacrifices.

I have a passion for what I do for this industry because of what it's done for me. Frankly, it doesn't feel like work because I'm always doing it with the best intention. We're not always going to succeed. We're going to make mistakes. We're going to come short. But my intention is always to provide the greatest good for the greatest number of people through everything that we do.

Alfredo Bala is the CEO of Mannatech and a world leader in the network marketing industry. You can find more information about his team, coaching, and speaking on Facebook and at www.alfredobala.com.

KELLI CALABRESE
Fearlessly Pursuing What Sets Her Soul on Fire

Kelli Calabrese is a 34-year health coach, bestselling author of Mom & Dadpreneurs, *international speaker, MLM top achiever, and former gym owner. She has appeared on all of the major networks as a lifestyle expert and is a spokesperson, entrepreneur, and the founder of Intentionally Fabulous.*

Moving Away From Pain and Towards Pleasure

I grew up in New York. My parents met at 10, married at 20, and truly are among a handful of people I personally know who were deeply in love throughout their entire marriage. They were inseparable, and over the years had 10 different businesses in the restaurant and deli industry while my dad worked his construction company during the day and operated equipment for the city of New York in the landfill on the 4-12 shift. To say I learned to have a good work ethic is an understatement.

By the age of 13, I realized that while they had accumulated things (boats, horses, sports cars) they rarely took the time to enjoy them. My dad and his family were all smokers and had a strong family history of alcoholism, cancer, and heart disease, and my mom's family suffered with obesity. I made a commitment at 13 years old to move away from that pain.

I also loved biking, cheerleading, dancing, swimming, and playing softball. The endorphin rush was a high for me that I wanted to always have and share with others. I wrote in my journal that I would be an exercise therapist.

The Voracious Quest Began

I had to wait until the age of 17 to get certified as a fitness professional. Over the next 14 years, I acquired three college degrees including a master's in clinical exercise physiology and cardiac rehabilitation with high honors. I studied for and passed 27 certifications including medical exercise specialist, post-rehab technician, strength and conditioning specialist, lifestyle and weight management consultant, and nutrition specialist.

I became a partner in a chain of health clubs, and we opened up four locations in addition to managing corporate fitness centers for companies like Calvin Klein. I also founded a school and prepared over 3,000 people to become certified fitness professionals.

This was in the infancy of the personal training industry, and I was committed to offering quality services and changing lives. I was blessed to train local celebrities like the New Jersey governor and Miss New Jersey. Looking back now, that quest for knowledge is something I highly value and continue to pursue. I'm actually completing a new certification as I write this. Jim Rohn said, "All leaders are readers."

The Turning Point

Sometimes things happen in a moment that shifts everything. My son was born in 2000. I thought I would put him in daycare at six weeks old. I pulled into the parking lot and knew I could not lay him down in a crib and return to work. I called my partner, and thankfully, he was able to buy me out.

The internet was just getting started. I went home with my son, and my daughter arrived 14 months later. I didn't know how, but I knew I would figure something out. I wanted to contribute to my industry on a high level both in helping people get fit as well as coaching trainers to be professionals and run profitable businesses.

I became the lead fitness expert for eDiets and became the online trainer of the year. I started speaking at industry conferences. I wrote my first book *Feminine, Firm & Fit*, trained clients in my home gym, was a lifestyle expert on the major networks, and became a spokesperson. I edited our industries leading magazines and became a master trainer for Adventure Boot Camp opening up camps in the US and in eight other countries. I was on infomercials, was a consultant, became the fitness expert for Montel Willliams, and also became a top achiever in an international nutrition company.

That also led to meeting Kyle Wilson at an event he hosted, The Billion Dollar Mastermind, where he invited me to collaborate on a book, which became a bestseller, *Mom and Dadpreneurs*. The book features 29 moms and dads who shared their stories of hope and overcoming to lead a lifestyle where they could work from home, still earn executive pay, and enjoy family time.

Disrupt-Her

My entire life was committed to my family and helping people be well. In another pivotal moment, my husband of 24 years came home and said his commitment to our marriage was zero. A few months later, he moved out, and within a short amount of time, he was engaged and remarried, and I was ripped out of my world as I knew it.

In a 12 month period, I sold our primary home and moved four times to keep my children in the school system, and my son moved across the country three times to live with my mom and was in four different schools. Between the kids and I, we had five car accidents, my daughter's horse coliced twice, my daughter wound up in the emergency room three times. I worked for someone for six months with a contract and never got paid. Things that normally came easy to me were unreasonably difficult, including work. I was healthy my entire life, but now I had PTSD and was barely functioning.

Navigating two teenagers who were hurting was the most challenging. They needed a safe place to let out their anger, disappointment, and resentment, and I was the target. I was served divorce papers on my 49th birthday and sent the final papers on what would have been our 25-year anniversary. The pain was excruciating.

While all of this hardship was happening, there were still miracles happening. I was constantly being encouraged by an act of kindness, a word, a song, or an answered prayer.

The Grief Cycle

Being a knowledge person served me. I did a deep dive to learn how to heal. I went to Divorce Recovery, read the books, journaled, listened to sermons, watched podcasts, joined a Bible study, went on retreats, did breath therapy, energy healing, and massage, surrounded myself with wise friends, went to counseling, and ultimately, learned the hardest lesson, to be still.

At a retreat, I learned about the grief cycle. I had no idea what that was. The leader said I was depressed and that was good news because that meant I was on the upswing of the curve and was moving closer to healthy. Somehow, that encouraged me!

The grief cycle includes shock, numbness, denial, sadness, fear, anger, panic, depression, isolation, and eventually new strengths, new patterns, hope, helping others, and loss adjustment.

I had experienced them all. I kept replaying the injustice, the unmet expectations, and the dreams that had died over and over in my head. It was so unhealthy!

Awaken-Her

In November of 2019, I arrived at my word for the year for 2020. *Awaken*! I was excited. I was ready, or so I thought. I bought a new home. The kids were getting settled with one in college and one graduating high school. I thought surely, I was ready to start getting back to a sense of normalcy and thriving again.

Then a friend and branding expert Roy Smoothe did one of his exercises with me. I quickly realized I had not yet arrived at *awaken*. There was still a big gap from where I was to where I wanted to be. I was not yet fully healed or "owning" *awaken*.

So, I did a deeper dive. I began to study identity. I realized my identity was in being a wife, a mom, a leader in my industry, and in the neighborhood I lived in. All of those things slipped away in a moment. When I realized my identity was in the Creator of the universe, it gave me peace.

Then I studied forgiveness and realized it started with self-forgiveness. I had been feeling like a huge failure and was being hard on myself. I studied the mind and learned how to renew mine to forget the past, be consciously present, and envision a very bright future.

I studied self-love and gratitude. Those were both things I needed to increase in practice to set myself up for living in joy. I was pressing in to understand my purpose, how to live in divine health, abundant wealth, and ultimately a life that was resurrected and one that included celebrating.

It took about another eight months, but I arrived at a place of peace, joy, love, fulfillment, and excitement for life.

Intentionally Fabulous

When I finally got to a place where I owned my part in the divorce and peeled back the layers of enabling, control, judgment, and self-criticism, I arrived at a place where I felt fully alive, refreshed, restored, and better than I have ever been enjoying singleness... for a season.

As a health coach, I wanted to help others. Over a dozen of my friends got divorced the same year I did. 54% of first marriages end in divorce. I joined the social communities and felt the torment of both men and women navigating the fear, suffering, and unknown of the process. I wanted to help them do something healthy to be a better person on the other side of divorce.

I became certified as a divorce coach and created a community, a coaching program, and a course called Intentionally Fabulous, which takes the master level information I learned from a variety of sources over a two year period and delivers them in a practical way to help women move from fear to fearlessly pursuing what sets their soul on fire.

I'm committed to helping women heal and tap into their superpowers to live an intentionally fabulous life that brings them extraordinary health, wealth, and joy.

To get more information on Kelli Calabrese's health coaching, speaking, online training, nutrition plans, Intentionally Fabulous, Mom & Dadpreneurs, or to join her community, go to

Web: https://kellicalabrese.com/

FB: https://www.facebook.com/IamIntentionallyFabulous

LI: https://www.linkedin.com/in/kellicalabrese/

Email: Kelli@KelliCalabrese.com

ANDREW LANOIE
Deliberate Focus (and Why It Is My Secret Weapon)

Andrew Lanoie was a talent agent at William Morris for 16 years representing celebrities including Tim Allen, Taylor Swift, Steve Martin, and Tom Petty. In 2009, he discovered the massive demand for affordable housing in the US and within five years became a Top 100 Owner of manufactured housing communities.

"We know there are many great things to accomplish, create, and explore, but not with a lot of time."

– David Allen, author of *Getting Things Done*

By the time I graduated from high school, I had sold over 100,000 albums in my band, and we were fielding attractive offers from some of the biggest record companies in the world—but, more importantly, I'd also learned a simple lesson that would allow me to replicate this same massive level of quick success in any area for the rest of my life. The lesson I learned was something I now refer to as *Deliberate Focus*, and it is, quite simply, my #1 secret weapon. This same strategy is what allowed me to land a job as a Hollywood agent in my early 20s, placing me in the top 1% of wage earners nationwide. It's also what allowed me to quit that job a decade later after replacing my entire agency salary with passive income.

Deliberate Focus has three main components.

1. Carefully consider which skills you most want to improve at

2. Delegate and eliminate activities that are not helping you improve

3. Track your progress and demand constant improvement

Today, I go through this process automatically, evaluating every new opportunity that comes my way and declining or strategically delegating anything that doesn't align with my current goals. But back in high school, I hadn't quite mastered the technique. In fact, I was struggling. The band I'd formed with three high school classmates, GrooveChild, was gaining a decent following in the New Hampshire area. Our demo album, *Children of the Groove*, was doing alright, and we had some moderate success at some local battle of the bands contests. But we wanted more.

Our philosophy was that the entire band needed to be involved in every decision, and we should all contribute equally to every initiative. We wanted to ensure fairness. But I started to notice that we were wasting a lot of unnecessary effort. For instance, we had long practice sessions scheduled every weekend for writing new music, but I played drums so I mostly found myself sitting around during these sessions while the other band members talked about chords and lyrics. And I was dragging the other guys around to meetings with club owners and promoters, but they really didn't need to be there.

That was when I learned the first step of Deliberate Focus. I saw that the way I was spending my time wasn't helping me improve at the things that mattered most. So I had to make some decisions about what was most important to me. After a bit of soul searching, I concluded that I wanted to get better at selling our records and getting us bookings. That was the secret ingredient we needed.

So we decided to change our policies. I brought up my concerns with the band and the other guys agreed. We ended up voting that my band mates would focus their attention on writing the music and lyrics for our second album while I managed the business side of things. This meant I could spend my weekends working on our promotion strategies rather than attending songwriting sessions.

Without realizing it, I was implementing the second step in Deliberate Focus: I eliminated the activities that weren't helping me improve at promoting our music. This freed me up to focus. I started studying everything I could find about other successful local and regional acts. I looked at exactly what the biggest bands in our area had done to become popular, and I put together a plan for how to sell and market our music in the same way. The key, I realized, was to break into the college circuit and to get radio airplay.

Every day after school, while the band practiced, I would spend hours on the phone calling every bar, club, venue, college, and high school within 500 miles. Most of the time, they hung up on me or told me to get lost. But every now and then my calls resulted in a booking. And I kept detailed records of everyone who booked us so that I could follow up with them later about potentially booking us again. I also called every radio station and college radio station on the east coast to pitch them on adding our music to their lineup. For a few smaller stations, I was actually able to get through to some DJs who asked me to send over a cassette of our music.

Keeping detailed records allowed me to accelerate our progress, which is why tracking is the third step in Deliberate Focus. I reported back to the band at the end of each month, and we would look through the numbers together and decide what was working and what wasn't. This kept me accountable for showing constant progress.

When our second album, *Sick at Last*, was finished in 1992, I sent copies to all of the club, bar, and radio contacts I'd been gathering, and then I called them all to follow up. The effort resulted in a wave of new bookings. Also, a few college radio stations started playing a song called "Riverside" off the new album. "Riverside" was catching on with fans at our live shows too.

Soon, we were playing three or four shows a week all around the greater New Hampshire region. We'd hit Portland once a month, Boston, once a month, Providence and New York every 45 days, and a handful of college campuses in Pennsylvania and New Jersey in between. GrooveChild was also starting to get airplay. The college radio stations I'd been in contact with were giving our songs a lot of play. Then, a larger regional station, WHEB, started playing "Riverside" too. And listeners loved it. At one point, "Riverside" was the station's number one most requested song for seven weeks straight.

That's when record companies started to take notice, leading to a development deal with IRS Records. The band continued to tour for a while, but by the time I was 22, I realized my true passion had been in the business of selling records, not in making them.

I knew I could succeed at anything I set my mind to using the steps of Deliberate Focus. So I decided to shoot for the stars. I moved to Hollywood and called every talent agency in Los Angeles, told them my story, and asked what I could do to get a job. Impressed by my hustle and real-word experience selling over 100,000 records, some of the people I got in touch with were willing to give me a chance. I wound up with an incredible position at William Morris, the top agency in the world.

Over the next few years, I applied the steps of Deliberate Focus again to quickly rise to the top of the entertainment industry. First, I recognized that negotiating deals was the most important thing for my success as an agent. Second, I delegated and canceled everything I possibly could that wasn't directly related to negotiating more deals (thankfully, the agency hired me an assistant, which made this much easier). Finally, I kept careful records of all my activities and regularly reviewed my progress to adjust my approach.

In 2009, I met a real estate mogul, and I started applying these same steps to the world of real estate investing. He pulled back the curtain on his deals to show me how they worked, and I took careful note of what he focused on and what he delegated. I spent a full year studying every piece of academics and advice he threw at me. Finally, I put together a five-year plan to purchase enough real estate to completely replace my salary with passive income. I tracked my progress closely to make sure I was on schedule, and I ended up accomplishing my goal in about four years. During that time, I bought over a hundred single-family homes.

It was a surreal moment when my passive income actually surpassed my agency salary. It was hard to believe that I could now make more money doing nothing than I was making at one of the highest-paid jobs in the world. In 2013, I left William Morris and opened an investment group, and today Four Peaks Partners manages a massive portfolio of homes and developments. I get to be highly selective about who I work with, I'm doing what I love, and I live well. And it's all because of the three step system I stumbled onto in high school that I call Deliberate Focus.

Lately, I've been applying the process to weightlifting, and the results have been equally astounding. The most important thing to master in order to improve at weightlifting is, of course, lifting weights. So I have delegated things like writing and scheduling my workouts to a personal trainer. I'm also tracking everything so that I can continue to systematically push myself harder.

In my experience, most people spend their time on the wrong things. Deliberate Focus is about removing activities from your day that aren't helping you progress toward important goals. Delegate and eliminate these things and then track your progress diligently and analyze the data often.

This simple habit will allow you to rise to any challenge you set your mind to.

Learn more about Andrew Lanoie, Four Peak Partners, and their opportunities to provide affordable housing in America by visiting www.fourpeakspartners.com, emailing team@fourpeakspartners.com, calling (844) 209-3153. You can also download The Impatient Investor podcast on all major podcast platforms.

NEWY SCRUGGS
Advice From a 7x Emmy-Winning Sportscaster

Seven-time Emmy-winner Newy Scruggs has been the sports director at KXAS-TV (NBC) in Dallas-Ft. Worth, Texas since 2000. Stops along the way have included gigs in Myrtle Beach, South Carolina; Austin, Texas; Cleveland; and Los Angeles.

My Parents and Growing Up

My parents grew up in segregated Birmingham, Alabama when it was known as Bombingham. It was THE worst city to be Black in America. My dad was sprayed by Birmingham's ultra-segregationist city commissioner of public safety Bull Connor's hoses for demanding equal treatment. In 1963, when Martin Luther King was in the Birmingham jail, my dad, who was just 17 at the time, was in the same jail with him. That was the same time Martin Luther King wrote the 1963 letter from the Birmingham jail. Black parents had to go to work; they couldn't take the day to go demonstrate. In the South, you would get fired. So, MLK used kids.

My dad was in jail for six days, and they were not letting these kids get bailed out. Dick Gregory was his block leader, and Harry Belafonte Jr. and Jackie Robinson were giving money and raising money to get these kids out of jail.

Growing Up as a Military Kid

I was born in Germany on the military base. My dad was in the military, so my family moved around a lot, and I got to experience many different places and met all kinds of people.

I could be at a school where I was one of maybe five Black kids in the class or I could be at a school where there were only five White kids in a class. One of the things I started to learn as I got older is that people try to put folks in boxes.

A military base is very different from the civilian world. My dad was strict. In the military, there's a standard. You go to school and you get good grades. That was our job as kids.

My dad got stationed at Fort Bragg, North Carolina, so we moved from Georgia back to Fayetteville, North Carolina, where rapper J. Cole is from. J. Cole consistently raps and talks about Fayetteville. That it is a place you've got to get out of.

Discovering My Dream

When I was 11 years old in Mr. McDuffie's 5th-grade class in Savannah, Georgia, we a did a mock newscast, and I absolutely loved it. That's when I knew what I wanted to do. But there's a difference between kind of knowing and hoping you'll get there and actually going through the action steps to get yourself there.

When I was 17 years old, I was in Mr. Stanton's class at Westover Senior High School in North Carolina. Nobody keeps notes from an English class they took as a junior in high school, but I have saved mine in a brown binder. I was inspired by Henry David Thoreau writing, "You should follow your genius closely enough and it will never fail you." In *Walden* he wrote, "By my experiment: that if one advances confidently in the direction of his dreams, and endeavors to live the life which he has imagined, he will meet with a success unexpected in common hours."

Ralph Waldo Emerson dropped what would become major motivational nuggets for me in *The Essay on Self-Reliance*. His rule of greatness was so epic because it really was simple. "What I must do is all that concerns me, not what the people think." Boom! Mic drop! I was on my way. At 17, Emerson was advising me to run my own race and to forget the voices, peer pressure, and expectations of others. After soaking in that education, I was a changed and clear headed individual.

Reading the Book *Showtime*

Later that year in high school, I read the book, *Showtime: Inside the Lakers' Breakthrough Season* by Lakers Coach Pat Riley. It was life-defining and really solidified the wisdom I had been catching on to.

Pat famously quotes his dad, "Every now and then, somewhere, someplace, sometime, you are going to have to plant your feet, make a stand firm, and kick some ass. And when that time comes, you do it."

The lesson in that quote for me was that you have to believe in and fight for your dreams and goals. Who are you going to be? What are you going to be? What are you chasing? I figured out at 17 years old that I didn't have to please everybody including the friends around me.

I had this dream about being a sportscaster. That's all I needed to work on—my dream.

Pat Riley's best chapter in *Showtime* is chapter 13, Motivation. I still have the beat up paperback copy published in 1988 with yellow highlighter marking his words on how he stays motivated: "...when you can put those two things together, what you need and what you want—there's your motivation. Keep that situation alive. Be so good at it that they can't even think about replacing you."

Chapter 13 is only two pages, and I reread it often. That book helped me define what I wanted for my life. You have to have self-confidence to not let other people's doubts get to you.

Getting Into Broadcasting

My dad wanted me to be a lawyer. He discouraged me from newscasting. You don't want your kids to chase some dream. You want your kids to do something secure.

Honestly, I was too stupid to expect anything but success and too stupid to know what I didn't know. I would not recommend trying to do this. There are only four sports television jobs in Dallas, the fifth largest TV market in the nation, like the job I have. I'm glad I didn't know how hard it was going to be or how improbable it would be for me to succeed!

In February of 1987, at another high school in town, the top sports anchor in Raleigh, Tom Suiter, was giving a speech to the student government group. I loved Tom and used to watch him every night on WRAL's six o'clock news and Football Friday at 11:30 at night. I went and met him. He was kind, and we developed a relationship and even became pen pals. Eventually, he let me come up to the television station, and I was able to tap into him for knowledge about becoming a sportscaster.

My dream was to attend University of North Carolina, the best broadcast journalism school in the state. I was a major Tar Heels basketball fan and still am today. But Tommy told me that Carolina might not be the best choice. He said, "They don't touch anything there. They don't DO anything. Go someplace where you can get hands-on experience." I never applied to Carolina.

God works in mysterious ways. Two weeks later in the local paper, *The Fayetteville Observer*, there was a big spread about Pembroke State University's television program WPSU. The article told of how the Pembroke State students did everything and ran everything in the program. That was the experience Tom Suiter was talking about. This small regional college in Southeastern North Carolina was the place I needed to go to learn the craft. I got a scholarship to go to Pembroke State.

I wish I could say people didn't question my decision. Those around me said a degree from Carolina would open more doors for me because it had a reputation for producing journalists. Pembroke State did not. Without the lessons of Thoreau and Pat Riley in *Showtime*, maybe I would have listened to them. Instead, I had the confidence to listen to my mentor and focus on gaining experience. Sure enough, in my freshman year I was working at WPSU-TV. I even served as a TV color commentator for two basketball games for the PSU Braves.

I was attacking this television program and sportscasting the way a basketball player or tennis player works on their game. I was in it every day, all the time doing it. The professor who recruited me told me though, "You need to not just think about sports. You're not going to get a job in TV sports when you leave here." So, I was the guy looking out for internships, trying to figure out where I could go and how I could get more experience. I made my own business cards and was constantly asking what I could do to get my foot in the door. I talked to as many people as possible because I wanted to do this. And he was right. I didn't get a job in TV or sports when I left school. I got that job before I left!

Having The Drive And Dedication

I sacrificed to work full-time at CBS in Florence/Myrtle Beach, South Carolina while going to college full-time my senior year. I was not a guy who went out and partied. As a weekend sports anchor and reporter, you can kiss a social life goodbye. The schedule means you work nights on Fridays, Saturdays, and Sundays. Holidays were just regular days for new folks in the business.

Time flies, and it wasn't long before I realized that I had achieved more success than I had ever dreamed of. I had worked my way up from South Carolina to Austin, Cleveland, and then Los Angeles as an award-winning weekday lead sports anchor. These days, I am the sports director at KXAS-TV (NBC) in Dallas-Ft. Worth with seven Emmys under my belt.

My mom and dad always told me, "We want you to take care of yourself." I know I've made my parents proud. I can attribute my success to the work ethic and standards they raised me with and the ability to run my own race.

I have a very strong work ethic. But when you're around military people the way I was, you're surrounded by high-achievers. My dad was in the First Cavalry, the 82nd Airborne, and an Army Ranger. That's the crème de la crème. In my family, *I'M* the lazy one. My work ethic has nothing on my parents, but my work ethic helped me keep going. I wasn't making a lot of money. There are a lot of people who start out in television who quit, because in television news, you start out in low TV market cities like a Minor League Baseball player. If you want to live this dream, you are tested early on.

I succeeded because of my willingness to work—all the time. I work in a job of inconvenience. You just can't plan it. Things just happen, and you have to figure it out. My wife had our second child on July 25, 2006, and six days later, I was at the Dallas Cowboys training camp in Oxnard. It was the controversial Terrell Owen's first year, and my boss wanted all the coverage we could get, so I left my wife with my mom and two kids aged 22 months apart. I am lucky that I have a partner who understands that this is the job.

I showed up. I showed up on days I didn't have to show up. My off day was a workday for me and was still a day I needed to go places, talk to people, and be seen. After a while, you build up your Rolodex of contacts and gain opportunities to tell good stories and have inside information. You'd be surprised how many people don't want to work hard in my industry. I find the trend today is a lot of people just want to be on TV and gain the perceived celebrity of the job.

Living My Dream

I'm proof Thoreau was right. I put in the time to advance confidently in the direction of my dreams, and I have lived the life I imagined. From covering Super Bowls, NBA Finals, college football playoff games, World Series, championship boxing matches, and men's and women's final fours, I have lived the dream.

I had the vision that this is what I wanted to do. I listened to the things that I like, and I still do to this day. I'm not going to let anyone else define me and put me in boxes. As Steve Martin says, "Be so good they can't ignore you."

Follow seven-time Emmy-winning sportscaster and sports director at KXAS-TV (NBC) in Dallas-Ft. Worth, Texas Newy Scruggs on Twitter: @newyscruggs | Facebook: NewyScruggsSports www.newdawg.com

CHRIS MASCARIN
What Caregiving Taught Me About Living

Chris Mascarin is a Renaissance man that connects to life with poetic integrity. A caregiver for 50 years, today, Chris is an entrepreneur and multifamily real estate investor passionate about housing solutions for seniors and adults with developmental disabilities. Chris lives his life in service.

Early Responsibility

Just after my ninth birthday, my mother took sick and the roles of everyone in the family quickly changed forever. I missed my time with my friends to prepare the renal dialysis machine four times a week for many years. Mom revered her role as an Italian mother preparing family dinner while she was attached to that life-saving machine. Instead of Little League, I was learning how I could make life easier for everyone at home. I became quite proficient in short order.

Flexibility Creates Control

Flexibility is mandatory to thrive in caregiving.

Mom had just received a kidney transplant, and I was starting college at Brown University. This was a dream, as Brown allowed me complete freedom in my selection of all my courses. I took classes in every academic discipline I could, and I even convinced my academic advisor that a semester abroad in Florence, Italy and completing my thesis obligation with an internship would be far better for my educational career than the prescribed curriculum. To my surprise, my caregiving guile was serving me well. The summer after graduation, Mom took sick again, and I chose to return home to California.

Sensing Opportunity With Intuition

Caregivers learn quickly to refine their intuitive skills and become sensitive opportunists.

Among all my interests, I had one professional love—real estate. The creative and intellectual challenge of "the deal" and building something that changes lives was exciting. As a commercial real estate broker, I grew my addiction to entrepreneurism while caring for my mom, who, after an amazing nine-year run with her kidney transplant, was back on dialysis.

My next professional move surprised even me. I found myself pitching one of the oldest corporations in America, Santa Fe Railroad. Over years of serving as their real estate broker, I realized their need for an internal real estate marketing function. I pitched my services to them for two years. If it were not for the blind faith I developed as a caregiver, I may have given up. Finally, they agreed. And their office was two miles from my mom. I like to call it synchronistic adaptation.

Curing Isolation with Exploration

Caregiving is a test of endurance with much isolation. The antidote is exploring human diversity in the world and the people around us.

As an antsy entrepreneur, I was not at the railroad for long. After four years, I had developed some wonderful and supportive relationships, including one of my most cherished friendships now of 25 years. For the first time, I understood how sacred and generous social relationships are.

I teamed up with my father by overseeing the legal management of his private pharmacy practice. He had developed a niche in filling medications for workers' compensation injuries.

It proved challenging because of the political influences in the system in the 1990's. But when I came in, we worked together to grow the practice to be the largest in California. It was challenging because I was creating something never seen before. And I loved it. I remember most how I felt helping the patients. And of course, with Dad as the boss, I was free to support Mom in any way she needed.

When the laws changed again, I told Dad it was time to retire the Workers' Compensation portion of the practice. With Christmas morning enthusiasm, I was on to my next endeavor. However, Mom's health had deteriorated, and she was tired. She asked to go home directly from the intensive care unit where she died in the summer of 1999.

Frivolity Has Its Place

Caregivers spend the day forging resilience. But all work and no play…

I found pleasure in the subsequent years renovating beautiful older homes in downtown Los Angeles and moving to Napa Valley, where I studied and taught at one of the world's best culinary schools in the heart of the world's best wines. As amazing as that sounds, I found a far greater treasure while I lived there. I met and fell in love with a woman who was divinely unique, of her own beautiful design, with an unconditional heart, and a passion for people. Her name is Ana, and she is the woman that fulfills my life still today.

I started to realize how all the skills I developed as a caregiver were positively influencing who I was and how I was living. Talk about making lemonade. Caring for Mom was emotionally exhausting, but as I cared for her, I reflected, and I started to see my role differently. When my perspective changed, Mom sensed it too. I truly believe my life has led me exactly where I need to be, with the people I want to be with, and living the values I cherish.

Finding Strength with Intention

In my 40s, with a chronic beginner's mind, I identified my next horizon thousands of miles away. With the partnership of an old college roommate, I found myself starting a new business venture in communist Vietnam in the city of Hanoi. After securing the national rights to the century-old real estate firm Knight Frank, we quickly had multiple offices, and within three years, we had over 150 employees. It was a wonderful experience. After three years, it was time to return home. Dad was beginning to slow down.

Caregiving for Dad was a contentiously negotiated arrangement with many gray areas. He knew the sacrifices we made for Mom, and he was adamant that "I should live my life." He opted to relocate to Boston to be closer to his two grandsons. There he was formally diagnosed with amyotrophic lateral sclerosis (ALS). At the time, Ana and I owned and operated a holistic health spa in northern California. My dad's prognosis was terminal, and I knew we needed to close our health care practice and relocate to Boston. This one decision serves me to this very day.

I also knew I needed to work on myself, so Dad and I made an agreement that I would only visit after 4pm on weekdays and on the weekends. This left us plenty of time to spend together but also ensured that I would not get lost in a caregiving role. I knew that could happen very easily. I learned to trade stocks, much to my dad's chagrin, and managed to earn a profit. Time with Dad was precious. We shared our birthdays, Christmas, New Year's, and hockey in the specialized hospice unit where he lived for eight months. The Veterans Administration staff there built my caregiving strength ten-fold. My life is forever changed by their unconditional respect and tender love. Dad died in early 2017 with Ana and me at his side.

Peace Springs From Serving

Tomorrow will be better than today, and in caregivers' speak—that is hope.

Assessing our resources, passions, and commonalities, Ana and I chose a direction born from my analytical brain and her deeply grounded heart. We both love caring for people and real estate, so we have embarked on endeavors in alignment with our goal to serve.

There are two populations that are growing exponentially that will need housing and medical care in the coming years, the aging baby boomers and young adults living with intellectual and developmental disabilities like autism. It is our intention to serve these two groups by joining others to design the challenging financial models to fund fiscally sound housing with sustainable, thriving communities.

Currently, we are working with two wonderful families to build housing communities and employment opportunities for young autistic adults. One project is in Sacramento, CA and the other is just north of Philadelphia, PA.

I am also developing a caregivers' support system online with a podcast and virtual outreach. Ana and I want to help caregivers reconnect to a thriving, balanced lifestyle that is free from emotional exhaustion, stress, and guilt.

Lastly, we will continue to promote the benefits of breast thermography as an early detection tool for breast cancer.

Because of our caregiving attitude, we are blessed with self-belief and driven to serve even people we may never meet. We never plan to retire because we are doing exactly what we want. We are living in gratitude for the opportunities we have to connect with others and help them live the best lives possible. Ironic how with illness we truly understand the beauty of life.

While it may seem paradoxical, positively contributing to another person's life is where we all can find contentment. It is rare to connect with a fellow human being and actively participate in manifesting their desires. "Beautiful life" happens regardless of health.

The future needs active participants. Give to yourself and find your place to serve.

"Change is the end result of all true learning."

– Leo Buscaglia

Chris Mascarin invites all forms of engagement. You can find him at chris@TrinityPropertyInc.com. Nosotros hablamos español. Recommended resource: breastthermography.com.

BRIAN TRACY
You Can Change Your Life

Brian Tracy is the top-selling author of over 70 books, has written and produced more than 300 audio and video learning programs, and has spoken, trained, and traveled in over 107 countries on six continents. Brian speaks four languages and is happily married with four children.

Early Years and Learning to Be an Entrepreneur

I grew up in Edmonton, Canada. It's not the North Pole, but they say you can see it from up there. It's really cold, 35 degrees Fahrenheit below zero in the wintertime.

I began my entrepreneur journey early at the age of 10. Because of my family situation, I had to earn my own money, so I went out and did jobs in the neighborhood to buy my clothes and school supplies.

So, for me, to go out and work, to start something and make it work, is as natural as breathing. I've started and built 22 businesses in different enterprises including hiring, recruiting, training, producing, selling, and marketing.

When I was 32, I saw an ad in the paper for an executive MBA at the University of Alberta. So, I applied, got in, and spent two years and $4000 to get an MBA.

Getting Paid to Speak

After university, I put together the content to what eventually became *The Psychology of Achievement*. Early on, when people went through the course, the feedback was fantastic. They basically said, "Oh my God, this is great," and they began to tell their friends.

The first seminar I gave, I had seven people, and six of them were family members. The seventh was a paid customer for $295. My next seminar was 12 people, and my next was 15 people in Canada. I then hired a guy for three months to sell for me full-time. Business grew and grew. Soon I was speaking to 100, then 200 and 500. And then, people started to invite me to speak to their entire audience.

The Power of Our Thoughts

In my seminars, I talk about the superconscious mind and understanding how you can activate the incredible mental power that you already have. You can turn on this switch and start to attract into your life everything that you want: opportunities, ideas, people, resources, and more, just simply by using the power that you already have within your brain.

Every single great accomplishment in history has been an accomplishment of superconscious thinking where people have learned how to turn on this switch.

Imagine that you live in a nice home and there is a garage, but you've never been into the garage. You're making an average living, as most people are. Then, one day, you go into the garage and turn on the light. And to your great surprise, there's this massive supercomputer there that is capable of answering any question you come up with. You just turn on this supercomputer, and suddenly you're producing 5, 10, 20, 50, 100 times more.

Perhaps you say, "I want to be wealthy, successful, and highly-respected. Maybe I don't have a university degree, and I don't have any money right now, but I do have my brain and my ability to **work**. And that's what I'm going to do," If you actually do the work, you set up a force field of energy in the universe that conspires to get you what you want.

The Power of Goal Setting

The most common occurrence when I travel and speak is audience members coming up and saying, "You changed my life. You made me rich. Thank you!" They grab my hand with both of their hands. "Thank you, Mr. Tracy. You changed my life." Because I speak on so many subjects, I then ask what about my material was so helpful to them. And almost always, they beam and say, "It was the goals. I'd never heard about goals before. I never understood how central they are to success."

You build your whole life around your goals. There is a wonderful quote from a dear friend of mine, Vic Conant: "Success is goals, and all else commentary." Wherever I've been able to persuade a person of that, their life changes.

I now have thousands of self-made millionaires and three self-made billionaires who have told me personally, "You made me rich. I was struggling. I was going nowhere. And after I learned about goals, here I am."

The Story Behind *Eat That Frog*

I was asked by a publisher to write a book on time management. I came up with 21 great ways to double your income and double your time off. The publisher loved the title of chapter 21, "Eat That Frog." It was from a story by Mark Twain where he said, if the first thing you do in the morning is eat a live frog, you'll have the pleasure of going through the day knowing that was the worst thing that could possibly happen to you.

Then I added the two corollaries of eating a frog. If you have two frogs, eat the ugliest one first. And if you have to eat a frog, it doesn't pay to sit and look at it for too long.

I followed the publisher's advice and included in all 21 chapters aspects of eating that frog, which means doing the worst and most important task immediately when you get up and start your day. They were a great publisher. *Eat That Frog* went on to sell 10 million copies and is still one of my best sellers.

Take Action

One idea can change your life—if you take action on it. One of the most important things I teach over and over again is action. Action! It's not enough to have good ideas or the best information. There are a lot of average people who are self-made millionaires. I have a really great hour-long program called *The 21 Success Secrets of Self-Made Millionaires*. I spent two months preparing before recording it. I buried myself in research on self-made millionaires. What I found is that they had characteristics and qualities that made it inevitable that they'd be successful. And if you simply practice the same things they practice, you become the same people they are. And action is one of the main traits of self-made millionaires.

Zero-Based Thinking

Every time I do a strategic planning program worldwide, we start off with an exercise called zero-based thinking. In zero-based thinking, wherever you are in life, you draw a line under your life to this date. You imagine that you're starting over and ask yourself:

> Is there anything that you are doing that, knowing what you now know, you would not start up again today?

> Is there any investment that you have that you would not make again today?

> If you had to do it over, is there any relationship that you would not get into?

> Is there any person that you would not hire?

You keep going through each area of your life, and you keep asking. And if the answer is "No, I would not get into this again." Then the next question is, how do I get out? And how fast can I get out? Because once you've reached the point where you have that intuitive feeling that you would not get into this again, you cannot save it.

I often say to my friends to ask themselves that question. Is there anything you're doing in your life that, knowing what you now know, you wouldn't get into?

If the answer is yes, get out and get out now.

We Make Our Living By Contributing Value to Other People

Today, we have this big thing in politics about inequality. It's not inequality of money. It's inequality of contribution. We make our living in a free country. We make our living by contributing value to other people. Sometimes I ask my audience how many people work on straight commission, and maybe 10% will raise their hands.

I then say, "Well, that's interesting. Maybe I didn't phrase the question properly. Let me ask it again. How many people here work on straight commission?" And then there's a pause, and it's wonderful, the light goes off! Absolutely everybody works on commission.

Everybody works for themselves. And each person creates value. You get a piece of the value that you create. So if you want to earn more money, create more value. Make a greater contribution. Do more.

The great line from Napoleon Hill that brings tears to my eyes still decades later is, "Always do more than you're paid for. Always go the extra mile. There is never a traffic jam on the extra mile." The one thing nobody can stop you from doing is doing more than you're paid for.

Earl Nightingale said, if you want to earn more than you're earning, contribute more than you're contributing, and an increase in earnings is automatic.

If you're not happy with your income, go to the nearest mirror and negotiate with your boss, because you are your own boss. You make your own contribution. You make your own decision. If you don't like your income, earn more.

Closing Thoughts

The happiest people in the world are those who feel absolutely terrific about themselves, and this is the natural outgrowth of accepting total responsibility for every part of their life. They make a habit of manufacturing their own positive expectations in advance of each event.

Never complain, never explain. Resist the temptation to defend yourself or make excuses.

Develop an attitude of gratitude, and give thanks for everything that happens to you, knowing that every step forward is a step toward achieving something bigger and better than your current situation.

To learn more about Brian Tracy's book and audio programs, go to BrianTracy.com.

Additional Resources

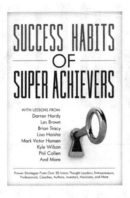

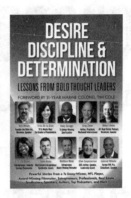

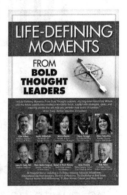

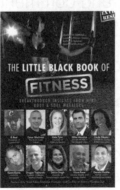

Order in Quantity and SAVE
Mix and Match
Order online KyleWilson.com/books

SUCCESS HABITS
— OF —
SUPER ACHIEVERS

Join the Success Habits Book Facebook Community!

Share with us your testimonials and comments and get daily insights from authors in the book.

Access the *Success Habits of Super Achievers* Podcast

Receive Special Bonuses When Buying The *Success Habits of Super Achievers* Book

To access bonus gifts, plus links to the *Success Habits* Book Facebook Group and the *Success Habits of Super Achievers* Podcast, send an email to

gifts@successhabitsbook.com